I, Me, Mine

Béatrice Longuenesse presents an original exploration of our understanding of ourselves and the way we talk about ourselves. In the first part of the book she discusses contemporary analyses of our use of 'I' in language and thought, and compares them to Kant's account of self-consciousness, especially the type of self-consciousness expressed in the proposition 'I think.' According to many contemporary philosophers, necessarily, any instance of our use of 'I' is backed by our consciousness of our own body. For Kant, in contrast, 'I think' just expresses our consciousness of being engaged in bringing rational unity into the contents of our mental states. In the second part of the book, Longuenesse analyzes the details of Kant's view and argues that contemporary discussions in philosophy and psychology stand to benefit from Kant's insights into self-consciousness and the unity of consciousness. The third and final part of the book outlines similarities between Kant's view of the structure of mental life grounding our uses of 'I' in 'I think' and in the moral 'I ought to,' on the one hand; and Freud's analysis of the organizations of mental processes he calls 'ego' and 'superego' on the other hand. Longuenesse argues that Freudian metapsychology offers a path to a naturalization of Kant's transcendental view of the mind. It offers a developmental account of the normative capacities that ground our uses of 'I,' which Kant thought could not be accounted for without appealing to a world of pure intelligences, distinct from the empirical, natural world of physical entities.

Béatrice Longuenesse studied at the Ecole Normale Supérieure, the University of Paris-Sorbonne, and Princeton University. From 1979 to 1993, she taught in France at the Ecole Normale Supérieure (Paris), the University of Paris-Sorbonne, the University of Franche-Comté, and the University of Clermont-Ferrand. Longuenesse then moved to Princeton University in 1993, as Associate Professor (1993–1996) then Professor (1996–2004) before moving to NYU in 2004. She has been visiting professor at the Ecole des Hautes Etudes en Sciences Sociales (Paris, spring 2008); faculty member in a 2010 summer school at the Central European University (Budapest), on Problems of the Self; Silver Professor at NYU since 2010; and is a Fellow of the American Academy of Arts and Sciences.

I, Me, Mine

Back to Kant, and Back Again

Béatrice Longuenesse

OXFORD
UNIVERSITY PRESS

Great Clarendon Street, Oxford, OX2 6DP,
United Kingdom

Oxford University Press is a department of the University of Oxford.
It furthers the University's objective of excellence in research, scholarship,
and education by publishing worldwide. Oxford is a registered trade mark of
Oxford University Press in the UK and in certain other countries

© Béatrice Longuenesse 2017

The moral rights of the author have been asserted

First published 2017
First published in paperback 2019

All rights reserved. No part of this publication may be reproduced, stored in
a retrieval system, or transmitted, in any form or by any means, without the
prior permission in writing of Oxford University Press, or as expressly permitted
by law, by licence or under terms agreed with the appropriate reprographics
rights organization. Enquiries concerning reproduction outside the scope of the
above should be sent to the Rights Department, Oxford University Press, at the
address above

You must not circulate this work in any other form
and you must impose this same condition on any acquirer

Published in the United States of America by Oxford University Press
198 Madison Avenue, New York, NY 10016, United States of America

British Library Cataloguing in Publication Data
Data available

Library of Congress Cataloging in Publication Data
Data available

ISBN 978-0-19-966576-1 (Hbk.)
ISBN 978-0-19-882272-1 (Pbk.)

Links to third party websites are provided by Oxford in good faith and
for information only. Oxford disclaims any responsibility for the materials
contained in any third party website referenced in this work.

Pour Madi et Max
qui se sont envolés sur les Plaines

Contents

Preface and Acknowledgments   xi
Conventions   xix

1. Introduction   1

Part I. Back To…

2. Uses of 'I'   19
   - 2.1 Wittgenstein and His Critics on the Use of 'I' as Subject   20
     - 2.1.1 Wittgenstein's Distinction   20
     - 2.1.2 Shoemaker's Amendment   21
     - 2.1.3 Uses of 'I' as Object   21
     - 2.1.4 Evans on 'I'-Thoughts   23
   - 2.2 Kant on Consciousness of Oneself as Subject   26
   - 2.3 Psychological Case Studies   32
   - 2.4 Concluding Remarks   37
3. Non-Thetic Self-Consciousness and Uses of 'I'   44
   - 3.1 Sartre on "Positional" or "Thetic" Consciousness of Object and "Non-Positional" or "Non-Thetic" (Self-)Consciousness   45
   - 3.2 Wittgenstein on "Use of 'I' as Subject" and "Use of 'I' as Object"   48
   - 3.3 Uses of 'I' and Consciousness of One's Own Body   51
   - 3.4 Sartre on Non-Thetic Consciousness (of) the Body   54
   - 3.5 Anscombe on 'I' and Sartre on Non-Thetic Self-Consciousness   59
   - 3.6 Taking Stock   64

Part II. …Kant

4. Kant on 'I Think'   73
   - 4.1 Descartes's 'Cogito, Ergo Sum'   74
   - 4.2 Kant's 'I Think'   77
   - 4.3 'I Think' = 'I Exist Thinking'   82
     - 4.3.1 Kant on Descartes's *Cogito* Argument   82
     - 4.3.2 Three Kinds of Consciousness of My Own Thinking   86
       - 4.3.2.1 The Mere Consciousness of the Act of Thinking   86
       - 4.3.2.2 The Indeterminate Perception that I Think   87
       - 4.3.2.3 The Empirically Determined Consciousness of the Sequence of My Mental States   91
     - 4.3.3 Kant and Descartes on Perceiving that One Thinks   92
   - 4.4 Interlude: Anderson on Longuenesse on Kant on Descartes' *Cogito* Argument   93
   - 4.5 Concluding Remarks   94

5.	Kant on 'I' and the Soul	102
	5.1 Ambiguities in Kant's Terminology	103
	5.1.1 Transcendental Unity of Apperception	103
	5.1.2 I Think	104
	5.1.3 I	107
	5.1.4 Subject	108
	5.1.5 Soul	109
	5.1.6 Self	111
	5.2 "The First Paralogism, of Substantiality"	112
	5.2.1 The First Paralogism in A	113
	5.2.1.1 Comments on the Major Premise	113
	5.2.1.2 Comments on the Minor Premise	115
	5.2.1.3 Where is the Paralogism?	115
	5.2.1.4 Another Way to Go	121
	5.2.2 The First Paralogism in B	121
	5.2.2.1 Kant's Statement of the Paralogism in B	121
	5.2.2.2 About the Major Premise, Comparison of A and B	124
	5.2.2.3 About the Minor Premise and the Conclusion, Comparison of A and B	124
	5.3 "The Second Paralogism, of Simplicity"	125
	5.3.1 The Second Paralogism in A	125
	5.3.1.1 The Major Premise	126
	5.3.1.2 The Minor Premise	128
	5.3.2 The Second Paralogism in B	129
	5.3.3 Logical Subject and Subjective 'I'	130
	5.4 Concluding Remarks	131
6.	Kant on the Identity of Persons	140
	6.1 Kant's Criticism of the Paralogism of Personality	141
	6.2 "I, as Thinking," and Consciousness of Identity in Different Times	142
	6.3 Consciousness of Identity and Personhood	146
	6.4 Kant's Person, and the Moral Standpoint	152
	6.5 Kant and Strawson on Persons	158
	6.6 Concluding Remarks	163

Part III. ... And Back Again

7.	Kant's 'I' in 'I Think' and Freud's "Ego"	173
	7.1 Preliminary Remarks	173
	7.2 Kant on 'I' in 'I Think'	176
	7.2.1 'I,' Discursive Thinking, and Being Conscious of One's Representations	176
	7.2.2 Discursive Thinking and Synthesis of Imagination	181
	7.2.3 We are "Seldom Even Conscious" of the Synthesis of Imagination	181
	7.2.4 'I' and Consciousness of One's Own Body	183
	7.3 Freud on "das Ich" ("the Ego")	185
	7.3.1 Consciousness and What is Unconscious	185
	7.3.2 "Ego" and "Id"	186

	7.4 Kant's '*Ich*' in '*Ich denke*' and Freud's '*Ich*'	188
	7.4.1 'I,' Discursive Thinking, and Consciousness of One's Representations	189
	7.4.2 Kant's Synthesis of Imagination and Freud's Perceptual Images Organized According to the Rules of the Ego	190
	7.4.3 Mental Activities of Which We are "Seldom Even Conscious"	191
	7.4.4 'I' and the Body	193
	7.5 Concluding Remarks	194
8.	Kant's 'I' in the Moral 'I Ought To' and Freud's "Super-Ego"	204
	8.1 Preliminary Remarks	204
	8.2 Kant's 'I' in 'I Ought To'	209
	8.2.1 The Moral 'I Ought To' and Mental Conflict	209
	8.2.2 'I Ought To' and Pre-Discursive Determination of the Will	212
	8.2.3 Motivated Blindness to the Grounds of One's Actions	213
	8.2.4 'I' in 'I Ought To' and Consciousness of One's Body	216
	8.3 Freud's Super-Ego	218
	8.4 Kant's 'I' in 'I Ought To' and Freud's Super-Ego	220
	8.4.1 Mental Conflict	220
	8.4.2 Discursive, Pre-Discursive, Non-Discursive Mental Activity	221
	8.4.3 Motivated Blindness	222
	8.4.4 'I' in 'I Ought To,' Freud's "Super-Ego," and Embodiment	224
	8.5 Concluding Remarks	226
9.	Epilogue	231
Bibliography		239
General Index		247
Name Index		255

Preface and Acknowledgments

1.

This book has been long in the making. I became interested in writing about self-consciousness and the first person some fifteen years ago, after reading Quassim Cassam's *Self and World*. In that book, Cassam mounts a systematic challenge against Immanuel Kant's claim that being conscious of oneself as a thinking subject is not, and cannot be, having intuitive awareness of oneself as an object. Kant was right, Cassam maintains, insofar as by 'object' he meant a Cartesian soul, distinct from the body. But there is an object one is aware of, indeed one must be aware of, in being aware of oneself as a thinking subject. That object is a physical thing among other physical things: an embodied, living being. A few pages into Cassam's book, one finds the provocative statement: "Awareness of oneself, qua subject, as a physical object, is a *necessary* condition for self-consciousness" (Cassam 1997, 3). The project of the present book grew out of my effort to understand Cassam's statement, to figure out the extent to which Cassam agreed and the extent to which he disagreed with Kant's view, and whether the types of arguments he deployed were even compatible with Kant's types of arguments. That initial interrogation soon developed into a more systematic exploration of Kant's account of self-consciousness and its relation to contemporary analyses of self-consciousness and our use of the first-person pronoun 'I.'

My first foray into the topic was a paper entitled "Self-Consciousness and Consciousness of One's Own Body: Variations on a Kantian Theme." Against Cassam, I defended the view that what Kant means by consciousness of oneself as a thinking subject is not and cannot be consciousness of oneself as a physical entity, although it is, in most instances, intimately connected with the consciousness one has of one's own body. In other words, whereas Cassam presented his view as a friendly amendment to Kant's view, I argued that, in fact, it could not be such an amendment because the amendment Cassam proposed was not compatible with what Kant means by "consciousness of oneself as subject."

After many rounds of discussion in departmental colloquia and invited lectures, the paper appeared in 2006 in a special issue of *Philosophical Topics* on "Analytic Kantianism," edited by James Conant. I am grateful to Quassim Cassam for discussing his view with me over the years. Thanks also to Christopher Peacocke and Galen Strawson, whose remarks, when I presented the paper in the CUNY Philosophy Department's colloquium in 2006, played a significant role in the development of my view. My conversations with Christopher Peacocke have hardly ceased since then, about this paper and many others, his as well as mine. I have learned a great deal from those conversations.

Unlike other papers I will mention below, the 2006 paper did not morph into a chapter of the book. One reason is that, in a sense, the whole book grew out of the paper, so that it seemed redundant to include it. But another reason is that the paper contained what I now think were quite a few confusions, for instance about the relation, for Kant, between the proposition 'I think' and what Kant calls the "transcendental unity of apperception"; or what Kant means when he claims that in thinking, I am conscious of the numerical identity of myself in different times. On the first point, I did not distinguish with enough consistency the *proposition* 'I think,' the *concept* 'I,' which occupies, says Kant, the position of the logical subject in the proposition 'I think,' and the transcendental unity of apperception which the proposition *expresses*. On the second point, I did not distinguish clearly enough between *being aware* of myself as numerically identical in different times, and *conceiving* myself to be numerically identical in different times. The former expression (being aware of myself as numerically identical) suggests a factive meaning, indicating that necessarily, in thinking, I am, as a thinker, numerically identical at different times as the agent of my thinking, and I am aware of just that fact. The latter expression (*conceiving* myself to be numerically identical), in contrast, suggests no such factive meaning: it may well be the case that necessarily, in thinking, I have a concept of myself as numerically identical in different times, without this concept offering any answer whatsoever to the question whether I do in fact remain, in thinking, one and the same entity, the agent of thinking, numerically identical in different times. Although Kant's terminology is less than perspicuous, it is clear from the general line of his argument that he holds the latter view, not the former. He holds that necessarily, in thinking, we conceive ourselves, or think of ourselves, as numerically identical in different times. This is different from being (factively) aware of ourselves as numerically identical agents of our thinking. The distinction is a difficult one, and was not clear to me in the earlier phases of my work on this project. It became clearer as I progressed.

A related point on which my view has evolved concerns the extent to which a notion much discussed in recent philosophy of language and mind is applicable to Kant's analysis of our use of the first-person pronoun 'I' in 'I think': the notion of "immunity to error through misidentification relative to the first-person pronoun" (see Shoemaker 2003c; the notion will be explained and discussed in Chapter 2). I thought then, and I still think now, that the notion *is* relevant to Kant's analysis, although of course these are not the terms in which he presented his view. But my view has changed on the extent to which the notion is applicable. This point is related to the previous one. Clearly, understanding what Kant means by "consciousness of one's own numerical identity in different times" has consequences for the answer one may give to the question whether that particular form of self-consciousness is immune to error through misidentification relative to the first person, or whether it even makes sense to ask such a question. Both points will come under discussion on multiple occasions in the course of this book.

Those differences notwithstanding, I continue to endorse the central thesis I defended in discussing Cassam's view. There is, according to Kant, a fundamental difference between the self-consciousness proper to the thinking subject in the course of her thinking, and her consciousness of herself as an object in the world, even more so if, by the latter, one means her consciousness of herself as an embodied entity. In the 2006 paper, I mostly tried to clarify Kant's distinction and to make a case for its plausibility. In this book, the case is considerably developed both as an interpretation of Kant's view and as a systematic argument.

One of the attractive features of the discussion engaged by Cassam was that it drew resources not only from the discussion of Kant's *Critique of Pure Reason*, but also from contemporary philosophy of language and mind, from the history of early modern philosophy, and from the Continental tradition in Western philosophy, a tradition that has long been occupied with concepts of consciousness, self-consciousness, subject and object of consciousness, and the relation between mind and body. Cassam acknowledged in his book the proximity between his position and that of the French philosopher Maurice Merleau-Ponty, who, in his *Phenomenology of Perception*, first published in 1945, maintained that consciousness of oneself as the subject of thinking just is consciousness of oneself as an embodied entity (see Merleau-Ponty 1962). For my part, in concluding my discussion of Cassam's view, I suggested that one finds a descendant of Kant's view of 'I' and its relation to the unity of consciousness, in Sigmund Freud's concept of 'ego,' which refers to an organization of mental events whose contents are ordered according to logical rules under what Freud calls the "reality principle." The suggestion made a brief and cautious appearance at the end of the paper. I have now extensively developed it in Chapters 7 and 8 of this book.

Most of the chapters in the present book draw part of their material from previously published papers. In what follows, I will indicate the ancestors of each chapter. These indications do not count as an explanation of the structure of the book. Nor do they count as an explanation of the content of its particular chapters. Those explanations will be offered below, in Chapter 1 ("Introduction").

2.

The earliest ancestor of some of the material appearing in Chapter 2 ("Uses of 'I'") was presented under the title "I, Self, Identity" in the weekly fellows' seminar at the Wissenschaftskolleg in Berlin, in the spring of 2007. I am grateful to Pierre-Michel Menger for serving as a helpful sparring partner during the preparation of the paper and as the moderator of the seminar discussion. A revised version was presented in spring 2008 in François Recanati's seminar at the Institut Jean Nicod in Paris. I am grateful to Recanati for his invitation to present in his seminar, and for the invitation that followed, to contribute to the volume *Immunity to Error through Misidentification: New Essays* (Prosser and Recanati 2012). The title of the published paper was "Two Uses of 'I' as Subject?" Material from that paper is reprinted with permission of Cambridge University Press.

Some of the material for Chapter 3 ("Non-Thetic Self-Consciousness and Uses of 'I': Sartre Meets Wittgenstein") appeared in 2008 in the *European Journal of Philosophy* under the title "Self-Consciousness and Self-Reference: Sartre and Wittgenstein" and is reprinted with permission of Wiley-Blackwell, publisher of the journal. The paper was first presented in 2007 at the University of Oxford, as the invited annual lecture of the *European Journal of Philosophy*. The public lecture was followed by a seminar in which we discussed "I, Self, Identity," mentioned above. I am grateful to participants in both events for their helpful comments. One mistake

I made in the *European Journal* paper is corrected in Chapter 3. I wrote that only in his 1943 *Being and Nothingness* did Sartre include under his concept of non-thetic self-consciousness, consciousness of one's own body. The idea was absent, I claimed, from his 1938 *The Transcendence of the Ego*. In fact, as I now indicate in Chapter 3, the idea was already present in *The Transcendence of the Ego*. This historical point had no consequences for the general argument of the paper, which I still endorse in its general line but have, I hope, improved not only in terms of historical accuracy but also in the formulation of its systematic points. Some of the material was presented again at a conference organized at Université Bordeaux Montaigne by Jean-Philippe Narboux, on "Sartrian Themes in Analytic Philosophy." I especially benefited from the comments of Jean-Philippe Narboux, Matthew Boyle, and Richard Moran. Richard Moran also sent me detailed and extremely useful comments on the penultimate draft of Chapter 3.

Some of the material for Chapter 4 is drawn from a paper published in the volume *Kant and the Early Moderns* (Garber and Longuenesse 2008) under the title "Kant's 'I think' versus Descartes' 'I am a thing that thinks'." The relevant material is reprinted with permission of Princeton University Press. The volume resulted from a conference Daniel Garber and I organized at Princeton University in the spring of 2004. I am grateful to Jean-Marie Beyssade for his insightful comments on my presentation at the conference. In the fall of the same year, I presented a French version of the paper under the title "Cogito Kantien et Cogito Cartésien" at the conference "Descartes dans Kant" organized at the Sorbonne and the Università degli Studi di Lecce (Italy). The French version was published in 2006 in the volume *Descartes dans Kant* co-edited by Michel Fichant and Jean-Luc Marion.

Some of the material for Chapter 6 ("Kant on the Identity of Persons") originated in a paper presented at the meeting of the Aristotelian Society held at the Senate House, University of London, in January 2007, and subsequently published in the *Proceedings of the Aristotelian Society* (see Longuenesse 2007) under the title "Kant on the Identity of Persons." The relevant material is reprinted by courtesy of the Editor of the Aristotelian Society © 2007. The paper was discussed at a conference on "Self, Agency, and Self-Awareness," organized by Michael Nelson at the University of California, Riverside, in 2008. Houston Smit was my commentator. His generous and challenging comments were instrumental in my revising the paper for the chapter of this book. Also helpful were discussions at Humboldt Universität in Berlin. Special thanks to Rolf-Peter Horstmann and to Tobias Rosefeldt for their invitations and for countless conversations on all the issues discussed in the book. Thanks also to Dina Emundts, Stefanie Grüne, Hannah Ginsborg, Daniel Warren, and Wayne Waxman, for our many conversations in Berlin, New York, and many other places.

An earlier version of some of the material for Chapters 7 and 8 was first presented, under the title "Kant's 'I' and Freud's 'ego'," as a keynote address at the Asilomar Conference on Phenomenology and Cognitive Science in 2008. I especially benefited from the comments of William Blattner, Hubert Dreyfus, Rebecca Kukla, Robert Pippin, and Charles Siewert. That version was presented again at the UNC–Chapel Hill philosophy conference in 2008. Richard Moran was the commentator. I am grateful for his comments, which gave me a lot to think about in continuing to work on that material.

As the paper grew, I divided the material and treated separately, on the one hand Kant's 'I' in the theoretical 'I think' in relation to Freud's "ego"; and on the other, Kant's 'I' in the moral 'I ought to,' in relation to Freud's "super-ego". The first part of the material was presented in 2010, as a keynote address to the 11th Congress of the International Kant Society in Pisa and published in 2013 in the proceedings of the conference. Chapter 7 is a revision and expansion of that paper. The relevant material is reprinted by courtesy of De Gruyter, © 2013.

The second part was presented in 2012 at the joint session of the Aristotelian Society and the Mind Association at the University of Stirling and published in the 2012 Supplementary Volume of the Aristotelian Society. Chapter 8 is a revision and expansion of that paper. The relevant material is reprinted by courtesy of the Editor of the Aristotelian Society, © 2012. Sebastian Gardner was my commentator in the joint session. I am grateful for his comments, which were instrumental in my preparing Chapters 7 and 8. My heartfelt thanks to Allen Wood for his extensive written comments and correspondence on Chapter 8, interspersed with "sermons" making me aware of my sins in textual interpretation or systematic claims. The reader will find traces of my discussions with Allen throughout Chapter 8. I am sure the chapter is much better from those discussions. The shortcomings that remain are entirely mine.

I benefited from presenting portions of the whole book project at various stages of its development. I am grateful to Vincent Descombes for inviting me to hold a one-month visiting professorship at the Ecole des Hautes Etudes en Sciences Sociales in Paris in spring 2008, during which I presented material from each of what became the three main parts of the book; to Tobias Rosefeldt for inviting me to give the annual weeklong "Kant-Kurs" at the Universität Konstanz, in spring 2009; to the Department of Philosophy at the University of British Columbia for inviting me to give the Landsdowne lectures in spring 2012, in which I presented ancestors of Chapters 2 and 8; to Hong Yu Wong and Natalie Sebanz for inviting me to present my work in the workshop on "Problems of the Self" at Central European University in 2012.

In April 2014 I presented the Hempel Lectures at Princeton University. Special thanks to Michael Smith for extending the invitation to present the lectures; and to Daniel Garber, Mark Johnston, Des Hogan, Gideon Rosen, John Burgess, Jeffrey Stout, and Dale Jamieson for their insightful comments. I am grateful to Christopher Peacocke for sending me very helpful written comments, continuing once again our conversation.

In May 2014, I presented the Kant Lectures at Stanford University. Special thanks to Lanier Anderson for extending the invitation to present the Kant Lectures and the accompanying seminar; for convening an additional seminar in which we discussed the differences in our interpretations of Kant on Descartes's *cogito* argument; and for his incisive comments throughout. Many thanks also to Michael Bratman, Graciela De Pierris, David Hills, Helen Longino, Tamar Schapiro, Ken Taylor, and Johan Van Benthem for their comments and contributions to the discussions. My correspondence with Johan Van Benthem in the weeks that followed was extremely helpful when working on the final draft of Chapter 2.

I have benefited from many more visits to philosophy colloquia, conferences, departmental seminars, and personal exchanges. All participants in those occasions should know how grateful I am for those countless and continuing conversations.

3.

Academic research would be impossible without the institutions that support it. My gratitude goes first to the two philosophy departments that have been home to my research and teaching while preparing this book.

Princeton University and its Department of Philosophy first welcomed me into the academic world in the United States, and were home to the first steps that led to this book. Tragically, Margaret Wilson passed away just five years after I arrived at Princeton. I never had a chance to discuss this project with her. And yet she is never far from my mind as an example of integrity, fierce independence, and intellectual as well as personal generosity. I am fortunate and honored to have had her as a colleague and a friend.

Throughout my years at Princeton, and in the years that followed, Paul Benacerraf has been an indefatigable friend and mentor. To this day his example continues to influence my work. My conversations with Harry Frankfurt have been a constant spur to think outside of the beaten track. As I progressed in this book project, I have also benefited from discussions with Sarah Buss, John Cooper, Daniel Garber, Richard Moran, Alexander Nehamas, Gideon Rosen, Mark Johnston, and Bas Van Fraassen.

The Department of Philosophy at New York University has been an exciting intellectual environment during the bulk of my work on the book. Paul Boghossian made me feel welcome, and throughout my years at NYU my conversations with him have been unfailingly challenging and rewarding. Richard Foley has been a constant support and an inspiring mentor and interlocutor. Don Garrett has been the best possible colleague, friend, and source of intellectual and personal inspiration. Conversations with Ned Block, Samuel Scheffler, and David Velleman have directly influenced my work on this book. I have also learned in countless ways from all my colleagues in the department, as well as from our graduate and undergraduate students. To all, I am deeply grateful. Special thanks to our guardian angels, the members of the staff, without whose help we could not keep the Department of Philosophy the vibrant place it is.

New York University has been exceptionally generous in allowing me to take leaves of absence at the Wissenschaftskolleg in Berlin in 2006-7, at the American Academy in Berlin in 2012-13, and at the national Humanities Center in 2015-16.

The first germs of this book began to sprout during my 2006-7 fellowship at the Wissenschaftskolleg, where I wrote the papers that eventually became ancestors to Chapters 2, 3, and 6. Dieter Grimm was the gracious and inspiring Rektor of the Wissenschaftskolleg during the fall of 2006, the final semester of his tenure there. I count myself exceptionally fortunate to have spent the first half of my fellowship under his gentle, intelligent, and generous leadership. Conversations with Frank Rösler influenced my work on this book and resulted in joint projects which I hope to continue (see Longuenesse and Rösler 2008; Longuenesse 2012a).

PREFACE AND ACKNOWLEDGMENTS xvii

Throughout the year I especially benefited from my conversations with Pierre-Michel Menger, Paul Schmidt-Hempel, and Helmut Lachenmann. In the years that followed, Pierre-Michel Menger remained a constant sounding board for the ideas that eventually made it into the book.

My 2012–13 fellowship at the American Academy in Berlin was spent in great part struggling with Kant's Paralogisms of Pure Reason. I wrote drafts of what eventually became Chapters 4, 5, and 6. I also revised the draft of Chapter 3, which benefited from written comments from Dean Moyar.

The final draft of the book was completed during my year at the National Humanities Center in the Research Triangle Park, North Carolina. I benefited from conversations with Owen Flanagan, who gave me insightful comments on Chapter 2 and on an earlier paper, "'I' and the Brain" (Longuenesse 2012b), when I was agonizing over the decision whether to revise it for inclusion as Chapter 9 in the book. In the end I decided not to, but my conversations with Owen remain a source of inspiration for continued research in that area. Bill Schwarz was a generous and upbeat brother in arms and a generous reader who helped me push through to the final completion of this book. I also benefited from the kindness of Paul and Lynn Otto, and from the warm and supportive community of fellows. The enthusiastic help extended by the whole staff (a special shout out for the library staff: the indomitable Brooke Andrade, as well as Sarah Harris and Sam Schuth) made the Humanities Center a joyful home for the final stages of the project.

I submitted a complete draft of the book to Oxford University Press in January 2014. I am grateful for the extensive and helpful comments I received from two readers for the press. One of them, Quassim Cassam, went the extra mile in allowing the press to lift his anonymity. There followed an email correspondence in which we discussed his already very detailed comments. The whole process was exceptionally helpful as I was working on the final draft for publication.

Thank you to Karen Carroll, the gifted copy editor of the National Humanities Center, for her invaluable help in giving decent shape to the final draft I sent the Press; and to Chris Prodoehl, my research assistant during the final phase.

I know I join a long cohort of authors in my expression of gratitude to Peter Momtchiloff, the magician of OUP, who commissioned this book and kept faith in its completion. Thanks also to Joanna North for her work in copy editing the book for Oxford University Press; to Vaishnavi Venkatesan, the project manager for SPi; and to Martin Noble for his invaluable help in putting together the index.

* * *

A word about the title, "I, Me, Mine." As people of my generation will know, it is the title of a song by George Harrison, the last song the Beatles recorded together before the group split up. It was suggested to me many years ago by Dale Jamieson, in one of those inspiring and mischievous conversations we have about everything and especially about philosophy. I'm not sure what his intention was in suggesting the title. Surely he was aware that the song is an indictment of our narcissistic obsession with the self. Now, one conclusion I have derived from my work on the first person is that there are all types of gradation in the use of the first person, from the use of 'I' that is sunk in what Kant called "the dear self," incapable of rising above its individual standpoint, egoistic motives, and archaic fears; to the use of 'I' that speaks for all, a use that belongs in the effort to rise above individual standpoints and egoistic motives and to develop the voice of what Kant called "the proper self." I relish the exasperated tone of the Beatles' song, and I endorse its exasperation. But what I try to understand with this book are the ways in which we human beings are capable of combining to good effect, in our uses of 'I' and its cognates, the most individual conception of ourselves and the most universal conception of our abilities and values. I have tried to understand the ways we combine a use that is sunk in the individual self, and a use that elevates us to a realization of what we universally share and ought to share.

Conventions

1. Use of quotation marks

I use single quotation marks when mentioning terms, concepts, sentences, or propositions, e.g., the word 'I,' the concept 'I,' the proposition 'I think.' I use double quotation marks when citing terms or sentences as used by specific authors, e.g., Kant's "transcendental unity of apperception."

2. Use of bold letters or italics for emphasis

I use italics in citations for emphasis. I indicate in each case whether the emphasis is mine or the author's. In citations from the *Critique of Pure Reason*, I follow the translators' format and always use bold letters for Kant's emphasis and italics for my own emphasis. In those cases, I will therefore not specify whose emphasis, mine or Kant's.

3. Use of capital letters

I use capital letters when referring to the title of a section in the *Critique of Pure Reason*, e.g., The Paralogisms of Pure Reason. I use lowercase letters when referring to an argument developed in the corresponding section, e.g., Kant's criticism of the paralogisms of pure reason.

4. Citations
   - Works of Kant are cited using an abbreviation of the title, followed by reference in the Akademie Ausgabe by volume and page (e.g., *Prol.*, AA4, 258). See abbreviations and complete reference to the Akademie Ausgabe in the bibliography at the end of this volume. One exception is the *Critique of Pure Reason*, cited by A and B, referring to the first (1781) and second (1787) original editions.
   - Works of Freud are cited using an abbreviation of the title, followed by reference, for the English edition, to the *Standard Edition* (e.g., *SE*, 12:20), and for the German edition, to the *Gesammelte Werke* (e.g., *GW*, 14:37). See complete reference to the *Standard Edition* and to the *Gesammelte Werke*, and abbreviations used for individual works, in the bibliography at the end of this volume.
   - Works of Descartes, Leibniz, Locke, and Wolff are cited by date of the edition used followed by the original date of publication. See complete references in the bibliography.
   - All other works are cited by date of the edition used.

1

Introduction

1.1 The Problem

The question at the core of the present book found its first formulation in Immanuel Kant's *Critique of Pure Reason* and has known a spectacular revival in recent analytic philosophy of language and mind: What is self-consciousness, and in what ways does it relate to our use, in language and in thought, of the first-person pronoun 'I'?

Kant was especially interested in a specific kind of self-consciousness, the kind that finds conceptual formulation in the proposition 'I think.' In thinking 'I think,' he claimed, we give conceptual expression to our consciousness of being engaged in a mental activity we take to be our own: the activity of combining and comparing representations according to logical rules. Keeping track of such mental activity, Kant claimed, is inseparable from being conscious of being engaged in that activity, and accountable for the correctness of its outcome. This consciousness is what we express in predicating 'think' of 'I' in 'I think.' Now, in being conscious of ourselves in this way, Kant claimed, we are not conscious of ourselves as an object among other objects in the world. I may, on other grounds, be conscious of myself as an object, indeed as a physical object, a particular entity among other entities located in space and time. But this kind of consciousness of myself is not, says Kant, what I am expressing when I use 'I' in 'I think.' Does this mean, then, that in using 'I' in 'I think' I am conscious of myself as another kind of entity, an immaterial object, a Cartesian soul? On the contrary, Kant takes great pains to argue that nothing in our consciousness of thinking provides justification for the view that we are souls, distinct from bodies. In short: the consciousness I have of myself, as the *subject* of thinking (the consciousness I have of myself in being conscious that I think), is not a consciousness of myself as any kind of *object* at all, whether material or immaterial.

In the second half of the twentieth century, a number of philosophers who otherwise acknowledged the importance of Kant's analysis of self-consciousness, nevertheless vigorously challenged Kant's claim that the consciousness of oneself expressed in thinking 'I think' is not consciousness of oneself as an object in the world. Kant was right, they said, to claim that the consciousness we have of ourselves in thinking is not consciousness of ourselves as an object, if by that he meant that we are not conscious of a Cartesian soul, distinct from the body. But there is an object we are conscious of when we are conscious of ourselves as thinking. That object is a physical thing among other physical things: our own body.

The discussion has often been framed in the terms of a more recent distinction, which we inherit from Ludwig Wittgenstein. In the preparatory notes for the *Philosophical Investigations* that were published posthumously in 1953 under the title *The Blue Book*, Wittgenstein distinguished between what he called the "use of 'I' as subject" and the "use of 'I' as object."[1] Whereas Kant's distinction is a distinction between two kinds of consciousness, Wittgenstein's distinction is a distinction between two ways in which we use the word 'I.' Nevertheless, just as Kant insists that consciousness of oneself as a subject of thinking is not consciousness of an object given in space and time, so Wittgenstein insists that in its use "as subject," 'I' is not used to refer to myself as a particular person. Rather, in its use "as subject" 'I' has no other function than to express the self-ascription of a subjective state (for instance, tooth-ache, in: "I have tooth-ache"), without any reference at all being made to a particular entity, distinguished from other entities in the world. In this respect, Wittgenstein provocatively maintained, saying "I have tooth-ache" is no different from moaning.

Many recent discussions of the uses of 'I' have challenged Wittgenstein's view. While accepting as important and illuminating Wittgenstein's *Blue Book* distinction between two uses of 'I,' some philosophers have claimed that even in its use "as subject," 'I' is used to refer to a particular entity, a person, distinguished from other persons. The difference between the two uses only lies in the kind of information on the basis of which the proposition is thought and the statement made, and therefore the kind of error to which an expression of the proposition is liable, or not. This argument against Wittgenstein's interpretation of his own distinction then easily morphs into an argument against Kant's interpretation of his own distinction. Just as it was a mistake, on Wittgenstein's part, to think that in its use as subject, 'I' does not refer to a particular person, so it had been a mistake, on Kant's part, to think that consciousness of oneself as subject is not consciousness of oneself as an object at all, distinguished from other objects in the world.

In this book, I argue that the force of Kant's view has been partly missed in the line of discussion just sketched out. My argument turns on two main points.

First, it is a mistake to think that Kant's distinction between consciousness of oneself as the subject of thinking and consciousness of oneself as an object in space and time is directly parallel to Wittgenstein's distinction between the use of 'I' "as subject" and the use of 'I' "as object," or to any of the more recent developments and reinterpretations of Wittgenstein's *Blue Book* distinction. I attempt to clarify the differences between the argumentative contexts in which the distinctions inspired by Kant and Wittgenstein, respectively, appear.

Second, behind both distinctions and their competing interpretations looms a question that is central to contemporary philosophy of mind: What are the respective roles, in self-consciousness, of consciousness of one's own body and consciousness of mental unity? I argue that the controversies just outlined rest in large part on a lack of understanding of Kant's contribution to an elucidation of these roles.

But there is more. If, as I argue, Kant's analysis of 'I' in 'I think' connects this particular use of 'I' to the consciousness of a logically ordered unity of mental contents, then Kant's analysis of 'I' in 'I think' does not find its most direct descendant in questions we inherit from Wittgenstein, concerning the referent, or lack of referent, for 'I.' Rather, surprisingly enough, Kant's analysis of the way our use of 'I' in 'I think' is grounded in the unity of consciousness finds a more direct descendant in Freud's psychological concept of "ego." For Freud's concept of ego, like Kant's concept of the unity of consciousness or unity of apperception, is the concept of an organization of mental events whose contents have a specific type of unity. The organization of mental events Freud calls "ego" is governed by what Freud calls the "reality principle," and its contents are structured according to elementary logical rules, allowing us to acquire a reliable perceptual representation of the world. Kant's "unity of apperception" or "unity of consciousness" is governed by rules of imagination as well as logical rules of judgment and inference, according to which the contents of one's representational states are reliably related to independently existing objects. Thus, Freud's concept of the ego, albeit belonging in the context of a psychological/clinical investigation, offers a striking parallel, in that context, to Kant's concept of the unity of apperception, which belongs in the context of a transcendental investigation into the necessary conditions for knowledge of independently existing objects.

It may seem at best arbitrary and unnecessarily provocative, or at worst jejune, to take Freud's view of the mind to be relevant to a discussion of Kant's legacy on self-consciousness and the use of 'I.' The chapters I devote to this question will have to speak for themselves. As a preliminary, let me just make the following remarks. Undoubtedly, recent advances in cognitive psychology and neuroscience provide so much unprecedented insight into the unity of consciousness that appealing to Freud may seem like an arbitrary and unnecessary detour. And yet a closer look will show that Freud's metapsychology, with its grounding in both folk psychology (the ordinary psychology of sensory perception, beliefs, desires, emotions, and fantasies) and in neurology (in its incipient stage in the first half of the twentieth century), is a significant intermediate step between Kant's and our own contemporary approach to the mind. For this writer, stumbling upon the connection between Kant and Freud was unexpected, and proved to be fruitful. I have found Kant and Freud mutually illuminating, and I form the hypothesis that the same will be true of the relation between both Kant and Freud, properly understood, and contemporary psychology and philosophy of mind. This last relation (Kant and Freud to contemporary philosophy of mind and psychology) is a program that remains to be explored, but to which I hope to further contribute, after the beginning steps I am taking in this book.

The sequence of questions just outlined explains the unusual structure of the present work. The book starts with a discussion of recent and contemporary analyses of self-consciousness in connection with analyses of our use of 'I' in language and thought (Part I: Back to...). It works its way back in time to Kant's view (Part II:...Kant). Finally, it works its way back again to our time, via an analysis of the similarities and differences between Kant's explanation of the role of 'I' in relation to mental unity, on the one hand, and Freud's concepts of "ego" and "super-ego," on the other (Part III:...and Back Again).

Let me now give a brief overview of each chapter. The reader may opt to jump directly to Chapter 2, or for that matter, to any other chapter, using the abstracts I am about to offer as independent summaries while she works her way through the book in the order that most suits her interests. Or she may read through the whole sequence of abstracts, thus getting some sense of what to expect from the book as a whole. Each chapter presents a relatively independent argument that can be read separately. But all of them together present a unified line of argument, whose results I assess at the end of the book.

1.2 Part I: Back to...

In **Chapter 2**, I introduce Wittgenstein's and Kant's respective distinctions outlined above. I explain to what extent they map each other, to what extent they don't. Kant's 'consciousness of oneself as subject'[2] is expressed in the proposition 'I think.' That proposition, I point out, covers only one of the examples Wittgenstein offers, in the *Blue Book*, of the "use of 'I' as subject" ("I think it will rain"). This should already alert us to the fact that Kant's and Wittgenstein's respective distinctions do not exactly map.

In 2.1, I examine Wittgenstein's distinction between the use of 'I' as subject and the use of 'I' as object. I endorse Sydney Shoemaker's argument according to which, *pace* Wittgenstein, the correct way to distinguish the two kinds of uses of 'I' is *not* to say that in its use as subject, 'I' does not refer to a particular entity at all. Rather, the distinction turns on the fact that a judgment in which 'I' is used as subject is "immune to error through misidentification relative to the first person pronoun,"[3] an error to which the use of 'I' as object is not immune. I then argue that, this distinction notwithstanding, even uses of 'I' as object *partly* depend on the kind of information that, if it were expressed in a judgment, would be expressed in a judgment in which 'I' is used as subject. The next question is: What is that information? I discuss Evans's claim that for 'I' to be used at all, that information must be information about one's own body. Evans claims Kantian ancestry on this point: Kant saw, Evans maintains, that absent a background understanding of the reference of 'I' to our own body, we would have "at most a formal 'I think,'"[4] where 'I' would not refer to any entity at all. My own view is that Evans is wrong both about the systematic point he is defending and about the view he attributes to Kant.

In 2.2, I examine Kant's view of 'I' in 'I think.' I argue that, according to Kant's groundbreaking thesis in the Transcendental Deduction of the Categories, the self-consciousness that grounds the use of 'I' in 'I think' is a consciousness of being engaged in an activity of binding one's representations in such a way as to come up with concepts, combined in judgments, connected in inferential patterns.[5] I argue that this particular kind of self-consciousness may be, but is not necessarily, connected to the particular kind of consciousness of one's own body that (in the terms of Wittgenstein's distinction, amended by Shoemaker and Evans) also grounds a use of 'I' as subject. I moreover argue that the kind of self-consciousness that, according to Kant's analysis, is consciousness of oneself as subject, is a necessary condition for any use of 'I,' whether as subject (in all the different cases of the latter I examine earlier in the chapter) or as object.

Kant's argument in the Transcendental Deduction is an epistemological argument (or more precisely, a "transcendental" argument, in a sense explained in 2.2), not a psychological description. Nevertheless, it had better not run afoul of psychological descriptions. In 2.3, I argue that the distinction between consciousness of the reason-giving unity of one's mental activity and consciousness of one's own body finds support in descriptions of pathological cases in which the two may come apart. I cite a case described by Oliver Sacks as "the disembodied lady," and similar cases of deafferented patients described by Jonathan Cole. Sacks concludes his discussion of the case of the "disembodied lady" by noting that consciousness of one's own body is the "mooring of the self," and relates this remark to Freud's own statement that the ego is "first and foremost a body-ego."[6] I argue that the connection Sacks makes between his view and Freud's converges with my own view that Freud's account of what he calls "the ego" offers a developmental account of the relation between the two aspects of self-consciousness I examine in Chapter 2. I defend this claim further in Chapters 7 and 8 of the book.

In **Chapter 3**, I take up again the question: What different kinds of self-consciousness support what Wittgenstein and his followers have called the use of 'I' as subject? When pressing his claim that any use of 'I' depends on consciousness of one's own body, Gareth Evans briefly mentions the affinity between his view and that of Jean-Paul Sartre. In order to assess Evans's suggestion, I examine Sartre's analysis of self-consciousness, in particular the variety of self-consciousness Sartre calls "non-thetic" or "non-positional" self-consciousness. I argue that Sartre offers a rich phenomenological description of self-consciousness as consciousness of one's own body, an account that indeed puts him close to Evans's view. But Sartre shares with Evans a lack of attention to the dimension of self-consciousness that is at the core of Kant's analysis of consciousness of oneself as subject: consciousness of a rationally unified mental activity one takes oneself to be accountable for.

In 3.1, I examine Sartre's view of consciousness and self-consciousness as expounded in *The Transcendence of the Ego* and in the opening sections of *Being and Nothingness*. In 3.2, I argue that the kind of self-consciousness Sartre calls "non-thetic self-consciousness" is the kind of self-consciousness that grounds what Wittgenstein and his followers call the "use of 'I' as subject." The claim may seem surprising, since in *The Transcendence of the Ego*, Sartre insists that in non-thetic self-consciousness, "there is no room for 'I.'" I point out that on Sartre's own description, there are nevertheless uses of 'I' that are specifically expressive of non-thetic self-consciousness. What is true is that those uses are not expressive of consciousness of oneself *as an object*. The examples Sartre gives of such uses include statements that depend on non-thetic consciousness of oneself as an embodied agent ("I am hanging a picture," "I am repairing a tire") as well as statements that depend on non-thetic consciousness of being engaged in a mental activity one is keeping track of ("I am counting cigarettes").[7]

Evans is correct in pointing out the proximity between his view, according to which consciousness of one's own body is a necessary condition for judgments that are immune to error through misidentification relative to the first-person pronoun, and Sartre's view of non-thetic consciousness of one's body. In 3.3, I analyze this proximity. I argue that Sartre's view of consciousness of one's own body is richer than Evans gives it credit for. I support this claim in 3.4. I note, moreover, that in addition to consciousness of one's own body, Sartre accepts another kind of non-thetic self-consciousness, the one that grounds the "pre-reflective cogito." In 3.5, I argue that Sartre's analysis of non-thetic self-consciousness in both its aspects (consciousness of one's own body, consciousness of one's mental activity or "pre-reflective cogito") offers tools for understanding the force of Anscombe's surprising statement: "I am

6   INTRODUCTION

E.A. is not an identity proposition," even while giving us reason *not* to endorse her claim that 'I' is not a referring expression.

In 3.6, I take stock of the lessons of the chapter. I conclude that Sartre's insufficient attention to the second kind of non-thetic self-consciousness he has identified (that which grounds the pre-reflective cogito) is parallel to both Evans's and Anscombe's neglect of a use of 'I' that is *not* based on bodily consciousness, but rather, on consciousness of one's mental agency. This takes me back to the conclusion of Chapter 2, in which I stressed the importance of Kant's legacy. It also opens the way to Part II of the book.

1.3   Part II: ... Kant

In **Chapter 4**, I discuss Kant's analysis of the proposition 'I think' and its relation to Descartes's *cogito* argument. Kant's analysis of 'I think' is offered in two main chapters of the *Critique of Pure Reason*: the Transcendental Deduction of the Categories, in the Transcendental Analytic; and the Paralogisms of Pure Reason, in the Transcendental Dialectic. In the Paralogisms, one of Kant's explicit targets is Descartes's *cogito* argument in the Second Meditation, and Descartes's view of the soul as a thinking substance really distinct from the body. It is therefore important to understand the relation between Kant's and Descartes's respective views of 'I think.'

In 4.1, I discuss Descartes's *cogito* argument and the role played in that argument by the fact that 'think' is asserted of 'I.' I argue that the role of 'I' in Descartes's *cogito* argument is quite different from the role assigned to 'I' in 'I think' by Kant's Transcendental Deduction of the Categories. Nevertheless, it is important to recognize that those two roles are not incompatible.

In 4.2, I discuss the role Kant assigns to the proposition 'I think' in the Transcendental Deduction. I take up again and develop the central point I made in Chapter 2: according to Kant, using 'I' in the proposition 'I think' expresses the consciousness of being, oneself, engaged in a mental activity whose contents are unified according to logical rules. Kant's explanation of the role of 'I,' I argue, is, as it were, upstream from Descartes's use of the ascription of 'think' (or 'am thinking') to 'I' in the *cogito* argument. I argue that predicating 'am thinking' of 'I' is essential to Descartes's antiskeptical argument in the Second Meditation. But *why* is 'think' or 'am thinking' predicated of 'I,' and what does this predication express? These questions are not asked, much less answered, by Descartes. They are by Kant.

In 4.3, I argue that Kant agrees with Descartes's *cogito* argument: for Kant, just as for Descartes, 'I think,' whenever actually asserted in thought or expressed in language, entails 'I exist.' Even the fact that Kant takes such an assertion to depend on *perceiving* that I think does not put him at odds with Descartes's *cogito*. What does put him at odds with Descartes are two main points. The first is that, for Kant, perceiving that I think is not only the active consciousness of a purely intellectual act, but also a self-*affection* in which I am, even while acting (while being engaged in mental action), in some sense passively affected by my own agency. There is no such idea of self-affection in Descartes. The second difference is that Kant does not think that from the pure consciousness of oneself expressed in 'I think,' or more precisely, 'I am thinking,' one can derive any knowledge of the nature of the referent of 'I.'

Nevertheless, 'I think' entails, for Kant just as for Descartes, 'I exist.' And for Kant, the consciousness of thinking expressed in 'I think' is a consciousness of myself as an "I, or he or it (the thing) that thinks,"[8] namely, as an entity that thinks and is individuated, for itself, by its consciousness of thinking. Thus, *pace* Evans, according to Kant, using 'I' in 'I think' expresses the consciousness of oneself as a particular entity (oneself, the entity currently thinking, whatever that entity is), a consciousness that does not depend on consciousness of one's own body, not even on that particular consciousness of one's body that grounds those judgments that Evans and Shoemaker call "immune to error through misidentification relative to the first person pronoun," or judgments in which 'I' is used as subject. Rather, using 'I' in 'I think' is premised on nothing but the consciousness of a mental activity one takes to be one's own in virtue of the fact that one takes oneself to be accountable for the correctness of its contents and their connections.

The order of dependence just stated may seem paradoxical. Isn't it the other way around? Isn't it, rather, that one takes oneself to be accountable for the correctness of the contents of some mental activity, and their connections, in virtue of taking the activity to be one's own?[9] I will argue that, in fact, the order is one of mutual dependence. Representing the activity as one's own *just is* acknowledging and endorsing the normative character of its contents and their connections. To frame the point in terms that are not Kant's but that are true to Kant's intention in the Transcendental Deduction of the Categories, as I will analyze it in 4.2: Being committed to thinking 'p&q' in virtue of thinking 'p' and thinking 'q' just is representing oneself as the thinker that thinks 'p,' the thinker that thinks 'q,' and the thinker—indeed the very same thinker—that is thereby committed to thinking 'p&q.'

Now, according to Kant's argument in the Paralogisms, in representing myself (in thinking 'I think') as the author of the rationally connected contents of my thoughts, I do not have any answer to the question, What kind of entity am I? Substance or accident? One or many? I am certainly not a material entity, Kant maintains, if by "material" we mean an entity that has the strictly mechanical properties of the bodies studied by Newtonian physics. Am I, then, mind? Or am I, rather, a third kind of entity that is neither mind nor Newtonian/corpuscular body? Thinking 'I think' and thus expressing my consciousness of my own thinking provides no answer to such questions. According to Kant, the error of rationalist metaphysics was to think that, from the mere thought 'I think,' I could in fact derive answers to those questions.

In **Chapter 5**, I discuss Kant's criticism of what he takes to be the rationalist error that consists in claiming one can derive from features of the mere concept 'I' in 'I think,' metaphysical knowledge of the kind of entity I am, as a thinking being. I discuss the first two of Kant's antirationalist arguments in the chapter of the Transcendental Dialectic entitled "The Paralogisms of Pure Reason." What gives those arguments their enduring relevance, I argue, is Kant's analysis of our use of 'I' in 'I think,' on which Kant bases his diagnosis of the rationalist illusion.

I suggest that some of the disagreements among scholars commenting on Kant's argument come from an insufficient clarification of the ambiguities in Kant's own use of expressions central to his analysis—for instance, 'unity of apperception,' 'I think,' 'I,' 'subject.' I try to clarify Kant's use of those expressions. I then offer an analysis of the first two fallacious inferences Kant takes to be implicitly at work in generating the purported knowledge of our metaphysical nature as thinking beings. Those first two inferences are the "paralogism of substantiality" and the "paralogism of simplicity." I lay out the differences between Kant's account of the general structure of the paralogisms in the first and second editions of the *Critique of Pure Reason*. I argue that, despite those differences, Kant's argument in the two editions is fundamentally the same, while being greatly clarified in the B edition. In support of my claim, I reconstruct a structure of the paralogisms I take to support Kant's argument in both the A and the B editions, explaining what makes the rationalist inference, as understood by Kant, a "paralogism": a formally defective inference in which the author of the inference is deceiving not only others, but also herself.[10] Obviously, this brief introduction is not the place to recount the details of the reconstructions I offer in Chapters 5 and 6. But it may help orient the reader to give at least a brief outline of those reconstructions.

The paralogisms of pure reason, as presented by Kant, have the classic form: "All As are B. All Bs are C. So, all As are C." What makes them "defective in their form," he claims, is that they display an equivocation on their middle term ('B' in the schematization I just gave). In the rationalist inferences, the term 'B' only apparently expresses the same concept in the major and in the minor premise. It in fact does *not* express the same concept. This being so, there turns out to be no middle term at all. In all four paralogisms, the inference is invalid.

Here's a rough approximation of the invalid inference. A detailed account, including an analysis of the differences between the two editions, will be given in 5.2. In the first paralogism, the inference reads: 'Something that cannot be represented otherwise than as subject, is substance. I, as thinking, cannot be represented otherwise than as subject. So I, as thinking, am substance.' Here, the equivocation is on '—cannot be represented otherwise than as subject.' In the major premise, the expression has a metaphysical meaning. It is a definition of what counts as substance. Implicit in the definition is the presupposition that an object is *presented* to us in such a way that it cannot be represented otherwise than as subject, not predicate of something else. In the minor premise, in contrast, the expression 'cannot be represented otherwise than as subject' has a "merely logical" meaning. It indicates the position that, necessarily, a concept (the concept 'I') occupies in a proposition, and the corresponding word 'I' occupies in a sentence, without any reference to *the way an object is presented* for that concept. The expression that occupies the place of the middle term in the syllogism ('—cannot be represented otherwise than as subject') thus only apparently expresses the same concept in the major and in the minor premise. It really expresses two different concepts, one metaphysical, the other "merely logical." The inference therefore has no middle term: the conclusion is invalid.

Kant makes a similar argument in the Second Paralogism, the Paralogism of Simplicity. A detailed analysis of the argument in both editions is given in 5.3. The general outline of the paralogisms, pending precisions to be provided in 5.3, is roughly this: 'Something whose action cannot be represented as the composition of the actions of several things, is simple. I, as thinking, am something whose action cannot be represented as the composition of the actions of several things. So I, as thinking, am simple.' Here, the equivocation is on '—whose action cannot be represented as the composition of the actions of several things.' Again, in the major premise, the expression has a metaphysical meaning. In the minor premise it has a "logical" meaning (to be explained in 5.3). This being so, the same phrase, '— whose action cannot be represented as the composition of the actions of several things,' expresses two different concepts. Again, there is no middle term: the inference is invalid.

The contrast between the "merely logical" and the metaphysical meaning of the words appearing in the position of the middle term in the inference, is not the only contrast Kant draws between the major and the minor premise of the paralogisms. Just as important is the contrast between what we would call the *first-person standpoint on her own thinking, of the thinker who thinks 'I think,'* expressed in the minor premise; and the *third-person standpoint*, which is the standpoint from which metaphysical propositions are asserted in the major premise. *For the thinker*, the referent of 'I' in 'I think' cannot be represented otherwise than as subject of the predicate 'think' in the proposition 'I think.' *For the thinker*, her action, in thinking and in expressing her consciousness of thinking in the proposition 'I think,' cannot be represented as the composite of the actions of different entities, so that she thinks of herself as indivisibly present in any instance of her act of thinking. These are necessary conditions on our consciousness of thinking, but they give no access to the ontological nature of the thinker, which would require the third-person standpoint of knowledge, including metaphysical knowledge.

While denouncing an equivocation between the metaphysical and the "merely logical" use of the concept expressed by the middle term, Kant thus also brings to light the contrast between the third-person, objective standpoint and the first-person, subjective standpoint, a standpoint that is necessary to the very act of thinking but tells us next to nothing one way or the other about the nature of the entity that thinks. I argue that this contrast between first-person standpoint on the activity of thinking and third-person knowledge of "the thing that thinks" is Kant's groundbreaking discovery in his discussion of the paralogisms.

In giving pride of place to this contrast, my interpretation of Kant's intention in the Paralogisms of Pure Reason differs from interpretations that see Kant's argument as more friendly to the rationalist metaphysical views of the mind whose arguments he is criticizing. This disagreement gives me reason to beg readers to have patience for the detailed textual analysis of Kant's argument I offer in Chapter 5, and again in Chapter 6. Settling interpretive disagreements depends on painstaking textual analysis. Analyzing Kant's arguments as they are stated in the text, with as much precision and care as we can muster, is a necessary condition for being in a position to draw on the resources they offer for our own reflections on the first person. Being responsible to the text in its proper conceptual framework and seeking the contemporary import of an argument, especially when it comes from as towering a philosophical figure as Kant, are not mutually exclusive, but on the contrary mutually reinforcing efforts.

In **Chapter 6**, I discuss Kant's argument in the Third Paralogism of Pure Reason, the Paralogism of Personality. According to rationalist metaphysics, as thinking beings we are immediately aware of our own numerical identity at different times. As such, we are persons. Here again, Kant criticizes the rationalists for engaging in the same kind of invalid inference as those he denounced in the first two paralogisms of pure reason.

Like the first two paralogisms of pure reason, the third trades on an equivocation on the middle term of a syllogistic inference. In this case, the inference is roughly this: 'What is conscious of the numerical identity of itself in different times is, to that extent, a person. I, as thinking, am conscious of the numerical identity of myself in different times. So I, as thinking, am a person.'[11] Here, the concept only apparently common to the major and the minor premise is the concept expressed by the phrase: "conscious of one's numerical identity in different times." Kant's line of argument is similar to what it was in the first two paralogisms. The phrase "conscious of (one's) numerical identity in different times," he maintains, does not have the same meaning and thus does not express the same concept in the major and in the minor premise. In the major premise, the phrase includes the implicit clause that the subject of consciousness *is* numerically identical in different times and is conscious of what is, *in fact*, its own numerical identity *as the entity it, in fact, is*. This implicit clause is absent from the minor premise. Here, "conscious of one's numerical identity in different times" does not have any factive meaning. The only thing the minor premise is entitled to assert is that, necessarily, in using 'I' in 'I think,' *I am assuming that* in each instance of its use, 'I' refers to one and the same entity, myself. "Being conscious of one's numerical identity" thus means "representing oneself as numerically identical," or even more precisely, "thinking oneself to be numerically identical in each instance of one's thinking, and of thinking 'I think.'"

This assumption, Kant argues, has its ground in the very nature of the activity of thinking. But considered on its own, this assumption of the continued existence through time of the entity I now represent as being, in the present instance of thinking 'I think,' the referent of 'I,' in no way guarantees that as a matter of fact, one and the same numerically identical, continuing entity is (has been) the bearer of the activity of thinking I take to now result in my thinking 'I think.' For such an identity *of the entity* that bears the activity of thinking to be justifiably asserted, the first-person standpoint of the thinker on her thinking is not sufficient. It needs to be supplemented with a third-person standpoint in which one's identity as a spatiotemporal entity can be assessed. I argue that in the course of his negative argument against the rationalist metaphysicians' invalid inference, Kant thus offers resources for an argument to the effect that we are aware of our own numerical identity at different times *not* in virtue of mere thinking (and thinking 'I think'), but insofar as, as thinking beings, we are capable of consciousness of our continued existence as spatiotemporal, empirically given, embodied entities. If I am correct, then in the course of debunking the rationalist inference, Kant offers resources for developing a positive notion of persons as embodied entities, endowed with unity of apperception.

This is not, however, the conclusion Kant himself draws from his criticism of the rationalist notion of a person. Rather, his conclusion is that once the rationalist inference has been debunked, the rationalist notion of a person can remain, albeit not as an object of knowledge, much less an object of a priori metaphysical knowledge. Rather, it can remain on behalf of the practical, not the theoretical use of reason. I offer an analysis of this surprising about-face, connecting it to Kant's own pre-critical attempt to derive a notion of person from the mere analysis of our use of 'I' in 'I think' and 'I do.'

In claiming that we can derive from Kant's criticism of the rationalist inference the resources for substituting, for the rationalist concept of a person, the concept of a person as an empirical, spatiotemporal entity, albeit endowed with unity of apperception and the capacity for second order assessment of her actions, I am not staying true to Kant's own conclusion. As I recalled above, Kant thinks one can, indeed one must, retain the rationalist concept of a person, derived from the mere concept 'I' in 'I think,' as "necessary and sufficient" for practical use. This conclusion connects Kant's argument in the Paralogisms of Pure Reason to Kant's practical philosophy. In *Groundwork for the Metaphysics of Morals*, Kant appeals to the concept of a "pure intelligence," belonging in an intelligible world, to ground the concept of practical freedom he takes to be indispensable for moral accountability. And in the *Critique of Practical Reason* he takes the postulate of the immortality of the soul to be a necessary condition for thinking the possibility of the highest good. In the final part of the chapter, I argue, *pace* Kant's arguments, that it is possible to do justice both to the role Kant assigns to the unity of apperception in cognition and to his conception of moral responsibility, without appealing to a purely intelligible world grounding the world of appearances.

This takes me back to an argument begun in Chapter 2. There I argued that one could find striking structural similarities between Kant's transcendental account and Freud's psychological account of the structures of our mental life. In Part III of the book, I explore this parallel in greater detail. I argue that the empirical concept of a person one can derive from Kant's criticism of rational metaphysics finds a descendant in Freud's account of the structural features of our mental life. This is true not only of Kant's concept of the transcendental unity of apperception with respect to Freud's concept of ego, but also of Kant's account of the structures of mental life yielding the categorical imperative of morality, with respect to Freud's concept of super-ego.

1.4 Part III: ... and Back Again

In **Chapter 7**, I offer support for my claim that there are significant parallels between Freud's "ego," on the one hand, and Kant's "transcendental unity of apperception," expressed in the thought 'I think,' on the other. I focus on four main features, the fourth of which will take us back to the relation between consciousness of the unity of mental activity and consciousness of one's own body in grounding the use of 'I' "as subject," and therefore in grounding any use of 'I,' whether "as subject" or "as object," as those expressions were analyzed in Chapter 2.

I first spell out four features of Kant's view of the transcendental unity of apperception, which grounds the use of 'I' in 'I think.' I then explain Freud's "ego" and review those of its features that are relevantly parallel to those of Kant's "transcendental unity of apperception." The four relevant features are the following.

(1) For Kant, the unity of apperception that grounds the use of 'I' in 'I think' is a necessary condition for the acquisition of concepts, for combining concepts in judgments and inferences, and for coming up with systematically connected representations of external objects. For Freud, the ego is that aspect of our mental life whose intentional contents obey elementary logical rules and are ordered according to the "reality principle." For both Kant and Freud, I argue,

the unity of consciousness yielding logically structured mental contents, the ordering of mental contents yielding a representation of independently existing objects, and the capacity for thinking first-person thoughts, are fundamentally connected. For Freud, this is an empirical fact explored in the context of his clinical practice. For Kant, this is a necessary condition of knowledge explored in his transcendental investigation.

(2) For Kant, the discursive thinking made possible by the transcendental unity of apperception depends on a pre-discursive activity of the mind, the "transcendental synthesis of imagination," which produces images of objects to be reflected under concepts. For Freud, the ego, governed by the reality principle, includes in its contents not only judgments according to logical rules, but also perceptual images and representations of imagination that are subject to rules of consistency according to the reality principle.

(3) For Kant, the pre-discursive activity of the mind, namely, the synthesis of imagination that generates mere images, is something of which we are "seldom even conscious." I argue that these productions of imagination of which we are "seldom even conscious" may be seen as a precursor to Freud's notion of "pre-conscious" representations, which, according to Freud, may become representations we are conscious of when they are associated with words and thus with concepts.

(4) For Kant, the transcendental unity of apperception, expressed in the thought 'I think,' is, as it were, indexed to a particular living, sensing body. Similarly, as we saw in Chapter 2, for Freud, the information from the outside world stored and ordered in the ego is information received via the surface of one's own body: one's skin and sensory organs.

Those parallels notwithstanding, Kant's and Freud's projects in offering a structural view of the mind are of course entirely different. Kant's project belongs in epistemology and aims at grounding a new kind of metaphysics. Freud's project aims at grounding a new kind of psychological therapy. I am not claiming that Freud answers Kant's questions, nor do I claim that Kant's philosophy is a new brand of psychology. Nevertheless, if the parallels I am suggesting are correct, then Freud's account of mental life and the structure he calls "ego" (the logically structured unity of mental events governed by the reality principle) put us on the path to a naturalized account of Kant's unity of apperception, an account that makes no appeal to Kant's unknown and unknowable "transcendental subject of thoughts = X,"[12] and directly challenges Kant's claim that our normative capacities cannot be accounted for in terms of our belonging to a natural world governed by natural causal laws.

An obvious objection is that considering only Freud's "ego" and its relation to Kant's 'I' in 'I think' leaves out the lion's share of both Kant's and Freud's accounts of the structure of mental life. It leaves out the role of 'I' in the moral 'I ought to,' for Kant. It also leaves out the mental structure called "super-ego" and its relation to "id" and "ego," for Freud. Here, my claim to a possible naturalization of Kant's view along Freudian lines might well fall apart, given the apparent incompatibility of Kant's and Freud's respective views of morality. To answer this objection, in Chapter 8 I consider the relation between Kant's moral 'I ought to' and Freud's "super-ego."

In **Chapter 8**, I argue that the parallels between the structure of mental life grounding the moral 'I ought to' according to Kant, on the one hand, and the structure of mental life Freud calls "super-ego," on the other, are just as striking as those I outlined in Chapter 7 between Kant's transcendental unity of apperception, grounding the thought 'I think,' and Freud's "ego." Admittedly, this is prima facie an even more shocking claim than those I made in Chapter 7. Freud's thesis that the moral attitude originates in what he calls the "the Oedipus complex" seems to undermine Kant's thesis that the categorical imperative of morality has its origin and justification in our rational nature. How can one possibly find parallels between Kant's and Freud's respective views of the structure of mental activity in generating moral attitudes?

I first lay out the structural parallels. I then examine the question: Does the Freudian account of the origin of the moral attitude undermine Kant's attempt to find a purely rational principle of moral determination and moral evaluation of our actions?

Just as Kant's 'I' does in 'I think,' Kant's 'I' in 'I ought to' expresses the consciousness of a mental activity for the contents of which one takes oneself to be accountable. In this case, the activity in question is not only an activity of reflecting and assessing reasons for belief, but also an activity of reflecting and assessing reasons for action. This is true both for the hypothetical 'If I want X, then I ought to Y' of instrumental and prudential reasoning, and for the categorical statement of moral duty: 'I ought to Z,' determined under Kant's various formulations of the categorical imperative of pure practical reason.

But the use of 'I' in the moral 'I ought to' has an additional dimension, one that is absent from the use of 'I' in 'I think.' In ascribing to myself the 'ought' of the moral imperative, I am taking myself to be both the author and the addressee of the moral command. I am both a rationally motivated agent who finds in herself the unconditional command of the moral law; and an agent motivated by the ends determined by her sensible nature. For Kant, these two kinds of motivations are in fundamental conflict: *either* I make the moral law the overriding motive of my actions *or* I let the sensible motives of self-love take precedence over the moral law. The 'ought' of morality expresses the consciousness that the former is unconditionally demanded of me—indeed is demanded *by* myself (as a rational being) *of* myself (as a being whose rationality is limited by her sensible nature).

I argue that Freud's concept of "super-ego" offers a developmental account of both aspects of Kant's moral 'I ought to'—it expresses the consciousness of being engaged in an activity of assessing reasons, and it is fundamentally conflicted—even while undermining Kant's claim that morality has its origin in pure practical reason.

On the one hand, Freud offers his own account of the insuperably conflicted nature of the moral attitude. The super-ego has its root in the id, the archaic and emotional aspect of our mental life. It is the internalization to the ego of the unconditional norms presented by the parental figures, limiting the libidinal and aggressive drives of the infant. The hold of moral attitudes on us is thus rooted in emotion, not reason. But on the other hand, in virtue of being internalized to the ego, the super-ego comes under the purview of that aspect of our mental life that makes us capable of endorsing or rejecting reasons. Where the rational capacities of the ego take the lead, subservience to the categorical imperatives inherited from the superego out of fear, grief, and guilt, may yield to the search for rationally motivated categorical imperatives. In Freud's statement that "Kant's categorical imperative is the direct heir of the Oedipus complex," I argue that we find both an acknowledgment of Kant's insight into the fundamental structure of the moral attitude, and a challenge to Kant's claim that the moral attitude finds its origin in pure practical reason. As for the structure of justification Kant claims for the categorical commands of morality, Freud has no more to say about it than he has about the structure of justification provided for objective knowledge by Kant's "transcendental unity of apperception" and its system of categories. These are not his questions. They are Kant's questions. Freud's naturalistic account of the development of human minds does not offer an answer to Kant's questions, nor does it make Kant's questions irrelevant. My only claim is that it offers a compelling model for what a naturalization of Kant's view of the structure of human minds might look like.

In **Chapter 9**, I take stock. I consider possible questions concerning the path I have taken in this book. I argue that the account of 'I' offered in Part III, drawing on Freudian metapsychology and its ramifications in contemporary psychology and moral psychology, is in no way incompatible with the account in terms of analytic philosophy of mind and language offered in Part I. On the contrary, they complement each other. It is a striking fact that Kant's transcendental approach to the mind, analyzed in Part II, should be the common ground on which a conversation can be established between those very different approaches to language and mind.

Notes

1. Wittgenstein 1958a, 66.
2. I put the expression 'consciousness of oneself as subject' in single rather than double quotation marks because, to my knowledge, this exact phrase does not appear in Kant's texts, although some of Kant's own phrases are very close to it (see for instance *Prol.*, AA4: 334), and the distinction between the consciousness we have of ourselves as subjects of thinking, and the consciousness we have of ourselves as objects (the determinate sequence of our inner states, in relation to the determinate sequence of the states of objects in space, especially our own body), plays a central role in Kant's arguments concerning self-consciousness. The distinction as Kant analyzes it will be extensively discussed in this book, especially in Chapters 4 through 6.
3. See Shoemaker 2003c, 8; and my discussion in Chapter 2, 2.1.2.
4. Evans 1982, 226; discussed in Chapter 2, 2.1.4.
5. Here, I use the term 'binding' to translate Kant's "Verbinden," usually translated into English as "combining" or "act of combination." I agree with the usual translation. But I sometimes say 'binding' to indicate that Kant's "combining" bears an interesting connection to the contemporary "binding problem" in cognitive psychology. On this point, see Chapter 2, 2.2, n. 29.
6. See O. Sacks 1998, 52. Freud *Ego and Id*, *SE* 19:26, *GW* 13:253. James Strachey translates Freud's expression "körperliches Ich" as "bodily ego," which is more faithful to the German than Sacks's "body-ego."
7. Sartre 2004, 40; 2003a, 9; discussed in Chapter 3, 3.1.
8. See the introductory paragraphs to the Paralogisms of Pure Reason, A346/B404.

9. Thanks to Quassim Cassam for pressing me to clarify this point.
10. This is the characterization Kant gives of a paralogism in *Logic*, §90, AA9, 134–5. See Chapter 5, 5.2.1.
11. This is not the exact formulation of the third paralogism in A: I am replacing the subject-term in the minor premise, "the soul," by "I, as thinking." This reformulation in the first person appears in the B edition. In Chapter 6, 6.1 and 6.2, I explain why it is legitimate to interpret the minor premise in the same way in A.
12. A346/B404.

PART I
Back To...

2
Uses of 'I'

We inherit from Wittgenstein's *Blue Book* a distinction that Wittgenstein did not take up again in other writings, but which subsequently acquired a life of its own: the distinction between "the use as object" and "the use as subject" of the word 'I.' It is tempting to compare this distinction with one we inherit from Kant: the distinction between consciousness of oneself "as subject" and consciousness of oneself "as object." The connection between the two distinctions has played an especially important role in recent analyses of the "use as subject" of 'I' as well as in recent interpretations of Kant's view.[1] I agree with those readings that the connection between Wittgenstein and Kant is illuminating. Nevertheless, I will argue that the two distinctions do not exactly map. It does seem plausible that the proposition 'I think,' which, in Kant's analysis, is an expression of consciousness of oneself as subject, is, in the terms of Wittgenstein's distinction in the *Blue Book* and of later analyses inspired by it, an instance of the use of 'I' "as subject": it meets the criterion of immunity to error through misidentification relative to the first-person pronoun (henceforth IEM) by which Shoemaker has characterized this use.[2] However, in the terms of Wittgenstein's distinction, 'I think' is only one of many cases of the use of 'I' "as subject." In contrast, the other cases cited by Wittgenstein would count for Kant as expressions of consciousness of oneself not as subject, but as object (e.g., "I have tooth-ache," "I see so and so," "I try to lift my arm").[3] My goal in this chapter is to make some progress toward understanding why the two distinctions do not exactly map and what we can learn from their comparison.

I will proceed as follows.

In the first part of this chapter, I will recall Wittgenstein's original distinction in the *Blue Book*. I will examine two influential amendments to Wittgenstein's distinction by Sydney Shoemaker and by Gareth Evans. I will explain why I endorse the former and only partly endorse the latter.

In the second part, I will explain Kant's notion of consciousness of oneself as subject and its relation to the proposition 'I think.' I will argue that Kant was right to claim that the self-consciousness expressed in the proposition 'I think' is a consciousness of being engaged in a specific kind of mental activity. I will argue that in making this point, Kant offers resources for understanding an aspect of the use of 'I' "as subject" that has been, until recently, insufficiently analyzed.[4] Finally, in the third part, I will draw on a clinical example borrowed from Oliver Sacks to investigate the relation between the two different uses of 'I' "as subject" and the two corresponding kinds of immunity to error through misidentification relative to the first-person pronoun analyzed in the first two parts of the chapter: one (emphasized by Evans) that rests on consciousness of oneself as an embodied entity, or at least on having a concept of oneself as an embodied entity; the other (emphasized by Kant) that rests on consciousness of a specific kind of unity of one's mental activity.

2.1 Wittgenstein and His Critics on the Use of 'I' as Subject

I will briefly recall Wittgenstein's original distinction in the *Blue Book* (2.1.1); I will then explain why I endorse Shoemaker's amended version of that distinction (2.1.2). I will defend the view that every use of 'I,' even its use "as object," depends partly on a way of knowing that supports a use of 'I' as subject (2.1.3). I will examine Evans's argument, in chapter 7 of *The Varieties of Reference*, "Self-Identification," to the effect that a necessary condition for any use of 'I' is that the 'I'-user be aware of herself as an entity individuated in space and time and thus as an embodied entity, or at least that she have available the concept of herself as such an entity (2.1.4). In the course of making this argument, Evans compares his view to Kant's. The comparison he offers helps to put in relief what is specific about Kant's view. It will thus prepare the ground for my argument, in 2.2, that Kant's characterization of what he calls "consciousness of oneself as subject" may offer a distinctive contribution to contemporary discussions of our uses of 'I.'

2.1.1 Wittgenstein's Distinction

Wittgenstein's examples, in the *Blue Book*, of what he calls the "use of 'I' as object" include "my arm is broken," "I have grown six inches," "I have a bump on my forehead," "the wind blows my hair about."[5] Examples of what he calls the "use of 'I' as subject" include "*I* see so and so," "*I* hear so and so," "*I* try to lift my arm," "*I* think it will rain," "*I* have tooth-ache." The difference between the two uses, says Wittgenstein, is manifest in the fact that in the first, there is room for a certain kind of error for which there is no room in the second. The error in question is an error in identifying *which person* the predicate is true of, if it is true of anyone at all. It may be true, and I may be justified by my perceptual experience in believing it to be true, that *someone* has a broken arm, that *someone* has grown six inches, that *someone* has a bump on her forehead, that *someone*'s hair is blowing about; and, nevertheless, I may be mistaken in believing that someone to be *me*. Even if the predicate is true of something and I have the right kind of justification for believing it to be true of something or someone, I can still be mistaken in this, and in this alone: asserting the predicate to be true of *me*. The possibility of this kind of error is characteristic of the use of 'I' as object. In contrast, the impossibility of an error of this kind is characteristic of the use of 'I' as subject:

> There is no question of recognizing a person when I say I have tooth-ache. To ask "are you sure it's *you* who have pain?" would be nonsensical.... And now this way of stating our idea suggests itself: that it is as impossible that in making the statement "I have tooth-ache" I should have mistaken another person for myself, as it is to moan with pain by mistake, having mistaken someone else for me. To say "I have pain" is no more a statement *about* a particular person than moaning is. "But surely the word 'I' in the mouth of a man refers to the man who says it; it points to himself..." But it was quite superfluous to point to himself.[6]

Thus, on Wittgenstein's account, the explanation for there being "no room" for an error of identification, that is, no room for an error in recognizing whom the predicate is true of, if justifiably asserted to be true of *someone*, is that using 'I' in these sentences does not indicate that one has recognized a particular person as the entity of which the predicate is true. And this, in turn, is explained by the fact that "the statement is not *about* a particular person."

2.1.2 Shoemaker's Amendment

This last explanation has been widely challenged. It's one thing to say that, in the case of judgments in which 'I' is used as subject, no recognitional capacity and no criterion of identification have been in play in order to determine *whom* a predicate is true of. It's a much stronger claim to say that this is because those judgments are "not about a particular person."[7] According to Shoemaker's amended version of the *Blue Book* distinction, judgments in which 'I' is used as subject are characterized *not* by the fact that they are not about a particular person, but rather by the fact that, even while asserting a predicate to be true of a particular person (and in this sense being *about* a particular person), they are "immune to error through misidentification relative to the first-person pronoun." This is because, given the kind of information these judgments are based on, knowing, on the basis of that information, the predicate to be true of anyone at all just is knowing it to be true of oneself, without any additional warrant being needed for knowing that the entity the predicate is true of, is identical to oneself.[8]

The information in question grounds knowledge "from the inside." Knowledge "from the inside" is knowledge of predicates one asserts to be true of oneself on the basis of a kind of information that is not available as a basis for knowledge of other people's states. For instance, I may be justified in asserting, on the basis of my own subjective experience, that I see a canary, whereas I cannot be justified in this way, but can only be justified on the basis of her overt behavior, in asserting that someone else is currently seeing a canary (for instance, she cries, 'Look, a canary!,' or she starts cooing as she usually does when she sees her pet canary). Similarly, I am justified on the basis of my own subjective experience in asserting that I am in pain, whereas I cannot be justified in this way, but only on the basis of her overt behavior—grimacing, screaming, or what have you—in asserting that someone else is in pain. So if I say or think, on the basis of my subjective experience, that I see a canary or feel pain, there is no room for the question: 'Someone sees a canary all right. But are you sure it's you? Someone is in pain all right. But are you sure it's you?'

2.1.3 Uses of 'I' as Object

Clearly, not all first-person judgments are such that in them, 'I' is used in the way just explained. Consider Wittgenstein's examples of the use of 'I' as object. On the basis of my visual experience of seeing a person in the mirror who looks like me and has a bump on her forehead, I may be justified in saying 'the person now standing next to the staircase in my house has a bump on her forehead,' and the statement may indeed be true. Nevertheless, I may still be mistaken in believing that person to be *me*—the individual currently thinking 'I have a bump on my forehead.' The mistake consists in believing the identity statement, 'the person standing next to the staircase = I' to be true. All uses of 'I' as object depend, implicitly or explicitly, on such identity statements, since in such uses, knowing the predicate to be true of someone is not ipso facto knowing it to be true of *me*, the current believer of the thought or speaker of the corresponding sentence. The relevant identity statement calls for a justification of its own: recognizing a uniquely identifying feature of the entity of which I am justified in believing the predicate to be true, to be a feature that is true of *me*—the believer of the thought and speaker of the sentence. It is precisely on this point that uses of 'I' "as subject" and uses of 'I' "as object" irreducibly differ: in the latter and not the former, an intermediate premise that consists in a statement of identity (e.g., 'The person I see standing next to the staircase = I') must be justified on objective grounds, namely, on the kinds of grounds you might call upon to justify any judgment concerning objects in the world.[9] Such intermediate premises are *not* needed in uses of 'I' as subject, where knowing the predicate to be true of anyone at all just is knowing it to be true of *me*.

Nevertheless, even uses of 'I' as object are partly supported by the kind of information that, if formulated in a judgment, would be formulated in a judgment that is immune to error through misidentification relative to the first-person pronoun, namely, a judgment in which 'I' would be used as subject. Of course, uses of 'I' as object do not depend *only* on those sources. They also depend on sources of information that would be apt to justify any kind of objective knowledge (knowing of someone that she is standing next to the staircase, knowing of something that it is big, and so on). But they depend *also* on those sources that make the use of 'I' immune to error through misidentification.

As a case in point, consider John Perry's famous example, "I am making a mess!"[10] In the situation described by Perry, the use of 'I' is not immune to error through misidentification relative to the first-person pronoun. It is true, and I am justified in believing it to be true on the basis of the information gathered by following the trail of sugar through the aisles of the supermarket, that someone is making a mess. And still, I may be mistaken in coming to the conclusion that *I* am the person making the mess. Someone else might have followed the same path just before me and gone round and round through the aisles, my bag of sugar may not be broken after all or not in a position to spill sugar out of my cart into the aisle, and so on. In short, my belief 'I am making a mess' is backed by an implicit belief whose content is the identity proposition 'The person who has just been walking through these aisles spilling sugar from her cart is *me*.' That proposition may be false even while I am undoubtedly justified in believing that the person who has just been walking through these aisles spilling sugar from her cart is making a mess. In the terms of Wittgenstein's *Blue Book* distinction, in the statement 'I am making a mess,' 'I' is used as object.

Nevertheless, formulating the belief in the first person is possible only because the use of 'I' is in part backed by the kind of information that, if expressed in a judgment, would be expressed in a judgment that includes a use of 'I' as subject. For the implicit train of thought that led to the judgment 'I am making a mess!' might run something like this: '(i) Someone is making a mess! (ii) The person who is making a mess has been pushing her cart through this aisle. (iii) My gosh, *I* have been pushing my cart through this aisle. (iv) The person who is making a mess = I. (v) *I* am making a mess!' This is only an inference to the best explanation. The identification of the guilty party with *me* is not failproof: the judgment is not immune to error through misidentification relative to the first-person pronoun. But the reason the judgment can be formulated in the first person at all is that the crucial implicit premise 'I have been pushing my cart through these aisles' is a judgment that is immune to error through misidentification relative to the first-person pronoun. On the basis of the information provided by proprioception, kinesthesis, self-location, and first-person memory, knowing of anyone that someone has been pushing her cart through the aisles is knowing it *of me*.[11] And this provides me with the crucial intermediate premise for the justification of the belief 'the person who pushed her cart = I' and thus 'I am making a mess.'

In other words, for the current believer and speaker to believe of herself, the believer and speaker, that she is the person making the mess, there needs to be a point at which no more search for objective criteria is called for in order to establish the identity between the entity of which the predicate is true, and the believer and speaker of the current thought asserting the predicate to be true. This is possible only if the speaker or believer has access to information about herself that she could not have about anyone else: access that uniquely identifies who the predicate is true of, if it is true of anyone at all.

2.1.4 Evans on 'I'-Thoughts

Although he made no mention of the distinction between "use of 'I' as subject" and "use of 'I' as object," recognizing the dependence I just laid out is clearly what motivated Evans to devote several pages, in chapter 7 of *The Varieties of Reference* ("Self-Identification"), to examining what kind of information may ground first-person judgments that are immune to error through misidentification relative to the first-person pronoun. Surely he did not mean that all first-person judgments are so immune. What he meant is that all uses of the first-person pronoun depend in part on information that is apt to ground its use "as subject," namely, its use in judgments that are immune to error through misidentification relative to the first-person pronoun. Evans, moreover, insists that not only the self-ascription of psychological states (which alone appear in Wittgenstein's examples of the use of 'I' as subject) but also the self-ascription of physical states (bodily states, positions, and motions) can be so immune. Indeed, Evans claims, it is a necessary condition for the possibility of any I-thoughts at all that the self-ascription of some of our bodily states be so immune.[12,13]

Evans defined "I-thoughts" as thoughts in which "a subject of thought and action has thoughts about *himself*—i.e. about a *subject* of thought and action."[14] This characterization of "I-thoughts," or self-consciousness, draws on the fundamental reference rule for 'I' (FRR): 'I' is a word or concept that refers, in any instance of its use, to the author of the thought or the speaker of the sentence in which 'I' is being used. In other words, in using 'I' in the argument-place of her judgment, the judging subject is representing the fact that she, the judging subject, is the entity of which the predicate of her judgment is asserted to be true. Now, for thoughts to be about the very subject of those thoughts *qua* subject of those thoughts, the subject must "think of an object in a way that permits it to be characterized as the subject of that very thought."[15] Most philosophers, Evans deplores, have considered only information about one's psychological states and mental properties as providing possible contents for such thoughts. They have neglected to consider information about one's bodily state via proprioception, feeling, and sense of balance; and most importantly, self-location (ibid., 212–13, 216–17).

As we saw, both of the latter sources of information played a role in grounding the judgment 'I have been pushing my cart through these aisles' that served as an implicit premise for the conclusion 'I am making a mess!' as I analyzed it earlier (see 2.1.3). I have proprioceptive knowledge that I have been moving through the aisles. I have self-locating knowledge of positions I have successively occupied, eliciting beliefs such as: 'there's the produce section, so I am in aisle 1; I am in aisle 1, so the spices are not far away; dairy is in aisle 2, this is where I now turn,' and so on. These first-person statements are all immune to error through misidentification relative to the first-person pronoun. As Evans insists (here, I substitute my example for his): 'None of the following utterances appears to make sense when the first component expresses knowledge gained in this way: someone is in aisle 1, but is it I? Someone now turns, but is it I?'[16]

Such self-locating beliefs play an essential role in our representation of the world around us as a world of independently existing objects, for they allow us to discriminate between perceiving one and the same object in one and the same place at different points in time; perceiving one and the same object at different places at different times; and perceiving two numerically different but generically identical objects at the same place *or* different places at different times.[17]

But there is an even more fundamental reason for the central role Evans assigns to self-location in our 'I'-thoughts. Like all thoughts about individuals, 'I'-thoughts stand under what Evans calls the "Generality Constraint," stated earlier in the book as follows:

We cannot avoid thinking of a thought about an individual object x, to the effect that it is F, as the exercise of two separable capacities; one being the capacity to think of x, which could be equally exercised in thoughts about x to the effect that it is G or H; and the other being a conception of what it is to be F, which could be equally exercised in thoughts about other individuals, to the effect that they are F. (ibid., 75)

In other words, any thought about an individual, of the form Fa, is, as it were, at the crossroads of two sequences of possible contrasting thoughts: (1) Fb, Fc, Fd, and so on (where understanding the thought Fa is understanding also what it would mean for the predicate F to be true of b, c, d, e, etc.); and (2) Ga, Ha, Ka, and so on (where understanding Fa is understanding also what it would mean for G, H, K to be true of a). Applied to 'I'-thoughts, the Generality Constraint means that,

One's Idea of oneself must also comprise, in addition to the information-link and the action-link, a knowledge of what it would be for an identity of the form $\lceil I = \delta \rceil$ to be true. (ibid., 209) My thought about myself does satisfy the Generality Constraint; and this is because I can make sense of identifying a person, conceived from the standpoint of an objective view of the world, as myself. (ibid., 210)

Evans's position is quite radical. It means that having available a concept of oneself as a physical thing located in space is involved even in the self-ascription of beliefs and experiences, namely, in the self-ascription of *mental* predicates. For the general conditions for understanding a judgment of the type 'I am F' apply also when '– am F' is specified as '– believe that p,' or for that matter, any other mental predicate.

Understanding of the content of the judgment ['I believe that *p*'] must involve possession of the psychological concept expressed by 'ζ believes that p,' which the subject must conceive as capable of being instantiated otherwise than by himself.... Without this background, we might say, we secure no genuine 'I think' ('think that p') to accompany [the subject's] thought ('p'). The 'I think' which accompanies all his thoughts remains purely formal. (ibid., 226)

Later in the same chapter, Evans explicitly refers to Kant when repeating the same point:

I believe we may have here an interpretation of Kant's remark about the transcendental 'I think' which accompanies all our perceptions (B131–32). Without the background, we have at most a formal 'I think'; it yields nothing until embedded within a satisfactory theory. (ibid., 228)

The passage in Kant to which Evans refers in the corresponding footnote to his remark (B131-2) is the beginning of §16 in the Transcendental Deduction: "The *I think* must be *able* to accompany all my representations." There, Kant does not say, as Evans has him say, that the 'I think' is "formal." Evans might have in mind other passages, which belong to the Paralogisms of Pure Reason.[18] Here are several examples:

The identity of the consciousness of myself in different times is only a formal condition of my thoughts and of their coherence, but does not prove at all the numerical identity of myself as *subject*. (A363)

The formal proposition of apperception, **I think**, remains the entire ground on which rational psychology ventures to extend its cognitions. (A354)

This I is no more an intuition than it is a concept of any object; rather, it is the mere form of consciousness, which accompanies both sorts of representations and which can elevate them to cognitions only insofar as something else is given in intuition. (A382)

Because... the only condition accompanying all thinking is the I, in the universal proposition 'I think,' reason has to do with this condition insofar as it is itself unconditioned. But it is only the formal condition, namely the logical unity of every thought, in which I abstract from every object; and yet it is represented as an object that I think, namely I itself, and its unconditional unity. (A398)

From these passages it is tempting to conclude that 'I' in 'I think' represents only a form of thought and is not used to refer to any entity at all. But other passages indicate unambiguously that Kant does take 'I' as used in 'I think' to refer to an entity. That entity, however, remains indeterminate as long as the only concept by which we represent it is 'I':

Through this I or he or it (the thing) that thinks nothing further is represented than a transcendental subject of thought = X. (A346/B404)

Kant's point, I will suggest, is that, absent any further information about the properties of its referent, *from the mere concept 'I,'* and a fortiori from the concept

'I' as used in 'I think,' one cannot derive any feature or property of the entity 'I' refers to. His point is *not* that the concept 'I,' merely as such and even in the context of the proposition 'I think,' is not used to refer to an entity at all.

* * *

To take stock: Evans makes an important point when he argues that properties and states whose self-ascription is IEM are not limited to mental states but include bodily states. He is justified in claiming that in most cases of such self-ascriptions, our conception of ourselves *as ourselves*, namely, as the referent of 'I,' is that of an embodied entity.[19] But this is distinct from the much stronger point he wants to maintain concerning conditions on the meaningfulness of the concept 'I' itself, namely, conditions on the very possibility of a referential use of 'I.' I shall argue in 2.2 that understanding FRR *and* being engaged in the activity of thinking are sufficient for a meaningful use of 'I'; and that anything further we might need to know about the referent of 'I' for the self-ascription of a predicate to go through depends on the content of the *predicate*, not on a priori conditions for a meaningful use of 'I.' I shall argue that this was essentially Kant's view, and that Kant was right about this.

2.2 Kant on Consciousness of Oneself as Subject

The context in which Kant developed his explanation of the concept 'I' and its use in the proposition 'I think' is not that of a theory of self-consciousness as self-reference;[20] nor is it that of an empirical investigation into psychological states or psychological concepts. Rather, the context is that of an epistemological investigation into the possibility of cognition,[21] especially those particular kinds of propositional cognition Kant took to be both synthetic and a priori: pure mathematics; some necessary background propositions of natural science, for example, the principle of conservation of substance or the causal principle; and metaphysics, especially metaphysical propositions about the nature of the mind and the mind/body distinction, the fundamental structure of the world, and the existence of God. In the course of that investigation, Kant developed an explanation of what makes perceptual cognition possible, namely, how our perceptual mental states come to be directed at empirically given objects we take them to be perceptions of. He defended the view that perceptual knowledge, however elementary, depends on mental capacities having complex a priori structures and that those same a priori structures explain the possibility of pure mathematics and knowledge of the a priori principles of mathematical natural science. Moreover, he argued, all these modes of cognition (perceptual knowledge, "pure" mathematics, mathematical natural science) depend on a unifying activity by which all mental contents (intentional objects of mental states) are bound together, concepts are combined in judgments, judgments are connected in inferences, inferences are connected in a system of thought, and knowledge. We represent conceptually our consciousness of this unifying activity when we preface the statement of a mental content with the proposition 'I think.'

For instance, suppose I say 'This is a tree,' and someone asks 'Are you sure?' I might reply 'Yes, I think this is a tree.' Coming up with the proposition 'I think' here does not depend on turning my attention back on to myself. My attention is still directed at the tree. 'I think' expresses my endorsement of the earlier proposition, backed by my reviewing the reasons for asserting it in the first place: combining the pieces of sensory information available, comparing them to others, forming recognitional concepts, and coming up with the proposition 'this is a tree,' which is now available as a premise for use in further reasoning.[22] Note also that 'I think' may have different degrees of epistemic force. It may mean, cautiously, 'yes, it seems to me this is a tree' or, more strongly, 'yes, I'm sure it is a tree!' or some intermediate statement such as 'I have no reason to think it's anything other than a tree.' These different degrees of epistemic force depend, according to Kant, on the relation between the particular proposition 'this is a tree' and other propositions that belong to the system of knowledge available to me to back my statement, whether or not I am, currently, consciously accessing the truth of those propositions.[23]

The predicate '—think this is a tree' is a concept that refers to the activity of reviewing the reasons for asserting this is a tree. The term in the argument place, 'I,' is a concept that refers to the current thinker of the thought 'I think this is a tree,' namely, the current agent of the activity of reviewing the reasons for asserting 'this is a tree.' Nothing further is needed for 'I' to meaningfully refer to an individual: the current thinker of the thought 'I think this is a tree.' Although Kant uses different terms, I submit that this is what he has in mind when he says that in the proposition 'I think,' 'I' represents nothing further than "the I or he or it (the thing) that thinks."[24]

Here, one might object that in saying or thinking 'this is a tree' one is aware of oneself as located in space. This self-locating awareness is implicit in the reinforcing statement 'I think this is a tree' (even more if one adds 'I can see this is a tree!'). If I were to list my reasons for identifying what I dimly see in front of me as *a tree*, those reasons might include the distance that separates me from the object I see as a tree, my own position and orientation with respect to the object I see, the quality of the light, and so on, all reasons that imply that I am aware of myself *not just* as the agent of the synthesizing activity which results in identifying the object as a tree and makes it possible for me, if pressed, to list *reasons* for identifying the object as a tree. Rather, I am aware of myself *also* as being, myself, whatever else I am, at least individuated by my location in space. Isn't Evans just correct in saying that absent such a component, Kant's 'I think' expresses a "merely formal unity" while no reference is made to *ourselves*, as individual entities?[25]

I would reply by recalling the distinction I offered earlier in my discussion of Evans. One should distinguish the information about oneself (the referent of 'I') that justifies the self-ascription of a given predicate, and the concept of oneself that conditions the very use of 'I' in the argument place of one's judgment. It is correct to say that 'think this is a tree' is asserted of oneself partly on the basis of information concerning one's location and one's physical properties. In this case, being embodied and located becomes part of the concept one has of oneself when ascribing the predicate 'think this is a tree' to oneself. But this does not mean that a conception of oneself as spatially located and embodied is a condition for the very use of 'I' in the argument place of one's judgment.

Consider this other case. I painstakingly go through the steps of a difficult logical proof. I triumphantly reach the final step of my proof, and then I have a doubt: 'Oh no, this proof is invalid.' I think again, I retrace the steps of my demonstration, I fill in the missing lines of proof. With some relief I conclude: 'I think the proof is valid!' Again in this case I am not directing attention—my own attention or that of others—to myself. Even less am I intending to bring attention to myself in contradistinction to another person.[26] My attention is wholly directed to—the proof! Asserting 'I think the proof is valid!' is making explicit my consciousness of being accountable for the sequence and connection of the steps of the proofs, and of my commitment to providing more justification if challenged to do so. Here, the use of 'I' need be supported by nothing more than the consciousness of my going through and checking the steps of the proof, leading to the assertion of my endorsement, 'I think the proof is valid.'

A problem of identity is looming here: how do I know I am one and the same author of the sequence of steps throughout the proof? This question will be discussed in Chapter 6 ("Kant on the Identity of Persons").[27] For now, I am content to say: the thinker of the thought 'I think the proof is valid' is asserting of herself, the thinker of that thought (the referent of 'I' in 'I think the proof is valid') that she is conscious of being accountable for the proof and committed to justifying it further if challenged to do so. I do not need to know what kind of entity I am, I who currently think 'I think the proof is valid,' or what kind of spatiotemporal unity and identity I may or may not have as an agent producing and endorsing the proof, in order to be able to assert of 'I' the predicate 'think the proof is valid,' namely, to ascribe to the referent of 'I' the state of thinking that the proof is valid.

One might object that it is not irrelevant that the proof is written out on the blackboard or on paper. There is no way to keep in view the sequence of the proof without such material props. Similarly, I am aware of my own activity of generating the proof with the help of my material connection to the blackboard or my piece of paper or my computer—think of our panic when a file gets lost or worse, our hard disk freezes. Even so, what is relevant to my using 'I' when I say or just think—'I think the proof is valid!'—is not my consciousness of being the particular person now standing in front of the blackboard or typing away at the computer. Even if my consciousness of being this person holding the chalk or typing away, like my consciousness of the blackboard or the computer in front of me, is an indispensable prop to my activity of thinking, my use of 'I' in the judgment 'I think the proof is valid' is supported *not* by my consciousness of my body, but by my consciousness of checking the steps and demonstrating the validity of the proof.

How does the judgment 'I think,' so considered, fare with respect to the test of immunity to error through misidentification relative to the first-person pronoun? Clearly, it would make no sense to ask, 'Someone thinks this proof is valid, but is it me (the current thinker of the thought "I think this proof is valid")?' Or, 'Someone thinks this is a tree, but is it me (the current thinker of the thought "I think this is a tree")?' Any proposition of the form 'I think p' is immune to error through misidentification relative to the first-person pronoun. In fact, as I said at the beginning, this is the only case where Kant's "consciousness of oneself as subject" plausibly maps one case of Wittgenstein's "use of 'I' as subject": the case 'I think it will rain.' But what's interesting about Kant's position is the reason he would give for the immunity to error through misidentification relative to the first-person pronoun in this case. It's not only (although it may also be) that I am predicating a state (the occurrent state of thinking) of which I am aware in such a way that there is no room for being justified in asserting it of *someone* but mistaken in this, and this alone, that I am asserting it of *myself*, the current thinker of the thought and speaker of the sentence 'I think this proof is valid' or 'I think this is a tree' or 'I think it will rain.' Rather, Kant's view is that the capacity to refer to myself via the concept and word 'I' and the process of connecting my representations in such a way that I can form thoughts (combinations of concepts) and account for my reasons, are mutually conditioning. In other words, having available the concept 'I' and being engaged in the kind of unifying activity that makes possible reason-giving thought are mutually conditioning. For this reason, it is nonsensical to suppose that I could wonder, 'Someone is thinking [that this proof is valid, that this is a tree, that it will rain] but is it me?' In this case, and in this case alone, the reason there is no place for this question is *not* that the judgment is justified by a particular kind of awareness. Rather, the reason is the very nature of the process of thinking.[28]

This is a controversial point. It will be discussed in more detail in Chapter 4. Let me nevertheless say a little bit here about the twofold conditioning: binding for thinking ("synthesizing," in Kant's vocabulary) being a necessary condition for having available the use of the concept 'I' in 'I think'; and conversely, having available the use of the concept 'I' in 'I think' being a necessary condition for the kind of binding necessary for thinking.[29]

Here's Kant on the first conditioning relation: synthesis (or what I call above "binding for thinking") being a necessary condition for access to 'I,' call this the I → SY principle:

Only because I can comprehend the manifold [of my representations] in one consciousness [SY] do I call them all together *my* representations [I]; for otherwise I would have just as multicolored and diverse a self as I have representations of which I am conscious. (B134)

I am ... *conscious of the identical self* [emphasis mine] with respect to the manifold of representations given to me in an intuition, because I call all of them *my* representations, which make *one*. But this is as much as to say that I am *a priori* conscious of an original synthesis of these representations, which is called the original synthetic unity of apperception, under which all representations stand but under which they must also be brought by a synthesis. (B135)

Here's Kant on the second (access to 'I' being a necessary condition for synthesis, call this the SY → I principle):

The synthetic proposition that every different **empirical consciousness** [Kant's emphasis] must be combined into a single self-consciousness is the absolutely first and synthetic principle of our thinking in general. But it should not go unnoticed that the mere representation **I** in relation to all others (the collective unity of which it makes possible) is the transcendental consciousness. Now it does not matter here whether this representation is clear (empirical consciousness) or obscure, even whether it be actual; but the possibility of the logical form of all cognition necessarily rests on the relationship to this apperception as a faculty. (A117n)

According to I → SY, there would be no representation 'I' unless an activity of binding representations that leads to their being thinkable, namely, recognizable under common concepts, were going on in our minds. In other words, the representation of oneself via the concept 'I' in 'I think' is conditioned by there being such an activity underway in our minds. But conversely, according to SY → I, representing oneself, explicitly or not (whether the representation is "clear or obscure, even whether it be actual"), via the concept 'I' (making possible the "collective unity of [all other] representations" and thus "the logical form of all cognition") is a condition for that activity going on in our mind at all.

Again, I will offer a more complete elucidation of these points and thus of Kant's view of the proposition 'I think' in Chapter 4. What matters to me in the current chapter is what Kant's I → SY and SY → I theses mean for the claim of immunity to error through misidentification relative to the first-person pronoun of propositions such as 'I think p.' Why is it the case, in light of these two principles, that on the basis of going through the proof and checking it step by step, or on the basis of checking what I see and how I see it, knowing 'think p' (e.g., 'think the proof is valid' or 'think this is a tree') to be true of someone just is knowing it to be true of *me* (the current thinker of the thought 'I think p')? The reason is that a sufficient condition for the entity referred to by 'I' to be able to refer to herself in this way (that is, a sufficient condition for her having 'I' available as a mode of presentation of herself to herself), is precisely that she be, herself, engaged in the activity which is asserted as the predicate of the proposition ('think p'). Checking the proof (in the case 'I think the proof is valid') or assessing my reasons (in the case 'I think this is a tree') just is what makes me (the current thinker of the thought 'I think the proof is valid' or 'I think this is a tree') an entity of which it is true to say that she thinks the proof is valid or this is a tree, as well as an entity that knows 'think the proof is valid' or 'think this is a tree' to be true of *someone* just in virtue of knowing it to be true of *herself*.

A natural objection is that this is an extremely thin notion of immunity to error through misidentification, perhaps to the point of leaving the notion utterly empty. True, it is thin compared to the cases we considered in section 2.1 and its subsections, where the claim was that 'I' was used with immunity to error through misidentification in self-ascription not only of psychological predicates, but also of bodily predicates or spatial location. In the case of the self-ascription of bodily predicates or self-location, immunity to error through misidentification relative to the first-person pronoun had the following feature: on the basis of proprioception, sense of balance, or self-location, I cannot know F (a bodily predicate or a location) to be true of *something or someone* and yet be mistaken in believing it to be true of *me* (the current believer of 'I am F'). In such cases the IEM is far from thin because it rests on the claim that, on the basis of a specific kind of information, if I know a bodily predicate or spatial location to be true of something or someone, I cannot fail to be correct in believing the something or someone of which the predicate is true, to be identical to *me*, the referent of 'I,' which in virtue of the FRR for 'I' is individuated as the bearer of an occurrent *psychological* state: the occurrent state of thinking the proposition 'I am F' and believing it to be true.

In contrast, saying that 'I think the proof is valid' or 'I think this is a tree' is immune to error through misidentification relative to the first-person pronoun is saying that, on the basis of checking the steps of the proof or reviewing my reasons for stating that the object I see is a tree, knowing of anyone that she thinks the proof is valid or that she thinks this is a tree just is knowing it of a referent (the referent of 'I') whose essential individuating characteristic, in virtue of the FRR of 'I,' is that of being the subject of an occurrent mental state (thinking 'I think the proof is valid,' thinking 'I think this is a tree'), which is the very same state as the state asserted in the proposition. Moreover, something counts as the referent of 'I' (= the current thinker of the thought and speaker of the sentences 'I think the proof is valid,' 'I think this is a tree') precisely in virtue of being engaged in the activity that is predicated of it in the proposition 'I think p': the activity of thinking, premised on an activity of binding for thinking. In contrast, it is of course not the case that something counts as the referent of 'I' (= the current thinker of the thought 'I am sitting cross-legged') just in virtue of her sitting cross-legged.[30]

But there's more: if it is true, as per Kant's I → SY, that some individual counts for herself as a referent of 'I' (namely, is in a position to use 'I' as a mode of presentation of the entity she happens to be) only in virtue of her being engaged in the activity of binding for thinking; and as per Kant's SY → I, that conversely, there is binding for thinking only if the agent of that activity ascribes that activity to herself (the referent of 'I'); then it is plausible to think that both capacities have a common ground, a ground that makes it the case that one is not available unless the other is available as well, and vice versa.[31] For Kant, that ground is what he calls the transcendental unity of apperception: the unity of self-consciousness that makes possible *both* our synthesizing representations into conceptualizable wholes (what I call here 'binding') and our ascribing thoughts to ourselves in the proposition 'I think.' The unity of apperception is, then, the ground for *any* use of 'I,' whether in 'I think' or in any of the other cases of self-ascription, whether IEM or not, namely, whether the use of 'I' is a use of 'I' as subject or a use of 'I' as object. For the unity of apperception that grounds the binding activity and the corresponding consciousness of oneself as subject is what makes possible the very concept 'I' with its fundamental reference rule: 'I' refers, in any instance of its use, to the author of the thought or the speaker of the sentence in which 'I' is a component (figures in the argument place).[32]

I said at the beginning of this chapter that Kant's distinction and Wittgenstein's distinction do not exactly map. Kant's proposition 'I think' is certainly a case of use of 'I' as subject in Wittgenstein's sense, amended by Shoemaker and Evans (namely, with the assumption, which I endorse, that there is a referring role for 'I' even in its use 'as subject'). But all other cases of use of 'I' as subject—those cited by Wittgenstein, which concern the self-ascription of psychological predicates, as well as those cited by Shoemaker and Evans, which concern, in addition to the self-ascription of psychological predicates, at least some cases of self-ascription of bodily predicates— all those cases are cases where the use of 'I' as subject is backed by what Kant calls a consciousness of oneself *not* as subject, but *as an object*, even though that consciousness, in terms of our IEM criterion, backs a use of 'I' as subject. Maybe we can now see why. 'I think,' or rather 'I think p' (on my examples: 'I think the proof is valid,' 'I think this is a tree . . . ') is the only type of case where what is asserted of the referent of 'I,' namely, of the individual currently thinking the proposition 'I am F,' is precisely the activity of thinking that makes 'I' available as a mode of presentation of that individual. All other uses of 'I,' whether they are uses of 'I' as object or those uses other than 'I think' that, in the terms of Wittgenstein's distinction, are uses of

'I' as subject, *depend* on that original binding-for-thinking (synthesizing) activity that makes possible any judgment at all. Even a judgment as immediately grounded in a subjective psychological state as 'I feel pain,' or (even more) 'I have tooth-ache' depends, as a judgment, on the activity in which alone, in Kant's terms, I am "conscious of myself as subject": the activity of thinking. And this means also that, unless they are bound, compared, and conceptualized in the course of such an activity, subjective mental states are *not* self-ascribed: they do not and cannot count as predicates in a proposition in which the subject is 'I.' And when they are self-ascribed, the relevant judgment expresses in each case, in Kant's terms, a consciousness of myself *as an object*—albeit as an object not of outer sense, but of inner sense.[33]

I argued in 2.1.3 that even the uses of 'I' as object partly depend on the kind of information that, expressed in a judgment, would ground a use of 'I' as subject. I now want to add that any use of 'I,' whether as subject or as object, depends on what Kant calls consciousness of oneself as subject, namely, the self-consciousness that is expressed in the proposition 'I think' or more completely, 'I think p.'

If this is correct, then not only should we distinguish the use of 'I' as object from the use of 'I' as subject, but we should also distinguish significantly different uses of 'I' as subject, with different grounds for the immunity to error through misidentification relative to the first-person pronoun in our use of 'I.' First, the Kantian type in 'I think' and its cognates ('I believe,' 'it seems to me,' and so on), based on consciousness of binding for thinking. Second, the self-ascription of subjective mental states—what Shoemaker called P* predicates. Third and fourth, the two types I mostly focused on in the first part of this chapter, based on proprioceptive/kinesthetic awareness on the one hand, and self-location on the other. If Kant is right, even while distinguishing these four kinds of uses of 'I' as subject in virtue of the four kinds of information about oneself on which they rest, one should still acknowledge that the latter three (self-location, self-ascription of bodily predicates, self-ascription of P* predicates) depend on the kind of self-consciousness which alone Kant calls consciousness of oneself as subject, and which in our terms grounds its own brand of use of 'I' as subject in propositions of the generic form: 'I think p.' This does *not* mean that the latter use of 'I' is *itself* a condition for all other uses of 'I.' The other three kinds of uses of 'I' as subject can of course occur without being prefaced by 'I think that...' (e.g., 'I think that I am sitting cross-legged,' 'I think that I am in front of the table,' 'I think that I am in pain'). But the *self-consciousness* on which 'I think p' rests is presupposed in all other uses of 'I.' And this definitely gives a special status to the corresponding use of 'I' as subject, as I shall have more occasions to argue in the rest of this book.

I would like now to offer empirical-psychological support for the distinctions I have discussed and for the dependence relation I have suggested between the different kinds of self-consciousness grounding our uses of 'I' as subject.

2.3 Psychological Case Studies

In his popular book *The Man Who Mistook His Wife for a Hat, and Other Clinical Tales*, Oliver Sacks tells the story of a young woman he calls Christina and describes as "the disembodied lady."³⁴ Following an antibiotic treatment in preparation for a relatively minor surgery, Christina started gradually losing the sense of her own body. She could stand only if she looked down at her feet and hold things only if she kept her eyes fixed on her hands. She reported that she could not feel her body any more. It was as if the parietal lobes of her brain were not processing the sensory information from her body. In fact, tests showed that the parietal lobes were working, but they had no information to work with. She was, says Sacks, in a state of total proprioceptive deficit, going from the tips of her toes to her head. The diagnosis was one of acute polyneuritis, not the one known as the Guillain-Barré syndrome, which affects motricity, but a version that affected the proprioceptive fibers only.

Christina undertook to compensate for the loss of proprioception by using vision to monitor the movements of her body. As a result, her "visual automatism and reflexes [became] increasingly integrated and fluent." A plausible explanation, says Sacks, is that "the brain's visual model of the body, or body image, [which is] normally subsidiary to the proprioceptive body-model was gaining, by way of compensation, an enhanced force."³⁵ The same was happening with her auditory feedback. She had lost her proprioceptive control of vocal tone and posture, so she had to use her auditory feedback instead. She had to artificially manufacture a voice for herself; she had to check how it sounded and then appropriately correct it. Similarly for her posture: she was acquiring information from vision and using it to control and correct her movements. As a result, she developed elegant and clearly artificial postures that gradually became second nature. But when she stopped paying attention, when she stopped monitoring her own posture, she just slumped like a rag doll. The same, strikingly, happened with her face: she had lost proprioceptive sense of her facial muscles and thus had to use "artificial enhancement of expressions."³⁶

I suggest one way to describe Christina's situation is to say that she experiences herself as being, with respect to her own body, just what Descartes claims we are *not* when, in the Sixth Meditation, he emphasizes the *inseparable unity* of mind and body as a "third substance." Descartes insists we are not "merely present in [our] body as a sailor is present in a ship." Rather, he says, we are intermingled ("intimement mêlés") with our body.³⁷ But Christina experiences herself as being present in her own body as a sailor is present in a ship. As Sacks describes her, she doesn't even remember how it feels to feel. Christina is, in her de facto relation to her own body, a more radical dualist than Descartes is in his explanation of the relation between mind and body. She has no experience of being "intermingled with [her body], so that [she] and the body form a unit."³⁸

Here's Sacks's account of what she says:

'What I must do then,' she said slowly, 'is use vision, use my eyes, in every situation where I used—what do you call it?—proprioception before. I've already noticed,' she added, musingly, 'that I may "lose" my arms. I think they're one place, and I find they're another. This "proprioception" is like the eyes of the body, the way the body sees itself. And if it goes, as it's gone with me, *it's like the body's blind.* My body can't "see" itself if it's lost its eyes, right? So I have to watch it—be its eyes. Right?'

'Right,' I said, 'right. You could be a physiologist.'

'I'll *have* to be a sort of physiologist,' she rejoined, 'because my physiology has gone wrong, and may never *naturally* go right.' (ibid., 47–8)

How should we understand Christina's use of 'I' here? It is clearly a use of 'I' as subject. It would make no sense to ask: 'Someone sees my arm, but is it me?' Her self-ascription of visual experience is immune to error through misidentification relative to the first-person pronoun. So is her self-location. In locating the arm she also locates *herself* (the individual thinking and saying "I think my arms are one place and I find they're another") with respect to the arm, with respect to the rest of the body, and with respect to the environment in relation to which she wants to control the movement of her arm. But that experience of self-location is not an experience of herself as a physical entity; rather, it is an experience of herself as the bearer of a point of view on the body, a point of view that can locate *that body* in space, where it cannot locate itself any longer.

Presumably, she calls the arms "my arms" because they are the arms whose movement she controls as long as she can keep her eyes on them. But she has no proprioceptive sense of those arms. She controls their movements "as a sailor is present in a ship." Compare with Evans's characterization of our awareness of our movements: "I do not move myself. I, myself, move" (Evans 1982, 207). In contrast, Christina's experience is not that she, herself, moves. In fact it is not even that she moves herself. Rather, it is that she moves *this body*. The difference between this body and other bodies is only that she moves the former without the mediation of another body, whereas she would move any other body (a car, or a wheelchair) through the mediation of the body she moves 'immediately' and which, at least in that sense, is her own. Christina's use of 'I' in "I think my arms are one place and I find them another" is not backed by an awareness of herself as an embodied entity that might back a use of 'I' as subject. At most, she is aware of herself as having a privileged connection to *that body*.

Most importantly, whatever other experience it rests on, Christina's use of 'I' in the statements reported above clearly depends on what Kant called "consciousness of oneself as subject." Her use of 'I' is backed by her awareness of herself as engaged in the reasoning in light of which and in virtue of which a unity of agency is painstakingly retrieved and a plan for action is adopted.[39] Whatever the nature of the referent of 'I' (the current speaker and thinker of "I have noticed...," "what I must do...," etc.), the basis on which she ascribes to herself the predicates of those statements is her awareness of the logically connected steps through which *she, herself* (the referent of 'I') tries to understand the situation she is in and to find a way to act on it.

I should add, however, that on Sacks's account, Christina gradually retrieves some experience of her own body through sensitivity in her skin. Nevertheless, in her own tragic description of her condition, she experiences herself as "pithed like a frog—disembodied."[40] Sacks comments:

She had lost, with her sense of proprioception, the fundamental organic mooring of identity—at least of that corporeal identity, or 'body-ego' which Freud sees as the basis of self. "The ego is first and foremost a body ego." (ibid., 52)

So here's the paradox in Sacks's description of Christina. She has lost the "fundamental organic mooring of identity...the body-ego." And yet she uses 'I' effectively and powerfully, albeit with a keen sense of loss, which she experiences as the loss of her very *self*—any meaningful referent for 'I.' This raises once again the question of the connection between the two most fundamental kinds of consciousness of oneself on which the use of 'I' as subject depends: consciousness of a body one experiences as one's own; and consciousness of the unity of one's mental activity.

Sacks's reference to Freud in this context is especially significant. The quotation is from Freud's 1923 essay in metapsychology, *The Ego and the Id*. The passage cited occurs just after Freud has expounded his notion of "Ich" (translated by Strachey as "ego") as an "organization of mental processes."*Within* that organization of mental processes, the representation of the body plays a central role, emphasized in the statement just cited. Freud's model of the mind thus seems to be offering resources for a psychological account of the sources of information that ground the use of 'I' as subject as I have analyzed it in the first two parts of this chapter: the unity of consciousness that grounds, according to Kant, the use of 'I' in 'I think'; and the proprioceptive/kinesthetic awareness of our own body that grounds the use of 'I' in statements such as 'I am standing in front of the table' or 'My legs are crossed.' To show this, let me briefly recount Freud's account of "das Ich" in his 1923 essay *Das Ich und das Es*.

The specific "organization of mental processes [*Vorgänge*] in a person"[41] that Freud calls "Ich" obeys what Freud calls the "reality principle." This means that the concatenation of representations belonging to the ego is gradually structured, in the development of the individual, in such a way as to yield information about the world that is sufficiently reliable to serve life-preserving action. As such, the ego is developed over against the mass of representations Freud calls "the id," "das Es." In contrast to the ego, the id is structured according to the "pleasure principle": very roughly, unpleasurable representations are avoided and pleasurable representations are promoted, even at the cost of privileging fantasy over reality.

Note that Freud's notion of "Ich" has prima facie very little to do with our use of the first-person pronoun. When we use the first-person pronoun we do not take ourselves to refer to an organization of mental processes or events. We refer to *ourselves*, individual persons. But it seems plausible to think the reason Freud chose the term "*Ich*" to name the organization of mental events governed by the reality principle is that he took that organization to be what makes us capable of thinking in the first-person at all.[42] If this is correct, then like Kant but in the context of a different investigation, Freud came to think that the capacity to come up with an objective, reasoned, logically ordered view of the world and the capacity to think in the first-person are mutually conditioning. This does not mean that Freud's concept of ego (*Ich*) is the counterpart of Kant's 'I' in 'I think.' Rather, it is the counterpart of Kant's concept of "transcendental unity of apperception" that jointly grounds what I called earlier our capacity to synthesize representations and our capacity to come up with the thought 'I think.'[43]

Now according to Freud, representations of our own body are at the core of the organization of mental events he calls "ego." This is because all the information we receive from the outside world passes through some state of our body. Freud writes:

> A person's own body [*der eigene Körper*], and above all its surface, is a place from which both external and internal perceptions may spring. It is *seen* like any other object, but to the *touch* it yields two kinds of sensations, one of which may be equivalent to an internal perception. Psychophysiology has fully discussed the manner in which a person's own body attains its special position among other objects in the world of perception. Pain, too, seems to play a part in the process, and the way in which we gain new knowledge of our organs during painful illnesses is perhaps a model of the way by which in general we arrive at the idea of our body. The ego is first and foremost a bodily ego; it is not merely a surface entity, but it is itself the projection of a surface. ([*Ego and Id*], SE 19:25; GW 13:253)

Freud said earlier that the ego is the "surface" of the psyche, by which the psyche communicates with the external world. He now says that it is also the projection of a surface. In other words, the representational *contents* of the organization of mental processes he calls "ego" represent some aspect of a "surface," namely, the surface of the body, its skin, eyes and ears, nose and so on. Because of this, "the ego is a bodily ego."

I suggest that this is a striking psychological counterpart to the two fundamental uses of 'I' as subject we have been considering. For in Freud's account of the organization of mental events he calls "ego," we have on the one hand the source of the consciousness of unity of mental activity that grounds the subject-use of 'I' in 'I think p,' and on the other, the source of the consciousness of one's own body that grounds the subject-use of 'I' in 'I see the tree in front of me,' 'I feel the wind blowing my hair about,' and so on.

It might be, after all, that this psychological account is not that far from Evans's epistemological + semantic account of the use of 'I' as subject. For if, as Freud says, the representation of our own body plays a central role in our ego as an organization of mental processes whose functional role is to direct us to a world of objects and guide our action, then, as Evans said, there is no use of 'I' that does not include at least a disposition to locate its referent as a physical thing among other physical things in an objective spatiotemporal world. Nevertheless, it is equally true that this self-location and self-reference would not even get off the ground unless our mental representations were ordered in what Freud calls "ego" and Kant "transcendental unity of apperception," a unity that makes possible what Kant calls the consciousness of oneself as subject and thus the use of 'I' in 'I think.' If Kant and Freud are right in their respective accounts, this organization of mental events is a necessary condition not only for the use of 'I' in 'I think,' but also for any other use of 'I' as subject and thus any use of 'I' at all, whether "as subject" or "as object." Granted, it is of course not a *sufficient* condition for all uses of 'I': for some of them, other sources of information are necessary for justifying self-ascription, whether in judgments in which 'I' is used as subject (with IEM) or as object (without IEM). Nevertheless, information about our own body or even self-location that is immune to error through misidentification are not necessary *semantic* conditions on a meaningful use of 'I.' They are *epistemological* conditions for most of our uses of 'I,' and as such they are so fundamental that in their absence any use of 'I' is deeply unsettled ("unmoored," to take up Sacks's expression), as is shown in the cases recounted by Sacks and Cole cited above. The unity of consciousness, on the other hand, is an absolutely necessary condition for any use of 'I' at all.[44]

2.4 Concluding Remarks

In this chapter, I have endeavored to clarify the differences and connections between the use of 'I' as object and the use of 'I' as subject. I have argued that all uses of 'I,' even uses of 'I' as object, depend at least in part on the kind of information on which the uses of 'I' as subject depend. I have granted to Evans that many uses of 'I' as subject depend on an awareness of oneself as an embodied entity, a person. But when this is so, it is because of the content of the predicate that is asserted of 'I' in a judgment that is IEM, *not* because having available a concept of oneself as an embodied entity is a necessary condition on the very meaningfulness of 'I,' as Evans maintains. I have also argued that all uses of 'I' as subject ultimately depend on the kind of information that grounds Kant's "consciousness of oneself as subject," in which the subject is conscious of being engaged in generating a unity or connectedness of her representations that makes them both *directed at the world* and *ascribed to the thinker* referring to herself by the concept and word 'I.' That particular brand of self-consciousness is not consciousness of oneself as an embodied entity. Rather, it is the consciousness of oneself as committed to the current reason-giving process of thinking. A healthy ego, as Freud would have put it, is one in which both fundamental kinds of self-consciousness grounding the use of 'I' as subject are in place: consciousness of oneself as a particular embodied entity, and consciousness of oneself as committed to the unity and consistency of one's mental contents. Moreover, the former (consciousness of one's own body) finds its proper place in the ordering of our representations expressed in the latter (consciousness of the unity of one's mental contents). But they are clearly distinct; and indeed they can, in extreme circumstances, come apart.

I have cited an empirical case for such coming apart (Sacks's "disembodied lady"). And I have called upon Freud's definition of the ego ("das Ich") and upon the place of the body image within the ego, as a possible psychological account of the distinction *and* connection between the two fundamental uses of 'I' as subject. But the main support for the view I have recommended is Kant's transcendental investigation into the proposition 'I think.' And this, in itself, might be a major objection to the approach I have taken here. What, one might object, does Kant's transcendental investigation into the conditions of possibility of experience and cognition have to do with either a semantic analysis of our use of 'I' or—even less—with a psychological account of the varieties of self-awareness? In this chapter I hope to have given some support to the claim that Kant's transcendental investigation (his investigation into the conditions of possibility of certain types of a priori knowledge), contemporary epistemological and semantic investigations into the justification of first-person statements, and clinical/psychological investigations into the workings of the mind can converge in producing a better sense of the richness and complexity of first-person thinking.

Notes

1. See Wittgenstein 1958a, 66–74; Kant, B421–2, B155–9 (as is customary, the *Critique of Pure Reason* is hereafter quoted with reference to its first edition ("A") and second edition ("B")); Strawson 1966, 164–6; Shoemaker 2003c, 11 and 1996b, 8; Evans 1982, 215–20; McDowell 1996, 87–107; Cassam 1997, 60–1. For a dissenting view, see Kitcher 2011, 1–5.
2. See Shoemaker 2003c, 7–8, and section 2.1.2.
3. Cf. Wittgenstein 1958a, 66–7.
4. Some recent analyses of the use of 'I' bear interesting connections to this aspect of Kant's view. See, for instance, Bayne 2010; and esp. Peacocke 2012a, 2012b, and 2014a. See also n. 32 in this chapter.
5. Evans has challenged the classification of this last example as one in which 'I' is used as object. If it is based on proprioception, the use of 'I' is immune to error through misidentification and is thus a use as subject. See 2.1.4.
6. Wittgenstein 1958a, 66–7.
7. In the *Investigations*, Wittgenstein makes no further mention of the distinction between "use of 'I' as subject" and "use of 'I' as object" and instead says of *all* uses of 'I' that in them, "'I' does not name a person" (see Wittgenstein 1958b, 410). My view is that the reason Wittgenstein generalized the point in this way is related to the claim I will defend in 2.1.2: even the use of 'I' "as object" partly depends on the kind of information that, if expressed in a judgment, would back a use of 'I' as subject. This seems to be the reason Wittgenstein maintains that 'I' does not function as a name or a definite description and thus that statements in the first person are not *about* a particular entity. I don't think Wittgenstein is correct in deriving the latter (the non-referring role of 'I') from the former ('I' does not function as a name or a definite description). I discuss this again in Chapter 3.
8. Cf. Shoemaker 2003c, 8.
9. On the various kinds of statements of identity that are implicit or explicit premises in uses of 'I' as object, see Coliva 2012b, 29–40. The issue is complicated by the fact that some uses that are, in normal circumstances, uses of 'I' as subject can arguably be taken to rest on implicit *background* identity propositions. Only those that don't rest on such background identity propositions are, according to Coliva's analysis, *logically* or *de jure* IEM. Those that do rest on such presuppositions are only *de facto* IEM. On this point, cf. also Shoemaker 1996b.
10. See Perry 1993b. Recall the circumstances: I am pushing my cart through the aisle of a supermarket and notice a trail of sugar on the ground. I follow the trail to warn the shopper I assume to be spilling sugar from his grocery cart. As I continue down the aisle the trail thickens, until it dawns on me: '*I* am making a mess!' In analyzing this example, Perry makes no use at all of the distinction between the two uses of 'I' laid out above. I don't think the analysis I propose is incompatible with his, but his purpose in this particular paper is quite different. Perry argues that the difference between a belief formulated in the first person ('I am making a mess') and a belief formulated in the third person to describe the same state of the world ('John Perry is making a mess') is not a difference in the *contents* of the belief, since one and the same state of the world is described in both propositions, but a difference in the belief *state* and its *relation to action*. In contrast, in importing into my analysis of Perry's example the distinction between use of 'I' as subject and use of 'I' as object, I am focusing on the *sources of information* on which the justification of the proposition depends. My point is that Perry's example offers a telling illustration of the dependence, *even* of the use of 'I' as object, on information that, if expressed in a judgment, would ground a use of 'I' as subject. In other words, even in uses of 'I' as object we must suppose implicit premises that contain a use of 'I' as subject.

Even though my approach in this example is different from Perry's in the cited article, it is compatible with it. In fact, the analysis I propose is close to Perry's analysis, in later writings, according to which all uses of 'I' are backed by what he calls "normally self-informative ways of knowing" (see Perry 2002b, 193, 202–5).

11. Following Shoemaker 2003b, I take first-person memory to preserve, in normal cases, the immunity to error through misidentification of self-ascriptions based on proprioception, kinesthesia, self location, and subjectively experienced sensory states. In normal cases, i.e., barring situations in which first-person memory is a particular case of quasi-memory, which does not preserve immunity to error through misidentification relative to the first-person pronoun. See ibid., 27.

12. See, for instance, Evans 1982, 212: "A subject's self-conscious thoughts about himself must be informed (or must be liable to be informed) by information the subject may gain about himself in each of a range of ways of gaining knowledge about himself." "It is essential if a subject is to be thinking about himself self-consciously [i.e., in a judgment where 'I' figures in the argument-place] that he be *disposed* to have such thinking controlled by information which may become available to him in each of the relevant ways" (ibid., 216). "The bearing of the relevant information on our I-thoughts is constitutive of our having an I-Idea" (ibid., 220). Evans then goes on to consider the different kinds of information that give rise to judgments that are IEM, and argues that some information about one's bodily states, and especially self-location, are among the kinds of information that are so immune and thus play an essential role in the meaning of 'I'-thoughts. On Evans's notion of an Idea, see ibid., 104: "An Idea of an object is something which makes it possible for a subject to think of an object in a series of indefinitely many thoughts, in each of which he will be thinking of the object in the same way." Evans adds, in a footnote to this passage (n. 24): "We cannot *equate* an Idea (a particular person's capacity) with a Fregean sense, since the latter is supposed to exist objectively (independently of anyone's grasp of it). But there is a very close relation between them. Two people exercising their (numerically different) Ideas of an object may thereby 'grasp' the same Fregean sense. What this means is that they may think of the object in the same way. (And the way of thinking would be available even if no one ever thought of the object in that way)."

13. Quassim Cassam has objected to my claim that *all* uses of 'I' depend at least in part on the kind of information that, if expressed in a judgment, would ground a use of 'I' as subject. He has offered me as a counterexample the judgment 'I am six feet tall,' based purely on the testimony of a reliable source. This, he rightly notes, is an "as object" use of 'I.' In what sense does it depend on a way of knowing that supports an "as subject" use of 'I'? My response is to dig in my heels and maintain that in this case, too, the use of 'I' as object is partly supported by a kind of information that is apt to ground a judgment in which 'I' is used as subject. The referent of 'I,' whoever or whatever she is, forms her judgment 'I am six feet tall' on the basis of hearing the statement 'you are six feet tall' or of reading the number on a chart; she is also conscious of being embodied so that a statement about her height makes sense to her. All of these are kinds of information that, if expressed in judgments, would be expressed in judgments in which 'I' is used as subject: 'I hear what you say,' 'I see the number on the chart,' 'I stand tall,' and so on. In the judgment itself, 'I am six feet tall,' 'I' is used as object: I might wrongly identify the person to whom the statement is addressed as being *me* (the person hearing the statement and thinking about it). The chart might not be about *me* (the person reading the chart), and so on. In other words, the general point I made in the main text applies: implicit *identity* statements (I, who hears the information, am the person about whom this information is asserted; I, who reads the chart, am the person described in the chart, and so on) have to bottom out somewhere. They have to bottom out in information that, if expressed in a judgment,

would be expressed in a judgment in which 'I' is used as subject. In such a judgment there is no further need to justify an identity statement in order to determine that *I*, the author of the judgment, am the person of whom the predicate is true.
14. Evans 1982, 207. See also 213: "The essence of self-consciousness is self-reference, that is to say, thinking, by a subject of judgment, about himself, and hence, necessarily, about a subject of judgment."
15. Ibid., 213.
16. Ibid., 222.
17. On this point, see also Evans, "Things without the Mind," in 1985, 249–91.
18. The role of "the *I* think" in Kant's Transcendental Deduction of the Categories and Kant's Paralogisms of Pure Reason will be analyzed in Chapters 4, 5, and 6 of this book.
19. An additional issue here is whether the self-ascription of bodily predicates that is immune to error through misidentification relative to the first-person rests on an implicit premise stating the self-ascription of what Shoemaker would call P* predicates, namely, psychological predicates that refer to subjective mental states; or whether it is *directly* the self-ascription of bodily predicates, without the implicit mediation of the self-ascription of P* predicates. Against Shoemaker, Evans maintains the latter view (Evans 1982, 216n23, and 220). But Shoemaker is arguably correct to maintain that, e.g., 'I am standing in front of the table' depends on the kind of information expressed in the statement 'I have a table in my field of vision,' to which I would suggest adding: 'I (proprioceptively) feel I am standing.' In other words, Shoemaker is right to claim that the self-ascription of bodily predicates depends on the implicit self-ascription of the relevant P* predicates. It remains, of course, that this merely epistemic fact does not commit us to any metaphysical view concerning the nature of the referent of 'I,' e.g., to a dualist view of the self. See Shoemaker 2003c, 8 and 16–17.
20. Cf. again, Evans 1982, 207, 213.
21. I am using 'cognition' here as translating the term "*Erkenntnis*" in Kant. As such it designates any representational state directed at an object or having what we would call intentionality.
22. This explanation may seem implausible in light of the common meaning of the phrase 'I think.' In ordinary language, 'I think that p' would carry the connotation of pulling back from the original statement rather than endorsing it. But the use Kant makes of the phrase 'I think' in the statements cited above is not an ordinary language use of 'I think.' It is quite an idiosyncratic use, indicating that an activity of thinking, i.e., conceptualizing, was behind my statement all along and is now made explicit to reinforce it. It can have various degrees of force. It may mean either that I am uncertain about my statement or, on the contrary, that I assert it without any reservation. See above in the main text for further explanation. I am grateful to Quassim Cassam for pressing me on this point. For an excellent analysis of degrees of assent according to Kant, see Chignell 2007.
23. See esp. B132–44. For a more detailed explanation of this aspect of Kant's view, see Chapter 4 in this volume.
24. Cf. A446/B404, and 2.1.4 in this chapter.
25. See again, Evans 1982, 226, 228, 232; and cf. 2.1.4 in this chapter.
26. The situation would be different if I had a colleague at my side and she had said: 'Sorry to disappoint you, but the proof is invalid.' Suppose now someone came into the room and I said: 'This colleague thinks the proof is invalid, I think the proof is valid. What do you think?' My judgment 'I think the proof is valid' would be IEM for just the same reasons as in the case I describe in the main text; nevertheless, I would be identifying myself in contradistinction to another individual, the colleague standing next to me. In this case, I would *also* be aware of myself as an embodied entity, distinguished from others (my two colleagues) by my location in space and by other uniquely identifying properties. But

Evans himself insists, against Grice and Strawson, that it is a mistake to consider 'I' primarily as a communicative device. Rather, he claims, an analysis of 'I' should focus on the context of thought (Evans 1982, 208). This is certainly the context in which Kant analyzes 'I think.'

27. See 6.2, n. 9.
28. For a contemporary systematic development of a similar point that can claim Kantian ancestry, see Burge 2000. For more on Kant's analysis of the role of the first-person 'I' in 'I think,' see 4.2; 5.1.2; 5.1.3.
29. My use of the term 'binding' here may cause some eyebrows to rise. What I am here calling 'binding' is what Kant calls "combination" or "synthesis" (*Verbindung, Synthesis*). Now what Kant calls "combination" is an activity that occurs at the personal level and includes combination of concepts (in judgments) and combination of sensory manifolds (in imagination). Even though the latter is an operation of which we are "seldom even conscious" (A78/B103), it, too, just like the combination of concepts in judgments (acts of judging), is characterized in terms of folk psychology and thus belongs at the personal level. Not so with 'binding' in the contemporary 'binding problem,' which belongs at the subpersonal level and is an activity of the brain. When I analyze Kant's view in more detail (especially in Chapter 4) I will return to using Kant's own terms: combination, synthesis. In using 'binding' here I mean to call attention to an interesting connection between the problem Kant tries to address at the personal level, and the problem contemporary cognitive psychology addresses at the subpersonal level. For an early discussion of the binding problem, see Treisman and Gelade 1980. For a philosophical discussion of the binding problem in cognitive psychology, see Bayne and Chalmers 2003 and Bayne 2010. Bayne himself draws attention to the connections between the contemporary problem of the unity of consciousness and Kant's: see Bayne 2010, 14, 34, 229.
30. In insisting on the thin, to the point of vanishing, character of IEM in the case of 'I think p,' in contrast to the IEM of self-ascription of bodily properties and of self-location, I am close to Annalisa Coliva's view that the proposition 'I think' is *logically* immune to error through misidentification relative to the first-person pronoun, in contrast to self-ascriptions on the basis of proprioception, sense of balance, or other experiences of bodily states, which are only contingently or de facto IEM (see Coliva 2012b, 32–40). However, the ground on which I claim 'I think' has IEM in a 'thin' sense is different from hers. For Coliva, the self-ascription of *any* psychological state (Shoemaker's P* predicates) is IEM in virtue of the phenomenological character of that state: to be aware of perceiving, sensing, feeling, etc. just is to be aware of *oneself* perceiving, sensing, feeling, and so on. For Coliva, thinking is no different in this regard than perceiving, sensing, feeling, or any other subjective state (see ibid., 38, and n. 21). But Kant's point concerns exclusively the activity of thinking. Subjective sensory or affective states, in contrast, have no intrinsic connection to 'I,' nor do they in themselves make self-ascription rational. Only insofar as they are taken up into the synthesizing activity I have been outlining above, do they acquire a connection to 'I' such that they can be self-ascribed. This means also that the ground for self-ascription is not phenomenological but constitutive: it is constitutive of the very concept 'I' that it should have a referent only insofar as there is binding for conceptualizing, just as it is constitutive of the activity of binding for conceptualizing that it be ascribable to an entity referring to herself via the concept 'I.' That, for Kant, psychological states per se have no connection to the concept 'I'—and acquire it only via the activity of binding for conceptualizing—makes Kant's view closer to Peacocke's than to Coliva's. But I suggest Kant's view offers resources that Peacocke's lacks to answer what Coliva calls "a dilemma for Peacocke's account" (Coliva, 2012b, 40): given that Peacocke affirms the "representational independence" of mental states from the concept 'I,' how can he explain, other than by fiat, that they are ever

self-ascribed? Kant's account provides an answer. For Kant, even though psychological states are in themselves 'independent' of any I-concept or I-representation (whether conceptual or not), they nevertheless *become* self-ascribable in virtue of being taken up in the synthetic activity I have been describing. See Peacocke 1999, chap. 6; Peacocke 2008, chap. 3; Peacocke 2012a. But see also Peacocke 2014a, 21–2 and chap. 7, where Peacocke discusses the proximity and the differences between his view and Kant's.

31. Many thanks to Christopher Peacocke for pressing this point in correspondence.
32. This is a point Coliva misses when she attributes to Kant the view that "'I think' must accompany all my psychological states" (2012b, 36). Kant only says that "The **I think** must **be able** to accompany all my representations" (B131-2, emphasis Kant's). For more on this point, see Chapter 4.

    Here, it may be important to clarify: I am *not* claiming that FRR offers an argument in favor of Kant's SY ↔ I. Quite the contrary: FRR fixes the referent of 'I' without any mention of synthesis or binding. The point here is that FRR is not enough to understand what's going on with our use of 'I.' One might offer any number of philosophical views about what makes it the case that an entity counts as a referent for 'I,' e.g., Descartes's metaphysical account according to which, strictly speaking, only a mind distinct from the body counts as a referent for 'I,' or in contemporary philosophy Peacocke's metaphysical account according to which only an integrating apparatus can count as a referent for 'I.' Kant's transcendental account of *our* use of 'I' consists in claiming that whatever kind of metaphysical entity we are, the fact that we are capable of synthesizing for judgment and the fact that we are capable of self-ascribing the predicate 'think' are mutually conditioning, and jointly grounded in the transcendental unity of apperception. But he would probably accept that an entity endowed with intuitive intellect, thus needing no step-by-step synthesizing of her representations in order to think, would also count as a referent for 'I' (an entity capable of referring to herself as the 'I'-user). But in our case—in the case of human beings—only by being capable of synthesizing for judging are we also 'I'-users. In other words, the claim here is not that one can derive the idea of synthesis for judging from FRR. The claim is that Kant offers an independent argument for what makes it possible for us, human beings, to count as a referent for 'I,' namely, an entity capable of self-reference. I am grateful to Quassim Cassam for pressing me to clarify this point.
33. Cases such as 'I feel pain' will be further discussed in Chapters 3 and 4. What Kant means by "object of inner sense" will be clarified in Chapter 4.
34. See O. Sacks 1998, chap. 3, 43–55. My account here is closely based on Sacks's narrative. The story of Christina was first published by Sacks in 1985. The onset of Christina's condition was eight years earlier: 1977. Since then, as Sacks already noted in the 1998 edition of the book, many other similar cases have been registered (see Sacks 1998 [1985], 54–5). Among the best documented are the cases of I.W. and G.L., recorded in Cole and Paillard (1995). I.W.'s story is told in greater detail in Cole (1995). In what follows I have mostly drawn on Christina's story as recounted by Sacks. But I have used information I derived from Cole and Paillard (1995) to comment on the case and to support my interpretation of Christina's use of 'I.' I am grateful to Hong Yu Wong for having directed me to Cole's and Paillard's publications.
35. Sacks 1998 [1985], 49.
36. Ibid., 50.
37. Descartes 1984 [1641], 56: "Nature also teaches me, by these sensations of pain, hunger, thirst, and so on, that I am not merely present in my body as a sailor is present in a ship, but that I am very closely joined and as it were intermingled with it, so that I and the body form a unit."
38. Similarly, Cole and Paillard note that "G.L. occasionally talks of her body as being a machine on which she imposes commands.... A more accurate description may be that

she uses her body as a tool, a passive instrument that can be used to move and to interact with her environment (a machine, though it must be started and controlled, is taken to have some autonomous performance)" (Cole and Paillard 1995, 261). They add, however, that even a tool "is not a satisfactory simile, in that when we use tools they rapidly become elaborated into a motor schema, and hence are hardly attended to." In contrast, G.L. can control the movements of her body only if she constantly attends to them, compensating for the lack of proprioception by calling on her visual body image.

39. Sacks himself does not point out this aspect of her use of 'I,' nor does he make any reference to Kant in this connection. But I suggest that it vividly emerges from the story he recounts. He does make reference to Kant a contrario when describing a case where the unity of consciousness has been lost: the "Lost Mariner." See O. Sacks 1998, 23–43.
40. Ibid., 52.
41. Freud, *Ego and Id*, SE 19:17; GW 13:243.
42. The term '*Ich*' was commonly used by brain anatomists contemporary with Freud (including his own teacher at the University of Vienna, Theodor Meynert) to designate the system of brain traces that are constitutive of an individual's character. I say more about what is specific to Freud's use of the term in Chapter 7. See esp. n. 52 in that chapter.
43. This point will be developed in Chapter 7, where I will also discuss the contrasts between Kant's transcendental investigation and Freud's clinical-psychological investigation.
44. This claim may seem implausibly strong, both at the personal and at the subpersonal level. At the personal level: what about split personalities or even milder cases of mental conflict? At the subpersonal level: can't it be the case, indeed is it not the default case, that *apparent* unity (at the personal level) is really a surface phenomenon for what is really a plurality of subpersonal agencies? I grant both points but take neither of them to challenge grounding the use of 'I' in mental (rational) unity. For more on this point, see my discussion in the introduction (Chapter 1). See also my discussion of Kant on the soul in Chapter 5. Thanks to Johan van Benthem for having pressed this question in correspondence.

3

Non-Thetic Self-Consciousness and Uses of 'I'
Sartre Meets Wittgenstein

In Chapter 2, I argued that Wittgenstein's *Blue Book* distinction between use of 'I' as subject and use of 'I' as object, and Kant's distinction between consciousness of oneself as subject and consciousness of oneself as object, do not exactly map. More precisely, Kant's consciousness of oneself as subject or "transcendental unity of self-consciousness" seems to map just one of the uses of 'I' that Wittgenstein describes as a use of 'I' as subject: the use of 'I' in 'I think.' I argued against Evans that this particular use of 'I' as subject does *not* entail consciousness of oneself as an embodied entity. I also argued that the kind of self-consciousness that backs the use of 'I' in 'I think' is a necessary condition of *any* use of 'I,' whether 'as subject' or 'as object.' This does not mean, of course, that thinking the thought 'I think' is *itself* a necessary condition for any use of 'I.' Rather, the suggestion is that the kind of unity of consciousness that grounds the thought 'I think' is itself—whether or not it comes to be expressed in the thought 'I think'—a necessary condition for any use of 'I' and, for that matter, any judgment at all. This is why, when pressed, we are disposed to reinforce any judgment 'p' by prefacing it with 'I think,' thus yielding: 'I think p.'

In this chapter, I will revisit the question: to what extent, and in what ways, is our use of 'I' backed by consciousness of ourselves as an embodied entity? What is the connection, if any, between that kind of self-consciousness and the self-consciousness Kant called "consciousness of oneself as subject," whose conceptual representation is the proposition 'I think'? In revisiting these questions, I will draw on resources offered by Sartre's analysis of self-consciousness in *The Transcendence of the Ego* and *Being and Nothingness*. In both texts, Sartre offers a phenomenological description of a kind of self-consciousness he calls "non-thetic" or "non-positional" self-consciousness. Of that non-thetic self-consciousness he offers examples that include, on the one hand, awareness of one's own body, or what Sartre calls "body for itself"; and, on the other, awareness of the unity of a mental activity that finds expression in what Sartre calls a "pre-reflective cogito." Sartre thus seems to offer his own version of not just one but both fundamental kinds of self-consciousness that I argued, in the previous chapter, ground the use of 'I' as subject. I will argue that Sartre's phenomenological description sheds light on those uses of 'I' and thus also on the uses of 'I' as object.

Evans briefly discusses Sartre's view of embodied self-consciousness in his preparatory notes for chapter 7 of *The Varieties of Reference*, "Self-Identification."[1] I will argue that Sartre's view is actually richer than Evans gives it credit for, and that it offers a more plausible account of the relation between self-consciousness and consciousness of oneself as a physical entity than the one offered by Evans.[2] But I will also argue that some of Sartre's paradoxical statements concerning non-thetic self-consciousness reveal a lack of clarity on his part concerning both kinds of non-thetic self-consciousness (consciousness of one's own body, consciousness of the unity of one's mental activity), and especially concerning non-thetic consciousness of the unity of one's mental activity.

The structure of the chapter is as follows.

In 3.1, I briefly explain Sartre's notions of consciousness and self-consciousness, in particular Sartre's distinction between "thetic" consciousness of object, "non-thetic" self-consciousness, and "reflective" self-consciousness.

In 3.2, I explain what I take to be the connections between Sartre's varieties of self-consciousness and Wittgenstein's distinction between the use of 'I' as subject and the use of 'I' as object.

In 3.3, I examine Evans's view of the connection between self-consciousness and consciousness of oneself as an embodied entity. I evaluate Evans's comments on the connections between his own view and Sartre's.

In 3.4, I examine Sartre's complex view of self-consciousness as consciousness of one's own body. I evaluate again its connection to Evans's view.

In 3.5, I argue that Sartre's description of the use of 'I' in what he calls "pre-reflective" judgments helps us understand (but not endorse) Elizabeth Anscombe's "extraordinary conclusion,"[3] according to which 'I' never has a referring role. Finally, I argue that Sartre's hesitation concerning the nature of non-thetic (self-)consciousness[4] and the related uses of 'I' are due to a shortcoming he shares with Wittgenstein and his followers: paying insufficient attention to the kind of self-consciousness Kant called "consciousness of oneself as subject," expressed in the proposition 'I think.'

3.1 Sartre on "Positional" or "Thetic" Consciousness of Object and "Non-Positional" or "Non-Thetic" (Self-)Consciousness

Sartre borrows from Husserl the categorical statement that "all consciousness is consciousness *of* something," that is to say, consciousness is *intentionality*.[5] Husserl meant thereby to stress the fact that consciousness is a standing mental attitude that is *directed at* something. In *Being and Nothingness*, Sartre accuses Husserl of maintaining an ambiguity on the question of whether this directedness or intentionality of consciousness relates it to a content *internal to consciousness* through the mediation of which consciousness is related to an external world, or whether, on the contrary, consciousness reaches directly "outside," into the world. For Sartre, there is no doubt that the "something" consciousness is directed at is outside, in the world, not an object internal to our mental life. "Everything is outside, everything, even ourselves: outside, in the world, among others."[6]

A second, equally important feature of consciousness is that while being directed at the world, it is always at the same time consciousness of itself, or self-consciousness. Being conscious (being in a particular attitude or state of awareness directed toward an object) without being at the same time conscious of being in this very state of awareness would be, according to Sartre, an oxymoron. However, the self-consciousness (the property of being conscious of one's consciousness of an object) that is thus inseparable from consciousness of an object is quite different from the latter. Sartre characterizes it as "non-positional" or "non-thetic" as opposed to consciousness of an object, which is "positional" or "thetic." In other words, in the non-thetic self-consciousness that accompanies all consciousness of object, consciousness is not directed at itself as if it were another object, added to the external object it is directed at. Sartre puts parentheses around the 'of' that characterizes the relation to itself of non-thetic consciousness (of) self, to underline the non-intentional character of this self-relatedness, or rather this immediate self-presence of consciousness.[7]

Now, if consciousness, insofar as it is consciousness (of) self, is not an object for itself, even less does it have an internal object that one might call 'I' ('*je*') or 'me' ('*moi*'). Thus, Sartre writes, in *The Transcendence of the Ego*:

> The type of existence that consciousness has is that it is consciousness of itself. And it becomes conscious of itself *insofar as it is consciousness of a transcendent object*.... The object lies opposite it, in its characteristic opacity, but consciousness, for its part, is purely and simply the consciousness of being consciousness of this object: such is the law of its existence. We need to add that this consciousness of consciousness—with the exception of cases of reflected consciousness, which I will be examining in detail later—is not *positional*, i.e. consciousness is not its own object.... I will call such a consciousness 'first order' or '*unreflective*' consciousness. My question is this: is there room for an *I* in a consciousness of this kind? The reply is clear: of course not. (Sartre 2004, 8)

Sartre devotes the totality of *The Transcendence of the Ego* and a large part of *Being and Nothingness* to explaining and justifying this categorical "of course not." Very roughly, the explanation is as follows.[8] The non-thetic consciousness (of) self that is inseparable from any thetic consciousness of objects draws the unity of the states it is made up of, not from itself, but from the object or objects it is directed at. Thus, it is not necessary to suppose an *I* that would be the source of the unity of conscious states. Indeed, supposing such an *I* would be the source of insuperable difficulties. If this *I* is an object of consciousness, it presupposes a non-thetic consciousness that is directed at it, and it cannot be the source of the unity of *that* consciousness. If it is not an object, but is entirely on the side of consciousness, then it introduces in the latter a point of opacity that is useless and even a source of confusion. For the unity of non-thetic (self-)consciousness is sufficiently ensured by the synthesis of conscious states generated by the directedness at an object, whether that object is a concrete object that is empirically given, or whether it is an abstract object such as a mathematical object.

Consciousness is defined by intentionality. Through intentionality it transcends itself, it unifies itself by going outside itself. The unity of the thousand active consciousnesses through which

I have added, now add, and will add in the future, two and two to make four, is the transcendent object 'two and two make four.' Without the permanence of this eternal truth, it would be impossible to conceive of a real unity, and there would be a multiplicity of irreducible operations—just as many as there are consciousnesses performing the operation. (Sartre 2004, 6)

So, thetic consciousness is consciousness of tables, chairs, and so on, but also of mathematical truths such as '2 + 2 = 4,' and is always at the same time non-thetic (self-) consciousness. But that non-thetic (self-)consciousness is not consciousness of an *I* in the way thetic consciousness is consciousness of tables, chairs, and so on. In fact, there is no *I* at all to be either the object of non-thetic consciousness or in some way within it as its unifying agent.

However, non-thetic (self-)consciousness can itself become the object of thetic consciousness: it can become an object of investigation for a second-order consciousness. Sartre calls this second-order consciousness directed at non-thetic consciousness: "reflective consciousness." Examples might be: directing my attention to my non-thetic consciousness (of) being in pain, perhaps also to my non-thetic consciousness (of) quickly withdrawing my hand from the fire, as well as to my non-thetic consciousness (of) screaming, and so on. Then an *I* appears as an object. But this *I* is again not an object internal to the non-thetic (self-)consciousness that is now inseparable from the new kind of thetic consciousness, reflective consciousness. Rather, the *I* is an object that reflective consciousness is directed at (like ordinary thetic consciousness is directed at tables and chairs and mathematical truths). That new kind of object, Sartre maintains, is a pole of unity of the conscious states and acts that reflective consciousness undertakes to examine, in just the way in which a material object is, for consciousness, a pole of unity of the aspects and states under which the object appears to consciousness.[9] But the non-thetic (self-)consciousness that accompanies the reflective consciousness, just as it accompanies all thetic consciousness of objects in general, remains, for its part, absolutely impersonal: in it, as in every non-thetic (self)-consciousness, there is "no place for an *I*."[10]

And yet it does sometimes happen that the formulation of non-thetic (self-)consciousness *as such*—not as an object for a reflective consciousness—should appeal to the first-person pronoun. What, then, is the status of this 'I'? In this context, says Sartre, 'I' is an empty concept.

It is however certain that the *I* appears on the unreflected level. If I am asked, 'what are you doing?' and I reply, preoccupied as I am, 'I am trying to hang up this picture,' or 'I am repairing the rear tire,' these phrases do not transport us on to the level of reflection, I utter them without ceasing to work, without ceasing to have in view just the actions, insofar as they have been done or are still to be done—not insofar as I am doing them. But this 'I' that I am dealing with here is not, however, a simple syntactic form. It has a meaning; it is quite simply an empty concept, destined to remain empty. (Sartre 2004, 40)

In both the examples Sartre gives here, the unreflective 'I' appears in the argument place in a judgment where I ascribe to myself an action or attempted action that involves my body: hanging up this picture or repairing the tire are physical actions. There is thus, for Sartre, accompanying the thetic consciousness of the picture to be hanged, and the thetic consciousness of the tire to be repaired, a consciousness (of) agency that is a consciousness (of) *oneself* acting, which finds expression in the judgments quoted in the citation above ('I am trying to hang up this picture,' 'I am repairing the rear tire.') Sartre does not comment on this use of 'I' beyond saying that "these phrases do not transport us on to the level of reflection." This lack of comment is a bit surprising, since in the passage previously cited he adamantly maintained that in non-reflective (self-) consciousness "there is no room for an *I*."[11] In the introduction to *Being and Nothingness*, which appeared six years after *The Transcendence of the Ego*, Sartre seems to accept without any reservation the idea of a legitimate use of the word or concept 'I' at the pre-reflective level. His example, this time, is that of the non-thetic consciousness (of) the activity of counting, a condition for the thetic consciousness of the cardinal number of the collection of objects I am currently enumerating.

> If I count the cigarettes that are in this cigarette case, I experience the unfolding of an objective property: there are twelve cigarettes. This property appears to my consciousness as a property existing in the world. I may very well have no positional consciousness of counting them. I do not 'know myself counting'.... However, while these cigarettes present themselves to me as being twelve cigarettes, I have a non-thetic consciousness of my activity of adding. If I am asked: 'what are you doing?' I will reply: 'I am counting', and this answer does not only track the instantaneous consciousness which I may reach by reflection, but also those that passed without being reflected, those that are forever unreflected in my immediate past.... There is a pre-reflective cogito which is the condition of the Cartesian Cogito. (Sartre 2003a, 9)

It is tempting to see a Kantian inspiration in this text, even though Sartre does not acknowledge it as such—his only explicit reference in the vicinity of the cited passage is to Heidegger. For in the text cited above, Sartre describes the (non-thetic) consciousness expressed in the phrase 'I am counting' as a "pre-reflective cogito," which is a condition of the Cartesian cogito. The latter is, in Sartrian terms, the expression of a *reflective* consciousness, namely, a consciousness that is *directed*, in an attitude of skeptical doubt, *at* the operations of thinking. In contrast with this reflective cogito, Sartre's "pre-reflective cogito" is close to the Kantian "I think" analyzed in the previous chapter, where there is no *object* I that is represented as falling under the concept 'think,' but rather 'I think' is the very expression of the act of thinking.[12]

The connections and differences between Kant's view and Sartre's will be considered again at the end of this chapter. My purpose for now is to examine the relations between Sartre's "non-thetic (self)-consciousness" and Wittgenstein's "use of 'I' as subject." Let me begin by briefly recalling Wittgenstein's *Blue Book* distinction.

3.2 Wittgenstein on "Use of 'I' as Subject" and "Use of 'I' as Object"

I recalled in the previous chapter Wittgenstein's distinction and the examples he offers. The difference between the use of 'I' as subject and use of 'I' as object, Wittgenstein urges, is that a kind of error is possible in the latter for which there is no room in the former. When I say 'I have a toothache,' there is no room for the question: someone has a toothache, but is it me? In contrast, there is room for such a question in a case such as 'I have grown six inches.'[13]

As is clearly indicated by the question Wittgenstein takes to be "nonsensical,"[14] the question with respect to which there is no room for error in the use of 'I' as subject is *not* the question: To what or to whom does the term 'I' refer? Rather, it is the question: Is this particular predicate, which I know to be true of someone, true of *me* (the current thinker of an I-thought or speaker of an I-sentence)? The impossibility of error in replying to that question in certain cases of first-person statements is what Shoemaker has called "immunity to error through misidentification relative to the first person pronoun" (IEM).[15] The immunity in question does not concern the word or concept 'I' on its own, independently of its use in the proposition. Rather, it concerns the *whole proposition* in which 'I' is used.

According to Wittgenstein, IEM in identifying the individual of whom the predicate is true indicates that in its use as subject, 'I' is not used to refer to someone in particular or to answer the question, 'Whom is F true of?' For instance, 'Who is feeling pain, who thinks, who sees?' Rather, 'I' is an inseparable component in the whole sentence that *expresses* a state or an action or an attempted action, without there being any question of identifying the particular individual who happens to be the subject of the state or the agent of the action or attempted action. This is why Wittgenstein writes, "To say 'I have pain' is no more a statement *about* a particular person than moaning is."[16]

The distinction between two uses of the word 'I' disappears from Wittgenstein's notes after the *Blue Book*. But the problem raised about 'I' does not disappear. Rather, it is generalized, since Wittgenstein declares that 'I' is *never* used to designate a person, thus transferring to *all* uses of 'I' the problem he had first identified by way of distinguishing between use of 'I' as subject and use of 'I' as object. In his "Notes for Lectures on Private Experience and Sense Data," he defends the radical position according to which "the word 'I' does not refer to a person."[17] And in the *Philosophical Investigations* he devotes several sections to elucidating the differences between 'I' and other personal pronouns, as well as definite descriptions and proper names, and he concludes: "'I' is not the name of a person."[18] In my view, the generalized denial that 'I' functions as the name of a person does not contradict the *Blue Book* distinction between two uses of 'I,' only one of which (the use of 'I' as subject) "is not the name of a person" or "does not refer to a person." For if it is true, as I have argued in the previous chapter, that *all* uses of 'I' depend at least in part on the kind of information that grounds a use of 'I' as subject, then it makes sense to generalize to all uses of 'I' the denial that 'I' is the name of a person.[19]

Wittgenstein's followers have gone in opposite directions in their accounts of what is unique about the role of 'I.' In a paper that has become a classic, Elizabeth Anscombe defended the view that 'I' never has a referential use.[20] At the opposite end of the spectrum, Gareth Evans defended the view that even in what Wittgenstein called its use as subject, 'I' has a referential use. Indeed, it is used to refer to the very same entity it refers to in its use "as object," namely, a person—a living, sensing, thinking body. But the difference between the two uses rests on the kind of information on which the attribution of predicate to subject depends.[21]

Now consider Sartre's "non-thetic (self)-consciousness." We saw above that Sartre considered two different kinds. One is consciousness (of) one's physical agency (where agency, of course, also includes some mental activity: figuring out how to hang the picture, how to repair the tire, and so on). The other is consciousness (of) one's mental agency (counting). Both kinds find expression in a non-reflective use of 'I' ('I am trying to hang this picture,' 'I am repairing this tire,' 'I am counting the cigarettes') where attention is directed, *not* at an I or an ego, but rather *at the object* the thetic consciousness is directed at. However, both non-reflective uses of 'I' can eventually become reflective uses: I can direct my attention at *my doing* what I am doing, whether in physical or in mental action and say, for instance, 'I am a pretty bad picture hanger,' 'I am a bad repairman,' or, like Descartes, 'cogito, ergo sum.' Note that whether pre-reflective or reflective, the uses of 'I' that either *express* (pre-reflectively) or *are directed at* (reflectively) non-thetic (self-)consciousness are instances of what Wittgenstein calls use of 'I' as subject.[22] If uttered on the basis of my non-thetic consciousness (of) hanging the picture, repairing the tire, counting the cigarettes, the judgment 'I am hanging the picture,' 'I am repairing the tire,' 'I am counting the cigarettes,' *whether pre-reflective or reflective*, is IEM. Not so in the contrast cases where the very same judgments might be based on what Sartre would call thetic consciousness of myself as an object: in an old photo I see myself, or someone I take to be myself, hanging the pictures in my then brand new home. Or I see, reflected in the glass door of the building, someone I take to be myself as I try to repair my bicycle tire. But maybe there is someone else next to me, also trying to repair her tire. These would be cases of thetic consciousness of myself that are neither pre-reflective nor reflective consciousness, but just an ordinary kind of consciousness of an object in the world. In these cases, the thetic consciousness is *not* directed at the non-thetic (self)-consciousness I have (of) my own action. Rather, it is (indirectly, through a photo or through my reflected image) directed at myself as an object in the world. In terms of Wittgenstein's distinction between use of 'I' as object and use of 'I' as subject, those instances of thetic consciousness of myself would ground uses of 'I' as object.

If this is correct, then there is a direct connection between Sartre's "non-thetic (self-)consciousness" and Wittgenstein's "use of 'I' as subject." Unlike Kant's "consciousness of oneself as subject," whose propositional expression maps only one case of the use of 'I' as subject (the use of 'I' in 'I think p'), Sartre's non-thetic (self-)consciousness seems to offer an account of the kinds of self-awareness that back *all* cases of the use of 'I' as subject. Indeed, in the following sections of this chapter, I will suggest that Sartre's analysis of self-consciousness and both of the opposed interpretations of the uses of 'I' inspired by Wittgenstein (Anscombe's and Evans's) are mutually illuminating in their strengths as well as in their weaknesses.

To show this, I will first recall Evans's view according to which all uses of 'I' as subject are premised on an awareness of oneself, or at least a conception of oneself,[23] as a corporeal entity, a physical thing among physical things (3.3). I will argue that Evans's view gains support from Sartre's description of non-thetic (self-)consciousness as consciousness (of) oneself as a corporeal entity or body for itself (3.4). But Sartre is more modest in giving the view an empirical/phenomenological rather than an a priori/semantic support.[24]

Sartre's view nevertheless remains unstable, since, on the one hand, he maintains that non-thetic consciousness (of) self is non-thetic consciousness (of) the body, but, on the other, he maintains a radical autonomy of non-thetic consciousness (of) self with respect to any bodily consciousness. Moreover, as we saw above, Sartre maintains that, whether embodied or not, when non-thetic (self-)consciousness finds expression in a first-person statement, 'I' is an "empty concept." I will argue that this aspect of Sartre's view can be compared with Anscombe's in her famous article "The First Person" (3.5). I shall argue that we can find in the tensions intrinsic to Sartre's view of non-thetic self-consciousness resources to understand the tension between the two opposed interpretations of the use of 'I' as subject: the one defended by Evans, according to which necessarily, any use of 'I,' including its use 'as subject,' is supported by consciousness of oneself as an embodied entity; and the one defended by Anscombe, according to which *no* use of 'I' at all, a fortiori not the use of 'I' as subject, has any referring role at all.

3.3 Uses of 'I' and Consciousness of One's Own Body

Contrary to Wittgenstein, Evans maintained that 'I'-thoughts are always thoughts *about* a particular entity. The reason Wittgenstein denied this, says Evans, is that, from the fact that in many cases of attributing to oneself mental or physical predicates, no criterion is needed for correctly identifying the entity of which the predicate is true, he mistakenly inferred that in those cases there is no identification at all and thus no referent for 'I.' But this inference is invalid, says Evans. The fact that there is no *criterion* of identification does not mean there is no *identification* at all.[25]

To understand Evans's thesis, it is important to keep in mind the distinction between two senses of the term 'identification.'

In one sense, (identification$_1$), one can say that asserting 'a is F' depends on an identification if knowledge of that proposition can be taken to depend on knowledge of two propositions, one predicative ('b is F'), and the other an identity ('a = b'). For instance, to know the proposition 'Elizabeth has a bump on her forehead' is to know two propositions: 'the person standing in front of the door has a bump on her forehead' and 'the person standing in front of the door is Elizabeth.' Of course, this identification may be erroneous. It may be true that the person I see in front of the door has a bump on her forehead but false that that person is Elizabeth. To confirm that she is Elizabeth, I must implicitly or explicitly appeal to criteria of identification, that is, criteria of the truth of the proposition 'the person standing in front of the door = Elizabeth.' The very same situation occurs in cases of the use of 'I' as object. If I say or think 'I have a bump on my forehead' while seeing in the mirror a person who looks like me and seems to have a bump on her forehead, my statement can be unpacked as 'the person reflected in the mirror has a bump on her forehead' and 'I am the person reflected in the mirror.' The predication may be true and the identity proposition false. I must make sure I have correctly applied the relevant criteria of identification, that is, criteria for recognizing the person I see in the mirror as being *myself*, the person who speaks or thinks the proposition 'I have a bump on my forehead.'[26]

But there is another sense of the term 'identification' (call it identification$_2$), where 'identifying' an object does not depend on verifying an identity proposition such as those I just gave as examples. In other words, it is not the case that all identifications depend on an identification$_1$ (on knowledge of an identity proposition), that is to say, on the application of identity criteria. When they don't, identifying is just having an answer to the question, 'Which entity is the predicate true of?' This second, broader meaning is the meaning that is in play in the expression 'immunity to error through misidentification.' According to Evans, since there is no room for errors of identification in the cases Wittgenstein thought about, Wittgenstein rightly concluded that there was no identification$_1$ grounding the corresponding first-person statements. But because Wittgenstein conflated identification$_1$ and identification$_2$, he wrongly concluded that in such cases, there was no identification$_2$ either (no answer to the question: *which*?) and thus no *referent* for 'I' in the use of 'I' as subject ("The word 'I' does not refer to a person," " 'I' is not the name of a person").[27]

According to Evans's explanation, cases of IEM depend on the kind of information on which the knowledge expressed in the proposition rests. This IEM and the information that makes it possible can be a feature of bodily just as much as of mental predicates. In the case of bodily predicates, proprioception and synaesthesis ground statements of the form 'I am F' such that knowing F to be true of something just is knowing it to be true *of me* (where 'I' or 'me' refers to the person thinking or saying 'I am F'). IEM is thus an *epistemic* property of some, but not all, first-person statements. Evans notes that, from this epistemic standpoint, attributions of mental predicates have no privilege over attributions of bodily predicates. It is the case just as much for bodily predicates as for mental predicates that, on the basis of certain kinds of information, they can be asserted of oneself in statements that are IEM. Conversely, it is the case just as much for mental predicates as for bodily predicates that, on the basis of certain kinds of information, they are liable to error through misidentification relative to the first-person pronoun. This situation occurs when the attribution of the relevant mental predicate to oneself depends on an identity proposition that may be false, for instance: 'this person in the picture is sad,' 'I am this person in the picture,' so 'I am sad in that picture'). This lack of epistemic privilege of mental predicates over bodily predicates is revealing of the fact, says Evans, that our use of the first-person pronoun supports a "firmly anti-Cartesian" conception of ourselves.[28]

Even more anti-Cartesian is Evans's thesis that, whatever the predicates (bodily or mental) that are asserted of it, necessarily, our conception of the particular entity to which the first-person pronoun refers is that of a bodily entity, individuated by its position in space and time. Evans supports this thesis with an argument derived from what he calls the "Generality Constraint." This argument was examined in Chapter 2; I will not repeat it here.[29] What is relevant to the current discussion is that, after producing his argument to the effect that necessarily, in any instance of its uses, 'I' is taken by its user to refer to a spatiotemporal, and thus to an embodied entity, a person[30] (or in Evans's terms: any use of 'I' depends on having a conception of oneself as an embodied entity), Evans remarks:

The idea that I can identify myself with a person objectively construed is often mis-expressed, e.g. in terms of the idea that I realize that I am an object to others (also an object of outer sense, as Kant says: *Critique of Pure Reason*, B145). This misleadingly imports an ideal verificationist construal of the point. (Evans 1982, 210)

Beyond the explicit reference to Kant's idealism, there is an implicit reference to Sartre in the cautionary dismissal of the "verificationist" view according to which acknowledging myself as an element in the objective order is acknowledging myself as an object to others. This implicit reference is confirmed if one looks at the added remarks taken from Evans's personal notes, which McDowell included at the end of the chapter when he edited the book. In these remarks, Evans cites the beginning of part 3 ("Being- for-Others"), chapter 2 ("The Body") of Sartre's *Being and Nothingness*. The chapter starts with a dismissal of the classical dualism between the "interiority" of consciousness and the "exteriority" of the body. Sartre writes:

If, after grasping 'my' consciousness in its absolute interiority and by a series of reflective acts, I then seek to unite it with a certain living object composed of a nervous system, a brain, glands, digestive, respiratory and circulatory organs whose very matter is capable of being analyzed chemically into atoms of hydrogen, carbon, nitrogen, phosphorus, etc., then I am going to encounter insuperable difficulties. But these difficulties all stem from the fact that I try to unite my consciousness not with *my* body, but with the body of *others*. In fact the body which I have just described is not my body as it is *for me* .... So far as the physicians have had any experience with my body, it was with my body *in the midst of the world* and as it is for others. My body as it is *for me* does not appear to me in the midst of the world. (Sartre 2003a, 327)

According to the notes recorded by McDowell, Evans cites this text in full.[31] Then he remarks that of course it is true that I can identify myself with a piece of matter only if I know that matter "from the inside" (this is Sartre's "body for me.") This knowledge "from the inside," Evans notes, is the groundwork for the identifications that go on in my ordinary self-ascriptive statements. But, he adds, "What this constitutes a groundwork for is an ability to identify myself with an element of the objective order—a body of others, if you like—unreservedly."[32]

We find here the two kinds of identification I argued are at work in Evans's reasoning about first-person thought. The "knowledge from the inside" that grounds the "identifications that go on in ordinary self-ascriptive statements" ('I feel pain,' 'I am sitting cross-legged') is the identification$_2$ that makes it possible to answer the questions: 'who is in pain?' 'who is sitting cross-legged?' without appealing to identity propositions and thus without appealing to criteria of identity$_1$. Nevertheless, this "knowledge from the inside" allows me to "identify myself unreservedly with an element in the objective order—with a 'body of others'" (see the quote from Evans cited above). This, Evans maintains, is because the body I know "from the inside" is the very same entity as the body "for others" and the body "of others." In contrast, Evans suggests, Sartre's new dualism of body "for itself" and body "for others" is just as unacceptable as the old dualism that Sartre rejects, between the interiority of consciousness and the exteriority of the body.

But in fact the standpoint Sartre defends in the rest of the chapter cited by Evans is itself a challenge to the rigid dichotomy between "body for me" and "body of others" or "body for others." Sartre's view is thus in greater agreement with Evans's than

Evans seems to think. However, where Evans claims to offer an a priori argument (based on the "Generality Constraint") in support of his view that having an Idea of oneself as a physical entity among other physical entities is a necessary condition for any use of 'I,' Sartre offers a phenomenological description of non-thetic (self)-consciousness that presents it as consciousness (of) the body, where body "for itself" and body "for others" are *in fact*, rather than in virtue of a purported a priori argument, inseparable. Despite its bombastic formulations, Sartre's argument is thus in some ways more modest in its ambition than Evans's. I will suggest, moreover, that because of its phenomenological nature it offers richer resources for understanding how we "identify ourselves with an element in the objective world, unreservedly" than Evans gives Sartre credit for, and perhaps richer than the resources Evans's own argument offers. Nevertheless, Sartre's formulation of his view does leave room for quite a bit of confusion, which I will try to sort out.

3.4 Sartre on Non-Thetic Consciousness (of) the Body

In part 3, chapter 2, of *Being and Nothingness*, "The Body," Sartre distinguishes three "modes of being" or "ontological dimensions" of the body: "The Body as Being-For-Itself, or Facticity," "The Body-For-Others," and finally what he simply calls "The Third Ontological Dimension of the Body," which consists in the unity of the first two: "I exist for myself as a body known by the Other."[33] Let me briefly comment on each of these three "ontological dimensions" or "modes of being" of the body.

The first is "being for itself." In characterizing the body as "being for itself," Sartre intends to contrast the conception of the body he is offering with a classically dualist view according to which the body is a physical thing that can ultimately be analyzed into chemical and microphysical components according to natural laws, while consciousness would be a mysterious awareness of one's "inner" states. Once one has set up the notions of body and consciousness in those terms, says Sartre, there is no hope of figuring out how they might relate. Now, of course, there are standpoints from which considering the body strictly as a thing obeying physical laws is legitimate, for example, the standpoint of the anatomist dissecting a corpse or the chemist analyzing tissues. But this is a third-person standpoint on the body, one for which the presence or absence of consciousness is irrelevant. To understand the body in its relation to consciousness, the starting point must be a different one. It must be that of the body *as* conscious body or what Sartre calls, borrowing Heidegger's terminology, "Being-in-the-world." To say that a human being is a "being-in-the-world" means, for Sartre, that she is not simply in the midst of the world as a thing among other things, but organizes a world of objects around herself, around the needs and projects that characterize her own existence. In that sense being-in-the-world *projects* a world, brings it into existence—a world of objects that are inseparably perceived and to be acted on.

Having defined, as we saw earlier, consciousness as intentionality, it is not surprising that Sartre should make consciousness the essential property of being-in-the-world.

We [ought to take as our point of departure] ... our being-in-the-world. We know that there is not a for itself on the one hand and a world on the other as two closed entities for which we must subsequently seek some explanation as to how they communicate. The for itself is a relation to the world....

... The for itself is-in-the-world,... consciousness is consciousness of the world. (Sartre 2003a, 330)

Consciousness is not a property or state one might attribute to an entity that can be defined by strictly physical laws independently of consciousness.[34] Rather, consciousness is the very mode of existence of that entity, the human body. In other words, the body is not an in-itself (a thing) that is the substrate or the material support of the for-itself. It is *as bodies* that we are *for-itself*. And it is in relation to the non-thetic (self-)consciousness we are, or we have, *as* bodies, that the things in the world acquire their apparent (to us) form and structure.

When he explained non-thetic consciousness (of) self in the introductory sections of *Being and Nothingness*, Sartre used parentheses around (of) (in French, *de*) to explain the non-positional and unreflected character of that (self-)consciousness. He now uses that same device to describe non-thetic consciousness (of) the body. Since it has been shown that necessarily, non-thetic consciousness (of) self is the correlate of the thetic consciousness of object, or in other words intentionality, non-thetic consciousness (of) the body is now itself designated as being, necessarily, the correlate of the thetic consciousness of objects. It is thus in relation to objects in the world or as intentionality that consciousness (of) the body exists. The role of a "point of view on the world," which Sartre originally assigned to non-thetic (self-)consciousness he now assigns to non-thetic consciousness (of) the body or to the body as for itself. But as consciousness (of) the body, this point of view is a situated and contingent point of view, as is the very existence of the body.

The body as for-itself, or conscious body, or being-in-the-world, is the point of reference with respect to which all objects appear. But insofar as it is such a point of reference, and insofar as it is only with respect to its active organization of a world of (perceived and acted on) objects around it that a world of objects appears at all, the body is not itself one of those objects. Nevertheless, the standpoint it offers is, of course, located among the objects it (perceptually and actively) organizes around its own projects.

For example, in a perspective scheme the eye is the point toward which all the objective lines converge. Thus the perceptive field refers to a center objectively defined by that reference and located *in the very field* which is oriented around it. Only we do not see this center as the structure of the perceptive field considered; we *are the center*. Thus the order of the objects in the world perpetually refers to us the image of an object which on principle [*par principe*, BL] cannot be an object *for us*. (2003a, 341; Sartre's emphasis)

So on the one hand, objects appear only in relation to the conscious body; but on the other, the body is conscious (of) itself only in virtue of the orientation, colors, sounds, and so on, in short, in virtue of the apparent features of the objects presented to it. The apparent features of the objects allow the body to be conscious (of) itself as the point of reference around which they appear.

This point leads Sartre to offer an analysis of sensory awareness and of action as the two ways in which there is a world for me. It is beyond the scope of this chapter to consider in detail this aspect of Sartre's view. Let me just cite two passages that are especially telling and will be useful for understanding Sartre's view of consciousness of one's own body:

The senses...are our being-in-the-world insofar as we have to be it in the form of being-in-the-midst-of-the-world. (Sartre 2003a, 343)

The body is not a screen between things and ourselves; it manifests only the individuality and the contingency of our original relation to instrumental-things. In this sense, we defined the senses and the sense organs in general as our being-in-the-world insofar as we have to be it in the form of being-in-the-midst-of-the-world. Similarly we can define *action* as our being-in-the-world insofar as we have to be it in the form of being-an-instrument-in-the-middle-of-the-world. (ibid., 349)

How can this text be reconciled with the text cited by Evans, "My body does not appear to me as an object in the midst of the world"?[35] In light of the texts just cited, we can now understand that Sartre is not denying that we appear to ourselves in the midst of the world. What he is denying is that our body *as it is for itself* appears *as an object* in the midst of the world. This is not in contradiction with Evans's claim that "I can identify myself without reservation with an element in the objective order of things." What Sartre is claiming is that *as* for itself, I do not appear *to myself* as such an element, although I have a non-thetic consciousness (of) myself as "in the midst of" the objective order of things.

Granted, Sartre's formulations are somewhat misleading when he presents the point as an *ontological* claim, as if there were two distinct *entities*, the body *for itself* and the body *as an object* in the midst of the world. In the same vein, he says about the eye, "Either it is a thing among other things, or else it is that by which things are revealed to me. But it cannot be both at the same time."[36] One is tempted to object that the eye *is* both at the same time: one and the same entity that is presented in those two different ways, and sometimes at the same time—for instance, if I see a detailed X-ray of my own eye. Moreover, Sartre's point might appear more acceptable if he presented it in epistemological and phenomenological terms, as a point about the different ways in which we *experience* the eye, rather than in ontological terms, as different entities or types of entity the eye *is*. However, for Sartre, phenomenology (the way we experience our own existence and the existence of things around us) just is fundamental ontology. It gives us access not just to ways of appearing but to ways of being: those ways of appearing *are* ways of being. Still, it would be consistent with Sartre's view to maintain that those ways of being, however irreducible to one another, are ways of being of one and the same entity. And *pace* Sartre's provocative statement, they can moreover be experienced at the same time.

The second "ontological dimension" of the body is "body for another" or "body of others." I perceive the body of others as an object among other objects. But it is an object capable of utilizing other objects and thus of organizing the space of objects around its own activity. The body of others is thus not perceived as a mere *thing*.[37] If I now consider my own body in light of the perception I have of other people's bodies, I will consider my own body, too, as an object among other objects, but nevertheless as that privileged kind of object which is not a mere thing, but rather an object capable of organizing around itself the world of objects it perceives and in the midst of which it acts.

Sartre characterizes the body *of others*, which is also my own body *for others*, as "transcendence transcended." By "transcendence" he means, in this context, an entity that organizes around itself the structure of the world, which it makes an instrument for the achievement of its own actions. Now, the body of another is for me such a transcendence only insofar as it is "transcended," namely, insofar as it is an object *for me*, who am also a transcendence. And again, being conscious in this way of the body of others is being conscious of my own body, which has that same mode of being. I am an entity among other entities that, like me, have the capacity of transcendence, and I am just as much an instrument for others as they are instruments for me. Thus, I can consider my own body as an instrument and adopt toward my body the attitude others have toward it.

This is where the "third mode of being" of the body comes into the picture. I am not on the one hand "body for itself" and on the other "body for others." It is also *as* body for itself that my non-thetic (self)-consciousness comes to be informed by the "body for others." Or in Sartre's terms, I exist *for myself* as known *by others*. This happens as a consequence of applying to my own body the knowledge I have of the body of others, and thus as a consequence of the fact that I thereby come to experience my own body differently. Think of the child who learns to swim by watching the swimming instructor and thus eventually acquires a swimming body, a body that in its non-thetic (self)-consciousness is a body for which water is a familiar and supporting element rather than a threatening element in which one might drown.

Moreover, internalizing to my own non-thetic consciousness (of) self as body the lessons I draw from the body *for others*, which is also the body *of others*, is a process that is mediated by language. We learn our own being, says Sartre, via the revelations of language. He gives the example of stomach pain. The pain one eventually comes to recognize as stomach pain first exists as a "pure quality of pain." It is distinguished, without any intellectual discrimination, from any other pain. At that level the stomach "is only this suffered figure which is raised on the ground of the body-existed."[38] In contrast, the reflective consciousness of stomach pain, which goes beyond the suffered pain (the non-thetic consciousness (of) pain) to the intentional consciousness of the stomach, which it names, is knowledge of the stomach in an aspect of its objective nature. It thereby leads to a discrimination not only of the stomach as an object, but also to a discrimination of the pain itself, as a lived pain. "Let us understand that the 'stomach' pain is the stomach itself as lived painfully."[39]

Sartre makes similar remarks about sensory discrimination. When we distinguish the five senses, it is not by discriminating different sensory experiences at a purely subjective level. The five senses are discriminated by learning to distinguish, with the help of language, one part of the body from other parts: eyes, ears, nose, etc. As a result, the discriminated quality of the sensory experience is part of the patterns of discrimination and action of the body in its entirety. The body "for others" becomes body for others *for me*, or becomes a discriminated pattern of my own non-thetic (self)-consciousness as non-thetic consciousness (of) the body.

What can we say in this context of Wittgenstein's example, "I have tooth-ache"? I suggest we have precisely an example of "for another for oneself." What is expressed is a lived pain. In the terms of the *Blue Book*, the experienced pain grounds propositions in which 'I' is used "as subject." In Sartre's terms, it is a case of non-thetic (self-)consciousness. But this non-thetic (self-)consciousness or body for itself is informed by the body for others learned through the mediation of language, and at least in this way, saying 'I have tooth-ache' is, *pace* Wittgenstein in the *Blue Book*, different from moaning.[40] This is a point the Wittgenstein of the *Philosophical Investigations* should accept. For it is in agreement with his thesis that our apparently most 'internal' experiences are informed by the fact that we belong to a world fashioned by others, in the context of which we discriminate our own states by means of a public language.

I conclude that Sartre is committed to maintaining, like Evans, that I can identify "without any reservation" with an element in the objective order. For according to his analysis of the three "modes of being" of the body, non-thetic (self-)consciousness or body for itself is, without any reservation, a non-thetic consciousness (of) the body-among-other-conscious-and-speaking-bodies as well as a consciousness of a body-among-instrumental-things. And yet it remains true that *for me*, and for me alone, the body I call mine provides the standpoint on the world *from which* any object is perceived and acted on, including that particular object, my body, that is an element in the objective order.

But as I indicated earlier, there is a tension in Sartre's view. Even while introducing the thesis that non-thetic (self)-consciousness is consciousness (of) the body, he claims there is a consciousness (of) self which is *not* consciousness (of) the body. He writes:

> The body belongs then to the structures of the non-thetic self-consciousness. Yet can we identify it purely and simply with this non-thetic self-consciousness? That is not possible,... Non-positional consciousness is consciousness (of the) body as being...something which consciousness is without having to be it,... The body is the *neglected*, the "*passed by in silence*" [*le négligé, le passé sous silence*]. And yet the body is what this consciousness is. It is not even anything except body. (Sartre 2003a, 353–4; Sartre's emphasis)

There are two ways of understanding these dramatic statements. The first is to take Sartre to mean that in non-thetic consciousness (of) the body, the body is "passed by in silence": it is not *itself* an object of consciousness; its presence is everywhere signaled by the way the world appears to us, without its appearing, itself, as an object. This is certainly part of what Sartre means. But I suggest that he is gesturing at a further meaning as well. Non-thetic consciousness (of) the body is not the only kind of non-thetic (self-)consciousness. As we saw earlier, the other kind is non-thetic consciousness (of) oneself present throughout the "unified theme" of a mental activity, for instance the activity of counting. In both cases, non-thetic consciousness (of) self grounds a use of 'I' that "does not reach the level of reflection," for example, "I am trying to hang this picture," "I am counting."

In his statement about the body that is the "neglected," the "passed by in silence," Sartre, I would like to suggest, is gesturing at both these dimensions of non-thetic (self-)consciousness without clearly distinguishing them. In non-thetic consciousness (of) the body, the body is "passed by in silence" because it is that in virtue of which objects appear, without appearing itself as an object. But this is not sufficient ground to challenge the idea that the body is non-thetic (self-)consciousness, as Sartre clearly does in the text cited above. The idea here seems to be that in non-thetic consciousness (of) self there is an aspect for which even non-thetic consciousness (of) the body is irrelevant. This aspect, I submit, is the kind of non-thetic self-consciousness that gives rise to the pre-reflective cogito.

The Sartrian afficionado may object that there is a simpler explanation of Sartre's dramatic statement. That explanation has to do with Sartre's theory of freedom. Non-thetic self-consciousness is a mode of being that transcends even non-thetic consciousness (of) the body, it is not bound or anchored to any facticity, it is absolutely pure and thus in charge of itself: radically free. That may be so. But my suggestion is that Sartre's theory of freedom is itself anchored in the intuition that non-thetic (self-)consciousness goes beyond consciousness (of) the body: that it includes consciousness (of) a certain kind of unity of mental activity that is *not* consciousness (of) the body, or body for itself.

I now propose to show that the difficulties Sartre struggles with in his attempts to characterize non-thetic (self-)consciousness are not far from the difficulty Anscombe struggles with in her famous article, "The First Person," when she makes the surprising claim that "I am E.A." is not an identity proposition, any more than "I am this body" is an identity proposition, although, she says, a proposition in the vicinity of both, namely, "this body is E.A." is an identity proposition.[41] Let me first recall Anscombe's view before explaining why I think her view and Sartre's are mutually illuminating.

3.5 Anscombe on 'I' and Sartre on Non-Thetic Self-Consciousness

The statement "I am E.A. is not an identity proposition" opens the final part of Anscombe's paper. If 'I am E.A.' were an identity proposition, Anscombe argues, then 'I' would function as a singular term referring to the same entity the proper name 'E.A.' refers to. One could say, for instance, that 'I' is a name, albeit one that obeys the peculiar rule that everyone uses it only to refer to himself.

But 'I' is not a name, Anscombe insists. Earlier in the paper, Anscombe introduced this claim by offering a thought experiment.[42] Imagine a population that uses two kinds of names. 'A' is a name, the same for all, stamped on the wrist of each individual and used by him to report on his own actions on the basis of observation, testimony, inference, and other usual sources of knowledge. 'B,' 'C,' 'D,' . . . are names stamped on the back and forehead of those same individuals and thus publicly accessible and used to report on other people's actions. Propositions predicating states or properties of an individual designated by 'A' are grounded on knowledge each individual has in the ordinary ways (namely, ways that could also be available for knowledge of any other entity: observation, inference, testimony . . .) of someone who is, in fact, herself. In other words, 'A' is a name, albeit one with an unusual rule for its use: everyone uses it only to refer to himself.

So, does 'A' in the language of Anscombe's fictitious population function in just the same way as 'I' in our language? No, says Anscombe. The 'A' users clearly lack something that we 'I'-users have: they lack self-consciousness.

> In my story we have a specification of a sign as a name, the same for everyone, but used by each only to speak of himself. How does it compare with 'I'?—The first thing to note is that our description does not include self-consciousness on the part of the people who use the name 'A' as I have described it. They perhaps have no self-consciousness, even though each one knows a lot about the object that he (in fact) is; and has a name, the same as everyone else has, which he uses in reports about the object that he (in fact) is.
>
> This—that they have not self-consciousness—may, just for that reason, seem not to be true. B is conscious of, that is to say he observes, some of B's activities, that is to say his own. He uses the term 'A', as does everyone else, to refer to himself. So he is conscious of himself. So he has self-consciousness.
>
> But when we speak of self-consciousness we don't mean that. We mean something manifested by the use of 'I' as opposed to 'A'. (1994, 145)

The argument seems circular. We want to know what the difference is between 'A' and 'I.' Reply: 'A'-users lack something 'I'-users have, namely, self-consciousness. Now we want to know what self-consciousness is. Reply: it is what is manifested by the use of 'I' rather than 'A.'

Now, Anscombe next step is precisely to examine what is meant by "self-consciousness." She first offers a negative answer: it is not consciousness of a particular type of object we might call "the self." If it were, then 'I' would be a referring expression. It would refer to that particular object, the self. But, Anscombe argues, all attempts to characterize that object, its identity conditions and the epistemic conditions under which it could be correctly identified, as well as all attempts at characterizing the type of singular referring expression 'I' might be, collapse into absurdity.[43] To this quandary there is only one solution:

> 'I' is neither a name, nor another kind of expression whose logical role is to make a reference, at all. (ibid., 154)

And yet, Anscombe endorses a rule she had earlier stated as the rule a proponent of the referring role of 'I' would offer. Let me cite first the rule she attributed to that proponent, then the very similar rule she reaffirms even while dissociating it from the claim that 'I' might function as a name or any kind of singular referring expression:

> Let me imagine a logician, for whom the syntactical character of 'I' as a proper name is quite sufficient to guarantee it as such....[44] To him it is clear that 'I', in my mouth is just another name for E.A, ... 'I' is a name governed by the following rule:
>
> If X makes assertions with 'I' as subject, then those assertions will be true if and only if the predicates used thus assertively are true of X. (ibid., 149–50)

Now immediately after offering the solution cited above ('I' is neither a name nor any kind of referring expression), Anscombe grants:

> Of course, we must accept the rule: 'If X asserts something with "I" as subject, his assertion will be true if an only if what he asserts is true of X.' But if someone thinks that is a sufficient

account of 'I', we must say 'No, it is not,' for it does not make any difference between 'I' and 'A'. The truth condition of the whole sentence does not determine the meaning of the items within the sentence. Thus the rule does not justify the idea that 'I', coming out of X's mouth, is another name for X. Or for anything else, such as an asserting subject who is speaking through X.

But the rule does mean that the question: '*whose* assertion' is all-important. (ibid., 154)

How can the rule hold without its being the rule for the use of a name? Reply: 'I'-thoughts are not thoughts *about* a particular object named by 'I' or to which 'I' refers. Rather,

'I'-thoughts are examples of reflective consciousness of states, actions, movements, etc., not of an object I mean by 'I', but of this body. These 'I'-thoughts... are unmediated conceptions (knowledge or belief, true or false) of states, motions, etc., of this object here, about which I can find (if I don't know it) that it is E.A., about which I did learn that it is a human being. (ibid., 156)

Thus, although it is true to say that when X says 'I am F' the proposition is true just in case X is F, this does not mean that 'I' is a name for the individual X. It only means that 'I am F' is the expression of the reflective consciousness[45] of the state F *of this body*. There is no more need to suppose that 'I' refers to a person in such a case than there is a need to suppose that 'it' refers to a thing in 'it rains.' That's why 'I am E.A.' is not an identity proposition, although when said or thought by E.A., 'I am E.A' is true. In contrast, if E.A. were a member of our imaginary population, when spoken by Elizabeth Anscombe, 'A is E.A.' would be true *and* an identity proposition.

We are to understand, then, that the "reflective knowledge of states, actions, etc., *of this body*," or "unmediated conceptions of states, motions, etc., *of this object here*," is the self-consciousness 'I'-users have and 'A'-users lack. It is illustrated *a contrario* by a character named "Baldy," described by Anscombe in the very last paragraph of the paper as having *lost* that kind of self-consciousness. Having just fallen out of a car, he is aware that someone just fell out but wonders *who*.[46] He has lost self-consciousness in the sense defined by Anscombe:

He did not have what I will call 'unmediated agent-or-patient conceptions of actions, happenings, and states.' (Anscombe 1994, 159)

Anscombe takes this case to be a confirmation *a contrario* that those "unmediated agent-or-patient conceptions" that Baldy has lost are subjectless. In her account, it is a sign of Baldy's impairment that he *looks for a subject* ("who fell"?) where there is none to be looked for.

This is a surprising interpretation of the case. It seems more plausible to say, rather, that the self-consciousness he has lost is the unmediated *answer* to the question, *who?*—an answer that is, without the mediation of any observation or inference, made available by precisely what she calls "agent-or-patient conception of actions, happenings, and states."

In other words, what Anscombe's analysis really shows is that FRR is not sufficient to characterize what is specific to the first-person pronoun in language or thought. For the rule is common to 'A' and 'I.' What is specific to 'I' is a particular *way of knowing* on the basis of which predicates are attributed to 'I,' not to 'A.' Those ways of knowing are included in the type of consciousness Anscombe calls "unmediated agent-or-patient conception of actions, happenings, and states." They are what Baldy has lost.

Suppose Baldy had *not* lost that way of knowing. Then he would be able to say "I fell." But how would this connect to "Baldy fell"? It would connect only if he was also able to think "I am Baldy," namely only if he was capable of thinking the *identity* of the individual of whose states he has unmediated agent-or-patient conception, and the individual whose name is Baldy, and who has a particular biography he acknowledges as his own.

This is where the connection with Sartre's notion of non-thetic (self-)consciousness is relevant. Let me recall one of Sartre's examples. In being thetically conscious of the picture I am trying to hang on the wall, I am non-thetically conscious (of) my own action of hanging the picture and thus non-thetically conscious (of) myself as hanging the picture. If asked what I am doing, I might answer, 'I am hanging this picture.' This answer, Sartre told us, "does not transport us on to the level of reflection."[47] It is pre-reflective. I am still absorbed in the action itself rather than observing it, much less observing myself as engaged in it. Nevertheless, this pre-reflective consciousness does find expression in a use of 'I.' *That* use of 'I' would be an instance of what Anscombe calls "unmediated agent-conception of action." Similarly, what Baldy has lost under the impact of his accident is the non-thetic consciousness (of) falling, namely, what Anscombe would call "unmediated patient-conception of being acted upon." This type of non-thetic (self-)consciousness is what might be expressed in the pre-reflective statement: "I'm falling!" and might allow Baldy, if he had it available, *also* to progress to the statement about himself as an object in the middle of the world: "I fell!"

As we saw, according to Sartre, in statements where 'I' expresses pre-reflective (self-)consciousness, 'I' is an "empty concept." What he presumably means is that this use of 'I' does not express consciousness of oneself as an object that one's attention is directed at. Nevertheless, when the non-thetic (self-)consciousness becomes itself an object of reflection, then the use of 'I' does express consciousness of oneself *as an object*. That object is what Sartre called a "for another for itself." Consciousness of oneself as such an object is presupposed in propositions such as "I am Jean-Paul Sartre" or "I am Elizabeth Anscombe." *Pace* Anscombe, such propositions are certainly identity propositions: one and the same entity is referred to on the one hand by the word and concept 'I' and on the other hand by a proper name. But it is not enough to say that the word 'I' is a singular referring expression by which everyone refers to him- or herself. Anscombe is quite right to say this would not distinguish 'I' from 'A.' It should be added that using 'I' is at least in part based on the kind of self-consciousness Sartre calls non-thetic (self-)consciousness and Anscombe calls unmediated agent-or-patient consciousness. As Sartre says, in such non-thetic (self-)consciousness "the body is passed by in silence." It is this being "passed by in silence" that Anscombe translates as "not needing a subject." But that the subject need not be expressly in view does not mean that the use of 'I' does not depend on silent consciousness (of) that subject, or what Anscombe calls "agent-or-patient conception." Even less does it mean that 'I' does not, as a matter of fact, refer to that subject (the entity that has agent-or-patient conception).

The connection between the two views goes even deeper. Anscombe notes that the examples she gave of 'I'-thoughts (other than the statement 'I am E.A.') were all examples of "postures, movements, actions." The examples were: "I am sitting," "I twitched," "I am writing," "I am going to stay still." She contrasts these examples with other examples she describes as "Cartesianly preferred [sic!]," which include "I have a headache," "I am thinking about thinking," "I see a variety of colours," "I hope, fear, love, envy, desire," all of which would be, for Descartes, instances of 'I think.'[48] Contrary to those "Cartesianly preferred" examples, she remarks, her own examples provide easier cases for her claim that 'I am F' expresses the reflective consciousness of states of *this body*. For about those cases it is possible to provide an answer to the question, *in happenings concerning what object* are those thoughts verified or falsified? The answer, according to her, is: in happenings concerning, not an object to which 'I' might refer, but rather in happenings concerning *this body*. Of course, she adds, the same kind of answer could in principle be given with respect to "Cartesianly preferred" 'I'-thoughts. But in these cases, the thoughts would be less easily verifiable, because the description of the events that might verify the thoughts is quite different from the description contained in the thoughts themselves:

> The Cartesianly preferred thoughts all have this same character, of being far removed in their descriptions from the descriptions of the proceedings, etc., of a person in which they might be verified. And also, there might not be any. And also, even when there are any, the thoughts are not thoughts of such proceedings, as the thought of standing is the thought of a posture. I cannot offer an investigation of these questions here. I only want to indicate why I go after the particular 'I'-thoughts that I do, in explaining the meaning of 'I am E.A.' This may suffice to show why I think the Cartesianly preferred thoughts are not the ones to investigate if one wants to understand 'I' philosophically. (Anscombe 1994, 158)

But it seems reasonable to request that a philosophical understanding of 'I' should rest on an account that is at least sufficiently attentive to the *differences* in the uses of 'I,' and, above all, to the *contrast* between the "Cartesianly preferred" examples and the examples one might describe as 'bodily.' Now a fairly natural way to account for both kinds of examples while acknowledging their differences would be to say, 'I' is a word or concept that refers, in any instance of its use, to the author of the thought or the speaker of the sentence in which 'I' is being used (FRR as defined above). But this characterization of its referential role is not sufficient to account for the peculiarities of 'I,' as is eloquently illustrated by Anscombe's fictitious population of 'A'-users. In addition, one needs to take into account the particular kind of access the subject who says or thinks 'I' has to herself. This is what Evans does when he considers the type of information that grounds propositions that have IEM. This is also what Sartre does when he talks about the non-thetic consciousness (of) self and its difference from thetic consciousness of object. This is what Anscombe herself does when she talks of the "reflective consciousness *of this body*"[49] or "self-consciousness" that distinguishes the use of 'I' from her fictitious population's use of 'A.'

Moreover, if one takes into account the kind of access on which our use of 'I' is uniquely grounded, in contrast to all other singular referential expressions, then one must explain why the "Cartesianly preferred" statements are not verifiable in the same way as the statements Anscombe chooses for her demonstration. One must also explain in what sense both kinds of examples nevertheless have in common that type of access to oneself Anscombe calls "self-consciousness," Evans calls "knowledge from the inside," and Sartre "non-thetic (self)-consciousness." Then it appears that Sartre's non-thetic (self-)consciousness cannot be limited to consciousness (of) the body; nor can Anscombe's "self-consciousness" be limited to what she calls "reflective consciousness *of this body*"; nor can Evans's "knowledge from the inside" be limited to that kind of body consciousness that is immune to error through misidentification relative to the first-person pronoun. Here again, Anscombe's and Sartre's views are especially mutually illuminating. For the "Cartesianly preferred" examples of uses of 'I' Anscombe acknowledges that she has not accounted for are precisely those cases for which, as Sartre acknowledged in his own terms, non-thetic (self-)consciousness *is not* the body for itself, *is not* non-thetic consciousness (of) the body.

3.6 Taking Stock

One of Sartre's groundbreaking achievements is his distinction between thetic, or positional, consciousness *of objects* and non-thetic or non-positional *(self)*-consciousness. Equally important, although less often noted—not even by himself!—is Sartre's distinction between two kinds of non-thetic (self)-consciousness: consciousness (of) one's own body or body for itself, and consciousness (of) the unity (the "unified theme") of one's mental activity. I have argued that Sartre's descriptions of each kind of non-thetic (self)-consciousness, on the one hand, and the semantic analyses of uses of 'I' offered by Wittgenstein, Evans, and Anscombe, on the other, are mutually illuminating.

I have argued that Sartre's phenomenological description of the body for itself and its connections with the body-for-others offers important insights into the kind of information that, according to Evans, supports a use of 'I' that is immune to error through misidentification relative to the first-person pronoun. Sartre's phenomenological description of consciousness of one's own body and its relation to the use of 'I' is in greater agreement with Evans's claim that in using 'I' we identify "without any reservation" with an element in the objective order of things, than Evans himself saw, and perhaps in greater agreement than some of Sartre's more dramatic statements would lead us to believe. For Sartre, the body for itself is "in the midst-of-the-world" and its non-thetic (self)-consciousness is informed by its own consciousness of other people's bodies, and thus by its consciousness of itself as a body for others. To that extent at least, in being conscious of our own body, even as body for itself, we identify with an element in the objective order of things. However, it remains true that, for Sartre, non-thetic consciousness (of) the body, or the body for itself, is irreducible to the body as an *object* of consciousness, and even more irreducible to a mere *thing*. Sartre calls those different ways in which we have access to our own body "ontological dimensions" of the body. He argues that they are irreducible to one another, sometimes even that they do not "communicate." His description of the "third ontological dimension of the body," the "for itself for another," shows that in fact they do communicate: *knowing* our body as an object, indeed even knowing it as a mere *thing* does influence the way we experience our own body or the body for itself. And it can happen that we experience the body as "for itself" and as "for another" *at the same time*. It remains, nevertheless, that these are different modes of access to one and the same entity, our own body. I have argued that Sartre's phenomenological descriptions give us an important insight into the different kinds of information that ground, respectively, a use of 'I' as subject (immune to error through misidentification relative to the first-person pronoun) and a use of 'I' as object (not so immune).

Sartre maintains that in non-thetic consciousness (of) the body, the body is "passed by in silence" so that non-thetic consciousness (of) the body, or body for itself, both *is* and is *not* the body. I have suggested that there were two ways to understand this statement. One draws on the irreducibility of "body for itself" to body as an object or body for another: the body for itself *is* fully body but it *is not* the body as an object. In contemporary terms, we might say that these are two irreducibly different modes of presentation of one and the same entity, the body. The other way to understand Sartre's dramatic statement, however, is to acknowledge—as he does in some of his examples—that there is a kind of non-thetic (self-)consciousness that is neither non-thetic consciousness (of) the body (or body for itself) nor (of course) thetic consciousness of the body as an object (body for another or body of the others). That second kind of non-thetic (self-)consciousness is consciousness of the unity (of) one's mental activity. Here the body is "passed by in silence" even more radically than in the non-thetic consciousness (of) the body.

I have argued that Sartre's views of non-thetic (self-)consciousness and the uses of 'I' that "do not reach the level of reflection" are apt to illuminate (but do not give reason to endorse) Anscombe's equally dramatic statements concerning the use of 'I': "'I' is neither a name, nor another kind of expression whose logical role is to make reference, *at all*," "'I am E.A.' is not an identity proposition," our use of 'I' expresses our "unmediated agent-or-patient conceptions of actions, happenings, and states."[50] The truth of those statements, I have suggested, lies in the fact that simply saying that in any instance of its use, 'I' refers to whoever says or thinks a proposition in which 'I' figures as subject, is not sufficient to capture what is specific to 'I' (whereas it would be sufficient to capture what is specific to 'A' in Anscombe's imaginary population). To capture what is specific to 'I,' one needs to take into account those modes of access to oneself that Evans called "knowledge from the inside," Sartre called "non-thetic (self-)consciousness," and Anscombe "agent-or-patient conception." If one adds that specification, I suggest, then it is legitimate to say that 'I' is a referring expression, and one can even understand *why* it is all right to say that 'I am E.A.' is an identity proposition even though it is not the same proposition as 'A is E.A.': 'I' and 'A' are different modes of presentation of the entity that is also referred to by the proper name, 'E.A.' 'A' is sufficiently specified by the description: 'name that refers to whoever is currently saying or thinking "A is F"'; but 'I' needs the further specification—'word that refers to whoever is currently saying or thinking "I am F" and whose use depends on non-thetic consciousness (of) whoever is saying or thinking "I am F".'

If this is correct, Sartre, because of his emphasis on non-thetic (self-)consciousness as grounding a use of 'I' in which the referent of 'I' is not an *object* of consciousness, helps us understand what is really motivating Anscombe's "extraordinary statement."[51] I have suggested, however, that it also gives us grounds to reject it.

But there is another convergence between what we learn from Sartre's phenomenological description and what we learn from Anscombe's semantic analysis of our uses of 'I.' As we saw, Anscombe acknowledges that her account of the truth conditions of 'I-thoughts' or 'I-statements' leaves out of consideration the "Cartesianly preferred" statements of the type: 'I think p.' Now such statements, on Sartre's account, are either instances of "pre-reflective cogito" or *reflective* statements *about* the non-thetic (self-)consciousness expressed in the "pre-reflective cogito." In both cases, the kind of (self-)consciousness expressed is *not* consciousness (of) the body but, rather, consciousness (of) being engaged in a specific kind of mental activity. Here I suggest that Sartre's insufficient attention to the second kind of non-thetic (self-)consciousness he identified is parallel to both Evans's and Anscombe's neglect of a use of 'I' that is *not* based on bodily consciousness. This takes me back to the conclusion of Chapter 2: Kant's legacy of consciousness of oneself as subject, which is consciousness of a specific kind of unity of mental activity, remains to be explored.

Notes

1. Evans 1982, 266.
2. Ibid., 208–15. Cf. 2.1.4 in this book.
3. The expression is Evans's in 1982, 212n.
4. Since there is, in the English expression 'self-consciousness,' no 'of' corresponding to the French 'de' in 'conscience de soi,' Hazel Barnes has opted for 'self-consciousness' to translate Sartre's "'conscience (de) soi'" (see Sartre 2003a, 10, n. 4). I prefer to keep parentheses around (self-) to remind us of Sartre's intention in using parentheses around (de) in "conscience (de) soi." I sometimes also use 'non-thetic consciousness (of) self' as well as 'non-thetic (self-)consciousness' to translate Sartre's "conscience non-thétique (de) soi." I explain the relevant distinctions in 3.4, and n. 7 in this chapter.
5. Husserl 2012 [1913], §§ 34–6.
6. Sartre 2003b, 89: "Tout est dehors, tout, jusqu'à nous-mêmes: dehors, dans le monde, parmi les autres." Coorebyter is right to note that in this article, just as in *The Transcendence of the Ego*, Sartre credits Husserl with the discovery of intentionality as an orientation to the external world (Sartre 2003b, 22). In *Being and Nothingness*, Sartre is more severely critical of Husserl, whom he takes to be a prisoner of a Cartesian conception of the "interiority" of consciousness, namely, a conception according to which the objects of conscious states and attitudes are internal to the mind, and only through the mediation of those "internal" objects do our conscious states reach out into the external world. On the evolution of Sartre's relation to Husserl's theory of consciousness and intentionality, see Coorebyter 2000, esp. chap. 1, 28–49.
7. I will follow Sartre's lead and sometimes use parentheses around (of) to characterize non-thetic consciousness (of) self. But I shall also, following the more familiar English expression, 'self-consciousness' rather than consciousness of self, put parentheses around (self-) in (self-)consciousness. See n. 4 in this chapter.
   Note that Sartre's non-thetic (self-)consciousness is close to the "what it's like (for the organism or the subject)," which is, according to Thomas Nagel, the fundamental characteristic of consciousness (see Nagel 1979b, 166, 170n6). One might object that, for Sartre, the fundamental characteristic of consciousness is precisely *not* "what it's like" or subjectivity, but intentionality. But Sartre's claim that all consciousness, as intentionality, is also non-thetic consciousness (of) self just means that there is no consciousness as intentionality without consciousness as a "what it's like" for the conscious being. Moreover, Sartre admits limit-cases of consciousness as pure affectivity, seemingly without intentionality (cf. Sartre

2003a, 354–5). Conversely, Nagel describes the "what it's like for the subject" character of consciousness as a "point of view" on the world, and calls on the Sartrian vocabulary of *in itself* and *for itself* to characterize the distinction between the "physical basis of mind" and its "what it's like" or conscious character (Sartre 2003a, 168). So there does seem to be a deep similarity between the two views.

8. See, in particular, Sartre 2004, 7–9.
9. More precisely, Sartre calls "I" ("je") the unity of conscious *acts* and "me" (*moi*) the unity of conscious *states*. He calls "ego" ("ego") the unity of I and me (cf. Sartre 2004, 21–41). We don't need to concern ourselves with these distinctions here. Note, however, that none of these objects are equivalent to Freud's ego (*Ich*) as I analyzed it in the previous chapter. Sartre's I, me, and ego are *objects* for consciousness. In contrast, Freud's ego or *Ich* is a mere organization of mental processes *in virtue of which* objects appear to consciousness: external objects in a perceptual representation of the world, abstract objects of reasoning, one's own mental states as objects for a reflective consciousness (see 2.3; see also 7.2.2 and 7.3.1). As I said in the previous chapter, Freud's ego, if close to any historical antecedent, is close to Kant's transcendental unity of self-consciousness, which is *not* an object of consciousness. The proximity between Kant and Freud will be explored in more detail in Chapters 7 and 8. As I will maintain immediately below in this section, Sartre actually does not stay true to his claim that I is entirely on the side of the objects for a thetic (reflective) consciousness, i.e., that it is an object for reflective consciousness. For as we will see shortly, there is a word and concept 'I' that appears in the context of a "pre-reflective cogito," that is to say a pre-reflective 'I think.'
10. Sartre 2004, 8, cited earlier in this section. Note that Sartre does not put quotation marks around 'I' here. This is because what he is talking about is not the concept or the word 'I,' but the object *I*, or more precisely, *ego* (see previous note).
11. Sartre 2004, 8, cited earlier in this section.
12. Kant, B158–9 and fn. Cf. 2.2. In 2.2, I described 'I think' as the *conceptual representation* of the activity of synthesis for judging. I am now describing Sartre's pre-reflective cogito as the *expression* of the act of thinking. I don't take the two formulations to be mutually exclusive. In using the term 'expression' I mean to indicate that there is a vanishing distinction between the act (thinking, or in the terms I used above to describe Kant's view, synthesis for thinking) and the conceptual representation of that act ('I think'). In Sartre's terms, the thought 'I think' is a pre-reflective cogito: the proposition is not *directed at* the act it represents, it is the expression of the non-thetic consciousness (of) being engaged in that act, i.e., in Kant's terms, consciousness of oneself as subject. In the opening pages of *The Transcendence of the Ego*, Sartre endorses the Kantian analysis of 'I think' and in particular the phrase from the Transcendental Deduction I analyzed in the previous chapter: "It must be possible for the 'I think' to accompany all my representations." See Sartre 2004, 2–3; Kant B131–2; and 2.2 in this chapter.
13. Wittgenstein 1958a, 66–7. Cf. 2.1.1.
14. Wittgenstein 1958a, 67: "Are you sure it's *you* who have pain?"
15. Shoemaker 2003c, 7–8. Cf. 2.1.2.
16. Wittgenstein 1958a, 67.
17. Wittgenstein 1993, cited by Glock and Hacker 1996, 95.
18. Wittgenstein 1958b, §410.
19. See 2.1, n. 7.
20. Anscombe 1994, 142, 152–3.
21. Strictly speaking, Evans does *not* distinguish between two uses of 'I' in the chapter of *The Varieties of Reference* I am referring to here. Because he nevertheless devotes a whole section to IEM, Glock and Hacker (1996) conclude that he endorsed the view that 'I' is

always IEM and nevertheless argued, against the late Wittgenstein and against Anscombe, that 'I' is a referring expression. But this interpretation seems implausible to me, given the content of the section. Even though Evans is not explicit about this, his argument seems to be that *all* uses of 'I' depend at least in part on *some* information that, if expressed in a judgment, supports a judgment that has IEM and thus a use of 'I' as subject. See Evans 1982, 215–20, and 2.1.4 in the present volume. In addition, Evans argues that all such judgments depend on having available a conception of oneself as an embodied entity, namely, either a direct *awareness* of oneself as, or at least a disposition to apply a concept of oneself as, an embodied entity. I have explained in Chapter 2 some of my reservations about his argument (see 2.1.4 and 2.2). I will return to these points later in this chapter.

22. Note also that non-thetic (self-)consciousness is not *itself* a use of 'I.' It *grounds* a use of 'I.' That use can be either pre-reflective or reflective. Either way, the use will be a use of 'I' as subject. That is because the source of information is in both cases non-thetic (self-)consciousness.
23. On these two formulations of his view, see 2.1.4.
24. By "a priori/semantic support" I mean support that consists in laying out universal conditions on the very possibility for a proposition to be meaningful and for its terms to have a referring role. I take Evans's "Generality Constraint" to count as such a universal condition.
25. Evans 1982, 218 and n. 25.
26. On the various kinds of statements of identity that are implicit or explicit premises in uses of 'I' as object, see Chapter 2, n. 9.
27. Cf. n. 16 and n. 17 in this chapter.
28. Evans 1982, 224.
29. See 2.1.4.
30. Evans's concept of 'person' is inspired by Strawson's concept as defined in *Individuals*: "What I mean by the concept of a person is the concept of a type of entity such that *both* predicates assigning states of consciousness *and* predicates ascribing corporeal characteristics, a physical situation &c. are equally applicable to a single individual of that single type" (Strawson 1959, 102). This is a very restricted concept of person, which does not include, in particular, the notion of moral status we usually associate with the concept of person. I discuss the richer concept of person in Chapters 6 and 8.
31. Evans 1982, 266.
32. Ibid.
33. Sartre 2003a, 330, 362, 375. What Sartre calls "ontological dimensions" are really different *ways of experiencing* the body. These amount, in his existential approach, to different *ways of being* that are proper to a human body.
34. Sartre is notoriously careless in his use of terminology. "Consciousness" may mean (1) the entity that is conscious, (2) the essential property of the conscious entity or body as "for itself," or (3) an occurrent state of that entity. Similarly, "for itself" and "being-in-the-world" designate (1) types of entities or (2) the essential property of those types of entities. The context generally settles which meaning is prevalent in each case.
35. Sartre 2003a, 327.
36. Ibid., 328.
37. Ibid., 363–74.
38. Ibid., 379.
39. Ibid.
40. Cf. Wittgenstein 1958a, 67. In all fairness, Wittgenstein does not say that there is no difference between moaning and saying 'I feel pain.' His claim is that saying 'I feel pain' is no more *about* a particular person than moaning is. But I suggest that what Sartre says

about stomach pain is also true of the use of 'I.' Even when, as Wittgenstein notes, the statement does not aim at directing attention to *me* (as would be the case if one were replying to the explicit question: 'Who's the one here who's in pain?') but to *the pain*, which is constitutively *mine*, it remains that saying 'I am in pain' rather than moaning depends on learning a language in virtue of which I know that saying (or thinking) 'I' is talking (or thinking) about the person saying (or thinking) 'I': myself if I am the person talking or thinking, someone else if she is the person talking or thinking. This capacity is sufficiently complex to be taken to be definitional of any use of 'I' and thus to be grounds for opposing Wittgenstein's view according to which "the word 'I' does not refer to a person" (cf. n. 16 in this chapter). That it is not the *name* of a person, on the other hand, is true and important. On this point, see Pariente 1973, 59–111, and esp. 100–4. Finally, note that the complex learning of 'I' as a unit of thought or language confirms my point in the previous chapter: something like Kant's "unity of apperception" is a condition for *any* use of 'I' as subject and background information for *any* use of 'I.'
41. Anscombe 1994, 155.
42. Ibid., 143–4.
43. Ibid., 153: "Our questions were a combined *reductio ad absurdum* of the idea of 'I' as a word whose role is to 'make a singular reference.' I mean the question of how one is guaranteed to get the object right, whether one may safely assume no unnoticed substitution, whether one could refer to oneself 'in absence' and so on. The suggestion of getting the object right collapses into absurdity when we work it out and try to describe how getting hold of the wrong object may be excluded." Examining this negative part of the argument is beyond the scope of my discussion in this chapter. I am interested in Anscombe's positive account of self-consciousness, and its connection to Sartre's. The issue of the referential or non referential role of 'I' will come back to the fore in light of that comparison.
44. Compare Shoemaker's characterization of 'I' at the beginning of "Self-Reference and Self-Awareness": "If we consider the logical powers of first person statements and the role played by the first person pronoun in communication, nothing seems clearer than that in all first person statements, including 'avowals', the word 'I' functions as a singular term or singular referring expression. Statements expressed by the sentence 'I feel pain' have in common with those expressed by sentences like 'He feels pain' and 'Jones feels pain' that they contradict the proposition 'nobody feels pain' and entail the proposition 'someone feels pain'. In these and other ways, 'I feel pain' behaves logically as a value of the propositional function 'X feels pain'" (Shoemaker 2003c, 6).
45. Note that what Anscombe calls "reflective consciousness of this body" is not Sartre's reflective consciousness. Rather, it is similar to what Sartre calls non-thetic consciousness (of) the body, or body for itself. I say more about this in n. 49 in this chapter.
46. This is supposed to be a true story, told by William James and recounted by Anscombe. See Anscombe 1994, 159.
47. Sartre 2004, 40. See 3.1.
48. Anscombe 1994, 155–7.
49. As I noted in n. 45 in this chapter, what Anscombe calls "reflective consciousness of this body" is not Sartre's reflective consciousness. It is, rather, what Sartre calls non-thetic consciousness (of) the body, or body for itself. This explains the striking parallel between Anscombe's claim that agent-or-patient consciousness is *without a subject* and Sartre's claim that, in its pre-reflective use, 'I' is an empty concept. In both cases, there is no *object* I am conscious of. But of course it does not mean that there is no entity 'I' refers to. What the comparison with Sartre reveals is that Anscombe confuses consciousness (and, therefore, mode of presentation) with reference. Moreover, what Anscombe does not consider

at all is the move from pre-reflective self-consciousness, to reflective (in Sartre's sense) self-consciousness, to consciousness of oneself as a full-fledged object, which can also be expressed by a use of 'I.' A statement such as 'I am E.A.' expresses a *thetic* self-consciousness. Such a statement expresses a consciousness of myself as an object (who am I in the world?). Moreover, I can misidentify that object. Suppose I have worked so hard on Anscombe's paper that I have lost my mind and started identifying with her. I would be thinking: 'I am Elizabeth Anscombe.' I would be *mis*identifying the object I am in the world. 'I am E.A.' is an identity proposition, and it is not IEM.

50. See Anscombe 1994, 154, 155, 159.
51. Evans 1982, 212n14.

PART II
…Kant

4
Kant on 'I Think'

Kant's explanation of the content and role of the proposition 'I think' is to be found in the Transcendental Deduction of the Categories, in the Transcendental Analytic of the *Critique of Pure Reason*. But Kant's explicit discussion of the concept 'I' in 'I think' occurs in the chapter of the Transcendental Dialectic entitled "The Paralogisms of Pure Reason," where Kant criticizes rationalist metaphysical doctrines of the soul and argues that they amount to attempts to derive an a priori doctrine of the soul from the particular features of the concept 'I' as used in the proposition 'I think.' The only names mentioned in the course of this discussion are Descartes and Mendelssohn. Especially relevant to the present chapter is Kant's discussion of Descartes's *cogito* argument,[1] namely, the argument in the Second Meditation that provides Descartes with his first step out of radical doubt.

Kant's response to Descartes's making 'I think, therefore I exist' the first certainty from which Descartes pulls himself out of radical doubt is largely positive. Kant agrees with Descartes that in virtue of the sole fact of thinking anything at all, I know with absolute certainty both that I think and that I exist. His criticism of Descartes and his rationalist successors starts downstream from the *cogito* argument. What he criticizes is their answer to the question: *What* am I, I who know with absolute certainty that I think and therefore also know with absolute certainty that I exist?

Understanding the relation between Kant's and Descartes's respective views of the semantic and epistemic features of the proposition 'I think' is especially important for the line of thought I am offering in the present book, for two main reasons. First, the role of the first-person pronoun in the context of Descartes's *cogito* argument is different from its role in Kant's 'I think' as introduced in the context of the Transcendental Deduction of the Categories. Clarifying this difference will help illuminate what is specific to Kant's 'I think.' Second, nevertheless Kant agrees with Descartes that 'I exist' is immediately entailed by 'I think.' But he claims to have a better account of the nature of the entailment than Descartes does. Examining Kant's claim will again help us better understand Kant's 'I think' and the role Kant assigns to 'I' in the proposition 'I think.'

The structure of this chapter is as follows.

(1) I will examine Descartes's *cogito* argument. I will explain why it is important to Descartes's argument that 'think' should be predicated in the first person.
(2) I will examine the role of the proposition 'I think' in Kant's Transcendental Deduction of the Categories. I will argue that, in this context, Kant's reasons for asserting 'think' of 'I' rather than 'it' are different from Descartes's in the argument of the Second Meditation, and those reasons throw a different light on the role of 'I' in 'I think.'

(3) I will examine Kant's discussion of Descartes's *cogito* argument in the Paralogisms of Pure Reason. I will argue that Kant endorses Descartes's derivation of 'I exist' from 'I think.' However, his formulations in discussing Descartes's argument leave somewhat unclear the extent to which Kant's justification for the derivation differs from Descartes's own. Clarifying this point will again help us get a better grasp of Kant's conception of the proposition 'I think,' the role of 'I' in 'I think,' and the nature of our epistemic access to the truth of that proposition. It will also help us understand why, even while agreeing with Descartes about the absolute certainty of *I think, I exist*, Kant criticizes Descartes's claim that I am thereby immediately certain of my existence as a mind, whereas the existence of bodies outside me is the object of an inferential knowledge that remains only probable.

Where Kant definitely disagrees with Descartes is in the latter's answer to the question: What am I, I who now have proved that, necessarily, if I think, I exist? Kant criticizes Descartes and his rationalist followers for having been under the illusion that they could derive not only 'I exist,' but also an answer to the question 'What am I?' from the mere consideration of the proposition 'I think.' That aspect of Kant's view, which is also the bulk of his discussion in the Paralogisms of Pure Reason, will be examined in Chapters 5 and 6.

4.1 Descartes's 'Cogito, Ergo Sum'

The context of Descartes's so-called *cogito* argument is well known: in the *Meditations on First Philosophy*, the meditator undertakes to accept as true only those beliefs that have survived the test of radical doubt, that is, all attempts at identifying a possible ground for disbelief. In the First Meditation, the meditator thus successively discards beliefs in the existence of ordinary objects of sensory perception, from the remotest to the closest and most familiar, including his own body. He finds reasons to discard belief in the existence of even the phenomenal components of those objects of sensory perception, even though one might initially have thought that those components could not possibly be mere fictions, however deluded the representations of their composition might be. Finally, he finds reasons to discard belief in what seem to be the most unassailable truths of mathematics. Reinforcing this stage of the doubt is the supposition of a malicious demon that deceives me even in the most careful exercises of my perception and reason. This last, desperate stage of the doubt is also what leads to light at the beginning of the Second Meditation:

> I have convinced myself that there is absolutely nothing in the world, no sky, no earth, no minds, no bodies. Does it now follow that I too do not exist? No: if I convinced myself of something, then I certainly existed. But there is a deceiver of supreme power and cunning who is deliberately and constantly deceiving me. In that case I too undoubtedly exist, if he is deceiving me; and let him deceive me as much as he can, he will never bring it about that I am nothing as long as I think that I am something. So after considering everything very thoroughly I must finally conclude that this proposition *I am, I exist*, is necessarily true whenever it is put forward by me or conceived in my mind. (Descartes 1984 [1641], 17)

Descartes's famous formulation "I am thinking, therefore I exist"[2] does not appear in the *Meditations*. It is present in this form in the *Discourse on Method* ("Je pense, donc je suis"),[3] and in the *Principles of Philosophy* ("Ego cogito, ergo sum").[4] In the *Meditations*, the emphasis is directly on the statement of existence, "I am, I exist," although of course what justifies this statement of existence is the indubitable fact that "I convinced myself of something," namely, the indubitable fact that I think, however deceived I may be as to the truth or falsity of the contents of my thoughts.

The exact nature of Descartes's transition from the proposition 'I think' to the proposition 'I am, I exist,' or indeed the question whether there is any inference at all from one to the other, has been the object of extensive discussion. Doing justice to that discussion is beyond the scope of this chapter. Let me just make two remarks that will be especially relevant when comparing Descartes's 'I think, therefore I am' to Kant's 'I think.'

The first remark concerns the nature of Descartes's account of the transition from 'I think' to 'I am, I exist.' Contrary to what Kant sometimes claims, Descartes does *not* derive the truth of the proposition 'I exist' by a syllogistic inference from the major premise 'Everything that thinks, exists,' and the minor premise 'I think.'[5] On the contrary, Descartes repeatedly insists that the proposition 'I exist' is known with certainty to be true by virtue of our knowing that *the particular proposition* 'I think' is indubitably true, and *not* from prior knowledge of the universal proposition, 'Everything that thinks, exists.' The classic reference that illustrates this point is from the Second Replies:

When we become aware that we are thinking things, this is a primary notion which is not derived by means of any syllogism. When someone says, 'I am thinking, therefore I am, or I exist,' he does not deduce existence from thought by means of a syllogism, but recognizes it as something self-evident by a simple intuition of the mind. This is clear from the fact that if he were deducing it by means of a syllogism, he would have to have had previous knowledge of the major premise: 'Everything which thinks is, is, or exists'; yet in fact he learns it from experiencing in his own case that it is impossible that he should think without existing. It is in the nature of our mind to construct general propositions on the basis of our knowledge of particular ones. (1984 [1641], 100)

However, the fact that the proposition 'I exist' is not derived from 'I think' by way of a *syllogistic* inference does not mean that our knowing it to be true depends on no inference at all. Granted, in the Second Meditation (contrary to the formulations of the *Discourse on Method* or the *Principles*), there does not seem to be any mention of *inference* from 'I think' to 'I exist.' Rather, the meditator directly asserts the certainty of the proposition 'I exist': "The proposition I am, I exist, is necessarily true *whenever it is put forward by me or conceived in my mind*" (1984 [1641], 17; emphasis mine). However, later in the *Meditations*, Descartes does speak of an inference when he sums up the argument of the Second Meditation: "Natural light has formerly shown me that, *from the fact* that I doubted, *I could conclude* that I was." Or again: "Examining these past days whether anything at all existed in the world and knowing that, *from the sole fact* that I examined this question, *it followed very evidently* that I myself existed...."[6] But the inference is not from the statement of something's having a property (thinking) to the statement of its having another property (existing). Rather, the inference is from the statement of *a fact* (*that I am thinking*) to the statement of an aspect of *this very same fact, (that I exist)*, which is a necessary condition for the obtaining of that fact.[7] This being so, the assertion of my existence is no more and no less indubitable than the assertion *that I think*. So what makes 'I think' indubitable?

This question leads to my second remark, which concerns the role of 'I' in Descartes's argument. There are two characteristics of the proposition 'I think' that make it indubitably true every time it is thought. One is the peculiar relation that obtains between the *predicate* of the proposition and the *thinking* of the proposition. The other is the peculiar role of the term in the argument place, 'I.' The latter is what is most relevant to my purpose in this chapter, but let me nevertheless first say something about the former.

The very fact of thinking the proposition 'I think' is an instantiation of the predicate 'think.' Of course the same point could be made about the proposition formulated in the third person: in being thought, the proposition 'there is thinking going on' is made true. Its truth-condition, that there *be* thinking going on, is satisfied by any instance of thinking the proposition: 'there is thinking going on.' However, compared to the impersonal proposition 'there is thinking going on,' the proposition 'I think' has two distinctive features, one semantic, the other epistemic. The distinctive semantic feature is that, whereas the proposition 'there is thinking going on' is made true by any episode of thinking, rather than just by the particular episode of currently thinking that very proposition, in contrast, the proposition 'I think' is made true by *the current thinker* of that proposition *in virtue of her thinking* that very proposition. In contemporary terms, we would say that this feature is to be traced back to FRR: '"I" is a word or concept that refers, in any instance of its use, to the author of the thought or the speaker of the sentence in which "I" is being used.' In the case where the predicate is 'think,' the proposition is made true by the fact that its predicate is said to be true of the very person currently thinking or asserting the predicate to be true of herself, the current thinker of the proposition 'I think.'

In the context of Descartes's antiskeptical argument, the distinctive epistemic feature of 'I think' is even more important: the proposition 'I think' is not only true in virtue of being thought by the thinker of that very proposition; it is also indubitably *known to be true* by that very thinker. For in using 'I' in 'I think' the thinker or speaker not only makes the proposition true but makes manifest *that* and *why* she knows it to be true: her using 'I' in the argument place indicates that she knows the predicate to be true *of herself*, the current thinker, in virtue of her thinking the proposition. This being so, the proposition 'I think' is the only proposition that is not only *true*, but also known to be true by the thinker of that proposition, mentioned in the content of the proposition.[8]

Let us now go back to the impersonal proposition 'there is thinking going on.' The current thinker of that proposition makes it true just in virtue of thinking it. But how does she *know* it to be true? She knows it to be true in virtue of being, herself, the thinker thinking it. This is just what is expressed by the proposition in the first person, 'I think.'[9]

I suggest, then, that to the question, why should we attribute 'think' to 'I' rather than asserting 'think' impersonally (e.g., 'there is thinking going on' or even 'it thinks'), as far as Descartes's *cogito* argument is concerned the answer is this: asserting the predicate 'think' of 'I' rather than asserting it in an impersonal mode just expresses the fact that thinking 'I think' is asserting the predicate 'think' to be true *of* the very subject by which that proposition is not only *made true* but also by whom it is indubitably *known to be true* every time it is asserted: the subject currently thinking the proposition 'I think.'[10]

Descartes's Archimedean point, lifting him out of radical doubt, thus rests on two pillars: that the truth of 'I exist' is a necessary condition of the truth of 'I think'; and that 'I think' is both *true* of the current thinker of the proposition and *known to be true* by the thinker of that very proposition, just by virtue of her thinking the proposition.

As we shall now see, the context in which Kant introduces the proposition 'I think' is quite different from the context in which Descartes introduces his *cogito* argument. In that different context, the role Kant assigns to 'I' is different from the role we have just seen it play in the context of the *cogito* argument. But it is not incompatible with the latter, quite the contrary. In fact, I shall suggest that when he proceeds to his discussion of rational psychology in the Paralogisms of Pure Reason, Kant basically accepts Descartes's *cogito* argument as I just analyzed it, although he rejects the syllogistic justification of it that he wrongly attributes to Descartes. But in virtue of his prior analysis of the role of 'I think' in the context of the Transcendental Deduction, Kant, I will suggest, goes further than Descartes in understanding the role of 'I' in 'I think.' This understanding explains his complex and sometimes puzzling formulations when endorsing the derivation of 'I exist' from 'I think.'

I will now proceed to Kant's introduction of 'I think' in the Transcendental Deduction before returning, in 4.3, to Kant's amended version of Descartes's derivation of 'I exist' from 'I think.'

4.2 Kant's 'I Think'

§16 of the Transcendental Deduction of the Categories in the B edition starts with the famous statement:

The **I think** must **be able** to accompany all my representations; for otherwise something would be represented in me that could not be thought at all, which is as much as to say that the representation would either be impossible or else at least would be nothing to me. (B131–2)

In Chapter 2, I offered a fairly minimalist explanation of what Kant meant in this paragraph. Let me recall one of the examples I gave there. For perceptual representations to be "something to me" is for them to be recognized under a concept, for instance 'tree,' which means that I can come up with the judgment 'this is a tree.' But I am able to come up with such a judgment only if I have bound ("synthesized") a variety of perceptual inputs and compared the resulting bundles in such a way that I can come up with a concept, in this case, 'tree.' The fact that my statement 'this is a tree' is backed by such a process of combining, comparing, and reflecting is what I am expressing when I say 'I think this is a tree,' thereby indicating that I am in a position to provide justification for my judgment.[11] Unless I had been through the process of combining, comparing, and reflecting that makes it possible for me to accompany my representations with the thought 'I think,' concepts would be impossible and intuitions would be nothing to me (they would not be recognizable *as* representations of something, e.g., a tree).

However, if this was all there was to Kant's 'I think,' we would understand neither its role in Kant's argument in the Transcendental Deduction nor how it becomes the cornerstone of his criticism of rational psychology in the Paralogisms of Pure Reason. More needs to be said about 'I think' in the Transcendental Deduction of the Categories.

The Transcendental Deduction is meant to answer the question: how are a priori concepts applicable to objects that are given? Another formulation of the same problem is: how are synthetic a priori judgments possible? Kant's strategy in the Transcendental Deduction is to argue that such judgments are possible, that is, the claim that empirical objects fall under pure concepts of the understanding is justified, because objects of experience would not be presented *as* objects in the first place unless the manifold of perceptual input from which we derive our representations of objects in the world had been ordered according to a priori concepts of the understanding. This being so, it is a priori true that those concepts are true of objects of experience. Of course, in any given case, we will have to rely on empirical investigation to determine *which* empirical objects fall under *which* categories. But, Kant argues in the Transcendental Deduction, at least we do know a priori that all empirically given objects fall under one or the other of each "title" of the categories (quantity, quality, relation, and modality).[12]

The argumentative path Kant takes to establish these points is slightly different in the A and the B deductions.[13] Let me give an outline of the path he follows in each edition.

In the A deduction, Kant's strategy is to follow the order of an empiricist account of the generation of our representations from the simpler to the more complex, and to argue that, for each step, an a priori condition is necessary. In the final stage of the demonstration, he argues that the a priori condition on which all other a priori conditions for objective representation ultimately depend is the "transcendental unity of apperception," which finds expression in the proposition 'I think.' Here, I will give only a very quick run through of each stage of empirical cognition and its a priori condition.

The first stage is the presence of an array of sensory information (a "manifold of sensory intuition" or "sensory manifold" in Kant's vocabulary). A necessary condition for the presentation of sensory information to the mind is that the sensory manifold be presented in one common spatial intuition. For instance, the perceptual input that will eventually be recognized as a house is presented at any given instant as an undifferentiated bundle spread out in space. Now, becoming aware of the presence to the mind of the sensory manifold *as such* rather than as an undifferentiated bundle depends on a mental activity of "going through and keeping together," which Kant calls the "synthesis of apprehension." This activity of synthesis is implemented not only on the sensory manifold (colors, sounds, and so on) but also on the parts of space in which that manifold is laid out. Space, time, and the "keeping together" of spatial parts through time are thus a priori conditions for the apprehension of a sensory manifold.

The second step is "reproduction in imagination" according to associative rules. According to those rules, a presently apprehended manifold may call to mind a manifold apprehended in the past. But this presupposes that some regularity should have been apparent in the presentation of the relevant manifold (this color regularly appears next to that color, this state of the object is regularly followed by that other state, and so on). Moreover, the presentation of these regularities would be to no avail unless the mind had the capacity to associate past rules of apprehension with similar current rules. This, then, is the second a priori condition: there has to be an original capacity of the mind to apprehend any given sensory manifold according to rules which, when presented again, call to mind relevantly similar manifolds.

The third step is "recognition under a concept": the relevant similarities, when recognized as such, yield empirical concepts, for example, the concept of a dog, a tree, a piece of metal (e.g., gold), or what have you. But for such "recognition under a concept" to occur, all past representations, their regularly occurring patterns, the reproductive associations those patterns have elicited, all those features must remain available for recognition. In other words, they must remain available for use in one and the same activity of apprehending, reproducing (according to associative rules), and recognizing. This is how concepts, and thus representations of objects as falling under those concepts, are eventually acquired. The unity of the mental activity at work throughout our mental life, from which concepts, and thus representations of objects under those concepts, are derived, is what Kant calls the "transcendental unity of apperception." It is the third a priori condition for the representation of objects, and unless this fundamental condition were satisfied, neither of the first two (presentation of sensory manifolds in one space and one time, a priori rules for association of sensory manifolds) would even get off the ground. This last, fundamental condition is also what makes concept acquisition possible. Whether or not we are explicitly aware of this fact, all the concepts we ever acquire are acquired against the background of associations we have previously formed and concepts we have previously acquired in the process of coming up with more or less systematically connected pieces of knowledge. *One* unity of apperception is thus at work throughout all our activities of apprehension, reproduction, and recognition, as the necessary conditions for those activities to yield mutually consistent concepts applicable to one world of empirically given objects. According to Kant, this unity of apperception that is the overall condition of any objective representation of the world or, for that matter, of any judgment at all, is what is expressed in 'I think.'[14] As we now see, the scope of 'I think' goes beyond any *particular* thought such as 'I think this is a tree' or 'I think this proof is valid.'[15] 'I think' is the expression of a unity of mental activity that conditions all the particular instances of 'I think p.'

This is a very rough outline of Kant's method of argumentation in Deduction A. In the B deduction, Kant's method is different. Not that he disavows the argument he provided in A.[16] The conditions for any representation of an object painstakingly laid out in A are quickly recalled in the initial section of Deduction B (§15). Three conditions are necessary, Kant claims, for any representation of an object: a manifold of intuition, the synthesis of that manifold, and the unity of the synthesis of the manifold. One can readily recognize here the three stages of the "threefold synthesis" expounded in detail in A: apprehension of a manifold in intuition (for which, as

I briefly recalled above, the a priori condition was the apprehension of space through time), associative synthesis of that manifold in imagination (for which the a priori condition was a priori rules of association and reproduction), and recognition of the reproduced manifolds in concepts (for which the a priori condition was the transcendental unity of apperception). But in the new version of the Deduction, Kant quickly mentions the three stages and their a priori conditions[17] and proceeds to ask: what is that "unity of synthesis" that is necessary for any representation of an object? §15 ends with the remark:

We must...seek this unity...even higher [than the categories], namely in that which itself contains the ground of the unity of different concepts in judgments, and hence of the possibility of the understanding, even in its logical use. (B131)

Kant then opens §16 with the sentence cited above, which for ease of reference I will cite again:

The **I think** must **be able** to accompany all my representations; for otherwise something would be represented in me that could not be thought at all, which is as much as to say that the representation would either be impossible or else at least would be nothing to me. (B131–2)

In the remaining part of §16 and in §17, Kant proceeds to argue that the proposition 'I think' is the expression of the transcendental unity of apperception, and that the logical form of judgment is the propositional form of that unity (§19). In standing under the unity of apperception, objects thus stand under the logical functions of judgment.[18] And in standing under the logical functions of judgment they also stand under the categories (§23), since the latter are just "concepts of an object, by means of which the intuition of that object is determined with respect to one of the logical functions of judgment" (§13, B128).[19]

Finally, Kant argues that the very same unity of apperception to which representations are brought in virtue of being synthesized according to logical functions of judgments and the categories that correspond to them—that unity of apperception is also what determines our intuition of space and time as *one* (*one* a priori intuition in which individual objects of intuitions are located and presented with a determinate shape and duration). This being so, any sensory manifold presented in those intuitions is such that it *can be* determined with respect to the categories defined above, indeed being so determined is a necessary condition for a sensory manifold to represent an object *as* an object. It remains, of course, that we can determine only empirically under which particular category any given object is to be cognized (what is a cause of what, and what is an effect of what; what is substance what is accident; what is the quantitative determination of any particular object; and so on).

The argument is thus the same in inspiration as that in A. The important difference is that in B, Kant structures his argument for the a priori validity of the categories around (1) the role of logical functions of judgment in giving *conceptual* structure to the unity of apperception and (2) the role of the unity of space and time, as "pure intuitions," in providing one common frame of reference for representations of objects in *intuition*.[20] The proposition 'I think' that must *be able* to accompany all my representations is the discursive expression (expression in the form of a combination of concepts in judgment) of the act of spontaneity that is responsible *both* for the imagined unity of space and time in which we locate objects of intuition, and for the presumption of unity, namely consistency, of the logical space in which the concepts we bind in judgments and inferences belong.[21] The fact that 'think' is predicated of 'I' in the thought 'I think' is the conceptual expression of the (mostly implicit) consciousness of an act of binding that the agent of that act takes to be her own just in virtue of being engaged in that act.

In the context of this argument, there is nothing at all we need to know about the metaphysical nature of the entity represented by 'I' in 'I think.' It matters not at all what kind of entity is the agent of the action expressed by the thought 'I think.' Attributing 'think' to 'I' in the proposition 'I think' is just expressing the fact that the thinker is aware of an activity of thinking (binding and reflecting) she experiences as her own.[22]

This all too quick summary of the role of 'I think' in Kant's transcendental deduction of the categories should at least make it apparent that the role of the thought 'I think' as it appears in this argument is quite different from its role in Descartes's Second Meditation. Kant's concern in the Transcendental Deduction is not with any kind of skeptical doubt about *existence*, either of the external world or of myself. 'I think' is not introduced as the vehicle of a solution to *that* kind of skepticism. Rather, it is part of Kant's response to a Humean brand of skepticism, a skepticism that is primarily (albeit not exclusively) directed at the objective validity of the idea (concept, in Kant's vocabulary) of causal connection.[23] In this context, when Kant states that a representation is my representation only if it can be accompanied by the thought 'I think,' he is not particularly interested in progressing to the claim that 'I think' cannot be true unless 'I exist' is true (Descartes's answer to the skeptical challenge he is addressing). Rather, he means to progress to the claim that all the representations I ascribe to myself are so ascribed in virtue of being taken up in one and the same act of combining and comparing them, an act that is determined according to some universal concepts of the understanding, among which is the concept of causal connection (Kant's answer to the skeptical challenge he is addressing). The role of 'I' in this context is thus quite different from what it was in Descartes's *cogito* argument. I argued that in the context of Descartes's argument, using 'I' in the proposition 'I think' indicated that the truth-maker of the proposition was the thinker of the proposition *in virtue of her currently thinking the proposition*, so that the proposition 'I think' together with the proposition representing the necessary condition for the fact that I think, namely 'I exist,' was beyond the scope of any possible doubt. In Kant's Transcendental Deduction, in contrast, using 'I' in 'I think' expresses the consciousness, by the subject of the activity of thinking, of the unity of the contents of her thoughts, and *thereby* of herself as the agent of that unity, whatever the metaphysical nature of that agent might be.[24]

It should be clear, however, that the role of 'I' in 'I think' in the context of Kant's Transcendental Deduction is by no means incompatible with the role of 'I' in the context of the *cogito* argument. For it is a short step from the claim I have attributed to Kant—namely, that 'I think' expresses the consciousness, on the part of the agent of the unifying activity, of being engaged in that unifying activity—to the claims (1) that the thinker of the thought 'I think' is, in virtue of her activity of thinking, the truth-maker of that proposition, and (2) that the proposition 'I think' expresses the thinker's awareness of being, in virtue of thinking the proposition, the truth-maker of that very proposition. Now these were the two points that, I maintained earlier, made the use of 'I' in 'I think' rather than 'it' in 'it thinks' or 'there is thinking going on' essential to Descartes's *cogito* argument.[25] This being so, if Kant is correct in his explanation of 'I think,' then Descartes's '*cogito, existo,*' is, as it were, directly downstream from that explanation. It is indispensable to Descartes's argument that 'think' should be asserted in the first person. What Kant adds is an explanation of what makes the thinker conscious of herself *as* the truth-maker of the proposition, designated within the proposition by the first person 'I.' In other words, what he adds is an explanation of the epistemic ground for asserting 'think' of 'I' in the first place, whether or not one is embarked on an enterprise of pulling oneself out of radical doubt.

Let me now examine Kant's account of the connection between 'I think' and 'I exist' and his assessment of Descartes's *cogito* argument.

4.3 'I Think' = 'I Exist Thinking'

4.3.1 Kant on Descartes's Cogito Argument

Kant's discussion of Descartes's *cogito* argument does not occur in the context of his discussion of any of the four paralogisms of pure reason. One might expect its context to be the discussion of the fourth paralogism, since the *cogito* argument concerns existence ("I think, therefore I exist" or "I am, I exist is necessarily true whenever it is put forward by me or conceived in my mind"),[26] and in Kant's table of the categories the category of existence belongs under the fourth title, that of modality. It should therefore be relevant to the fourth paralogism, since Kant's exposition of the four paralogisms follows the table of the categories in reverse order, starting with the category of relation (first paralogism, of substantiality) and working its way back through quality (second paralogism, of simplicity) and quantity (third paralogism, of personality). One would expect to have come full circle back to modality in the fourth paralogism.[27]

Kant does in fact discuss the issue of existence in the fourth paralogism, both in A and in B, but he discusses it under a more specific angle than that of the relation between 'I think' and 'I exist.' In A, the question under discussion is: are we justified in believing that the existence of outer objects is open to doubt while only the existence of inner perceptions is absolutely certain? In B, the question is: am I justified in thinking that I could exist only as a mind rather than as a human being, namely, an entity that is inseparably mind and body?[28] In Descartes's *Meditations*, both questions are answered in the affirmative. The first is settled as early as the end of the Second Meditation: "the mind is better known than the body," that is to say, we are certain of our own existence as thinking beings and of the existence of ideas in us even while the existence of bodies outside our ideas has yet to be established, which happens only in the Sixth Meditation.[29] The second question is resolved in the Sixth Meditation: I am a mind, really distinct from the body while being substantially united with it. I can thus exist as a mind independently of my body.[30]

Kant rejects Descartes's answers to both questions. The first, epistemic question is discussed in the fourth paralogism in A. In B, this epistemic discussion is transferred to the Transcendental Analytic, namely, to the Refutation of Idealism appended to the discussion of the modal category of actuality in the Postulates of Empirical Thinking in General.[31] The second, ontological question is discussed in the fourth paralogism in B. In both cases, those discussions occur only downstream from the discussion of the *cogito* argument. Kant's discussion of Descartes's *cogito* appears briefly in the introductory paragraphs common to A and B (A347/B405). It is extensively developed in several passages of the closing remarks in B (B420, B422n, B428–30). These are the passages I will mostly be discussing in this section.

'I think,' says Kant, is "the sole text of rational psychology" (A343/B401). He means by this that rational psychology derives its a priori doctrine of the soul merely from features of the concept 'I' in the proposition 'I think.'[32] 'I think,' here, is treated as a *type*, not as a proposition currently thought by an individual thinker. Or, in Kant's words, it is taken "problematically": as a proposition it is *possible* to think, indeed as a proposition it *must be possible* to think if my representations are to be related to an object that they are the representation of, as Kant argued in §16 of the Transcendental Deduction.[33] Now, in all possible instances of thinking 'I think,' thinking 'I think' is thinking of oneself under a concept ('I') that can only be subject, not predicate, in the proposition 'I think.'[34] In all possible instances of thinking 'I think,' thinking 'I think' is thinking of oneself as one rather than as many (the word 'I' is a first-person *singular* pronoun; correspondingly, the concept 'I' is the concept of some individual, whatever kind of entity that individual might be). In all possible instances of thinking 'I think,' thinking 'I think' is thinking of oneself as numerically identical through time. And finally, in all possible instances of thinking 'I think,' thinking 'I think' is thinking of oneself as a thinking entity that is distinct from other entities, including one's own body.[35] In other words, even while denouncing the rational psychologist's move from features of the logical/grammatical position of 'I' in judgment to supposedly real features of a thinking substance, Kant himself asserts that we are justified in taking 'I think' to be a type of thought universally shared by all thinkers, which entails ways of thinking about oneself that, necessarily, all thinkers share.

> I cannot have the least representation of a thinking being through an external experience, but only through self-consciousness. Thus such objects are nothing further than the transference of this consciousness of mine to other things, which can be represented as thinking beings only in this way. The proposition 'I think' is, however, taken here only problematically; not insofar as it may contain a perception of an existence (the Cartesian *cogito, ergo sum*), but only in its mere possibility, in order to see which properties might flow from so simple a proposition as this for its subject (whether or not such things might now exist). (A347/B405)[36]

I submit that this text confirms what I said above: Descartes's *cogito, ergo sum* does not belong in the context of Kant's discussion of any of the Paralogisms of Pure Reason. In fact, Descartes himself does not claim to offer, with the *cogito* argument, any answer to the question, "*What* am I"? For Descartes, the *cogito* argument is only the indispensable preliminary to raising that question.[37] Kant's quarrel with

Descartes and his rationalist followers is about their answer to that second question. So then, what is Kant's attitude toward the *cogito* argument itself?

For Descartes, just as the proposition 'I am thinking' can be thought by all thinkers considered merely as such, so the *cogito* argument is an argument that is available to all thinkers—otherwise it would not be the decisive Archimedean point from which any reader of the *Meditations* can be pulled out of hyperbolic doubt. *Cogito, ergo sum* is true not only of the individual Descartes, but of any individual using 'I' in 'I am thinking.' Nevertheless, 'I' has to be *actually in use* for the argument to take on its force. If what I suggested in the first part of this chapter is correct, the driving force of Descartes's argument is the role of 'I' in any *actual instantiation* of its use in 'I think' ('I am thinking'): 'I' refers to whoever is *currently* thinking the proposition 'I think,' so that thinking 'I think' entails the existence of the individual currently thinking 'I think,' whatever the nature of that individual might be.

Similarly, for Kant 'I think' is, for any thinker, a justification of the *assertion* 'I exist' only insofar as 'I think' is itself *not* problematic but assertoric. The thinker who thinks 'I think' thereby asserts that s/he is currently engaged in the act of thinking. She is thereby justified in asserting that she, the referent of 'I' in 'I think,' exists. So neither the mere understanding of 'I,' nor the mere understanding of 'think,' can ground the assertion of existence that Kant says is "contained" in 'I think.' Rather, the justification for 'I exist' is provided by the particular *perception* of thinking expressed by the proposition 'I think' when it is taken assertorically.

Kant makes this point in each of the crucial mentions of the *cogito* I indicated above: in the opening section of both A and B paralogisms (A343/B401), in Kant's comments on the connection between 'I think' and 'I exist' when recapitulating the paralogisms in B (B420), and in the closing sections in B (B422–3n, B428). The most complete, but also the most difficult formulation of the point can be found at B422–3n. There, Kant contrasts his view with Descartes's. But his ground for opposing Descartes's version of the *cogito* argument is that he attributes to Descartes a syllogistic inference from 'I think' to 'I exist.'

> The 'I think' is, as has already been said,[38] an empirical proposition, and contains within itself the proposition 'I exist.' But I cannot say 'everything that thinks, exists'; for then the property of thinking would make all beings possessing it necessary beings. Hence my existence also cannot be regarded as inferred from the proposition 'I think,' as Descartes held (for otherwise the major premise, 'everything that thinks, exists' would have to precede it) but rather it is identical with it. It expresses an indeterminate empirical intuition, that is, a perception (hence it proves that sensation, which consequently belongs to sensibility, grounds this existential proposition), but it precedes the experience that is to determine the object of perception through the category in regard to time. (B422–3n)

Kant is clearly mistaken in attributing to Descartes the claim that 'I exist' is derived from 'I think' via a syllogistic inference whose major premise is 'Everything that thinks, exists.'[39] As we saw, Descartes expressly denies this. If Kant had avoided that mistaken interpretation of Descartes's proof, he would have been in a better position to determine just where the difference lies between Descartes's derivation of 'I exist' from 'I think' and his own statement that 'I exist' is *contained* in 'I think.'

Recall Descartes's claim:

> When someone says, 'I think, therefore I am, or I exist,' he does not conclude his existence from his thought as if by the force of some syllogism, but as something known by itself; he sees it by a simple inspection of the mind. As it appears from the fact that, if he deduced it from the syllogism, he would first have had to know this major premise: Everything that thinks, is or exists. But on the contrary, it is taught to him from the fact that *he feels in himself that it cannot be the case that he thinks, unless he exists.* (1984 [1641], 100)

The fact that an "inspection of the mind" is needed to establish 'I think, therefore I am, or I exist' (or better, the less misleading formulation of the *Meditations*: 'I think, I exist') is a result of the method of hyperbolic doubt. Because, according to this method, I have resolved to suspend belief about everything about which the least reason for doubt could be manufactured, I have to methodically establish, first 'I think' and then, "by a simple inspection of the mind," 'I exist.' But Kant is not engaged in this kind of methodical doubt. So he can directly claim that *knowing* the proposition 'I think' to be true is also *knowing* the proposition 'I exist' to be true. This is because I know myself to exist *by perceiving myself to be thinking*, and perception is the sole source of any knowledge of existence. I would not think 'I think' unless I *perceived* myself to be thinking. That perception, and *not* a derivation from a universal premise, grounds my knowledge of my own existence.

After he has bootstrapped himself out of hyperbolic doubt, does Descartes say anything different about the connection between 'I think' and 'I exist'? Recall the text just cited: "He feels in himself that it cannot be the case that he thinks, unless he exists." And consider article IX of the *Principles of Philosophy*, which comes *after* the resolution of hyperbolic doubt in article VII:

> By the word thought, I understand all that which so takes place in us that *we of ourselves are immediately conscious of it* [tout ce qui se fait en nous de telle sorte que nous l'apercevons immédiatement par nous-mêmes]. (1985 [1644], 195; emphasis mine)

Descartes's notion of thought is broader than Kant's: any occurrent mental state is a thought. In contrast, for Kant only conceptual representations, and more specifically, judgments (combinations of concepts), are thoughts. Leaving this important difference aside, there are striking similarities between Descartes's claim in article IX and Kant's claim as recounted above. According to Descartes, we are immediately conscious of our being currently engaged in thinking ("*nous l'apercevons immédiatement par nous-mêmes*"). And according to article VII cited earlier, this "apercevoir immédiatement par nous-mêmes" that we are engaged in thinking is a sufficient epistemic ground for being certain that we exist. According to Kant, in any particular instance of its assertion, 'I think' is an empirical proposition, whose epistemic warrant is grounded in perception (the perception that I think). My occurrent act of thinking is a fact, and my access to that fact, as to any existing rather than merely possible or fantasized fact, is my perceiving it.[40]

Nevertheless, Kant's understanding of the connection between 'I think' and 'I exist' is importantly different from Descartes's. Unlike Kant, Descartes does not think that perceiving our own thinking is being "affected" by it. For Kant, perceiving that

86 KANT ON 'I THINK'

I think is being affected by my own (active) thinking, just as I can be affected by external objects.

What difference does this make?

Here, it will help to distinguish three ways in which, for Kant, I am conscious of my own thinking. The first is the pure intellectual consciousness that I think (which does not necessarily involve thinking the proposition 'I think'). The second is the mere "indeterminate perception" *that I think*, that is to say, the mere "indeterminate perception" of my pure act of thinking, considered merely as such. That "indeterminate perception" is what is expressed in the proposition 'I think,' which Kant takes, in his own revised version of the *cogito* argument, to "contain" 'I exist.' The third way in which I am conscious of my own thinking is the *determinate* perception, that is to say, the *experience*, in Kant's sense of the term, of the temporal succession of my mental states. The second way just listed is the one that grounds the Cartesian "cogito, ergo sum"—even though, according to Kant, Descartes was not aware of this and made the mistake of understanding the *cogito* argument as a syllogistic inference.

4.3.2 *Three Kinds of Consciousness of My Own Thinking*

Here's the textual support for my claim that Kant distinguishes the three kinds of consciousness of my own thinking I just outlined.

4.3.2.1 THE MERE CONSCIOUSNESS OF THE ACT OF THINKING

In the transcendental synthesis of the manifold of representations in general... hence in the synthetic original unity of apperception, I am conscious of myself not as I appear to myself, nor as I am in myself, but only **that** I am. This **representation** is a **thinking**, not an **intuiting**. Now since for the **cognition** of ourselves, in addition to the action of thinking that brings the manifold of every possible intuition to the unity of apperception, a determinate sort of intuition, through which this manifold is given, is also required, my own existence is not indeed appearance (let alone mere illusion), but the determination of my existence* can only occur in accordance with the form of inner sense.

 * The **I think** expresses the act of determining my existence. The existence is thereby already given, but the way in which I am to determine it, i.e., the manifold that I am to posit in myself as belonging to it, is not yet thereby given. For that, self-intuition is required, which is grounded in an *a priori* given form, i.e., time, which is sensible and belongs to the receptivity of the determinable. Now I do not have yet another self-intuition, which would give the **determining** in me, of the spontaneity of which alone I am conscious, even before the act of **determination**, in the same way as time gives that which is to be determined, thus I cannot determine my existence as a self-active being, rather I merely represent the spontaneity of my thought, i.e., of the determining, and my existence always remains only sensibly determinable, i.e., determinable as the existence of an appearance. Yet this spontaneity is the reason I call myself an **intelligence**. (B157 and 157n)

This is as close as Kant gets to admitting a pure action-awareness: a consciousness of being engaged in the act of thinking (and synthesizing: transcendental imagination) just in virtue of being engaged in that act. That consciousness is the consciousness of an existence ("the existence is thereby already given") but there is nothing we can *cognize* about either the act or its existence: is it substance or accident? What temporal magnitude or duration does it have? What degree of reality? And so on. To answer such questions I would need to intuit my own mental act of thinking, and assign it temporal determinations. This, according to Kant, would not be intuiting the act itself, but only the way it affects me. Such intuition leads to the second and third ways I am conscious of my thinking. Before getting to them, let me offer a second text in which Kant seems to admit self-consciousness as consciousness of the pure act of thinking. The text just cited was from the Transcendental Deduction in B. The one I will cite now is from the Paralogisms in B:

> If... I represent myself as **subject** of a thought or even as **ground** of thinking, then these ways of representing do not signify the categories of substance or cause, for these categories are those functions of thinking (of judging) applied to our sensible intuition, which would obviously be demanded if I wanted to **cognize** myself. But now I want to become conscious of myself only as thinking; how my own self is given in intuition, I set this aside...; in the consciousness of myself in mere thinking I am the being itself [*das Wesen selbst*], about which, however, nothing yet is thereby given to me for thinking. (B429)

Here again, Kant seems to accept a consciousness *of myself as thinking*, which as such is certainly consciousness of an existence, my own existence as a thinking being. But what is the ontological status of that existence? Is it substance or accident, cause or effect? It is meaningless to even ask that question, even though we can *think* of the existing thinking entity as being the subject or the ground of thinking. Moreover, even though we cannot cognize it (represent it *as an object*), nevertheless our consciousness of thinking, merely as such, gives us access to *the being itself,* or the very essence of what we are, without cognizing *what* that essence is: without being in a position to make any use of our categories to characterize it as an object.

4.3.2.2 THE INDETERMINATE PERCEPTION THAT I THINK

The second kind of consciousness of my thinking is the mere "indeterminate empirical intuition" or perception *that I think*, that is to say, the mere perception of an act of thinking I take to be mine. A perception is an empirical intuition. In the case of the empirical intuition of thinking, the form of the intuition is time, and its matter is the sensation elicited by the fact that I affect myself with my own act of thinking. The proposition 'I think,' then, expresses the perception (indeterminate empirical intuition) of thinking, which we are now disposed to locate in time in relation to other perceptions. But as long as it is not so located, the relevant empirical intuition remains "indeterminate." Here's Kant:

> One should not be brought up short by the fact that I have an inner experience [of the proposition **I think**], which expresses the perception of oneself, and hence that the rational doctrine of the soul that is built on it is never pure but is grounded in part on an empirical principle. For this inner perception is nothing beyond the mere apperception **I think**, which even makes all transcendental concepts possible, which say "I think substance, cause, etc." For inner experience in general and its possibility, or perception in general and its relation to another perception, without any particular distinction or empirical determination being given in it, cannot be regarded as empirical cognition, but must be regarded as cognition of the

empirical in general, and belongs to the investigation of the possibility of every experience, which is of course transcendental. The least object of perception (e.g., pleasure or displeasure), which might be added to the general representation of self-consciousness, would at once transform rational psychology into an empirical psychology. (A343/B401)

It is admittedly unfortunate that Kant should speak in this text of an "inner experience" of thinking, let alone of the proposition "I think." For what he calls "experience," in the Transcendental Analytic, is "a cognition that determines an object through perceptions." Of experience so defined, he offers a proof that it is possible "only through the representation of a necessary connection of perceptions" (A176/B218). Clearly, in the text above he is not talking about experience in that rich sense, introduced in the Transcendental Analytic. For he expressly says that the "inner experience" he is talking about here is *not* empirical cognition. It is, he says, "the mere apperception 'I think'" which is not itself an empirical cognition (is not connected to other perceptions in time) but rather is the "cognition of the empirical itself." In fact, it shouldn't even be called cognition at all, except in the minimal sense that in thinking 'I think' I am disposed to locate this thought in time and thereby make it, itself, an object of cognition, making relevant questions such as: when did this thought occur? How is it connected to other mental states and attitudes? And so on. This will be the third kind of consciousness of thinking, which I will analyze below. But the mere "indeterminate perception" of thinking is not there yet, even if it opens the way to that third kind. Here's Kant again on what I am here calling the second kind of consciousness of thinking:

Because my existence in the first proposition[41] is considered as given, since it does not say that every thinking being exists (which would at the same time predicate absolute necessity of them and hence say too much), but only "**I exist** thinking," that proposition is empirical, and contains the determinability of my existence merely in regard to my representations in time. But since for this once again I first need something persisting, and, just insofar as I think myself, nothing of the sort is given to me in inner intuition, it is not possible at all through this simple self-consciousness to determine the way I exist, whether as substance or accident. (B420)

The 'I think' is...an empirical proposition, and contains within itself the proposition 'I exist.'[42]...It expresses an indeterminate empirical intuition, that is, a perception (hence it proves that sensation, which consequently belongs to sensibility, grounds this existential proposition) but it precedes the experience that is to determine the object of perception through the category in regard to time; and here existence is not yet a category, which is not related to an indeterminately given object, but rather to an object of which one has a concept, and about which one wants to know whether or not it is posited outside this concept. An indeterminate perception here signifies only something real, which was given, and indeed only to thinking in general, thus not as appearance, and also not as a thing in itself (a noumenon), but rather as something that in fact exists and is indicated as an existing thing in the proposition 'I think.' For it is to be noted that if I have called the proposition 'I think' an empirical proposition, I would not say by this that the I in this proposition is an empirical representation; for it is rather purely intellectual, because it belongs to thinking in general. Only without any empirical representation, which provides the material for thinking, the act I think would not take place, and the empirical is only the condition of the application, or use, of the purely intellectual faculty. (B422–3n)

Three points need explaining here. First, why Kant says that, while 'I think' is an empirical proposition, 'I' is a "pure intellectual" concept. Second, whether the "sensation" that grounds the existential proposition 'I exist' is the same as the "material for thinking" without which "the 'I think' would not take place." Third, why Kant says that the 'existence' predicated of 'I' in 'I exist' "is not the category of existence."

'I' is a "pure intellectual concept" because having available the use of the concept 'I' has its origin not in experience, but in our pure spontaneity, as expounded above in 4.2. What puts us in a position to use 'I' is *not* any particular experience but our capacity to bind and conceptualize representations, a capacity that makes experience possible rather than being derived from experience. In that sense 'I' (in 'I think') is, like the categories, an a priori concept. Unlike the categories, however, it has no application rule or schema, because it is not the concept of an object. There is no feature we need to recognize in an object in order to be in a position to apply the concept 'I.' We just learn to use 'I' to refer to ourselves insofar as, necessarily, in thinking we ascribe thinking to ourselves, the individual currently engaged in the act of thinking, and aware of thinking by perceiving the fact that we think.[43] The "perception" here is just a state of awareness. In terms more familiar to us today, there is a "what-it's-like-for-the-subject-of-thinking" character of thinking, even if there is no determinate awareness of the process of thinking in its temporal development or in its underlying structure: the latter have both to be the object of a special investigation, empirical psychology for the first, transcendental philosophy for the second.

The 'perception,' or elementary qualitative awareness of thinking, is what grounds, in each instance of its *assertion*, the proposition 'I think.' One may then ask: is that "indeterminate perception" or "indeterminate empirical intuition" the empirical representation mentioned at the end of the text just cited? Let me cite the passage again:

Without any empirical representation, which provides the material for thinking, the act I think would not take place, and the empirical is only the condition of the application, or use, of the purely intellectual faculty. (B423n)

It is indeed possible that the "empirical representation" mentioned here is the "indeterminate empirical intuition" or "perception" that grounds the proposition 'I think.' If that's so, then the "act I think" that is thereby made possible is not just any act of thinking, but the act *of thinking 'I think.'* What Kant would be saying is that without the indeterminate empirical intuition, or perception, mentioned at the beginning of the text, namely, without the minimal qualitative awareness *that I think*, the act of thinking 'I think' would not take place at all. I would not think (or say) 'I think,' even as the expression of a pure intellectual act of thinking, such as the 'I think' that opens the way out of Descartes's radical doubt, or in the example I have offered earlier, 'I think the proof is valid.'

It is also possible that in the final sentence of the cited passage, Kant is just reiterating a point he has made throughout the Transcendental Aesthetic and Transcendental Analytic, indeed a point that opens the introduction to the *Critique of Pure Reason* and is in the background of Kant's Refutation of Idealism: without an empirical representation *provided by outer sense*, the act of thinking would never take place.[44] This is a possible but, I submit, not the most likely interpretation. For it is more consistent with the general point made in this footnote (B422–3n) that Kant should be talking specifically here of the minimal empirical component grounding the proposition 'I think,' namely, *the perception that I think*. This would be confirmed by the fact that he is not talking about the act of thinking in general, but rather the "act I think," namely—again consistently with the beginning of the passage—the act *of thinking 'I think.'*

The third and last question about this passage: why does Kant say that the type of existence whose assertion is "contained" in the assertion 'I think' "is not the category of existence," but rather a type of existence whose assertion "precedes the experience that is to determine the object of perception through the category in regard to time"? Kant explains: we use our category of existence in connection with objects of experience when, having a concept of an object that we represent as *possible*, we ask whether the object is also *actual*, or exists, that is to say, we ask whether the concept is *actually instantiated* in a particular object, or particular objects, of experience. To answer that question affirmatively ('yes, an object falling under that concept does exist') we need either to have a perception of it or to represent its existence as connected, according to known empirical laws, to the existence of objects we do perceive. But this is not what happens with 'I' in 'I think.' The perception of an act of thinking just is the perception of that act as being my own, and thus as being the ground of my use of 'I.' So this is not a case of the application of the *category* of existence, but rather an immediate, pre-categorial perception of existence that is a component in any individual perception of thinking.

In the *Prolegomena* (which appeared between the two editions of the *Critique*), Kant goes even further in claiming the empirical ground of our use of 'I' in 'I think.' The representation of apperception, the I, he says, is itself "a mere feeling."

> If the representation of apperception, the *I*, were a concept by which something, whatever it is, were thought [ein Begriff, wodurch irgendetwas gedacht würde], it could then be used as a predicate for other things, or contain such predicates in itself. But it is nothing more than a feeling of an existence without the least concept, and is only a representation of that to which all thinking stands in relation (*relatione accidentis*). (*Prol.*, AA4, 334n; translation modified)

'I'[45] is "the representation of apperception" (the representation of self-consciousness). If this representation were "a concept through which anything might be thought," then it could be predicated of other representations (whether intuitions or concepts); and other concepts would be contained in it, as its marks. This is just how Kant characterizes concepts, both in the *Critique* and in the *Jäsche Logic*.[46] But 'I,' in each instance of its use, is applied to one and only one individual: the individual using 'I' in that particular instance. So if 'I' is a concept (and Kant, as we saw, says elsewhere that it is), it is *not* a concept "by which something might be thought." If it is a concept, then, it is a very peculiar kind of concept. In fact, Kant says here, 'I' is not a concept at all,[47] but rather a "mere feeling." I submit Kant means that 'I' represents what it represents ("that to which all thinking stands in relation" in the proposition 'I think') only by virtue of what he will call, in the B Paralogisms cited above (posterior to the *Prolegomena*) the "sensation" that gives its representational matter to the "indeterminate perception" *that I think*.[48] The formulation of the B Paralogisms is more satisfactory in that it allows the transition from the sensation or feeling, which is radically individual and as such justifies the ascription of thinking to *myself*, to the "indeterminate empirical intuition," which locates the feeling in time and thus makes me disposed to acquire a determinate representation of my own thinking as a process occurring in time. But in merely thinking 'I think' I have no such temporal determination and the perception of my own existence is only an "indeterminate empirical intuition."

When and how does that intuition become "determinate"? This question leads us to the third kind of consciousness of my own thinking.

4.3.2.3 THE EMPIRICALLY DETERMINED CONSCIOUSNESS OF THE SEQUENCE OF MY MENTAL STATES

This third kind of self-consciousness is a consciousness of my own existence in time as a thinking being. It is a *determinate* consciousness, as opposed to the "indeterminate perception" of thinking that grounds the proposition 'I think' and makes it the case that 'I think' contains 'I exist.' That determinate consciousness is what is mentioned in the thesis of the "Refutation of Idealism" in the second edition of the *Critique of Pure Reason*:

The mere, but empirically determined, consciousness of my own existence proves the existence of objects in space outside me. (B275)

The restrictive term "mere" (bloße) appended to "consciousness of my own existence" is meant to indicate that here we are talking of that minimal consciousness of existence "contained in" the proposition 'I think.' However, that 'mere' consciousness of existence is now "empirically determined," that is to say, it is experienced as a temporal succession of mental states. 'First I thought this, then I thought that, but then my thinking was interrupted by that idiot who asked me what I was doing,' and so on. Kant's argument in the Refutation of Idealism is that the empirical cognition of such a succession is not possible except in connection with something permanent. Only in space can the existence of something permanent be experienced. Therefore, I have determinate cognition of the sequence of my mental states only under the condition that I have determinate cognition of the objective sequence of states of objects outside me, including the body I take to be my own in virtue of the systematic connection between its states and mental states "in me." Only the representation of bodies in space, and of my own body, can provide the (relatively) permanent, in connection with which the succession of its states, and the succession of mental states associated with them, can be empirically determined. Thus, Kant boasts that in his Refutation of Idealism "the game that idealism plays has with greater justice been turned against it." Kant claims to have proved not only that our experience of outer objects is just as immediate as our experience of the sequence of our own inner states, but that our experience of the temporal determinations of outer objects is a condition for our having any experience at all ("determinate perception") of the sequence of our own mental states.

My goal here is not to assess Kant's argument in the Refutation of Idealism. I am referring to it only to clarify the contrast between what Kant calls the "indeterminate perception" of my own thinking, expressed in 'I think,' and the determinate perception of the sequence of my mental states when thinking. This contrast completes Kant's account of the ways in which I may be conscious of my own thinking.

4.3.3 Kant and Descartes on Perceiving that One Thinks

We are now in a position to see why the difference between Kant and Descartes on *perceiving* that one thinks is important. For Descartes, any occurrent mental state is a thought (a thinking). Moreover, perceiving that one thinks and thinking are two aspects of one and the same fact. This identity between thinking and perceiving that one thinks is what grounds the epistemic certainty of 'I [currently] think' as opposed to any statement involving the body. Given the meaning of 'I think' (*I am currently engaged in the act of thinking*),[49] a "simple inspection of the mind" allows the move from 'I think' to 'I exist.' The "inspection of the mind" is nevertheless necessary to this move because Descartes is engaged in the enterprise of hyperbolic doubt.

Kant, who is not engaged in Descartes's enterprise of hyperbolic doubt, does not need the extra step of the "simple inspection of the mind" to progress from 'I think' ('I am thinking')[50] to 'I exist.' All he needs to say is: 'I think' *just means* 'I exist thinking.' And he adds: our epistemic access to 'I think' together with the 'I exist' it entails, is not secured by the *concept* of thought or of thinking, but rather by perceiving the *fact* that we think. This point is not, however, what makes Kant's position different from Descartes's. What makes his position different from Descartes's is that Kant characterizes the perception *that I think* as an act of self-affection, that is to say, an act of attention in which I become (1) *receptive* to my own act of thinking, thus (2) aware of it and (3) disposed to think the proposition: 'I think.' Moreover, only such an act of self-affection eventually yields an awareness of the temporal determinations of my activity of thinking, whose stages can now be located in time, insofar as they become, themselves, the object of attention, in connection to the temporal location of other mental states and attitudes, all of which are temporally located with respect to events occurring outside them, in space. This is how, as we saw, the third kind of consciousness of our thinking leads to the refutation of Cartesian idealism.

It may help here to compare Kant's account of the complex nature of self-consciousness with Sartre's, which was discussed in Chapter 3. Kant's mere (intellectual, spontaneous) self-consciousness, as the consciousness of a complex unity of synthesis (the first way in which I am conscious of thinking), is comparable to Sartre's non-thetic consciousness (of) self: while counting I am (non-thetically) conscious of (my) counting. Kant's account of my perceiving my own thinking, which finds expression in 'I think' (the second way in which I am conscious of thinking) is comparable to Sartre's "pre-reflective cogito": if someone asks me what I am doing I will say, without having to think about it: 'I'm counting!' Similarly in the examples I gave in Chapter 2, I may say, without explicitly turning my attention to myself: 'I think the proof is valid!' This kind of statement, although not an explicit *reflection* on myself and my thought, is what makes it possible later to say or think, for instance: yesterday I thought the proof was valid; now I see I was wrong. So it already locates my awareness of thinking *in time*, even though I do not, in the "pre-reflective cogito," have a determinate consciousness of the temporal sequence of my thinking. And finally, the explicit *reflection* on the sequence of my thoughts is comparable to Sartre's *reflective* self-consciousness. According to Kant, that reflection is conditioned by my consciousness of the objective temporality of things outside me, including, and above all, my own body. This is why Kant can *both* agree (unbeknownst to him) with Descartes that my immediate consciousness *that I think* is also an immediate consciousness *that I exist, and* disagree with Descartes's "problematic idealism": for Kant, as soon as what I have in view is the *determinate* sequence of my mental states—including the sequence of steps in an episode of reasoning, to which I pay no attention at all *while* reasoning but can retrospectively assess: how long did it take me to get from here to there? How hot I felt all that time! And so on—then my consciousness of that sequence is dependent on my consciousness of the objective temporal order of objects outside me: the "game of idealism is turned against itself."

4.4 Interlude: Anderson on Longuenesse on Kant on Descartes' *Cogito* Argument

In chapter 11 of his impressive monograph on Kant, *The Poverty of Conceptual Truth: Kant's Analytic/Synthetic Distinction and the Limits of Metaphysics*,[51] Lanier Anderson offers a rebuttal of the interpretation of Kant on *cogito* that I defended in my 2008 article "Kant's 'I think' vs. Descartes's 'I am a thing that thinks.'"[52]

Anderson and I agree that when Kant criticizes Descartes for having derived "ego existo" from "ego cogito" by a syllogistic inference, he just misses the nature of Descartes's argument. Anderson adds that Kant makes a second error in his assessment of Descartes's argument. It is highly unlikely, he says, "that Descartes would have been inclined to insist, with Leibniz and Kant's other rationalist targets, that the *cogito* was a purely logico-conceptual result."[53] As I mentioned earlier, I have my doubts about the claim that Wolff or Leibniz took the result of the *cogito* argument [*ego sum, ego existo*] for a purely logico-conceptual result, even though Wolff blunders in giving it syllogistic form.[54] Whatever the case may be on this point, it is precisely because I claim, like Anderson, that for Descartes the *cogito* argument does *not* rest on an analysis of the concept of thinking but rather on the perception of a *particular* act of thinking, and thus of existence as its necessary condition, that I also claim Kant endorses a version of the *cogito* argument which is closer to Descartes's than Kant realizes.

Anderson seems to think that in maintaining that there is for Kant an analytic connection between 'I think' and 'I exist,' I end up attributing to Kant the view that there is between "thinking" and "existing" just the kind of conceptual containment Kant denies. Loading Kant with this view, Anderson worries, amounts to attributing to Kant the view that existence can be derived from 'I think' taken "merely problematically," rather than from the empirical statement, 'I think,' which involves the full apparatus of the Refutation of Idealism.[55]

Now I expressly said, in 2008 and again above, that in the version of the *cogito* argument Kant endorses, 'I think' is *not* taken problematically. If there is an analytic derivation, it is of course *not* from 'I think' taken problematically to 'I exist.'[56] I note in my 2008 article that this would be engaging in just the kind of derivation of existence from a concept that Kant denounces in his refutation of the ontological proof. Rather, if there is an analytic derivation, it is the tautological derivation from 'I exist thinking' to 'I exist.' When Kant says 'I think' *just means* 'I exist thinking' he does not mean that existence is contained in thinking. Rather, he means that *when based on the perception that I am (currently) engaged in the act of thinking*, the proposition 'I think' has existential import. In other words, what we are really thinking when we say (on the basis of being conscious of our current act of thinking) 'I think' is: 'I am (currently) thinking,' that is to say, 'I (currently) exist thinking.' Anderson and I agree that the statement 'I exist thinking' cannot be grounded in concepts. Its ground can only be empirical.

It is on the nature of this *empirical* ground that Anderson and I disagree. Anderson thinks that "only the full apparatus of the Refutation of Idealism"[57] can ground the statement of existence contained in 'I think' taken assertorically (as an assertion that I am currently engaged in thinking), not problematically. In other words, only the full apparatus of my empirical consciousness of my own existence can explain how in thinking 'I think,' I also think 'I exist.' In contrast, I claim that the statement of existence "contained" in the 'I think,' which is involved in Kant's version of the *cogito* argument, rests *not* on "the full apparatus of the Refutation of Idealism" but only on the "indeterminate perception" *that I think*. That "indeterminate perception" is radically empirical: it depends on the *sensation* of thinking.[58] Kant is very explicit about the difference between this "indeterminate perception" and the full "experience" that would ground an assertion of existence in the case of empirically given objects.

I will argue in the next two chapters that Kant's distinction between two ways of justifying assertions of existence, on the one hand in the case of consciousness of objects, and on the other in the case of consciousness of one's own mental agency, is of fundamental consequence for Kant's argument in the Paralogisms of Pure Reason. It is also of groundbreaking *systematic* significance, as I argued in Chapters 1 and 2, and will argue again in the following chapters.[59]

4.5 Concluding Remarks

My goal in this chapter was to examine how far Kant went in his agreement with Descartes on the *cogito* argument. The conclusion I am offering is: he went very far indeed. According to Kant, my consciousness of my own thinking grounds a consciousness of my own existence in which I am to myself *das Wesen selbst*, the being itself. Nevertheless, this consciousness falls short of telling me anything at all about *what* I am, except for the fact that I (the individual currently engaged in thinking 'I think'), think. Knowing more depends on locating myself, the thinker, or more specifically locating my acts of thinking, perceiving, and so on, *in time*. And this in turn depends on locating myself and my acts of thinking, of perceiving, and so on, in relation to other temporally determinate beings *in space*. No a priori metaphysical conception of myself derived from the mere proposition 'I think' is thus possible at all.[60]

My purpose in the next two chapters will be to consider Kant's refutation of what he takes to be Descartes's and his rationalist followers' claim to derive an a priori metaphysics of the soul from the use of 'I' in 'I think.' In Chapter 5, I will examine Kant's criticism of the rationalist claim that the referent of 'I' in 'I think' is a thinking substance, indivisible and thus immortal. In Chapter 6, I will examine Kant's criticism of the rationalist illusion that the consciousness of one's own identity expressed in 'I think' is sufficient to warrant the assertion of one's personal identity in different times. Although Kant's explicit goal in both cases is only negative—refuting the rationalist claim to derive metaphysical knowledge of the soul from the mere proposition 'I think'—I will argue that, from his refutation of the rationalist argument, a positive account of the contrast between first-person and third-person standpoints on oneself emerges, as well as a groundbreaking concept of person and of personal identity in different times.

Notes

1. I call '*cogito* argument' or 'Descartes's *cogito* argument' the argument in the Second Meditation by which Descartes claims to establish both the absolute indubitability of 'I am thinking,' and the indubitability of 'I exist' premised on the indubitability of 'I am thinking.' I call '*cogito*' or 'Descartes's *cogito*' or 'Descartes's "I think"' the proposition 'I think' (in Latin, '*cogito*') as it appears in Descartes's *cogito* argument. On translating 'Je pense' by 'I am thinking' in preference to 'I think,' see n. 2.
2. Descartes 1985 [1637], 127. "I am thinking, therefore I exist" is Robert Stoofhof's translation for the French "Je pense, donc je suis" in the *Discourse on Method* as well as John Cottingham's translation for cogito, ergo sum in the *Principles of Philosophy* (see below, n. 4). They are right to offer this translation rather than the more famous: "I think, therefore I am." For as I shall argue below, it is essential to Descartes's argument that the first truth that survives his hyperbolic doubt is that of his own *existence*, guaranteed, for him, by the fact that he is *currently engaged in the act of thinking*. The latter is better rendered by translating "je pense" by "I am thinking" than by "I think." The French equivalent might be "Je suis entrain de penser," but the expression is heavier and less usual than the English "I am thinking," which is certainly why Descartes uses the formulation "je pense, donc je suis" in the *Discourse on Method*. I shall mostly use the phrase "I think" rather than "I am thinking" in describing Descartes's argument, partly because it is so well known under that phrase, and partly because it makes the relation to Kant's "I think" more perspicuous. But it should be kept in mind that in the context of Descartes's argument, "I think" always means "I am thinking." And as I shall argue below, this is certainly how Kant understands "I think" (*Ich denke*) when discussing Descartes's argument. Thanks to Allan Gabbey for pressing me to clarify this point.
3. Descartes 1985 [1637], 127.
4. Descartes 1985 [1644], 195.
5. See B422n. Kant's claim will be discussed in 4.3.
6. These texts are respectively from 1984 [1641], 27; ibid., 58. See also ibid., 176, and 160: "And what M. Arnauld adds is not contrary to what I say, namely that when I think *I come to conclude* that I am" (my emphasis). On these references, and for an illuminating analysis of Descartes's argument in these texts, see Pariente 1988.
7. For an insightful analysis of the "cogito, sum" argument as an analytic explication of "cogito" resting on meaning containment, see Katz 1990.
8. For a penetrating analysis of the structure of Descartes's argument, based on the "self-verifying" structure of the proposition 'I think,' see Pariente 2002b. See also Katz's

argument that the role of 'I' in the Cartesian *cogito* disqualifies Anscombe's claim that 'I' is non-referential (Katz 1990, 174).

9. I shall say more in 4.3 about what exactly that knowledge is supposed to be when I compare Descartes's and Kant's respective accounts of *Cogito, ergo sum*.

10. Here, by 'subject' I mean the metaphysical subject, the entity that bears the property of thinking. In early modern logic, by 'subject,' one might often just mean the 'logical' subject, namely the term in the proposition *of which* something (the predicate) is asserted, while the predicate is asserted *of* something (the subject). To avoid ambiguity, in the second to last paragraphs, I have said: "'I' is used in the argument-place in the proposition" rather than saying it is the (logical) subject of the proposition; and in this paragraph I have reserved the term 'subject' for the entity, the metaphysical subject. Nevertheless, in what follows, and especially in discussing Kant's position, I will often use the term 'subject' in both senses: logical, and metaphysical. This is unavoidable, since Kant's charge against the rationalist metaphysicians is precisely that they move seamlessly from the "merely logical" to the metaphysical sense of 'subject' in reasoning about 'I' or 'the I.' See 5.1.

11. On the role of Kant's "combination" in providing justification for judgments, see 2.2. On the relation between Kant's "combination" and our contemporary notion of "binding" in cognitive psychology, see 2.2, n. 30.

12. For an explanation of the four "titles" and three divisions of each title of categories, see Longuenesse 2005, chap. 4.

13. For an analysis of the argument of the Transcendental Deduction in A and B, see Longuenesse 1998, esp. chaps. 2, 3, 4, 8. For current purposes only a rough outline of the argument is necessary.

14. Readers may have noted that I sometimes say that 'I think' *expresses* the unity of apperception, and other times say that it *conceptually represents* the unity of apperception. I think both are correct, although in each case the emphasis is different. On this point see 3.1, n. 12.

15. These were the canonic examples I was using in Chapter 2: see 2.2.

16. On this point, see Longuenesse 1998, chap. 3.

17. See B129–30.

18. Kant defines 'function' as the "unity of the act of bringing different representations under one common representation" (A68/B93). That act is an act of judging. The act of judging (bringing intuitions under concepts, subordinating lower concepts to higher concepts) yields judgments (propositions) that have a specific logical form. So to each aspect of the function of judging corresponds a specific form of judgment. Kant sometimes uses the two terms, "function" and "form" of judgment, interchangeably. But the first refers more specifically to the act of judging, the second to the result of the act: judgments, or propositions. On this point see Longuenesse 1998, chap. 4.

19. Henry Allison has objected that my interpretation of the role of the logical functions of judgment in Kant's argument leaves no role for the unity of apperception; moreover, he has argued that in my interpretation, no distinction remains between logical functions of judgment and categories, so that the categories just disappear; "where have all the categories gone?" he asks (see Allison 2000; for a response to Allison's objections, see Longuenesse 2005, chap. 1). Let me very briefly recapitulate my answer to each charge. (1) According to my interpretation of Kant's view, there is a distinction between unity of apperception and logical functions of judgment, because the unity of apperception is the "higher unity" (B131) to which logical functions of judgment, each with its particular form or structure, jointly contribute. Acts of judging just are acts of bringing sensory representations directed at objects to a more and more complete and articulated "synthetic" (combinatorial) unity. This is what Kant says, at B135–6: "All representations

given to me stand under [the original synthetic unity of apperception] but... must also be brought [under it] by means of a synthesis." (2) Even though categories originate in logical functions of judgment, and even though, absent any relation to sensible intuition, they *reduce to* logical functions of judgment (A242/B299–300), they are concepts of actual or possible objects only insofar as the logical functions of judgment are operative *in synthesizing sensible manifolds for judgment*, namely, in synthesizing (combining, binding) sensible manifolds in such a way that they can now be reflected under concepts combined in judgment. Patricia Kitcher (2011, 234-7) seems to think that, according to my interpretation of Kant's view, the act of synthesis is the same as the act of comparison, reflection, abstraction by which empirical concepts are formed. I agree that this would be a bizarre view to hold. But it is not mine. Synthesis is a *condition* for analysis (that is to say, for comparison, reflection, abstraction): you need to put together ("bind") what you are then going to analyze into concepts. But these are two different stages or aspects of the act of judging. I give a detailed analysis of the kind of synthesis specific to each category in Longuenesse 1998, pt. III, chaps. 9, 10, and 11. The details of those explanations are not essential to my concern in the present book. What matters to my current argument is the role of the unity of apperception and its expression in 'I think.'

20. For more explanation of this structure of the argument in B, see Longuenesse 1998, chap. 3, 69–70.
21. Kant calls space and time, as pure intuitions ("empty intuitions, without an object"), *entia imaginaria*: imaginary entities (see A292/B348). He means by this that the unitary space and unitary time that provide one common framework for all empirical objects and their correlations are products of our imagination (our capacity to represent objects even without their being presented to the senses). Nevertheless, spatial and temporal relations of empirical objects are real: they are real determinations of those objects, as they appear according to our forms of intuition (space and time).
    In the main text I talk of the 'presumptive' unity of the logical space into which we bind concepts into judgments and inferences because that unity is assumed (we presume that we will come up with mutually consistent concepts and propositions) but also has to be achieved by our own acts of thinking: see for instance B131, B136, B143. Of course, what I call 'logical space' here is *not* space as a form of intuition. It belongs to understanding, not to sensibility.
22. Compare with Sartre's "pre-reflective *cogito*" in the introduction to *Being and Nothingness*: 2003a, 9. See 3.1. Kant's "I think," as the conceptual expression of the transcendental unity of apperception, and Sartre's "pre-reflective *cogito*," namely a *cogito* that does not express a *thetic* or *positional* consciousness of myself, are, in my view, closely related.
23. See the preface to *Prol.*, AA4, 257–60.
24. Cf. B157: "In the transcendental synthesis of the manifold of representations in general, and thus in the original synthetic unity of apperception, I am conscious of myself, not **as** I am in myself, but only **that** I am. This **representation** is a **thinking**, not an **intuiting**." B158–9: "For the cognition of myself I also need, in addition to the consciousness, or in addition to the fact that I think myself, an intuition of the manifold in me, through which I determine this thought; and I exist as an intelligence that is merely conscious of its faculty for combination, but which, in regard to the manifold that it is to combine, is subject to a limiting condition that it calls inner sense."
25. See 4.1.
26. Descartes 1984 [1641], 17.
27. About the order of the four paralogisms, see A344/B402 and A404. In B, Kant explains that once one has dissolved the illusion of deriving knowledge of an object (the soul as a

thinking substance) from the concept 'I' in 'I think,' then one can substitute for the sequence of paralogisms by which the soul is characterized (as a substance, simple, conscious of its own identity through time, really distinct from bodies) a sequence of the ways in which we think of ourselves via the concept 'I' in 'I think.' Then the sequence starts with the proposition 'I think' as an assertoric proposition (containing 'I exist'), which means we start with modality. The sequence then works its way back through the table of logical functions of judgment: I, e.g., the referent of 'I' in the proposition 'I think' or the thinking being, is thought (or rather, I think myself) to be subject, simple, numerically identical in each state of thinking. See B419.

28. The first formulation is a simplified version of the formulation of the fourth paralogism in A: see A404 (the fourth title) and A366-7 (the statement of the fourth paralogism). The second formulation is a simplified version of the very brief formulation of the fourth paralogism and its refutation in B: see B409.
29. Descartes 1984 [1641], 18.
30. Descartes 1984 [1641], 54.
31. See A366-81 (Fourth Paralogism) and B274-9 (Refutation of Idealism).
32. I use the term 'feature' as the most neutral possible. I shall attempt in the next two chapters to clarify what, in the concept 'I,' Kant thinks is the source of the illusions of rational psychology. The illusions cannot be derived from the marks or content of the concept, since Kant insists that 'I' is a representation that is "simple and in itself completely empty of content" (A346-7/B404). However, even though 'I' is an empty representation, its mere position and thus its role in the proposition 'I think' ends up being interpreted as determining marks for the concept: the concept 'I' is then supposed to be the concept of something that is subject, simple, numerically identical through time, distinct from the body and better known than it. Kant thus takes rational psychology to task for having confused features of the syntactical position of 'I' in language and thought for marks of the concept 'I,' and for having confused the concept 'I' for the concept of an object given in intuition (whether sensible or intellectual). Here I am in agreement with Proops 2010, who notes that an important part of Kant's diagnosis of the rationalist illusion "turns on the (correct) idea that certain grammatical (or quasi-grammatical) considerations do not... function as a guide to conceivability." See Proops 2010, 493. In Chapter 5, I shall say more about the agreements and disagreements between Proops's interpretation and my interpretation of Kant's argument.
33. Recall the first sentence of §16 in the Transcendental Deduction: "It must be *possible* for the **I think** to accompany all my representations" (B131-2).
34. And, of course, 'I' also has the position of logical subject (in an Aristotelian subject-predicate logic) in *any* proposition in which it figures. But the proposition relevant to the discussion of rational psychology is 'I think.' The generalization to any proposition will be discussed in 6.4.
35. See B407/409, B418.
36. In his comments on the table of logical functions of judgments, Kant characterizes "problematic" propositions in the following way: "**Problematic** judgments are those in which one regards the assertion or denial as merely **possible** (arbitrary [*willkürlich*])…. Thus, the two judgments whose relation constitutes the hypothetical judgment (*antecedens* and *consequens*)…are…merely problematic" (A75/B100). This is the strictly logical characterization of "problematic" judgments, namely, a characterization that rests only on the relation of the relevant judgment to "the unity of thinking in general" (B100). In this context, to say that the proposition 'I think' that is the "sole text" of rational psychology is "merely problematic" is to say that it occurs in hypothetical propositions such as: "Necessarily, if I think 'I think', then I represent myself as subject not predicate of something

else." "Necessarily, if I think 'I think' then I represent myself as simple not composite." And so on with the other titles.
37. See again 1984 [1641], 17.
38. See B420.
39. See 4.1. In (mistakenly) attributing to Descartes a syllogistic model for the derivation of 'I exist' from 'I think,' Kant was probably misled by the fact that such a derivation can be found in Wolff. In the Latin *Psychologia Empirica*, the inference Wolff offers is as follows: "Whoever is *in act* [*actu*, my emphasis] conscious of himself and of other things, is *in act* [*actu*], or exists. We are conscious of ourselves and of other things outside us. So, we exist." Although it is not repeated in the minor premise or the conclusion, the important term here is "in act," "*actu*." The major premise is stated at §13 of *Psychologia Empirica*: "Qui sui aliarumque rerum actu conscius est, ille etiam actu est sive existit." The minor premise and the conclusion are stated in §14: "Sumus enim nobis nostri rerumque aliarum extra nos conscii (§11). Qui sui rerumque aliarum extra se conscius est, ille existit (§13) [this is just a repetition of the major premise stated in §13, unfortunately leaving out the crucial term: *actu*]. Nos igitur existimus." §11, which the minor premise refers back to, said: "Nos esse nostri rerumque aliarum extra nos constitutarum conscios quovis momento experimur. Non opus est nisi attentione ad perceptiones nostras, ut ea de re certi simus." "We are conscious of ourselves and of other things outside us each time we have an experience. We need nothing but attention to our perceptions to be certain of this" (see Wolff 1968 [1738], 9–11). So, in defense of Wolff himself, one could say that he is *not* deriving existence from the *concept* of thinking. He is deriving existence from the fact that the concept *is instantiated in the actual occurrence of an act of thinking*. It is our immediate consciousness of that act that justifies us in asserting our own existence. This is what the final sentence in the text just cited says: "We need nothing but attention to our perceptions to be certain of this." Nevertheless, in formulating the *cogito* argument in syllogistic form, Wolff gravely misses its true structure, which is *not* from a universal premise to a particular instantiation of the premise. Rather, the argument proceeds from a particular truth, "I think," to the condition of possibility of that very truth, "I exist." As Lanier Anderson has convincingly argued, Wolff's reformulation of the *cogito* argument in syllogistic form is an especially glaring case of his understanding even empirical truths on the model of a priori conceptual truths, which makes all truths analytic. See Anderson 2015, chap. 3. Anderson's analysis of Wolff's version of the *cogito* argument is based on Wolff 1983 [1751] commonly known as the "German metaphysics" rather than on the *Psychologia Empirica* I just cited. In the German metaphysics, Wolff's blunder is even more apparent. The argument is formulated as follows: "Who is conscious of himself and of other things, is.—We are conscious of ourselves and of other things.—So, we are." (See Wolff 1983 [1751], §§6–7, and Anderson's excellent analysis in 2015, 81–2.) Thanks to Lanier Anderson for having led me to revise an earlier version of my comments on Wolff's version of the *cogito* argument, which were admittedly too charitable and missed the import of what Anderson calls the "Wolffian paradigm."
40. It is worth noting that Leibniz, too, in the *New Essays on Human Understanding*, described 'I think' as an empirical proposition: "[the *cogito*] is a proposition of fact, grounded on immediate experience, it is not a necessary proposition whose necessity is seen in the immediate agreement of ideas." Leibniz 1765, bk. 4, chap. 7, §7. Note also that Wolff's exposition of the *cogito* argument belongs in his *Psychologia Empirica*.
41. That is to say, the proposition 'I think': see B418–19.
42. The passage I am passing over here is the criticism of Descartes's supposed error in deriving "I exist" from "I think" taken as a minor premise and "everything that thinks, exists" taken as a major premise. This was discussed earlier: see 4.3.1.

43. Cf. 4.2.
44. See B1, A34/B20, B67, A50/B74, Bxln.
45. The quotation marks here are mine, but I submit they are true to Kant's meaning: he is talking about the *representation* 'I'. Kant never uses quotation marks to distinguish a representation from what it represents. This creates difficulties, especially in understanding his view of 'I' and 'I think.' At the beginning of Chapter 5, I attempt to resolve some of those difficulties by disambiguating some of Kant's formulations.
46. A68/B93; *Logic*, AA9, 91.
47. I will return in the next chapter to Kant's difficulties in characterizing 'I' in 'I think.'
48. In the *Critique of the Power of Judgment*, which appeared in 1788, Kant bemoans the fact that 'feeling' ['*Gefühl*'] and 'sensation' ['*Empfindung*'] are not clearly distinguished. He declares that he will from now on distinguish the two notions in the following way: "In the above explanation [Kant is referring to the explanation he has just given, of the various kinds of feelings of pleasure and displeasure] we understand by the word 'sensation' an objective representation of the senses; and in order not to run the risk of always being misinterpreted, we will call that which must always remain merely subjective and absolutely cannot constitute a representation of an object by the otherwise customary name of 'feeling.' The green color of a meadow belongs to **objective** sensation, as perception of an object of sense; but its agreeableness belongs to **subjective** sensation, through which no object is represented, i.e., to feeling, through which the object is considered as an object of satisfaction (which is not a cognition of it)" (*Judgment*, AA5, 207). Kant clearly thinks that the distinction he is offering here has not consistently been made before, including by himself. Indeed, in the *Critique of Pure Reason* he talks about a *sensation* of thinking, which is the empirical component in an "indeterminate perception" of thinking. In the *Prolegomena*, cited in the main text, he talks of "the representation of apperception" as being a feeling, a point I have explained as meaning that the representation of myself as thinking is a *feeling* before it becomes a concept of a very particular kind: a concept that can, in each instance of its use, be applied only to one entity, the entity currently thinking 'I.' If a feeling is distinguished from a sensation as "that which must always remain merely subjective and absolutely cannot constitute a representation of an object," then what the *Critique* calls the "sensation" that grounds the empirical proposition 'I think' is such a feeling. But insofar as it grounds the proposition 'I think' it is also the matter of an "indeterminate perception": as I suggested above, in thinking 'I think' I am reflecting my own existence as a thinking being *at each instant in time* in which I think, even though I am not thereby *determining* my own existence in time. At least at this point, this is the best I can do to make sense of Kant's fluctuating formulations.
49. See this chapter, n. 2.
50. See again this chapter, n. 2.
51. Anderson 2015.
52. See Longuenesse 2008, esp. 10, 17–19, 20. Some of the material for the present chapter is drawn from that article. I essentially stand by what I said in 2008 about Kant's relation to Descartes on the *cogito* argument. But I have considerably developed my analysis of Kant's own view of *cogito*.
53. Anderson 2015, 294n12.
54. See this chapter, nn. 39 and 40.
55. Anderson pressed this last point in a discussion of an earlier draft of this chapter, on the occasion of my visit to Stanford University to give the Kant Lectures in 2014.
56. See Longuenesse 2008, 18.
57. See this chapter, n. 55.
58. See again, A218/B266, B423n, and my comments in 4.3.2.2.

59. One might still wonder why Kant insists on the fact that we are aware of the existence of our mental agency by being *affected* by it. Why should Kant not be satisfied with stating that the consciousness of our own existence expressed in 'I think' is a consciousness of (mental) agency? A full answer to that question would have to involve a discussion of Kant's view of the duality and mutual indispensability of our representational capacities (sensibility and intellect). Here I will only note once again that a pure "action-awareness" finds its place in the first kind of consciousness of our own thinking, listed above (see 4.3.2.1). I am grateful to Quassim Cassam and to Christopher Peacocke for pressing me on this point.
60. On the statements of this paragraph, I take it that Lanier Anderson and I agree. As I understand it, our disagreement concerns the question: how much weight should one give to Kant's appeal to an "indeterminate perception" in grounding the assertion of existence contained in the mere assertoric proposition 'I think'? This question will come up again in the next chapters.

5
Kant on 'I' and the Soul

Chapter 4 focused on two main points: the role Kant assigns to the proposition 'I think' in the Transcendental Deduction of the Categories, and Kant's discussion of Descartes's *Cogito, ergo sum* in the opening and closing sections of the Paralogisms of Pure Reason. Examining Kant's treatment of the proposition 'I think' in both contexts confirmed a point I have been maintaining since Chapter 2: Kant recognizes the existence of a use of 'I' that may in some cases be premised only on the consciousness of being engaged in bringing rational unity to the contents of one's mental states.[1] In Chapter 4, I moreover argued that Kant endorses Descartes's claim that the proposition 'I think' entails the proposition 'I exist.' Indeed, in the terms of Kant's analysis, 'I think' *contains* 'I exist.'[2] Nevertheless, neither the consciousness of one's thinking, nor the proposition 'I think' supported by that consciousness, justifies the claim that I can exist *merely* as a thinking being, distinct from my body. In contemporary terms, nothing more needs to be known about the referent of 'I' in the context of the proposition 'I think' than the fundamental reference rule: in any instance of its use, 'I' refers to the individual currently thinking the proposition in which 'I' is used. In the context of the proposition 'I think,' the predicate 'think' adds nothing further to our knowledge of the nature of the referent of 'I.' It tells us neither that the referent of 'I' is *only* a thinking thing, nor that it is anything besides a thinking thing.

Now according to Kant, rationalist doctrines of the soul rest on a set of invalid inferences from characteristic features of the concept 'I' in the proposition 'I think' to purported answers to the question: what am I, I who have the ability to use 'I' in 'I think'? In this chapter and the next, I propose to examine Kant's criticism of those invalid inferences.[3]

Chapter 5 will be devoted to the first and second Paralogisms of Pure Reason, in the Transcendental Dialectic of the *Critique of Pure Reason*. In the first, Kant criticizes what he takes to be the fallacious inference by which rationalist metaphysicians support their claim that the referent of 'I' in 'I think' is a soul (*Seele*), a thinking substance (first paralogism). In the second, Kant criticizes the inference by which rationalist metaphysicians support their claim that the soul, as a thinking substance, is also a simple substance.

Chapter 6 will be devoted to Kant's criticism of the fallacious inference by which rationalist metaphysicians support their claim that in using 'I' in 'I think' we have immediate consciousness of our numerical identity through time as one and the same continuing entity, in other words, the rationalist claim that as souls (indivisible thinking substances) we are persons.

I will not devote a distinct chapter to the fourth Paralogism of Pure Reason. The particular problems raised by that paralogism have been discussed in Chapter 4 and will be discussed again in Chapter 6.[4]

Before embarking on our examination of the Paralogisms, it is important to acknowledge a difficulty in dealing with this chapter of the *Critique*. Kant's vocabulary in expounding his transcendental psychology and criticizing rationalist doctrines of the soul is not fully fixed. The ambiguities that result explain, I will suggest, some of the unresolved controversies concerning the correct interpretation of Kant's view.

In 5.1, I will endeavor to lay out some of those ambiguities and to offer preliminary solutions to them. Those solutions will be tested in the next sections, in light of the contribution they make to a consistent interpretation of Kant's criticism of the Paralogisms of Pure Reason.

In 5.2 and 5.3, I will offer interpretations of the first and second paralogisms.

In 5.4, I will offer a few concluding remarks, emphasizing the contrast between what Kant calls the "subjective I" and an objective representation of oneself.

5.1 Ambiguities in Kant's Terminology

Kant often seems to be using the following words or expressions interchangeably: 'transcendental unity of apperception,' 'I,' 'I think,' 'subject,' 'soul' (*Seele*), and 'self' (*Selbst*). And yet, more than once Kant's explanations make it clear that those expressions play a different role in his argument. Before entering the discussion of the first two paralogisms, it will help to offer some preliminary explanations of the relevant differences between those terms.

5.1.1 Transcendental Unity of Apperception

As we saw in Chapter 4, in the Transcendental Deduction of the Categories, Kant argues that we have representations of objects only if we bind the contents of our representational states through one and the same mental act of combination (*Verbindung*) or "unity of synthesis" (B130). Combination is "an act of the spontaneity of the power of representation."[5] In saying that combination is a *unity* of synthesis, Kant makes two related points. First, each particular act of synthesis (of a perceptual content, of a representation in imagination, of concepts in judgment) is performed according to a specific unifying form. Specific unifying forms are provided by logical functions of judgment, by the categories and their schemata, or by empirical concepts and their own schemata.[6] Second, all particular unifying acts (*Handlungen*) belong to one and the same mental activity. The transcendental unity of apperception is the consciousness of that overall unity of our mental activity.

This overall unity, Kant says, is higher than the category of unity; indeed, the category of unity, like all other categories, presupposes this higher unity (B131), which, Kant says, is

the unity of the comprehension of the manifold of cognition in thought, as, say, the unity of the theme in a play, a speech, or a fable. (B114)

Because this overall unity is a necessary condition for any representation of an object, it is called the *transcendental* unity of apperception. Because it is the unity of acts of synthesis, the *transcendental* unity of apperception is also called the *synthetic* unity of apperception.

The conceptual expression of that overall, synthetic unity of apperception is the thought: *I think*. With this, we encounter the first of the terminological ambiguities I wish to draw attention to.

5.1.2 I Think

As we have seen, combination is described as an *Aktus der Spontaneität der Vorstellungskraft* (B130), an "act of the spontaneity of the representational power." Now one might think that the proposition 'I think' is the *expression* of that act. But this is not how Kant describes it when he first introduces "the **I think**" in the B Deduction. Rather, what he says is that the **I think** is, itself, an *Aktus der Spontaneität*.

> All manifold of intuition has a necessary relation to the **I think** in the same subject in which this manifold is to be encountered. But this representation is an act of **spontaneity**, namely it cannot be considered as belonging to sensibility. (B132; Kant's emphasis)

Given the description of combination in the preceding paragraph as an "act of spontaneity of the representational power," it now seems that what Kant calls "the **I think**" just is that very act insofar as it is self-conscious. If that's so, then there is no distinction between the transcendental unity of apperception and what Kant calls "the I think." The latter is just the former, considered in its self-reflective aspect.

But on the other hand, Kant says that the former "brings forth" the latter. Immediately after the sentence just cited, he continues:

> I call [this representation] the **pure apperception**, in order to distinguish it from the **empirical** one, or also the **original apperception**, since it is that self-consciousness which, because it brings forth [*hervorbringt*] the representation **I think**, which must be able to accompany all others and which in all consciousness is one and the same, cannot be accompanied by any further representation. (B132; Kant's emphasis)

Here, "the **I think**" is not just the unity of apperception or even an aspect of it. It is a representation that is *brought forth* by "the original apperception." This seems more in tune with what Kant says when he distinguishes the original synthetic unity of apperception, which is an "act of spontaneity of the representational power," from the analytic unity of apperception, which is the conceptual outcome of that activity, its expression in concepts (see B133 and B133n). Indeed Kant goes on to describe 'I think' as the *expression* of the unity of apperception:

> I can grasp [all my representations] together, as synthetically combined in an apperception, *through the general expression* **I think**. (B138; Kant's emphasis in bold; italics mine)

Kant also describes 'I think' as the expression of an act of *determining my own existence*: "The **I think** expresses the act [*den Aktus*] of determining my existence" (B157n). What does this mean? In the Transcendental Aesthetic, Kant explained that although the contents of our sensory representations always come from outer sense, nevertheless they come to be contents we are aware of by being taken up into inner sense, whose a priori form is time. This means two things: insofar as we are aware of them, our representations are successive; and we become aware of them *as* successive by relating them to the objective temporal order of things outside us. But we thereby also become aware of our own act of combining *as an act that is continued through time*: this is just what it means to say that the act of combining is one and the same, or numerically identical through time. Its identity is that of an act whose effect appears at different points in time, and thus as continued, or as having temporal duration.[7] This being so, the act of combining that is expressed by 'I think' is also an act of determining the sequence of my states from one point to the next in time. 'Determining' here just means: producing a determinate representation of my successive states in connection with the successive states of objects outside me.[8]

Obviously, a lot more will have to be said about this "determination of my own existence," which is sometimes said to be "the **I think**" and sometimes the transcendental unity of apperception that "the **I think**" expresses. What I want to focus on for now is the second claim: the claim that "the **I think**" is the *expression* of the *Aktus* that is the transcendental unity of apperception. What does Kant mean by "expression"?

The term 'expression' also appears in Kant's characterization of the categories:

The same function that gives unity to the different representations in a judgment also gives unity to the mere synthesis of different representations in an intuition, which *expressed universally*, is called the pure concept of the understanding. (A79/B105)

The categories, then, are "universal expressions" of the specific forms of unity of synthesis. For instance, in synthesizing sensory manifolds in such a way that I become aware of the contrast between a (relatively) permanent object and its changing states, I delineate in the perceptual world (relatively permanent) substances whose accidents change. The relation between substance and accident is a universal way of representing the world, but that way of representing the world is also an *expression of my own act of synthesizing* sensory manifolds according to the category of substance. One could say, similarly, that 'I think,' as expressing the *overall unity* of the *Aktus* of combination, is the *expression* of an act by means of which we come up with a *representation* of the world to which we strive to give systematic unity.[9] Should we say, then, that 'I think' is a concept in just the way the categories are? Kant hesitates on this point, as shown in the opening paragraph of the Paralogisms of Pure Reason:

Now we come to a concept that was not catalogued above in the general list of transcendental concepts, and nevertheless must be assigned to it, yet without altering that table in the least and declaring it defective. This is the concept—or rather, if one prefers, the judgment—**I think**. (A341/B399)

As the universal representation of the unity of an act of synthesis, it would seem that 'I think,' like the categories, is a concept. But 'I think' has the form of a judgment, or proposition,[10] as confirmed a few lines later:

We have thus already before us a putative science which is built upon the single proposition **I think**. (A342/B400)

Moreover, the occurrence of the act expressed by the proposition in question is *perceived*. In contemporary terminology, we would say that it is experienced: there is something it feels like to be engaged in that act. In his own terminology, Kant says that the act is "perceived" rather than "experienced."[11] For according to Kant's own use of the term 'experience,' to say that the *Aktus* is experienced would be to say that it is an object of empirical cognition, which Kant does not want to say. According to his explanations, "perceiving" the act of thinking is not forming an intuition of it as a continuing state spread out through time, but only *being affected by it* in such a way that one knows that one thinks (one is currently engaged in the act of thinking) without necessarily turning one's attention to one's act and forming a cognition of it, that is to say, a temporally extended intuition thought under a concept. All we can say about the act itself is that it is an act we are conscious (of) at each instant, without its being itself displayed in time. This makes it "perceived" but not "experienced." And the proposition "I think" is the expression of that perception.[12]

Finally, the fact that Kant sometimes just identifies the proposition 'I think' with the unity of apperception (rather than saying it is the *expression of* the unity of apperception) explains bizarre statements such as:

> the proposition **I think**...contains the form of every judgment of understanding whatever and accompanies all categories as their vehicle. (A348/B406)

I suggest we should understand Kant to mean that *the unity of apperception* (as the unity of synthesis of sensory manifolds, and the systematic unity of the act of combination of concepts in judgments and inferences) "contains the form of every judgment." By this he means that it occurs according to the logical functions of judgment that find expression in specific *forms* of judgment. It thus "accompanies all categories as their vehicle," and makes possible all reflection of sensory manifolds under the categories. It would be absurd to say that the mere *proposition* 'I think' contains the form of every judgment, or that it is the vehicle of all the categories. But it is not absurd to say that *the unity of apperception*, which the proposition 'I think' expresses, plays both roles: it contains the form of all judgments (or more accurately: the form of all judgments originates in the unity of apperception), and it is the vehicle of the categories.

So, to sum up: 'I think,' or (in Kant's terms) "the **I think**" (the proposition 'I think'), is sometimes identified with the unity of apperception, sometimes described as the *expression of* the unity of apperception. Insofar as it is identified with the unity of apperception, it "contains the form of all judgments." Insofar as it, more plausibly, *expresses* the unity of apperception, it depends on the "indeterminate perception" of the mental act of unifying representations and is thus "an empirical proposition" (B421n). But it is not a judgment of experience, which would depend on a determinate perception, a temporally extended intuition of objects reflected under concepts. And of course, as we saw in Chapter 4, when it is taken "problematically," 'I think' is a proposition any thinker *can* think, indeed *must* be disposed to think, just insofar as she is disposed to think at all: insofar as she has a transcendental unity of apperception.

Unsurprisingly, the ambiguities that plague the expression 'I think' also plague the concept 'I,' '*Ich*.'

5.1.3 I

In the Transcendental Deduction in A, Kant says that "the mere representation 'I'" makes possible the collective unity of all other representations and the logical form of all cognition (A117n). The justification for this statement is the principle I called, in Chapter 2, SY → I. Only if I am capable of using 'I' in the proposition 'I think' am I capable of intuiting objects in one spatial and temporal framework, and of thinking them under concepts in one system of judgments and inferences. Using 'I' in 'I think' is just the conceptual expression of a consciousness of the rational unity of an act of thinking for which I take myself to be accountable.[13] Because the capacity to use 'I' in 'I think' is thus a condition of possibility of any cognition (representation related to an object), Kant calls the representation 'I' "transcendental consciousness":

> It should not go unnoticed that the mere representation I in relation to all others (the collective unity of which it makes possible) is the transcendental consciousness. Now it does not matter here whether this representation be clear (empirical consciousness) or obscure, even whether it be actual; but the possibility of the logical form of all cognition necessarily rests on the relationship to this apperception as a faculty. (A117n)

Kant builds on this argument when he says, in the concluding remarks of the Paralogisms in A:

> Because the sole condition that accompanies all thinking, [*alles Denken begleitet*], is the I, in the universal proposition **I think**, reason has to do with this condition, insofar as it is itself unconditioned. But it is only the formal condition, namely the logical unity of every thought, in which I abstract from every object. (A398)[14]

As we can see, here Kant seems to equate not just 'I think,' but even 'I' itself, with the "logical unity of every thought." This being so, when he says, as in the text from A114n cited above, that 'I' is "the transcendental consciousness," it is tempting to think he means by that, not just that 'I' (used in 'I think') is the expression of a self-consciousness that is the condition of any cognition and even any thought (any thinking), but also that 'I' is the transcendental unity of apperception itself. Indeed, at B419 Kant writes:

> In the third proposition [this is the proposition according to which I am "simple subject"], the absolute unity of apperception, the simple I... becomes important for its own sake. (B419)

Passages such as this one seem to justify some prominent interpreters' claim that, for Kant, "the I" just is the pure activity of thinking.[15] But I submit that such an interpretation is even more misguided than the interpretation that equates the thought 'I think' with the transcendental unity of apperception rather than understanding it to be an *expression* of the transcendental unity of apperception. 'I' can be equated neither with the transcendental unity of apperception nor even with 'I think.' Rather, it is an inseparable component of the proposition 'I think.' As such, many passages indicate that Kant takes it to *represent* an entity, whatever that entity might be. 'I' represents an entity that is conscious of itself in virtue of being conscious of its own thinking (synthesizing) activity. This is not the same as saying that 'I' represents that activity itself, much less that the I *just is* that activity itself. As testimony to this point, see for instance, in the Transcendental Deduction:

I exist as an intelligence that is merely conscious of its faculty for combination. (B158–9)

And as an echo, in the Paralogisms of Pure Reason:

Through I, or he, or it (the thing) which thinks, nothing further is represented than a transcendental subject of thought = X, which is cognized only through the thoughts that are its predicates, and about which, in abstraction, we can never have the least concept. (A346/B404)

Kant tells us in the first text cited (B158–9) that the entity represented by 'I' in 'I think' is conscious of itself only by being conscious of its activity of thinking. He tells us in the second text that the predicates this entity attributes to itself are the predicates that express that very activity. It is clear from both texts that the entity in question is the (unknown) subject or agent of the activity, rather than the activity itself.

One might ask: why should we privilege the last two texts over the preceding ones in interpreting Kant's view of 'I'? My answer is twofold. First, we have been able to identify a systematic chain of equivocations in Kant's transitions from 'unity of apperception' to 'I think' and to 'I.' Resolving those equivocations clearly helps make consistent sense of all the texts cited above and yields support for the interpretation of 'I' as a term referring to an entity, albeit one unknown and unknowable. Second, this understanding of 'I' is supported by Kant's argument in the Paralogisms, as we shall see in what follows.

Understanding 'I' to refer to an entity calls for clarifying yet another term: the term 'subject.'

5.1.4 *Subject*

'Subject' can mean logical subject of judgment (in the classical Aristotelian predicative form: S is P), or metaphysical subject, the bearer of properties and states that Kant calls "subject of inherence." According to Kant, the rationalist metaphysicians make the mistake of concluding from the fact that 'I' can occupy only the position of logical subject and not that of predicate in the proposition 'I think,' that the entity that 'I' stands for exists as something that is a "subject of inherence," a bearer of properties and states that does not itself exist as the mere property or state of something else: a substance.

However, it is worth noting that, in the Transcendental Deduction of the Categories, Kant himself uses the term 'subject' in a sense that is clearly metaphysical when discussing the activity of combination that gives rise to representations of objects:

The manifold of representations can be given in an intuition that is merely sensible, that is, nothing but receptivity, and the form of this intuition can lie *a priori* in our faculty of representation without being anything other than *the way in which the subject is affected*. Yet the **combination** (*conjunctio*) of a manifold in general can never come to us through the senses, and therefore cannot already be contained in the pure form of sensible intuition.... Among all representations **combination** is the only one that is not given through objects *but can be executed only by the subject itself*, since it is an act of its self-activity. (B130)

"The subject," here, refers to the entity, whatever that entity might be, that is, on the one hand, passively affected by external objects, and on the other, actively combining the manifold of sensory representations resulting from its being thus affected. This subject that is both passive and active is also passively affected by its own activity:

Under the designation of a **transcendental synthesis of imagination,** [the understanding] ... exercises that action on the passive subject whose faculty it is, about which we rightly say that the inner sense is affected by it. (B153–4)[16]

Now consider 'I' in 'I think.' The concept 'I' is a logical subject: it has the function of subject in the classical predicative form "S is P." Each thinker, in thinking 'I think,' refers to herself as a thinking entity and in doing so, thinks of herself as a subject in the metaphysical sense and as such, the agent of the act and resulting occurrent states of thinking. But she need not know anything further about that subject, not even whether it is appropriate to think of it as a subject in an absolute sense rather than as the predicate or state of some more fundamental kind of entity. The referent of 'I,' which we can only think of as a subject without having any determinate concept of the kind of entity it might be, is what Kant calls the "transcendental subject = X." According to Kant, the error of rational doctrines of the soul is to mistake the consciousness each thinker has of herself in being engaged in the act of thinking, for a purported knowledge of the transcendental subject, which is then mistaken for an object: the soul, an object of inner sense distinct from the body.

5.1.5 Soul

However pure from the empirical (from impressions of sense) it may be, [the concept 'I'] still serves to distinguish two kinds of object through the nature of our power of representation. I, as thinking, am an object of inner sense and am called 'soul.' That which is an object of outer sense is called 'body.' Accordingly, the expression 'I,' as a thinking being, already signifies [*bedeutet*] the object of a psychology that could be called the rational doctrine of the soul if I do not seek to know anything about the soul beyond what independently of all experience (which always determines me most closely and *in concreto*) can be inferred from this concept I insofar as it occurs in all thinking. (A342/B400)

This text is somewhat disconcerting. In the texts I cited above (see 5.1.3 and 5.1.4), Kant characterizes the concept 'I' in 'I think' as referring to, or representing, the thinker *as* thinker: as the entity that thinks, not as an object of thought. But now 'I' serves to distinguish two kinds of *objects*. It serves to distinguish myself as an object of inner sense: the soul, from another kind of object, distinct from myself as an object of inner sense, and instead, an object of outer sense: the body.

Here it helps to give due attention to the end of the first sentence in the text just cited: "through the nature of our power of representation." The power of representation Kant has in mind here is clearly sensibility, which includes outer sense and inner sense. The distinction between these two senses, the outer sense by which we have epistemic access to external objects in space, and the inner sense by which we have epistemic access to our own mental states and actions, is a distinction inherited from Locke and accepted both by Kant and by the rationalist metaphysicians he criticizes. Kant's complaint, formulated in the Transcendental Analytic, is that rationalist metaphysicians confuse inner sense and apperception, and thus confuse the consciousness we have of ourselves as objects of inner intuition, and the consciousness we have of ourselves in pure apperception.[17]

Now from Kant's standpoint, if bodies, as objects of outer sense, are mere appearances, so is the soul, as an object of inner sense. Indeed, Kant characterizes the soul as the object of a "physiology of inner sense," namely a natural science of objects of inner sense, just as bodies are the objects of a "physiology of outer sense," namely a natural science of objects of outer sense (A381). But the parallel is deceptive. For as Kant immediately adds, in outer sense we have "something standing and abiding," (at least relatively) persistent (or relatively persistent) bodies located in space, whose identity through time we can track while their positions and states change. But in inner sense we have no such subsisting entity, because the object of inner sense is not presented in space: all we have in inner sense is the temporal succession of mental states. So even though the very distinction between inner sense and outer sense calls for the distinction between the *object* of inner sense, called soul, and the *object* of outer sense, called body, strictly speaking we have no empirical object of inner sense *in the way* we have an empirical object of outer sense. The only (relatively) persisting objects are the objects of outer sense; in inner sense we just have the succession of mental states we take to be our own.

Now with the concept 'I' in the proposition 'I think,' whose referent is the thinking being considered merely as such, it looks like we do have the concept of an object that is an object of inner sense and not of outer sense, and an object that does subsist while its states change. So now we seem to have a concept of an object for a rational psychology, a purely rational doctrine of the soul, where "I do not seek to know anything about the soul beyond what, independently of all experience (which always determines me more closely and *in concreto*), can be inferred from this concept I insofar as it occurs in all thinking" (A342/B400, end of text cited above). But, as Kant will go on to argue, this is just one example of the way reason (ourselves, in exercising our rational capacity, or the rationalist metaphysician who might be any of us when we seek answers to our insatiable metaphysical questions) comes up with a fallacious way to support the claim that an actually existing entity (myself, as thinking) instantiates the illusory concept it has coined: an ultimate metaphysical subject for what is cognized only as a sequence of mental states.

In sum: the concept 'soul' is the concept of the object of inner sense (the object whose states are, for each of us, the sequence of our mental states, accessible through inner sense). As the concept of an empirical object, unlike the concept 'body,' the concept 'soul' has no abiding object presented in sensibility, even in a relative sense. Even less does the concept 'soul' as a pure concept of reason, the concept of the unifying subject of the sequence of my inner states (perceptions, acts, feelings, and so on), have any object at all. And yet, it is a concept that is indispensable both to the understanding (as a concept of the object of inner sense) and to reason (in its attempt to represent as an object of inner sense the ultimate subject of inner states, a subject that is not itself the predicate of something else).

I conclude, then, that for Kant 'I, as thinking' and 'soul' are not interchangeable concepts. In thinking 'I think,' I refer to myself as an entity I cannot cognize even though in thinking, I am conscious of my own existence. By the concept of soul, in contrast, I refer to an entity that I suppose to be distinct from the body. That distinction belongs in the world of appearances. But even in the world of appearances, the concept of a soul turns out to be empty. For, unlike the concept 'body,' it does not refer to any entity I might identify and reidentify as relatively permanent while its states change, as I can do in the case of bodies, whose continuing existence I can track in space while their states and positions change. The object thought under the concept 'soul' thus turns out to be, as the supposed object of inner sense, an object of mere thought. It is an object *of inner sense* because it is the object that is supposed to bear the states we experience as "inner" states rather than states of our body or of bodies outside us. But it turns out to be an object *of mere thought* because there is no way for us to individuate such an object, since we cannot track its persistence while its states change, as we do in the case of bodies.

Here, I am anticipating an argument Kant will make in the course of the Paralogisms of Pure Reason. It is enough for his opening argument in the Paralogisms to accept, with the rationalist metaphysician, that our concept 'I' in 'I think' opens the way to a distinction between two kinds of objects: bodies (objects of outer sense) and souls (objects of inner sense); and that features of the concept 'I' in 'I think' seem to support an a priori doctrine of the soul, as an object of inner sense.

> The expression 'I,' as a thinking being, already signifies the object of a psychology that could be called the rational doctrine of the soul if I do not seek to know anything about the soul beyond what independently of all experience (which always determines me most closely and *in concreto*) can be inferred from this concept I insofar as it occurs in all thinking. (A342/B400)

Now another concept that seems to be coined on the basis of our use of the concept 'I' is that of 'self' (*Selbst*).

5.1.6 Self

Kant does not offer any explanation of the concept of 'self' [*Selbst*] and yet he makes repeated use of it, not only in the first Critique but also in his moral philosophy. Here I will limit myself to the concept of self as it appears in the first Critique and thus is relevant to the discussion of Kant's argument in the Paralogisms of Pure Reason.

I suggest that Kant uses the concept of self in two different, but related ways. The first is as a substitute for the rationalist concept of the soul. The rationalist concept of the soul, which purports to represent an object of inner sense corresponding to the concept 'I', is in fact empty; no object is presented for it in inner intuition. And nevertheless, 'I' in 'I think' refers to an entity, which Kant calls 'a self.' In this first sense, 'the self' means the same as 'the I': it is the referent of the concept 'I' by which each thinker, in thinking, is disposed to refer to herself, without the referent of 'I' being an *object* of intuition or cognition. This concept of 'self' can be found, for instance, in the following passage from the concluding remarks of the Paralogisms of Pure Reason in A:

> Why do we have need of a doctrine of the soul grounded merely on pure rational principles? Without doubt chiefly with the intent of securing our thinking self [*unser denkendes Selbst*] from the danger of materialism. But this is achieved by the rational concept of our thinking self

which we have given. For according to it, so little fear remains that if one took matter away, then all thinking and even the existence of thinking beings would be abolished, that it rather shows clearly that if I were to take away the thinking subject, the whole corporeal world would have to disappear, as this is nothing but the appearance in the sensibility of our subject and one mode of its representations. (A383)

Note that here, "thinking self" and "thinking subject" are used interchangeably. Both concepts refer to the entity that is the referent of 'I' in 'I think': an entity we know to exist just in virtue of being, ourselves, engaged in thinking and thereby being in a position to think 'I think.' But we don't thereby know what kind of entity the self is. The concept 'self' just designates the entity the thinker refers to (herself, as thinking) when using 'I' in 'I think.'

However, Kant also uses the concept of 'self' as equivalent to the rationalist concept of the soul, derived, by the series of deceptive inferences Kant denounces in the Paralogisms of Pure Reason, from the mere concept 'I' in 'I think.' See for instance:

I relate each and every one of my successive determinations to the numerically identical self in all time, i.e., in the form of the inner intuition of myself. On this basis the personality of the soul must be regarded not as inferred but rather as a completely identical proposition of self-consciousness in time. (A362)

Here "the numerically identical self" seems to be the object of inner sense that the concept 'I,' in 'I think,' is supposed to have as its object. So understood, "the self" is just the same concept as the (rationalist) concept of "soul." As such, deriving features of the former from features of the concept 'I' is just as unwarranted as deriving features of the latter, even though, we are told, "the personality of the soul must be regarded... as a completely identical proposition of self-consciousness in time." But this is because the self as a purported object of inner sense is, like the soul, an inevitable illusion yielded by the mere features of our use of 'I' in 'I think,' grabbed upon by reasons in its search for an ultimate, absolute subject of thinking.

Kant seems often (including in A362, cited above) to move seamlessly from the first sense (the self as what 'I' in 'I think,' refers to, without its being presented as an object of intuition) to the second (the self as the object of inner sense supposed to be conceptually represented by 'I' in 'I think'). That the transition is so seamless is presumably meant to indicate how treacherously easy (and deceptive) is the move from the first sense of 'self' to the second. This point will be especially important for Kant's argument in the Paralogism of Personality.

It is now time to turn to Kant's argument in the Paralogisms of Pure Reason.

5.2 "The First Paralogism, of Substantiality"

Kant's statement and analysis of the paralogisms of pure reason differ significantly in the A and the B editions of the *Critique of Pure Reason*. The relevant chapter (book 2, chapter 1 of the Transcendental Dialectic: The Paralogisms of Pure Reason) is one of only two chapters of the *Critique of Pure Reason* Kant completely rewrote for the B edition.[18] I shall argue that differences in exposition notwithstanding, Kant's view remains the same from A to B, both in its negative aspect (Kant's criticism of what he takes to be the fallacious rationalist inference), and in its positive aspect (the view Kant defends as an alternative to the rationalist view). Nevertheless, it is important to understand why he changed the formulation of his argument from A to B. In this chapter, I will therefore devote a separate section to the A and the B versions of the argument for both the first and the second paralogisms, and explain why I think the changes from A to B do not indicate a shift in Kant's view.[19] Having done that groundwork, in Chapter 6 I will allow myself to offer only one version of Kant's argument in the third paralogism, reconstructed from a combined interpretation of the A and the B versions.

5.2.1 The First Paralogism in A

In the *Jäsche Logic*, Kant calls 'fallacies' (*Trugschlüsse*) inferences that appear to be valid when in fact their form is defective. He lists different kinds of such fallacies, among which is the *sophisma figurae dictionis*, a syllogistic inference that is apparently valid but in fact invalid because its middle term has a different meaning in the major and in the minor premise.[20] The paralogisms of rational psychology, he explains in the *Critique* (in both A and B) are fallacies of that kind: they appear valid, but they trade on an equivocation on the middle term. They thus belong to the kind of logical fallacy he calls *sophisma figurae dictionis*.[21] Such a sophism qualifies as a paralogism when its author deceives not only others, but even herself. In the case of the paralogisms of pure reason, the self-deception is rooted in the very nature of human reason. Finally, Kant makes clear that there is at least one sense in which both premises of the paralogism are true (A402).[22] The fallacy does not lie in the falsity of the premises but in the fact that what apparently counts as a middle term is in fact no middle term at all. The inference, says Kant, is "invalid in its form."

Any analysis of the Paralogisms, in both A and B, will therefore have to be consistent with these three aspects of Kant's description: each paralogism has a seductive force that stems from "having its ground in the nature of human reason"; each inference is apparently valid, but in fact invalid due to an equivocation on the middle term; in each inference, there is at least one sense in which both premises are true.

In A, Kant states the first paralogism as follows:

That the representation of which is the **absolute subject** of our judgments and hence cannot be used as determination of another thing, is **substance**.

I, as a thinking being, am the **absolute subject** of all my possible judgments, and this representation of myself [*von Mir selbst*] cannot be used as predicate of other things.

So I, as a thinking thing (soul), am substance. (A348)

5.2.1.1 COMMENTS ON THE MAJOR PREMISE

The major premise is endorsed as true both by Kant and by any rationalist metaphysician raised in the Aristotelian tradition. Substance is that in which essential and accidental properties inhere. In a judgment, the relation that properly maps the relation between substance and accident is the relation between the subject-concept and the predicate-concept. Indeed, this relation is definitional of the concept of substance.[23] Of course, logical operations of conversion can always reverse the position of subject and predicate and place the concept of the property in the position of subject, the concept of the substance in the position of predicate, as in the example cited by Kant (see B128-9): the proposition 'All bodies are divisible' properly represents the relation between substances (bodies) and what we would call a dispositional property (divisible). But a simple conversion rule may transform the judgment into: "Some divisible things are bodies."[24] Nevertheless, the relation in judgment that properly maps the ontological relation is that in which substance is represented by the subject-concept, property (accidental or essential) is represented by the predicate concept in the proposition, since subject is that *of which* something is asserted and predicate is that which is asserted of something. So the proper representation of the ontological relation between 'body' and 'divisible' is that in which 'body' is in the position of subject, 'divisible' in the position of predicate.

Because of this fundamental mapping of the concept of subject in the proposition onto that of substance, Kant, like the rationalist metaphysicians, often calls the substance itself 'subject.' It is a metaphysical subject, or substrate of properties and changing states. As I noted in 5.1.4 and as we shall see confirmed in our analysis of the first paralogism, this creates an ambiguity in the use of the term 'subject' that does not facilitate attempts to understand Kant's argument.

Now an entity may count as a substance only in a relative sense. For instance, the piece of wax, in Descartes's Second Meditation, counts as substance with respect to its changing shapes, odors, colors, sounds. But wax is really only a state of some more fundamental substrate or metaphysical subject: it is a composite of fundamental particles (a 'mode' in the vocabulary of early modern metaphysics). Any such composite is substance only in a relative sense. A substance that is not itself the temporary state (or mode) of a more fundamental entity or entities would be a substance "in the absolute sense." Only a substance "in the absolute sense" is substance properly speaking.[25] This is what the major premise asserts. Note in particular the modal "cannot": that whose representation *cannot* be used (namely: used in a judgment or proposition) as the predicate of something else, is substance. The modal is a normative modal: even if it is not grammatically or even logically impossible to use the concept of a substance in predicate position, the use that properly represents the relation between substance and its attributes, accidents, and modes, is that in which the substance-concept is in subject position rather than used as predicate of something else. What justification might be available to claim of any entity that it is substance, much less substance in this absolute sense, is a different matter, which we can set aside for now.

What we cannot set aside is the ambiguity in Kant's use of the term 'of' in "that whose representation is the absolute subject *of* our judgments."[26] In my explanation I have assumed that by 'subject of our judgment' Kant meant 'subject *in* our judgment,' namely subject-concept in the propositional content of our act of judging. This assumption is justified by the fact that Kant is talking about *the representation of* something, not the represented something itself. And he is talking about the *use* we make of that representation: ascribing it the place of subject, not predicate, in the propositional content of our judgment. Now of course 'subject of our judgment' might also mean the *metaphysical* subject, the entity that bears the act of judging as one of its properties or states or actions. It seems clear that Kant is not using the expression 'subject of' in this second sense in the major premise, however, since he talks of the *representation's* being the subject of our judgment. But the ambiguity remains, and is reinforced when we look at the minor premise.

5.2.1.2 COMMENTS ON THE MINOR PREMISE

In the first half of the minor premise, it seems obvious that 'subject of' should be interpreted in the second, ontological sense. "I, as thinking, am the absolute subject of all my judgments." How could we possibly understand this sentence otherwise than as: "I am the (absolute) metaphysical subject or substrate of which the act of judging is an actualized power"? But the second half of the sentence cancels this interpretation: "And this representation of myself cannot be used as predicate of other things." This takes us back to the first, logical interpretation: the *concept* 'I,' insofar as it refers to myself as a thinking being, can only be used in judgment as subject, and not as predicate of other things.

But why is that? Surely I am not the absolute subject *in* all my possible judgments? Tobias Rosefeldt proposes to interpret the sentence as meaning: "I am the absolute subject in all the possible judgments *in which 'I' appears*."[27] 'I' cannot appear in judgments otherwise than as subject, it cannot appear as predicate of something else. Now this is certainly true, but such an interpretation does not account for the fact that Kant expressly specifies "I, *as a thinking being*, am the absolute subject" (emphasis mine). Kant has something more specific in mind than Rosefeldt's interpretation suggests. Kant clearly means: "In the judgment 'I think', 'I' cannot be present otherwise than as subject, and cannot be predicated of something else." To understand what Kant makes of this statement, we need to return to the role of 'I think' in the argument of the Transcendental Deduction of the Categories.

In Chapters 2 and 4, I suggested that, according to Kant's argument in the Transcendental Deduction, thinking any proposition 'p' to be true is at the same time being in a position to think 'I think p,' a conceptual representation of the activity of synthesizing the manifolds presented to the senses, and of analyzing those synthesized manifolds into concepts, which are then bound in judgments. But this means that any act of judging, which yields a judgment or proposition as the content of the act of judging, puts me in a position to use the concept 'I' as "the absolute subject" in the proposition 'I think' *and thereby* to think of myself as the absolute subject, in the metaphysical sense, of my judgment. In other words, the ambiguity in the use of the term 'subject' that was present in the major premise is not only confirmed in the minor premise but also, if we refer back to the Deduction, explained. The concept 'I' is the absolute (logical) subject of the proposition 'I think,' a proposition that expresses my consciousness of an act of synthesis and analysis I ascribe to myself. But having and using that concept, I am thereby inclined to think of myself as the absolute *metaphysical* subject of all my acts of judging.

5.2.1.3 WHERE IS THE PARALOGISM?

Here's the situation we have so far: the major premise offers a characterization of the concept 'substance' that is a definition of that concept: that whose representation *cannot be used* as the predicate of something else, is substance. The minor premise predicates the subject-concept in the major premise, of the subject-concept in the minor premise. And that predication is true: 'I,' in 'I think' (the representation of myself, as thinking), *cannot be used* as predicate but only as subject in the proposition 'I think.' The inference to the conclusion seems valid: I, as a thinking being (namely as that whose representation is 'I,' used as the subject-concept in the proposition 'I think') am substance. Where is the paralogism?

Here it is worth looking at Kant's comments.[28]

Kant starts by reminding us of the lesson gained from the Transcendental Analytic: pure concepts of the understanding (categories) have no objective significance, namely no reference to a possible or actual object, unless a sensible intuition is subsumed under them, an intuition to which they can be applied as functions of synthesis of the manifold. Absent such an intuition, categories remain just what they are so long as they belong merely to the understanding: they are functions of judging without any content. According to such functions, says Kant, of any entity at all I can say that it is substance, and by this I mean only that I assign its concept the position of subject in my judgment, and distinguish it from what I think as its determinations, thought under the predicates of my judgments. Moreover, as I recalled above,[29] strictly speaking that alone is substance in the proper sense of the term or "absolute substance" (rather than mere *compositum substantiale*), whose representation (namely whose concept) can *only* properly occupy the position of subject-concept and *not* that of predicate-concept in the relevant judgment. But if we do not have the criterion in intuition that justifies taking a particular object as substance (that whose concept can *only* be subject, and not predicate, in our judgment), then the concept remains empty: no object whatsoever is known to fall under it.

Now this is just what happens with our use of the concept 'I' in the proposition 'I think.' As I just recalled from Kant's argument in the Transcendental Deduction, 'I' is merely *thought* as subject, albeit necessarily so, and indeed as absolute subject with respect to the predicate 'think.' This position of 'I' as necessarily subject, and not predicate, is not justified by any intuition or experience of permanence, but only by the role of 'I' as referring, *for* the thinking being, in any instance of its thinking 'I think,' to that very thinking being, conscious of being engaged in the activity of thinking, the outcome of which she assesses as valid or invalid, true or false.[30]

But if the concept taken to be necessarily subject not predicate is just as purely intellectual in the major and in the minor premise, where is the paralogism? Let me reformulate the inference again, making its AAA form even more explicit:[31]

> Everything whose representation can only be absolute subject, and cannot be predicate in our judgment, is substance.
> I, as thinking, am such that my representation ('I,' in 'I think') can only be absolute subject and cannot be used as predicate in my judgment ('I think').
> So I, as thinking, am substance.

Where is the invalidity "due to form"? Why is the inference invalid?

When, after criticizing all four paralogisms of pure reason, Kant explains the generic fallacy of the rationalist inferences, he says the following (for ease of reference I have identified by bracketed letters the crucial points in Kant's comments).

> If one wants to give a logical title to the paralogism in the dialectical syllogisms of the rationalist doctrine of the soul, insofar as they have correct premises, then it can count as a

sophisma figurae dictionis, in which [a] the major premise makes a merely transcendental use of the category, in regard to its condition, but in which [b] the minor premise and the conclusion, in respect of the soul that is subsumed under this condition, make an empirical use of the same category. [c] Thus e.g., the concept of substance in the paralogism of substantiality[32] is a pure intellectual concept, which in the absence of conditions of sensible intuition is merely of transcendental use, i.e., of no use at all. But in the minor premise [d] the very same concept is applied to the object of all inner experience, yet [e] without previously securing and establishing as a ground the condition of the application [of the concept], namely the persistence[of the object], [f] so that an empirical but improper [*unzulässiger*] use is made of the category. (A402-3)[33]

In [a] and[c], Kant claims that in the major premise a "merely transcendental use" and thus "no use at all" is made of the category (in this case the category of substance). In other words, the use of the category spins in the void. Saying that a "merely transcendental use" is "no use at all" should remind us of what Kant said in the Transcendental Analytic, in the chapter on the Schematism of the Pure Concepts of the Understanding (A146-7/B185-7) and in the chapter on Phenomena and Noumena (A238-41/B297-300): absent schemata relevant to each of them, that is to say, absent the rules for synthesizing sensible intuitions (and so, here, the schema of permanence), the categories have no application to objects at all.

The pure concepts of the understanding can **never** be of **transcendental**, but **always** only of **empirical** use, and ... the principles of pure understanding can be related to objects of the senses only in relation to the general conditions of a possible experience, but never to things in general (without taking regard of the way in which we might intuit them. (A246/B303)

Now in [b], Kant says that an "empirical use" is made of the category. This is surprising: according to the Transcendental Analytic, an "empirical use" of the category is a use in which the category—any category—is used in application to an object of experience through the mediation of a schema, a rule for the synthesis of a manifold of intuition. In the case of the category of substance, that schema is the distinction between what is permanent (the substance) and what changes (the alteration of the substance, the succession of its states). But now Kant claims, in [e], that no permanent entity, persisting through the changes of its states, is available in experience when we use the concept 'I.' When we apply the concept of substance to the object thought under the concept 'I,' the concept is applied "without previously securing and establishing as a ground the condition of the application [of the concept] *in concreto*, namely the permanence [of the object]" (A403). So how is this use of the category "empirical," if it is not grounded on the schema of the concept of substance, the rule distinguishing the permanence of an object from its changing states?

This is explained by [d]: the concept is then applied to "the object of all inner experience." Now recall the introductory section of the Paralogisms of Pure Reason, where Kant said: "I, as thinking, am the object of inner sense and am called 'soul.' As such I am distinct from the object of outer sense, called 'body.' A rational doctrine of the soul is a doctrine in which "nothing empirical is mixed" (A342/B400) except "the inner experience" that grounds the proposition 'I think.' As I explained in 4.3.2.2, what Kant calls here "inner experience" should more properly be called "indeterminate empirical intuition, that is to say, a perception" (B423). It is in virtue of being grounded on such an indeterminate empirical intuition that the proposition 'I think,' when asserted rather than just entertained "problematically," contains, according to Kant, the proposition 'I exist.' 'I think,' when it is not merely problematic, but assertoric, is not *purely* conceptual. Otherwise it could neither entail nor analytically contain an assertion of existence.[34]

But why not say, then, that this "inner experience" gives us just the permanent object that justifies the application of the category of substance? The reason is that all we have by way of empirical ground for the (assertoric) proposition 'I think' is an affection or impression of inner sense. For it to give us access to a permanent object, whether in an absolute or even in a merely relative sense, we would need the presence of the affection to be complemented by a determinate *experience* of the succession of thinking states, and this is possible only if we also have an intuition of objects in space, including our own body. Only spatial intuition allows us to experience the continued existence of an object while its states change and while our perceptions of it (our intentional perceptual states) continuously change. We do not have such an experience of persistence in the case of the "mere object of inner sense," the object for the concept 'I,' even though with each instance of thinking 'I think,' the *existence* of the thinker is attested, for the thinker, by the fact that she "affects" herself with her act of thinking and thus "feels" her own existence in inner sense.[35]

The affection of inner sense gives an immediate access to *existence*, that is to say, an immediate awareness of one's own existence. But that awareness is not sufficient to determine *what kind of existence* is thereby accessed: that of a substance, or of a contingent composite of substances only the composition of which yields the thought 'I think,' or of an accident of a substance. Thus, in applying the concept of substance to the object thought under the concept 'I,' Kant concludes, "an empirical but improper use is made of the category" (A403). It is empirical because it applies the concept to an *existing* entity, whose existence is attested, as any existence is, by the fact that it affects the thinker. It is improper, or illegitimate, because the condition for applying the category of substance to an existing thing—the cognition of its being permanent while its states change—is absent.

But again, none of this explains why the inference reconstructed by Kant is a paralogism in the form of a *sophisma figurae dictionis*. After all, the subject-concept of the major premise ("—whose representation is the absolute subject of my judgment and cannot be predicate of something else") is the predicate concept of the minor premise ("[I am such that] —the representation of me ('I') is the absolute subject of my judgment ('I think') and cannot be predicate of something else"). That concept in both premises is a pure concept of the understanding, or a mere form of thought (the representation can only occupy the place of subject in the judgment), deprived of its schema. The major premise asserts that, necessarily, anything thought under that concept is a substance. In the minor premise, the subject-concept of the major premise is said to be true of a particular, existing thing, the entity thought under the concept 'I' in 'I think' ("I, as thinking"). The inference is valid: necessarily, the predicate of the major premise applies to the subject of the minor premise.

One possible solution is to say that the paralogistic nature of the inference lies in the transition from the minor premise to the conclusion. In the major premise, the concept of "substance" that is predicated of "that whose representation can only be absolute subject in our judgments" is a purely intellectual concept. It *does not say anything more* than what is already said in the subject-concept. The statement, as I said earlier, is just definitional of the concept of substance. Thus, it does not tell us anything at all of any existing object unless it is applied under the justifying condition provided by the schema of permanence—recognizing an object as permanent while its states change. In the minor premise, the concept 'I' falls under the concept 'something whose representation is the absolute subject in all my judgments,' but no permanent entity is presented as the object falling under the concept 'I.' So even though we do know that entity to exist, we have no justification for asserting that it is a substance. For absent the condition of permanence, the syntactic and logical property of the representation 'I' (it can only occupy the subject place in all our judgments, and specifically in the judgment 'I think') tells us nothing at all about the ontological status of the existing entity thought under the concept. But the *existing entity*, not its concept, is what the conclusion is talking about: "So I, as thinking, [and so, as an existing entity], am substance." Thus, the concept of 'substance' predicated of it tacitly includes its condition of application to an existing entity: the schema of permanence.[36]

In other words, strictly speaking, the valid inference would be:

MP That which is represented by a concept that can only be absolute subject, not predicate in our judgments, is represented by the concept of substance, as a pure concept of the understanding (subject in the logical function of categorical judgment).
mP I, as thinking, am represented by the concept 'I,' a concept that can only be absolute subject, not predicate in my judgments.
C   So I, as thinking, am represented (I represent myself to myself) under the concept of substance, as a pure concept of the understanding (subject in the logical function of categorical judgment).

And this is valid. But it tells me nothing about what I *am*. It tells me that, necessarily, I think of myself under the concept of substance. Thinking, however, doesn't make it so.

Now instead of this valid inference, the rationalist metaphysician, and each of us insofar as we think of ourselves as thinkers, are drawn to the following invalid inference:

MP That which is represented by a concept that can only be absolute subject, not predicate, in our judgments, is represented by the concept of substance, as a pure concept of the understanding (subject in the logical function of categorical judgment).
mP I, as thinking, am represented by the concept 'I,' a concept that can only be absolute subject, not predicate in my judgments.
C* So I, as thinking, am substance.

The error here is precisely to have moved from the way in which, necessarily, I represent myself (I think about myself), to the way I exist—as if thinking made it so. Under this scenario, the paralogism lies in the transition from the major and the minor premise, both true and both making a purely intellectual use of the concept "represented by a concept that can only be absolute subject and cannot be used as predicate," to a conclusion that moves from "—am represented by a concept of substance, as a pure concept of the understanding (logical function of judgment)" to "—am (exist as) substance."

For this second inference to be valid, we would need to have talked all along, in both the major and the minor premise, of a concept that can only occupy the position of subject in judgments *justified by intuition and experience*: in judgments *in which the use of the concept of substance is justified by the presence in experience of its schema, permanence*. In other words, the conclusion is invalid because it sneaks into the use of the concept of substance the supposition of an underlying schema of permanence that has been absent from both the major and the minor premise. This invalid move is indicated quite explicitly by Kant:

> In all our thinking the I is the subject, in which thoughts inhere only as determinations, and this I cannot be used as the determination of another thing. Thus everyone must necessarily regard Himself as substance, but regard his thinking only as accidents of his existence and determinations of his states.
>
> But now what sort of use must I make of this concept of a substance? That I, as a thinking being, **endure** for myself, that I naturally **neither arise** nor **perish**—this I can by no means infer, and it is for that alone that the concept of the substantiality of my subject can be useful to me: without that I could very well dispense with it altogether. (A349; Kant's emphasis)

I cannot deduce permanence from the inference just laid out, and so I cannot deduce *any* use of the concept of substance *in the real sense*, as applied to an existing object, even though in the case of the concept 'I,' and in this case alone, in using a purely intellectual concept I *am* thinking of an existing entity.

Because, in criticizing the conclusion of the inference, Kant insists that one cannot *conclude* the permanence of an object from the merely intellectual use of the concept of substance, Karl Ameriks maintains that Kant's real target in the first Paralogism in A is *not* the assertion that the soul is a substance, but rather the assertion that the soul is persistent and thus immortal.[37] If I am correct in the analysis I just proposed, this is a mistake. Kant's target in the first Paralogism in A is the idea that from the use of 'I' in 'I think' one can derive the claim that as a thinking being considered merely as such, I am substance. We cannot derive from the use of 'I' *any* kind of argument to the effect that 'I,' in 'I think,' refers to something that exists as an absolute subject rather than as the mere state or mode of a substance or substances. Kant is quite explicit about this in the recapitulation of his criticism of the Paralogisms in A. He asks: why do we want a doctrine of the soul grounded on pure rational principles? And he replies: we think we need it in order to prevent the danger of materialism. But the fact is, he counters, that we do not need such a doctrine to escape the danger of materialism. For "our rational concept of a thinking self [*eines denkenden Selbst*: the referent of the concept 'I' in 'I think']"[38] does the job much more effectively.

> For according to it, so little fear remains that if one took matter away then all thinking and even the existence of thinking beings would be abolished, that it rather shows clearly that if I were to take away the thinking subject, the whole corporeal world would have to disappear, since the

latter is nothing but the appearance in the sensibility of our subject and one kind of its representations.

Thereby of course I obviously cognize this thinking self [*dieses denkende Selbst*] no better as to its properties, nor can I have any insight into its persistence, *or even the independence of its existence from whatever transcendental substrate of outer appearances there may be; for the latter is just as unknown to me as the former.* (A383–4; my emphasis)

Clearly, here, it is not just the persistence, it is the very ontological status of the referent of 'I' in 'I think,' the "thinking self," either as dependent on a substrate, whatever that substrate is, or as being itself the substrate on which everything else depends—it is that ontological status that remains unknown on the basis of the mere thought 'I' in 'I think.' Of course, Kant immediately adds that this ignorance at least leaves open the possibility that on other grounds I might "hope for an existence of my thinking nature that is self-sufficient and persisting through all possible changes of my states" (A383). Nevertheless, it remains that no resource in support of this view (or, for that matter, against it) can be derived from the mere use of 'I' in 'I think' or from the "indeterminate perception" that supports that use.

5.2.1.4 ANOTHER WAY TO GO

Now a more helpful way to make clear the paralogistic nature of the rationalist argument would have consisted in saying that the major premise makes a true statement about existing objects only if those objects satisfy the condition of application of the category of substance: if they persist while their states change. We would have to reformulate the major premise as:

> **MP**** That whose representation, *in virtue of the way it is presented in intuition*, can only be absolute subject in our judgment, and not predicate of something else, is substance.

Now the condition stated by the subject-concept in the major premise is not satisfied any more by the entity that is thought under the concept 'I' in 'I think,' even though the concept 'I' is such that it can occupy only the position of subject in the proposition 'I think,' and even though we know its referent to exist. But once one keeps in view the condition under which alone the concept of substance can be applied to actually existing objects, then the subject-concept in the major premise is only apparently the same concept as the predicate concept in the minor premise, and the inference becomes paralogistic not just in its conclusion (as it was in the original formulation in A), but in the equivocation on the middle term. Such a formulation of the paralogism would have been true to Kant's criticism of the rationalist view in the A edition, and it is in fact the formulation Kant adopts in B, which decisively clarifies the nature of his argument in all four paralogisms. I now turn to the first paralogism as stated in B.

5.2.2 The First Paralogism in B

5.2.2.1 KANT'S STATEMENT OF THE PARALOGISM IN B

In the B edition, Kant does not lay out explicitly the (fallacious) syllogisms that are supposed to ground the claims rationalist metaphysicians make about the soul. Rather, he lays out in four quick paragraphs the ways in which the position of 'I,' and thus its role in the proposition 'I think,' is translated into an illusory *content* of that representation, which is then supposed to reflect *objective features* of a purported object of knowledge: the soul. It is worth noting that this translation is exactly the transition, in the paralogism expounded in A, between the statement of the minor premise and that of the conclusion. According to the minor premise in A, the concept 'I' could only be used as subject not predicate in the judgment 'I think,' and this gave rise to the invalid conclusion that the *referent* of 'I' was a metaphysical subject, a substance. Now in B, Kant initially skips the full exposition of the fallacious syllogism and just expounds the slide from the (logical) use of 'I' to the fallaciously inferred metaphysical status of the referent of 'I.' Only after the exposition of the four fallacious transitions along this general line does he set up an inference in the form of a full syllogism, which makes explicit the major premise that seemingly grounds the transition from a logical point about 'I' to a metaphysical point about the referent of 'I.'[39]

Here's the paragraph that expounds the rationalist's transition from the claim that 'I' can only be used as logical subject, and not as predicate of something else, to the (fallaciously inferred) claim that I, as thinking, am a substance. I have added letters in brackets again to help identify the main steps of Kant's reasoning in this paragraph.

[a] In every judgment I am always the **determining** subject of the relation that constitutes the judgment. Now, that [b] I, who think [*Ich, der ich denke*], must in thinking always count as **subject**, and cannot be considered as something that is attached to thinking as a predicate, [c] is an apodictic and even an **identical proposition**; but [d] it does not mean that I, as **object**, am for myself [*für mich selbst*] a **subsisting** [*bestehendes*] **being**, or substance. [e] The latter goes very far and thus also demands data that are not at all encountered in thinking, perhaps (insofar as I consider merely what thinks as such) more than I will ever encounter anywhere (in it). (B407; Kant's emphasis; translation modified)[40]

[a], [b], and [c] make the same point as does the minor premise laid out in the A edition. Indeed, [a] is almost word for word the repetition of the first half of the minor premise in A. [b] and [c] develop the point and make even more explicit that what is in view here is the logical position and thus the role of the concept 'I.' But we also find the same ambiguity as in the A edition in the formulation of the point. To say (as in sentence [a]) that I am the absolute subject of the relation that constitutes the judgment might mean that [a_1] I am the metaphysical subject *of* the act of judging, or that [a_2] the concept 'I' is the subject-concept *in* the judgment. But Kant's new formulation of the point makes it even clearer than it was in the A edition that Kant means [a_2]. For "the relation that constitutes the judgment" (or proposition) is the relation of subject and predicate. I am, or rather the concept 'I' is the subject-concept in that relation. But it is also true that, in virtue of this position of the subject-concept 'I,' I (the referent of 'I' in the occurrent thought 'I think') think of myself as the subject, that is to say, the bearer or the agent of the thinking activity.

According to [c], the whole statement [b] "is an apodictic and even identical proposition." The "identical proposition" is that "I must, in thinking, always count as subject and as something that cannot be considered as predicate that is attached to thinking." Necessarily, in 'I think,' 'think' must count as the predicate of 'I' and not 'I' as the predicate of 'think.' What is "analytic," indeed "identical" here? One way to put the point would be to say that it is analytically contained in the very proposition

'I think,' in virtue of its form, that in it 'I' is subject and 'think' is predicate. Since, as we saw, Kant sometimes hesitates on the question whether he should call 'I think' a concept or a proposition, this is a plausible interpretation: it is analytic to 'I think' (concept? proposition? The concept of the proposition 'I think'?) that in it, 'I' is subject and 'think' predicate.

[d] is the dismissal of the conclusion that was attributed to the rationalist metaphysician in the A edition: *pace* the rationalist metaphysician, it is not the case that, from the fact that 'I' *must* count as absolute subject-concept and *cannot be* predicate in the proposition 'I think,' I can legitimately derive that I, as an entity (Kant now says "as object": I'll comment on this term below), am substance. The derivation of my being substance would need another justification than that provided by the position of 'I' in the proposition 'I think.' The nature of the justification that is needed, but missing, is hinted at, but not fully spelled out, in [e]: the justification would consist in "data that are not encountered in thinking," indeed that are "perhaps (insofar as I consider merely what thinks as such) more than I will ever encounter anywhere (in it)."

The missing justification is further explained only after Kant has laid out the four fallacious transitions from logical features of 'I' to purported properties of the referent of 'I' (repeating in each case, sometimes word for word, the fallacious transition from the minor premise to the conclusion of the relevant paralogism in A—at least for the second and third paralogisms). After expounding those four fallacious transitions, Kant offers one syllogism which, he says, "governs the procedure of rational psychology." The fallacy is then clearly located in an equivocation on the middle term, rather than (as in A) being pushed down to the transition between minor premise and conclusion.

Unsurprisingly, that fundamental syllogism is the paralogism of substantiality. This is not surprising because the first question to ask is: what kind of entity am I, substance, or state or mode of a substance? Then one can ask what properties that entity has: simple, identical through time, distinct or not from the body (the next three invalid transitions from 'I' to metaphysical entity in B, laid out as transitions from minor premise to conclusion in A, with the difference already noted where the fourth paralogism is concerned).

Here's how Kant now lays out the fundamental paralogism and his refutation of it.

What cannot be thought otherwise than as subject does not exist otherwise than as subject, and is therefore substance.

Now a thinking being, considered merely as such, cannot be thought otherwise than as subject.

Therefore it also exists only as such a thing, i.e., as substance. (B410–11; Kant's emphasis)

Kant explains:

The major premise talks about a being that can be thought of, in every respect, and consequently also as it may be given in intuition. But the minor premise talks of this same being only *insofar as it considers itself* [*sofern es sich selbst ... betrachtet*] as subject, *only relative to thinking and the unity of consciousness*, but not at the same time in relation to the intuition through which it is given as object for thinking. Thus the conclusion is drawn *per sophisma figurae dictionis*, hence by means of a deceptive inference.* (B411; translation modified) [* refers to the following footnote:]

> * Thinking [*das Denken*] is taken in an entirely different signification in the two premises: in the major premise, as it applies to an object in general (hence as it may be given in intuition); but in the minor premise, only as it consists [*besteht*] in the relation to self-consciousness, where, therefore, no object is thought, but only the relation to oneself, as subject [*die Beziehung auf Sich, als Subjekt*] (as the form of thought) [*als die Form des Denkens*]. In the first premise one talks of things that cannot be thought of otherwise than as subjects; but in the second premise one talks not about **things**, but about **thinking** [*vom Denken*] (in that one abstracts from every object), in which the I always serves as the subject of consciousness [*immer zum Subjekt des Bewusstseins dient*]; hence in the conclusion it cannot follow that I cannot exist otherwise than as subject, but rather only that in thinking my existence I can use myself only as the subject of the judgment [*nur zum Subjekt des Urteils brauchen*], which is an identical proposition, that discloses absolutely nothing about the manner of my existence. (B411n)

The emphasis is different from what it was in A, but I submit the core claims are the same. It is helpful to identify both differences and similarities.

5.2.2.2 ABOUT THE MAJOR PREMISE, COMPARISON OF A AND B

Whereas in A Kant said that in the major premise, a "merely transcendental use, namely no use at all" was made of the category, in B Kant writes that in the major premise "**thinking** is taken ... as it applies to an object in general (hence [*mithin*] as it may be given in intuition)." The reference to intuition is made necessary by the mention of *existence* in the statement of the major premise, which was absent from A. For it to be true that "what cannot be thought otherwise than as subject, does not *exist* otherwise than as subject, and is therefore substance," a condition must be satisfied: that the existence of the object be *presented in* intuition in such a way that the object cannot be thought otherwise than as subject; and, more specifically, that the object be experienced as something permanent whose states change. Only then does the concept have *any use at all*—as the Schematism chapter and the chapter on Phenomena and Noumena asserted.[41] Of course, Kant's point is that the rationalist metaphysician, too, assumes this condition to be satisfied when he states as the major premise that "what *cannot be thought otherwise than* as subject *does not exist otherwise than* as subject" and thus "is substance." But the rationalist leaves this condition (only *that which persists while its states change* can be thought only as subject not as predicate of something else, and thus *exists* as a substance) merely implicit.[42] The rationalist is thus in no position to notice that the condition is *not* satisfied in the case of our use of the concept 'I.'

5.2.2.3 ABOUT THE MINOR PREMISE AND THE CONCLUSION, COMPARISON OF A AND B

Here the relation between A and B is more puzzling. Whereas in A Kant emphasized, in his analysis of the minor premise, the *empirical* although *improper* [*unzulässig*] use of the concept "absolute subject," in B the term "empirical" has disappeared and the emphasis is on the impossibility of deriving from the position of 'I' in 'I think' any knowledge of the existing entity represented by the concept and word 'I.' This is what Kant means, I submit, when he says that in the minor premise, "**Thinking** is taken... only as it consists in the relation to self-consciousness, where, therefore, no object is thought, but only the relation to oneself, as subject (as the form of thought)." The "form of thought" is the form that the attribution of the predicate 'think' necessarily takes: necessarily, 'think' is, in each instance of thinking, attributed by the thinker to herself, in judgments in which necessarily, 'I' is, with respect to 'think,' subject not predicate. However, this tells us nothing at all with respect to the question: is the entity thereby represented a *real* subject, something that, *in its existence*, is an ultimate subject of determinations rather than the determination of something else? The *existence* of that entity, the referent of 'I,' is not thereby put into question. But to the question, *what kind of entity* is that referent?—to that question no answer can be offered on the mere basis of the nature of the representation 'I' in 'I think.'[43]

In short, despite the difference in emphasis between the two versions of the first paralogism, there is nothing in Kant's reconstruction of the rationalist fallacy in B that contradicts his reconstruction of it in A. One possible reason Kant left out the words "empirical" and "inner experience" in his B explanation is that he took them to be potentially misleading: neither of them has in this context the meaning they have when they are employed in connection with knowledge *of objects* given in intuition.

The lesson of Kant's criticism in both A and B, then, is that there is a striking disconnect between the way, necessarily, each thinker thinks about herself, on the one hand; and what she *knows* of herself, on the other. As we shall now see, that disconnect only grows as we progress through the Paralogisms. If this analysis is correct, its upshot is that the power of Kant's argument in debunking the rationalist paralogism lies primarily in the contrast between the third-person, objective standpoint of the major premise and the conclusion, and the exclusively first-person, subjective standpoint of the minor premise. The major premise, as restated in B, asserts that we are justified in taking the way we cannot but think of something, to be an indication of the way that something *is*. Such a move is legitimate only if *the way the thing is given in intuition and experience* grounds the way we cannot but think about it. And the way a thing is given in intuition and experience is precisely what the minor premise does not provide. Nevertheless, the minor premise expresses a way each of us, as a thinking being, *cannot but think about herself* when engaged in thinking. Since, in thinking, we also know ourselves to exist, the first-person standpoint is an all too fertile terrain for the errors of rational metaphysics.

I now turn to the second paralogism, in which the lack of fit between the way in which, necessarily, each thinker thinks of herself, and what she can *know* about herself, is, if anything, even more apparent than in the first paralogism, and at the same time reveals important aspects of the use of 'I' in our mental life.[44]

5.3 "The Second Paralogism, of Simplicity"

5.3.1 *The Second Paralogism in A*

The statement of the paralogism in A is as follows:

That thing whose action can never be regarded as the concurrence of many acting things, is simple.

Now the soul, or the thinking I, is such a thing.
Thus etc. (A351)

As is often the case, Kant is rather cavalier about following through on the argumentative structure he has set up: his formulation of the minor premise is less than satisfactory ("... is such a thing") and his formulation of the conclusion is non-existent ("Thus etc."). It will help to fill in the blanks.

Replacing, in the minor premise, "the soul, or the thinking I" by 'I, as thinking,' and completing the formulation of the predicates in the minor premise and the conclusion, we get:

MP_{sim}: Something whose action can never be regarded as the concurrence of many acting things, is simple.
mP_{sim}: I, as thinking, am something whose action can never be regarded as the concurrence of many acting things.
C_{sim}: So I, as thinking, am simple.

Let us now examine the major and the minor premise.

5.3.1.1 THE MAJOR PREMISE

If we apply to the paralogism of simplicity Kant's general explanation of the rationalist fallacy in A, we can say that "the major premise makes a merely transcendental use" of the concept of simplicity, "namely no use at all."[45] We saw what this means in the case of 'substance.' What does it mean in that of 'simplicity'? It means, I suggest, that what is under consideration in the major premise is the purely intellectual concept 'simple,' which means 'not composed of parts.' Moreover, the predicate 'simple' is attributed to the subject 'something that acts.' We thus get the statement: 'something whose action cannot be regarded as the composition of the actions of many things, is simple (is not a composite of things).' Both the rationalist and Kant endorse such a statement. For both accept that the action of a composite is the composition of the actions of its components. So if a thing's action *cannot be* regarded as the composition of the actions of many things, then it is not a composite, it is simple—indivisible. Kant offers that explanation for the major premise, in the form of a contraposition, immediately after the statement of the paralogism:

Every **composite** substance is an aggregate of many, and the action of a composite, or of that which inheres in it as such a composite, is an aggregate of many actions or accidents, which is distributed among the multitude of substances. (A351)

He immediately goes on to state that this composition is easy to empirically pick out in the case of things external to one another in space:

Now of course an effect that arises from the concurrence of many acting substances is possible if this effect is merely external (as, e.g., the movement of a body is the united movement of all its parts). (A352)

Now the rationalist view is that such a composition is impossible in the case of thinking. One thought (or one thinking) *cannot be* a composite of several separate thoughts (acts of thinking). Unlike motion, the rationalist claims, a thought *cannot* be *one thought* if it is the composition of different thoughts. Suppose a thought were divided into different, separate thoughts, like a line of verse is divided into different words. Then different substances would carry each component of the thought. Then each substance would think just one component of the thought, and the thought itself would not come out *as one thought*. The thinking of the thought has to be one action and thus, by equivalence of unicity of action and unicity of substance, the action of one simple substance.[46] Kant says, in a footnote, "it is easy to give this proof the usual dress of scholastic precision" (A352n). I suggest the "scholastic precision" Kant has in mind is something like: Necessarily, if the action of a thing *is not* (or even better: *cannot be*) the composition of the actions of several things, then the acting thing is not (or even better: *cannot be*) a composite thing. Now—the rationalist inference goes on—one thought (one thinking) *cannot be* the composition of several thoughts. So, it cannot be the thinking of a composite thing. So necessarily, thinking is the action of a simple thing.

But Kant rejects the rationalist claim that the case of thought differs from that of motions. The rationalist claims that unlike motion, which can be the composition of the motions of several things, one act of thinking *cannot be* the composition of the acts of the components of a composite thing, divisible into its parts. This claim, Kant says, is the fallacious interpretation of a true premise, the minor premise of the second paralogism. In his comments immediately following the statement of the second paralogism, Kant first explains why the rationalist's modal statement (a thought *cannot be* the composition of the actions of several things) is unsupported. He then explains under what correct understanding the minor premise nevertheless stands. Let me first consider his negative argument against the rationalist's modal statement. Then we will consider the minor premise, and Kant's comments on it.

The proposition "one thought cannot be the composition of the actions of a multiplicity of things" (and so can only be the action of one, indivisible thing—one substance, as per the first paralogism) is not analytic: it is not contained in the *concept* of thought that one thought (one act of thinking) cannot be a composition of actions and thus the composition of the actions of several things, in just the way a motion can be a composition of motions and thus the composition of the motions of several moving things. Is it, then, synthetic, but still a priori (as its modal force, "cannot be" would require)? If so, what could be its justification? The only possible justification of synthetic a priori propositions has been established in the Transcendental Analytic: a synthetic a priori proposition can be proved to be true only if by proving that its being true is a necessary condition of the possibility of experience and thus of the objects of experience. Of course, the rationalist offers no such argument, and neither does Kant: the proposition "The thought of a thinking thing cannot be the composition of the thoughts of its components" is not one of the principles of pure understanding that are, according to the Transcendental Analytic, the a priori conditions of the possibility of experience. Finally, the proposition is not an empirical proposition: the very fact that it states an *impossibility* indicates that no experience can justify it.[47]

So if the proposition 'one thought (one act of thinking) cannot be the composition of the actions of many thinking things' is justified neither a priori nor empirically, why does the rationalist claim have such a pull on us? Kant's answer is given in his analysis of the minor premise.

5.3.1.2 THE MINOR PREMISE

Kant, like the rationalist, accepts the minor premise, at least if formulated in the way offered above (see 5.3.1: mP_{sim}): "I, as thinking, am something whose action cannot be regarded as the concurrence of many acting things." Now his explanation of the point might trade simply on the feature of 'I' as a first-person singular, just as his explanation of the minor premise in the first paralogism traded on the role of 'I' as logical and grammatical subject in the proposition 'I think.' But in A, he does not rely on the grammatical feature of 'I,' at least not explicitly—the point will come up explicitly only in B.[48] In A, Kant explains *why* 'think' is attributed to a first-person singular by sending us back to the Transcendental Deduction. And, even more emphatically than he did in his analysis of the first paralogism, he contrasts the first-person standpoint we have on ourselves in thinking, with the third-person standpoint we have on objects in general, returning to a point he had made in the general introduction to the paralogisms:

> It is obvious that if one wants to represent a thinking being, one must put oneself in its place, and thus substitute one's own subject for the object one wants to consider (*which is not the case for any other species of investigation* [my emphasis]); and it is also obvious that we demand absolute unity for the subject of a thought only because otherwise it could not be said "I think" (the manifold in a representation). For although the whole of the thought could be divided and distributed among many subjects, the subjective I cannot be divided or distributed, and this I we presuppose in all things.
>
> Here, therefore, as in the previous paralogism, the formal proposition of apperception, **I think**, remains the entire ground on which rational psychology ventures to extend its cognitions. (A354)

This means, then, that when predicated of 'I' the concept 'simple' does not characterize the property of a thing, but just the way we have to think of ourselves, as thinkers, in using the concept 'I' in 'I think.'

> Through the I, I always think an absolute but logical unity of the subject (simplicity) but I do not cognize the real simplicity of my subject. (A356)

I suggest the "absolute but logical unity" of the subject is the unity of the subject-*concept* 'I,' expressed by the grammatical first-person singular pronoun, used in the proposition 'I think,' which expresses the unity of the act of thinking insofar as its contents are systematically connected. The "real simplicity of our subject" would be the metaphysical indivisibility of the *metaphysical* subject that bears the act of thinking. *Thinking* of the (logical) subject-concept as indivisible, and of the act as indivisible, in virtue of the fact that the intentional content of the act is formally one and indivisible, does not give us any clue to the real indivisibility, or lack thereof, of the entity thought under the concept 'I' or to which 'I' refers.

And now we are back in the situation we encountered in the first paralogism: as stated, the inference does not look like a paralogism, where the invalidity of the inference would be explained by the lack of a proper middle term. For the subject-concept in the major premise, "—represented as something whose action can never be regarded as the concurrence of many acting things" is exactly the predicate concept in the minor premise, where it is predicated of 'I.' And in both cases the concept is just this: a concept, without any consideration of the conditions that might make the concept applicable to an actually existing object. And, nevertheless, in applying the concept to 'I' in 'I think,' we appear to make an empirical use of the concept (applying it to an entity whose existence is warranted, for each thinker, by the mere fact of her currently being engaged in the act of thinking). But that application is "improper" since the entity is not given in a determinate intuition.

So, once again, the paralogism seems to occur not in the equivocation on the middle term but in the transition to the conclusion, which applies the concept 'simple' to the referent of 'I,' taken to be a soul: the object of inner sense. If we want to explain the transition as depending on an equivocation on the middle term, we would have to reformulate the paralogism in the following way:

MP_{sim}*: Something whose action can never be regarded, in judgments justified by intuition and experience, as the concurrence of many acting things, is simple.
mP_{sim}*: I, as thinking, am something whose action can never be regarded, in the judgment' I think,' as the concurrence of many acting things.
C*: So I, as thinking, am simple.[49]

Now one can see that the apparent middle term that seems to ground the attribution of simplicity to the soul is in fact no middle term at all: "regarded as" in the major premise includes intuition and experience as the justification for the judgment in which something's action is characterized. But no such justification is offered, in the minor premise, for the judgment ('I think') in virtue of which I am regarded as such that my action (of thinking) cannot be regarded as the concurrence of many acting things. The apparent middle term is thus no middle term at all: the inference is invalid.

This, again, is made clearer in B.

5.3.2 The Second Paralogism in B

Just as for the first paralogism, in B Kant quickly runs through the refutation of the rationalist view rather than laying it out step by step. In the following citation, and as I have done above, for ease of reference I have identified each step with a letter in brackets.

[a] That the I of apperception, consequently in every thought, is **a singular** [*ein Singular sei*] that cannot be resolved into a plurality of subjects, and so refers to [*bezeichne*] a logically simple subject, lies already in the concept of thinking, and is consequently an analytic proposition; [b] but that does not signify that the thinking I is a simple **substance**, which would be a synthetic proposition. The concept of substance is always related to intuitions, which in me cannot be other than sensible, and hence must lie wholly outside the field of understanding and its thinking, which is all that is really under discussion here when it is said that the I in thinking is simple. (B407–8; translation modified.)[50]

Kant adds:

> [c] It would also be miraculous if what otherwise requires so much care in order to distinguish, in what the intuition presents, what is substance; and even more to distinguish whether the latter can be simple (as in the parts of matter)—it would be miraculous if that could be given straight away in the poorest representation of all, as if by a revelation. (B408; translation modified)[51]

[a] is an explanation of what counts in A as the minor premise, which I commented on above. [b] is the denial of what counts as the conclusion, on the grounds that what is thought in [a] (that is, what is thought in the minor premise in the A edition) is not supported by intuition and thus cannot fall under the major premise as I have reformulated it (see mP_{sim} at the end of 5.3.1) along the model given by Kant at B410-11. The reformulated major premise remains implicit, but [c] makes it clear that asserting of any object of knowledge that it is simple would need to be supported by intuition and experience, and not just derived from a concept, let alone "the poorest concept": 'I.' Now as I suggested earlier, it is impossible to find support in intuition for applying the concept of substance in the absolute sense to a particular object: it can always be considered as a *compositum substantiale*, an object that is only relatively permanent with respect to its changing states, rather than a substance in the absolute sense. And now we also have to acknowledge that it is impossible to find support in intuition for applying the concept of simplicity or indivisibility, since the division of space and time, and thus of things as spatiotemporal appearances, can be pursued indefinitely.[52]

5.3.3 *Logical Subject and Subjective 'I'*

In the paralogism of substantiality, Kant argued that necessarily, the entity thought under the concept 'I' is represented as an absolute subject only in a 'logical' sense: in virtue of the logical use of the concept 'I' that refers to that entity rather than in virtue of the way the entity is given in intuition. Similarly, in the paralogism of simplicity, Kant argues that the concept 'I' is only 'logically' simple: it is a logically singular term, which expresses the thinker's consciousness of the logical connectedness of her thoughts. The concept 'I' is such that necessarily, the entity thought under it is thought to be simple (indivisible) in virtue of the fact that necessarily, its action is thought to be indivisibly one.

But the point that is made with renewed force is that this simplicity of the subject of the action is represented only *to that subject itself*: to the entity referring to itself by the concept 'I.' Kant's formulation of the second paralogism thus emphasizes the difference between what we today call the "first-person standpoint" and the "third-person standpoint." Any attempt at objective justification, justification "from a third-person standpoint" of the simplicity of the soul from the thought of the simplicity of the 'I,' is dismissed by Kant.[53] And, nevertheless, from the first-person standpoint, the standpoint of the thinker referred to by 'I,' it is both inevitable *and legitimate* to represent oneself as simple. Kant stresses the contrast between the two standpoints when he describes the concept 'I' as a "subjective" concept. See again the text cited earlier:

It is obvious that if one wants to represent a thinking being, one must put oneself in its place, and thus substitute one's own subject for the object one wants to consider (which is not the case for any other species of investigation); and it is also obvious that we demand absolute unity for the subject of a thought only because otherwise it could not be said: 'I think' (the manifold of representation). For although the whole of the thought could be divided and distributed among many subjects, *the subjective I* cannot be divided or distributed, and this I we presuppose in all thinking. (A353–4)

From an objective standpoint, the entity referred to by 'I' *might be* a divisible thing, a composition of (metaphysical) subjects or, for that matter, a composition of accidents of (metaphysical) subjects. Even if this is the case, *for* the entity referring to herself via the concept 'I' in the proposition 'I think,' not only is the entity referred to by 'I' in 'I think' thereby represented as indivisible, it is also appropriate, indeed indispensable, to represent the action of thinking as indivisible. Ascribing thinking to 'I,' i.e., to oneself represented by the concept 'I' as an indivisible subject of thought, is just the expression of the normative commitment to the unity of thinking, namely its connectedness and consistency ("We *demand* absolute unity for the subject of thought"). This first-person standpoint is not relative to particular subjects. If the argument of the Transcendental Deduction is correct, this "subjective I," namely the representation 'I' by which I refer to myself in thinking, is a universal condition, for any thinking being, of being engaged in the activity of thinking.

5.4 Concluding Remarks

As I suggested at the beginning of this chapter, from Kant's refutation of the first and second paralogisms of pure reason there emerges, beyond the *negative* argument against the claims of rationalist metaphysics, a groundbreaking *positive* account of the role of 'I' in 'I think.' As we saw in the previous chapter, according to that account, there is no possible doubt, *for the 'I'-user*, namely for all of us insofar as we think, that 'I,' used in 'I think,' represents (we would say: refers to) an existing thing. And as we have seen in this chapter, necessarily, the entity thus representing or referring to itself via the representation 'I,' represents *itself* as indivisibly present in all its thoughts. But this first-person standpoint, however universally (subjectively) indispensable to the act of thinking, tells us nothing about the objective nature of the thing that thinks, even though, in thinking, we do know it to exist.

Kant's reasoning in the first two paralogisms thus confirms, I submit, the claim I was making in Chapter 2. The use of 'I' in 'I think' presents a case of immunity to error through misidentification (there is no question of being mistaken in asserting 'think' to be true of the current thinker of the proposition 'I think') that is based solely on the consciousness of the activity of thinking, namely on the consciousness of being myself engaged in bringing rational unity to the mental contents I direct my attention to when I think 'I think p' or even just 'I think.' Should we then take Kant's view to be an ancestor of Anscombe's, according to which 'I' is a non-referential term that just expresses the reflexivity of the activity of thinking? What Kant says is that the predicate 'think' is, by each of us, predicated of a transcendental subject = X that is the referent of the logical subject (the concept 'I' in 'I think')—a transcendental subject we know to exist just in virtue of thinking the thought 'I think.' That the entity represented by 'I' remains thereby unknown does not mean that there is no such entity. Nor does it mean that the entity can be purely and simply identified with what is represented by the predicate 'think' in the judgment 'I think.'[54]

Nevertheless, just as the perception of thinking and (inseparably) of existing remains "indeterminate,"[55] so our consciousness of the entity referred to by 'I' in 'I think' remains indeterminate. 'I think' is an expression of self-consciousness (in Evans's terms: "thinking, by a subject of judgment, about a subject of judgment") and not an expression of self-knowledge. In using 'I' in this context, we need have no knowledge at all about the kind of entity we are, nor indeed any knowledge of our own identity through time as the individual entity we are. For such knowledge to obtain, the consciousness of one's thinking needs to be complemented by the consciousness of one's embodied existence. This point emerges with renewed force from Kant's criticism of the third paralogism, the paralogism of personality, to which I turn in the next chapter.

Notes

1. See 2.2, and 4.2.
2. See 4.3.2.2.
3. Michelle Grier (2001) has convincingly pressed the importance of the distinction between the two main steps in Kant's argument in the Transcendental Dialectic of the *Critique of Pure Reason*. In the first step (book 1 of the Transcendental Dialectic: "On the Concepts of Pure Reason"), Kant claims that reason (our rational capacity) inevitably generates its own brand of *illusions*, or illusory representations. In the second step (book 2 of the Transcendental Dialectic: "The Dialectical Inferences of Pure Reason"), Kant claims that metaphysical errors corresponding to each of the specific illusions of reason result from fallacious inferences in support of the claim that actual objects instantiate those illusory representations. The Paralogisms of Pure Reason (chapter 1 of book 2) are the first type of such fallacious inferences. They seem to ground the claim that I, as thinking, instantiate the illusory concept of a soul as a thinking substance, and moreover as a simple substance, distinct from the body. In the present chapter and the next, I will be discussing these fallacious inferences. I will not be discussing Kant's general theory of the illusions of reason, nor will I discuss the way the particular illusory representation 'soul' relates to Kant's general notion of an illusion of reason. This is because my primary concern is with Kant's analysis of 'I' in 'I think.' Kant's argument in the Paralogisms of Pure Reason is a key component of that analysis. However, as we will see, the relation between the fallacious inference and the general illusion does come up at key points in the argument of the Paralogisms of Pure Reason.
4. See 4.3.1; 6.4, n. 28.
5. "Ein Aktus der Spontaneität der Vorstellungskraft" (B130). Instead of the Latinate '*Aktus*' Kant more often uses the German '*Handlung*.' Kant seems to prefer to use '*Aktus*' when he has in mind the overall unity of all acts of the understanding; see B137, B158. Although for a use of '*Handlung*' even in that case, see A108. On the other hand, Kant prefers to use '*Handlung*' when he is talking of each particular act (of unifying a perceptual content [A99], of producing a representation in imagination [A102], and especially of thinking, i.e., judging [A68/B93]). Of course, given Kant's overall argument, each particular act

(*Handlung*) belongs within the overall "act of the spontaneity of the power of representation."
6. On the relation between logical function of judgments and categories, see Longuenesse 2005, chap. 4.
7. This point will be discussed in detail in Chapter 6. On the consciousness of identity of the act of combination, see Arthur Melnick's illuminating analysis in 2009, esp. chap. 9, II, 119–26.
8. This is Kant's argument in the Refutation of Idealism: see B274–9, and see 4.3.2.3 in this volume.
9. Admittedly, the distinction between *expression* (*Ausdruck*) and *representation* (*Vorstellung*) is not as consistent in Kant's text as the explanation I am offering might suggest. Kant uses the term '*Vorstellung*' to refer to any mental state, whether intentional or not, and whether we are conscious of it or not (see A320/B376–7). This being so, when he says that the 'I think' "expresses" the unity of apperception or that the unity of acts of synthesis is "universally expressed" by the categories, "express" might as well be replaced by "represent." However, I do think that Kant uses "expression" and "express" to refer to a specific kind of representation: the (non-intentional) representation of the act of representing itself, rather than a representation directed at an object. Rosefeldt (2000, 17–22) takes Kant to use "expression" to refer to linguistic representations (sentences and words) and "representation" to refer to the corresponding mental representations (propositions and concepts). This is true in some cases, but not generally and not in the quotes given above in the main text. Generally speaking, Kant claims that without language we would form neither concepts nor judgments, and he does not systematically distinguish between the mental representations and their linguistic formulations. See, for instance, *Jäsche Logic*, §§30–3, AAIX, 109. On my own use of the term 'expression' in accounting for Kant's view, see, 3.1, n. 13; and 4.2, n. 14.
10. A judgment can be an act of judging or the content of that act. Insofar as it is the content of an act of judging, Kant sometimes—not always—distinguishes a judgment (*Urteil*) from a proposition (*Satz*) by their modal qualifier: a judgment is problematic, a proposition is assertoric. Note that the 'I think' that is the "sole text" of rational psychology (A343/B401) is sometimes characterized by Kant as problematic (A347/B405), sometimes as assertoric (B418). It is only when it is assertoric, namely based on the *current perception* that I think, that it "contains" the proposition 'I exist.' See again 4.3.1. I say more about this later in this chapter.
11. Although see, as a counterexample, the statement that immediately follows the one just cited in the main text: "I have an *inner experience* of this proposition, which expresses an inner perception of oneself" (A342–3/B400–1). However, as we shall see, it is crucial to Kant's argument in the Paralogisms that 'I think' expresses an *indeterminate* perception and is *not* a judgment of experience. On this point, see also 4.3.2.2 (the second kind of consciousness of my thinking).
12. So what about the earlier statement: "I think" expresses the *Aktus* of determining my existence? Insofar as my existence is present to me via the *Aktus*, although the presence of that *Aktus* is *perceived* at each instant, that perception remains indeterminate. What I *determine* is the succession of perceptions I experience as my own and whose temporal order I experience by distinguishing it from the temporal order of objects outside me, including the states of my own body. On this last point, cf. 4.3.2.3 (the third kind of consciousness of my thinking). See also Chapter 6.
13. See 2.2. As I showed in 2.2, according to Kant not only is SY → I true, so is I → SY, so that the full statement of the principle is SY ↔ I.

14. Although Evans does not cite this passage, it is no doubt among those he had in mind when he attributed to Kant the view that, absent self-location and consciousness of oneself as an embodied entity, 'I' would be a "merely formal condition of thought" (Evans 1982, 228). See 2.1.4. In Chapter 2, I suggested that *pace* Evans, for Kant, even absent self-location and consciousness of oneself as an embodied entity, in using 'I' in 'I think' the 'I'-user is conscious of herself as an existing entity and even thinks of herself as distinct from any other entity. It is true, however, that passages like the one just cited seem to provide justification for Evans's claim that, absent self-location and consciousness of oneself as embodied, 'I' is a "merely formal condition of thought." My own view (further substantiated in what follows) is that *the unity of apperception* is a "merely formal condition of thought." 'I think,' on the other hand, is a conceptual *expression* of that formal condition, and 'I' is an integral part of that expression.
15. See, for instance, Horstmann 1993; Melnick 2009.
16. What can it possibly mean, to be affected by one's own act, or acts? I suggest it means: to become aware that one is engaged in that act and thus be disposed to locate it in temporal connection with other events in the world. One might object that the consciousness of one's mental actions is a species of action awareness, so that it makes no sense to talk of being *affected* by one's mental action. I would reply that Kant does have room for pure action awareness. This is the first kind of consciousness of one's own thinking I was mentioning in Chapter 4 (see 4.3.2.2, and n. 12 in the present chapter). But I suggest it is actually a deep insight on Kant's part to say that, to this pure action awareness, which is atemporal (as we acknowledge when we say, retrospectively, after having been deeply engaged in our intellectual endeavor: "I lost track of time!"), one should add the "passive" awareness that makes us disposed, when circumstances call for it, to locate our act in time, as an event of which we are aware. I am grateful to Quassim Cassam for pressing me on this point. This is not a complete answer, but it will have to do for now.

    Note that I have repeatedly helped myself to two terms where Kant uses only one. I sometimes say that we are 'aware' of our thinking, and sometimes that we are 'conscious' of our thinking (with the corresponding substantive forms, awareness, and consciousness), where Kant uses only '*bewußt*,' and the corresponding substantive form '*Bewußtsein*.' By states of awareness or states we are aware (of), I generally mean states such that there is "something it is like for us" to be in that state. My use of parentheses around (of) is a reference back to Sartre's notion of non-thetic (self-)consciousness: see 3.1. By states we are "conscious of" I generally mean states that are more complex. A state is something of which we are conscious when it not only has the qualitative feature that characterizes states (of) which we are aware; but it also is bound with other states in such a way that we may become conscious of the intentional object of those states *and* we become conscious of the states themselves, as empirical states and events, located in time with respect to other states and events located in space and time (bodily states). I cannot swear I am consistent in my use of these two terms (awareness, consciousness). I probably sometimes use them interchangeably, as we do in ordinary language. But insofar as I use them to capture a conceptual distinction, that's what the distinction is. I will say more about Kant on consciousness in 7.2.1 and 7.2.3.
17. The distinction is formulated most forcefully in the Transcendental Analytic in the B edition: see B155–6.
18. The other chapter Kant completely rewrote is the Transcendental Deduction of the Categories. In the latter, an important aspect of Kant's reformulation of his argument is the more prominent role given to "the 'I think'," which in turn gives more perspicuous support to the argument of the Paralogisms.

19. In claiming that Kant does not change his view between A and B, I differ from Ameriks (2000) and Horstmann (1993). Both Ameriks and Horstmann argue, albeit on different grounds, that the change in Kant's formulations from A to B does indicate a fairly significant evolution in his view. I will discuss their arguments later in this chapter. I do think that the B version of Kant's argument brings considerable clarification to the core of his criticism of what he takes to be the rationalist argument. Nevertheless, Kant's analysis of each paralogism is more detailed in A than in B. Considering each exposition separately is thus worth our effort.
20. *Jäsche Logic*, §90, AA9, 134–5.
21. See A402–3, B411.
22. Ibid. I say "at least one" because, as we shall see, for the major premise there are two senses in which it might be true.
23. See Aristotle, *Categories* 5, 11–14: "Substance in the truest and strictest, the primary sense of that term is that which is neither asserted of nor can be found in a subject." In Aristotle 1973, 19.
24. Note that Kant's particular judgment ('some S are P') is not our existential proposition. Unlike our existential proposition, particular propositions make no more existential claim than do universal judgments. This explains why a universal judgment such as "all bodies are divisible" can be converted into a particular judgment "some divisibles (divisible entities) are bodies." This would not be possible if the particular judgment had existential import. But a categorical judgment, for Kant, is just a relation of concepts, the extension of which can be either other (lower) concepts, or pure intuitions, or empirical intuitions (representing actually existing entities). About Kant's view of the logical forms of judgment, see Longuenesse 1998, chap. 4, esp. 86–90. About the forms of universal and particular judgment, see ibid., 247–9.
25. According to Kant's argument in the second Antinomy of Pure Reason, given that material things are empirical objects existing in space and time, ultimate components of matter (indivisible corpuscles) are not objects of a possible experience. This partly explains why Kant thinks the rationalist metaphysicians, in search of something that counts as an "absolute subject," resorted to believing that the only kind of entity that can count as "absolute subject," namely substance properly speaking, is something that is *not* spatial: a soul.
26. Note, however, that in the German text the word 'of' is not present. The word 'of' translates the mere genitive form in German: "Subject of our judgments" is in the original German "*Subjekt unserer Urteile.*" But what is ambiguous in the English 'of' is also ambiguous in the grammatical genitive.
27. Rosefeldt 2000, 52.
28. See A348–9.
29. See 5.2.1.1.
30. See 2.2 and 4.2. As I emphasized especially in 2.2, here Kant's analysis of 'I' in 'I think' strikingly anticipates a point that we can today formulate in terms of IEM: the use of 'I' in 'I think' is the surest but also the thinnest case of use of 'I' that is immune to error through misidentification relative to the first-person pronoun. See 2.2.
31. The so-called 'AAA' form, or form in Barbara, of categorical syllogisms is that in which both premises as well as the conclusion are universal. In the *Critique of Pure Reason*, in commenting on his table of logical functions of judgment, Kant notes that in the context of syllogistic inference a singular judgment can be treated as a universal judgment, since *all* of the instantiations of the subject-concept or subject-term in the minor premise fall under the predicate-concept of that premise (see A71/B96). This is why our paralogism can be considered as being in the form of Barbara, or AAA.

136   KANT ON 'I' AND THE SOUL

32. Following Adickes's correction in a footnote to the Meiner edition, I have substituted "substantiality" for "simplicity." The latter clearly seems to be an oversight in Kant's text. See A/B 1971, A403n.
33. I have translated "*unzulässig*" as "improper" rather than "unreliable," the term proposed in the Guyer-Wood translation. As I shall argue in the main text, Kant's point is not just that the use is unreliable. It is that it is improper, or illegitimate: absent an intuition, *no claim can be made at all* that any object is justifiably asserted to fall under the category of substance. I have also altered the Guyer-Wood translation for [e]. The German says, for [e]: "*ohne doch die Bedingung seiner Anwendung in concreto, nämlich die Beharrlichkeit desselben, voraus festzusetzen und zum Grunde zu legen.*" The German text does not say explicitly what "*seiner*" refers back to (the application of what?), nor does it say explicitly what "*desselben*" refers back to (the permanence of what?). But it is clear from the general sense of the passage that the application is that *of the concept* (to which "*seiner*" thus refers back to) and the permanence is that *of the object* (to which "*desselben*" thus refers back to). I have taken the liberty of making these two points explicit by introducing the genitive "of the concept" instead of just the adjective "its" in front of "application" and the genitive "of the object" instead of just the adjective "its" in front of "permanence." But my main correction to Guyer-Wood is to have also made clear that what is grounded, namely justified, is not the permanence (or persistence) of the object, but the application of the concept (which is grounded in, or justified by, the permanence of the object as presented in intuition, or more precisely in the temporal order of intuitions in experience).
34. See my explanations in Chapter 4, especially 4.3.2.2 and 4.4.
35. See again 4.3.2.2.
36. As Karin de Boer has suggested to me, one might account for the paralogistic nature of the inference by saying that the rationalist metaphysician subrepticely introduces the condition of permanence in the minor premise, thus yielding the conclusion: "So I am (or I exist) as substance." This would make the structure of the paralogism truer to Kant's general description of a paralogism, according to which the latter trades on an equivocation on the middle term. But it would also make the minor premise false, even though Kant says explicitly that "both premises are correct" (A402). This is why I submit it is overall preferable to say that in A, the equivocation is introduced in the conclusion. As we shall see, Kant certainly became aware of the problem, and solves it in his new formulation of the general structure of the paralogism in B (see B410–11). I am grateful to Karin de Boer for pressing me to clarify this point.
37. See Ameriks (2000), 68. Wuerth (2010), 210–20, and (2014), chap. 5, defends a similar view and extends it to both editions of the *Critique of Pure Reason*.
38. See 5.1.6 in this chapter.
39. In other words, in B the syllogistic (paralogistic) inference is offered in the form of an enthymeme, namely an inference in which one of the premises (the major premise) remains implicit, until Kant finally states the paralogism in its fully developed form (B410–11).
40. For the second sentence in this quote, the German says: "*Daß aber ich, der ich denke, im Denken immer als Subjekt und als etwas, was nicht bloß wie Prädikat dem Denken anhängend betrachtet werden kann, gelten müsse, ist ein apodiktischer und selbst identischer Satz; aber es bedeutet nicht, dass ich als Objekt ein für mich selbst bestehendes Wesen oder Substanz sei.*" Guyer and Wood translate "*Ich, der ich denke*" as "the I that I think." But the grammatical form "*Ich, der ich,*" which is not unusual in German, clearly makes '*ich*' grammatically nominative throughout, not accusative. This is important for Kant's point: it is the I who thinks (or more precisely: I, who think) that considers itself as subject

(consider myself as subject). I, who think, express my act of thinking in the thought 'I think,' in which, necessarily, 'I' is subject and 'think' predicate, not the reverse. The Guyer-Wood translation also misses the difference in the scope of the two modal verbs: "*nicht als Prädikat... betrachtet werden **kann***" and "*als Subjekt gelten **muß***." They make "*kann*" have "*als Subjekt betrachtet*" in its scope, and think "*gelten muß*" means "is valid." But this is clearly not how this sentence is constructed. What it says is that '*Ich*' *cannot be considered as predicate* **but rather** *must count as subject* (in the proposition 'I think').

41. Cf. 5.2.1.3.
42. Compare A184/B227: "I find that at all times not merely the philosopher but even the common understanding has presupposed this persistence as a substratum of all change in the appearances, and has also accepted it as indubitable, only the philosopher expresses himself somewhat more determinately in saying that in all alterations in the world the **substance** remains and only the **accidents** change. But I nowhere find even the attempt at a proof of this so obviously synthetic proposition, indeed it only rarely stands, as it deserves to, at the head of the pure and completely a priori laws of nature."
43. Here my interpretation is at odds with both Horstmann's and Melnick's interpretations, according to which what Kant calls 'the I' is an activity (cf. Horstmann 1993; Melnick 2009, chap. 1). Horstmann's and Melnick's interpretation seems to me to ignore Kant's insistence on the claim that, despite its position as subject-concept to which 'think' is attributed, the representation 'I' cannot legitimately be said to refer to anything that is known to be either substance or accident of a substance. Our use of the concept 'I' gives no indication at all about *what kind of entity* 'I' might represent, whether substance, mode, activity, or anything else. That 'I,' in 'I think,' does represent *some entity* (*Wesen*) is nevertheless as certain as the fact that 'I exist' is contained in 'I think' when taken assertorically.
44. My interpretation agrees with Proops (2010) in stressing the importance, in Kant's argument against what he takes to be the rationalist fallacy, of the grammatical position of 'I' in the sentence 'I think,' which is the linguistic expression of the logical position of the concept 'I' in the proposition 'I think.' However, in his reconstruction of Kant's analysis of the paralogisms, Proops puts no emphasis on the first-person formulation of the minor premise (see Proops 2010, 471). And he thinks the equivocation on the middle term that Kant makes clear in B (and did not make clear in A: on this, too, I agree with Proops) is the following: in the major premise, says Proops, 'being thought as' means 'being conceived as,' whereas in the minor premise it means 'being deployed (in judgment) as.' But for Kant, since, absent its schema, the pure concept of the understanding is reduced to the logical function of judgment, there is no distinction between '(necessarily) being thought only as subject, never as predicate of something else' and '(necessarily) having, in judgment, the position of subject and never that of predicate' (or in Proops's terms, '[necessarily] being deployed as subject never as predicate of something else'). All there is to the (logical) concept of subject *is* a function in judgment. Correspondingly (given Kant's view of the origin of the categories in logical functions of judgment), all there is to the concept of substance is the "concept of an object in general, by means of which its intuition is considered as *determined* with respect to [the] logical function of [categorical] judgment" (B128, which I have modified to introduce into Kant's general definition of the categories the specific case of the logical function in *categorical* judgment, namely the logical relation between subject and predicate, in which the category of substance originates). In other words, in my view there is, for Kant, a greater continuity than Proops acknowledges between saying that (necessarily) a thing is represented as (or thought as) subject and saying that (necessarily) its concept is deployed as (logical) subject in a subject–predicate judgment. Moreover, the fact that an object is thought to be subject, and never predicate of

something else, becomes more than the (empty) role of its concept in a logical function of judgment, *only if* the logical function (relating subject-concept to predicate-concept in judgment) is anchored in empirical intuition, or more specifically, in a specific a priori form of synthesis of a sensory manifold. In the case of substance, the category is the concept of a possible or actual object, and thus a category properly speaking, only if it serves to synthesize intuitions according to the relation of a permanent entity and its changing states. The latter is what is missing in the use of the logical function of the relation between subject and predicate in the minor premise of the first paralogism, and indeed Kant is quite explicit, both in A and in B, that the absence of a relation, in sensible intuition and experience, between a permanent entity and its changing states, means that the category is reduced to a mere logical function spinning in the void: and *this* is, according to the B edition, where the equivocation of the middle term, between major and minor premise, lies. The equivocation does not consist in moving from thinking as "conceiving" to thinking as "deploying in judgment," but rather in moving from thinking *justified by intuition and experience* to *mere* thinking, which means, inseparably, conceiving (as subject) and deploying in judgment (as logical subject). Unlike Proops, I don't think there are *three* concepts of substance at work in Kant's argument (see Proops 2010, 478–80). Nor do I think there are two. There is just one, which is the one cited above in this footnote (B128 and its specification to the case of the category of substance). Given this definition, in the absence of its schema, the category of substance does not apply to any actual or possible object: nothing is left but the concept of subject as a mere role in the logical function of categorical judgment, a role we may assign to the concept of an object, but according to which alone there is no sense at all in which an entity can be said to *be* substance, namely to be "something that can exist only as subject, not as a mere determination of something else" (B288, cf. also B149). In other words, in *no* sense is the rationalist metaphysician entitled to the conclusion that I, as thinking, am substance (nor, for that matter, is anyone entitled to the opposite conclusion).

45. Cf. A403. Note that, in my citation of A403 above, I had substituted (in agreement with Adickes) "paralogism of substantiality" for "paralogism of simplicity" (see n. 32 in this chapter). Here, conversely, we can have "paralogism of simplicity" and substitute "concept of simplicity" for "concept of substance." Just as the concept of substance in the major premise of the first paralogism, the concept of simplicity, in the major premise of the second paralogism, is a "purely intellectual concept" so that "a transcendental use, namely no use at all" is made of it.

46. For references to possible sources of the argument in Kant's rationalist predecessors, see the editorial note 24 to the statement of the paralogism at A351 in the Guyer–Wood translation. Guyer and Wood cite Wolff, *Psychologia rationalis*, §3, and Baumgarten, *Metaphysica*, §§745–7, both of whom take their inspiration from Leibniz, *Monadology*, §§1–6. For other sources, see also Rosefeldt 2000, 92n150.

47. This paragraph is fleshing out Kant's brief review, at A352–3, of the three types of support one might consider but that the rationalist cannot offer, for her claim that "many representations have to be contained in the absolute unity of the thinking subject to constitute one thought."

48. B407–8. See my comment in 5.3.2, n. 50.

49. The formulation "in judgments justified by intuition" versus "in judgments not justified by intuition" is Rosefeldt's. See especially Rosefeldt 2000, 29. I add "and experience" because intuition yields a representation of composition of actions only if perceptual intuitions are synthesized according to a priori concepts, a synthesis that yields experience (see A176/B218–A181/B224).

50. I have corrected the Guyer-Wood translation, which for [a] says: "That the I of apperception, consequently in every thought, is a **single thing** that cannot be resolved in a plurality of subjects, lies already in the concept of thinking, and is consequently an analytic proposition." The German says: "*Daß das Ich der Apperzeption, folglich in jedem Denken, ein **Singular** sei, der nicht in eine Vielheit der Subjekte aufgelöst werden kann, mithin ein logisch einfaches Subjekt bezeichne, liegt schon im Begriffe des Denkens, ist folglich ein analytischer Satz.*" "*Ein Singular*" and "*bezeichnet*" make it clear that "*das Ich der Apperzeption*" at the beginning of the passage, is the *concept* or *representation* or even just the *word* 'I,' which is the expression of apperception. It is not a *thing*. Because that concept is a "singular," namely a concept that has the peculiarity of referring in each instance of its use to just one entity, and is correspondingly a first-person *singular* pronoun in language, it may seem that the I, as the entity described (*bezeichnet*) or (in contemporary terms) referred to by 'I,' is a simple (indivisible) substance. But this would be a synthetic conclusion that is not justified, since there is no intuition to support any objective statement about the nature of the thing described by 'I.' It is true that Kant does not facilitate our understanding of his argument by moving seamlessly from *mention* to *use* of the term (and concept) 'I,' without giving us any conventional tool to distinguish his *mentioning* the concept 'I' (at the beginning of the passage) from his *using* it to describe the entity thereby thought. But for the textual reasons just explained, added to the explanations given above concerning the different meanings of 'subject' for Kant (see 5.1.4), it seems clear to me that we must, as much as possible, make these distinctions explicit where Kant implicitly presupposes them. On the same point, see Rosefeldt 2000, 84. See also Proops 2010, 473n40.
51. I have corrected the Guyer-Wood translation, which for [c] says: "It would be miraculous if what otherwise requires so much care in order to distinguish what is the substance and what is displayed in intuition, and even more to tell whether this substance could be simple (as in the parts of matter)...." The German says: "*Es wäre auch wunderbar, wenn ich das, was sonst so viele Anstalt erfordert, um in dem, was die Anschauung darlegt, das zu unterscheiden, was darin Substanz sei; noch mehr aber, ob diese auch einfach sein könne (wie bei den Teilen der Materie)....*" The idea is: it is so difficult to discern *in intuition* what is substance, even more to discern whether anything at all is simple—it would be truly miraculous if in the face of such difficulty one could acquire by the mere representation 'I' access to something that is both substance, and simple.
52. Compare with the argument of the second Antinomy of Pure Reason, A434/B462–A464/B472. And A523/B551–A527/B555.
53. A354–55; cf. 5.3.1.2.
54. See n. 43 in this chapter, my discussion of Horstmann (1993) and Melnick (2009).
55. See 4.3.2.2.

6
Kant on the Identity of Persons

For the rationalist philosophers Kant criticizes in the Paralogisms of Pure Reason, consciousness of one's own numerical identity at different times is a necessary and sufficient condition for being a *person*. For those same philosophers, only a thinking substance is a person. For only a thinking substance is both persisting through time (numerically identical at different times) *and* conscious of its own numerical identity at different times. In his *New Essays on Human Understanding*, Leibniz defends this notion of a person against Locke's. Contrary to Locke, Leibniz maintains that mere "consciosité," the mere fact of having an *idea* of self and of its identity at different times, is not enough to define some entity as a person. For an entity to be a person, its consciousness of its own identity at different times has to be consciousness of its *real* identity at different times, *as the entity it, in fact, is*. And that condition is satisfied only by the immediate consciousness a thinking substance has of its own identity at different times. Similar notions of person are defended by Wolff in his *Psychologia Rationalis* and by Baumgarten in his *Metaphysica*, both works that heavily influenced Kant in his pre-critical period.[1]

In the third Paralogism of Pure Reason, the "Paralogism of Personality,"[2] Kant argues that the consciousness of identity expressed in using 'I' in 'I think' is *not* sufficient to make me a person, an entity that is conscious of what is, in fact, its own numerical identity at different times as the entity it, in fact, is. According to Kant, supposing that it does is the result of an implicit and invalid inference from features of the concept 'I' in the proposition 'I think,' to purported properties of an entity: a substance, indeed a thinking substance. As we saw in Chapter 5, Kant calls this type of invalid inference a "paralogism of pure reason." He calls "paralogism of personality" the inference that leads from a particular feature of the concept 'I' in the proposition 'I think' to the assertion that I am a person in the sense just laid out: a thinking substance conscious of what is, in fact, its own numerical identity at different times. I will argue that in the course of criticizing the paralogism of personality, Kant delineates, against the rationalist view, a positive notion of person that is more complex and subtle than is often acknowledged.

I proceed as follows. First, I give a quick overview of Kant's criticism of the paralogism of personality. This allows me to identify two different meanings of "being conscious of one's numerical identity at different times" according to Kant. I further explore each of these meanings in 6.2 and 6.3. In 6.4, I explore the puzzling contrast between Kant's criticism of the rationalist inference and what seems to be, ultimately, his endorsement of the rationalist notion of person as an idea that has its proper role in the practical use of reason. In 6.5, I compare Kant's argument in the paralogism of personality to the amended version of Kant's argument that Peter Strawson offers in *The Bounds of Sense*. Finally, I return to the central question introduced in Chapter 2 of this book: in light of Kant's discussion of the third paralogism, what, if anything, do we stand to learn, beyond its historical significance, from Kant's analysis of our use of 'I' in 'I think'?

6.1 Kant's Criticism of the Paralogism of Personality

In the A edition, Kant's formulation of the paralogism of personality is the following:

What is conscious of the numerical identity of itself in different times, is to that extent a **person**.
Now the soul is, etc.
So it is a person. (A361)[3]

If we replace "the soul" by "I, as thinking"[4] and make the middle term explicit in the minor premise, we get the following formulation:

> What is conscious of the numerical identity of itself in different times is to that extent a person.
> Now I, as thinking, am conscious of the numerical identity of myself in different times.
> So I am a person.

The inference trades on the ambiguous meaning of "being conscious of the numerical identity of oneself in different times." In the major premise, the expression means: "being a numerically identical entity in different times *and* being conscious of one's numerical identity in different times," or again "being conscious of what is, in fact, one's own numerical identity in different times."[5] In contrast, in the minor premise, the same expression, "being conscious of one's own numerical identity in different times," does not presuppose any statement at all, one way or the other, concerning the question: Am I, in fact, an entity that remains numerically identical in different times?

It is important to note that Kant accepts the major premise, which he takes to be definitional of 'person': a person is an entity that is conscious of what is, in fact, her (its, his) own numerical identity in different times. To this extent at least, Kant accepts the rationalist notion of a person against the Lockean notion, according to which the psychological continuity provided by memory is sufficient to characterize the identity of person, whether or not the substrate of the relevant mental states remains numerically identical at different times. However, as we will see, against the rationalist metaphysicians, Kant denies that the consciousness of the numerical identity of any entity, including oneself, is possible for us human beings otherwise than by relying on criteria for identifying and re-identifying that entity in space and time. He therefore rejects the idea that the consciousness of identity expressed by the use of 'I' in 'I think' is sufficient to infer that I am, as an existing entity, a person. For contrary to what the rationalist thinks, that consciousness does not give me access to the identity of myself in different times as a persisting entity, a thinking substance. As was the case with the previous two paralogisms, the point is made especially clear in the more compressed version of Kant's argument in the B edition:

The proposition of the identity of myself in everything manifold of which I am conscious is... one lying in the concepts themselves, and hence an analytic proposition; but this identity of the subject, of which I can become conscious in every representation, does not concern the intuition of it, through which it is given as object, and thus cannot signify the identity of the person, by which would be understood the consciousness of the identity of its own substance as a thinking being in all changes of state; in order to prove that, what would be needed is not a mere analysis of the proposition 'I think' but rather various synthetic judgments grounded on the given intuition. (B408)

There are, then, at least two things we need to understand. First, what is this "consciousness of the identity of oneself at different times" which is not the *de re* consciousness of the numerical identity of an entity, and which is nevertheless grounded in the use of 'I' in 'I think'? Second, if the consciousness of oneself expressed in 'I think' does not count as consciousness of oneself as a person, what *does* count as such consciousness? In fact, do we count at all as persons, and if so, how? This second question will be addressed in 6.3. In 6.2, I offer an answer to the first question. This means examining the minor premise in the inference laid out above: "I, as thinking, am conscious of the identity of myself in different times."

6.2 "I, as Thinking," and Consciousness of Identity in Different Times

In the previous chapter, I argued that according to Kant, the rationalist metaphysician's mistake is to infer from the peculiar features of 'I' in 'I think' (features concerning its *role* in the proposition 'I think'), to the supposed *content* of that representation, and from the supposed *content* of the representation to the properties of a supposed *real object* of the representation.[6] I argued moreover that explaining the features of the representation 'I' consists in explaining two things: first, its role in the proposition 'I think' considered in its mere logical form (the way concepts are combined in it); second, its role in 'I think' considered as the conceptual expression of the transcendental unity of apperception. It will help to briefly recall what these two aspects of the explanation yielded in the case of the paralogism of simplicity, before considering the case of the third paralogism, the paralogism of personality.

In his discussion of the second paralogism, Kant rejects the rationalist claim that there cannot be a composition of several thoughts (the thoughts of several thinking things) into one thought in just the way there can be a composition of several motions (the motions of several moving things) into one motion (the motion of the composite of moving things). The rationalist refusal to consider the composition of thoughts on the same model as the composition of motions, Kant maintains, stems from the fallacious interpretation of a true premise, which is the minor premise of the second paralogism. The rationalist's error, Kant claims, is seemingly supported by the peculiarity of the pronoun 'I' as a first person *singular*. But that peculiarity of the pronoun 'I' as used in the proposition 'I think' is just the expression, by the thinker, of the unity of the activity of thinking she is conscious of being, herself, engaged in. It is *not* a warrant for asserting as an a priori truth (a proposition purportedly a priori inferred from the content of the concept 'I') that the referent of 'I,' the thinker, is itself a simple, indivisible entity. This is a mistake the rationalist metaphysician knows is not to be made in the case of motion (he would accept that one motion may result from the concurrent actions of multiple moving entities), but one he nevertheless makes in the case of thought (where he thinks *one thought* cannot result from the concurrent actions of multiple thinking entities).

Kant denounces a similar mistake in the third paralogism. He criticizes the rationalist metaphysician for inferring from the fact that, necessarily, in thinking 'I think' we take the concept 'I' to refer to one and the same thinker throughout the contents of our thought, to the numerical identity at different times of the entity that is the agent of the thought. Where, according to the second paralogism, the representation of myself as simple was derived from the synchronic unity (logical connectedness) of the content of the thought, now, in the third paralogism, the representation of myself as numerically identical at different times is derived from the diachronic unity of the content of the thoughts I take myself to have held, and which result in the current thought. But just as the synchronic connectedness of the content of a thought, which makes it one thought, could in fact result from the concurrent actions of a plurality of entities, so the connectedness of the contents of a thought may well derive from a diachronic plurality of actions and thus a diachronic plurality of acting entities, rather than from the action of one entity remaining numerically identical at different times, that is to say, one and the same, numerically identical agent of the thought. Such a scenario is possible, Kant claims, despite the fact that the unity of the thought finds expression in the use of 'I' as the subject of the proposition 'I think.' Just as, according to Kant's argument in the Second Paralogism, despite the fact that the word 'I' is grammatically a first-person *singular*, the concept 'I' might refer to what is, in fact, a plurality of entities whose actions collectively constitute one action producing the current thought; so, Kant now argues in the Third Paralogism, despite the fact that 'I' is a concept such that there is, on the part of the 'I'-user, a presumption of identity through time of its referent, in fact the entity now thinking 'I think' might be collecting, and attributing to itself, a sequence of thoughts successively carried by a series of distinct entities, whatever the metaphysical nature of those entities might be.

Why is there, for the 'I'-user, such a presumption of numerical identity at different times of the referent of 'I' in 'I think'? For the same reason there was a presumption of her being "absolute subject" and "simple": the *content* of her thought is, for each thinker of 'I think,' one collective whole appearing to her, in inner sense, as developing through time with logical connectedness. Here it will be useful to recall a passage from the Transcendental Deduction of the Categories we already analyzed in Chapter 4. In this text, "identity" of oneself (or of one's mind) is connected with "unity" of the contents of one's mental activity. It is that connection that I would like to go over again. For ease of reference, I have identified by letters in brackets the various instances of identity or unity.

Thus [a] the original and necessary consciousness of the ***identity*** of oneself is at the same time [b] a consciousness of an equally necessary ***unity*** of the synthesis of all appearances in accordance with concepts, that is, in accordance with rules that not only make them necessarily reproducible, but also thereby determines an object for their intuition, that is, the concept of something in which they necessarily hold together [*zusammenhängen*]; for [c] the mind [*das Gemüt*] could not possibly think the **identity** of itself in the manifoldness of its representations, and indeed think it *a priori*, if it did not have before its eyes [d] the identity of its action, which [e] subjects all synthesis of apprehension (which is empirical) to a **transcendental unity**, and first makes possible its holding together [*Zusammenhang*] in accordance with *a priori* rules. (A108; translation modified; bold italics are mine)[7]

Throughout this text, Kant maintains that the consciousness of the *identity* of oneself ([a], [c], and [d]) is nothing but the consciousness of the *unity* of one's representations ([b], [e]). The latter unity is the "holding together" of our representations according to rules. This "holding together" is a necessary condition for there being *objects* of our representations. Note that according to [c] and [d], the mind ("*das Gemüt*"),[8] *thinks* the identity of itself just in case it "has before its eyes" the identity of its action. But "having before its eyes" the identity of its action amounts to nothing other than acknowledging the "transcendental unity" that binds all synthesis of apprehension and makes it hold together in accordance with rules. The consciousness of identity of self is thus a merely intellectual consciousness, a *thinking* of one's own identity, or having a *concept* of one's own identity insofar as one is actively engaged in bringing about the *unity*, the "holding together" of one's representations.[9]

Now using the concept 'I' in the proposition 'I think' is expressing just that consciousness of the identity of oneself throughout the unity of one's representations analyzed above. This point is analogous to those we analyzed in the previous chapter. We saw that according to Kant, using 'I' in 'I think' is expressing the consciousness of oneself (that is to say, the thinking of oneself) as *the subject* of the unity of representations; this is the source of the first paralogism of pure reason. We also saw that using 'I' in 'I think' is expressing the consciousness of oneself (that is to say, the thinking of oneself) as the *unitary* agent of the *unitary* action that is presumed to generate the *unity* of representations; this is the source of the second paralogism of pure reason. Similarly, we now see Kant claim that using 'I' in 'I think' is expressing the consciousness of oneself (that is to say, the thinking of oneself) as *remaining identical* throughout the holding together of one's representations. This is the point Kant makes in commenting on the minor premise of the paralogism of personality. In the citation that follows, the numbers in brackets and the indication of the original German terms are meant to draw attention to the different ways in which Kant uses the reflexive "selbst," on which I comment below).

But now I am an object of inner sense and all time is merely the form of inner sense. Consequently I relate each and every one of my successive determinations to [1] the numerically identical self [*auf das numerisch identische Selbst*] in all time, i.e. [2] in the form of inner intuition of myself [*in der Form der inneren Anschauung meiner selbst*]. On this basis the identity of the soul must be regarded not as inferred but rather as a completely identical proposition of self-consciousness in time, and that is also the cause of its being valid *a priori*. For it really says no more than that in the whole time in which [3] I am conscious of myself [*mir meiner selbst bewußt bin*] I am conscious of this time as belonging to [4] the unity of my self [*der Einheit meines Selbst*], and it is all the same whether I say that this whole time is in me, as an individual unity, or that I am to be found with numerical identity in all of this time.

The identity of person is therefore unfailingly [*unausbleiblich*] to be encountered in my own consciousness. (A362)

The discussion of the rationalist paralogisms introduces a new dimension into the representation of the "identity of oneself." In the text from the Transcendental Deduction discussed above, the consciousness (conception) of one's own identity was the atemporal consciousness of identity of the thinker *qua* thinker, engaged in the process of thinking. Here, as befits the context of the third Paralogism, the thinker thinks of herself *as an object of inner sense*, and as such, as an object that remains identical throughout the changes of its states at different times. But really, the thought of that identity is just the same thought as the thought of the identity of the thinker throughout its thoughts, and as such is "a completely identical proposition of self-consciousness": *for the thinker aware of her current act of thinking*, 'think' can only be predicated in the first person, and predicating 'think' in this way just is thinking of oneself as one thinker throughout the mental contents one binds in thinking them. Conversely, using the concept 'I' just is thinking of oneself *as the thinker of the thought currently being thought*, and so as the numerically identical author of the "holding together" (*Zusammenhang*) of the representations that converge into the present thought.

By giving in brackets the original German variations on "*selbst*" in the citation above, I mean to draw attention to the fact that sometimes Kant uses the merely reflexive "seiner selbst," and sometimes he substantivizes "*selbst*" into "*das Selbst*," the self. [1] and [4] are instances of the latter; [2] and [3] are instances of the former.[10] The mere reflective consciousness of oneself involved in binding the contents of one's mental states (*Bewusstsein seiner selbst*) becomes, insofar as one thinks of oneself as an object of inner sense, consciousness of one's identical self (*seines identischen Selbst*) or of the unity of one's self (*der Einheit seines Selbst*). In fact, the concept of such an identical self is, for the reasons stated above, "analytically contained" in the concept of oneself as thinking, namely in the thought 'I think.' Or, as Kant writes in the text cited above, "the identity of the soul must be regarded not as inferred but rather as a completely identical proposition of self-consciousness in time, and that is also the cause of its being valid *a priori*." Since the concept of a person just is the concept of an entity that is conscious of its own identity at different times, then "the identity of person is therefore unfailingly [*unausbleiblich*] to be encountered in my own consciousness."

Kant cannot mean that the *assertion* of the identity of person is *justified* by my own consciousness. Rather, we must understand him as claiming that the *concept* of identity of person is unfailingly to be met in my own consciousness. Or in other words, given the role of 'I' in thought and what that role expresses, I inevitably *think* of myself as an identical person, an entity persisting as a numerically identical, metaphysical subject of all my representations. This is how the role of 'I,' as a representation, gives rise to the idea of a *content* for the representation 'I': a numerically identical object of the representation 'I.' However, the fact that in using 'I' I am necessarily represented to myself as numerically identical in each component of the connected whole that constitutes a thought, does not suffice to justify the claim that I am, as a real entity, numerically identical through all the states whose connected contents constitute the thought. Kant makes exactly this point in the short paragraph laying out the rationalist fallacy in B:

> The proposition of the identity of myself in everything manifold of which I am conscious is... one lying in the concepts themselves, and hence an analytic proposition; but this identity of the subject, of which I can become conscious in every representation... cannot signify the identity of the person, by which would be understood the consciousness of the identity of its own substance as a thinking being in all changes of state; in order to prove that, what would be demanded is not a mere analysis of the proposition "I think," but rather various synthetic judgments grounded in intuition. (B408)

What would it take for the consciousness (the thought) of my identity to be the consciousness of the *real identity* of an actually existing object? Kant's answer is the same as in the other paralogisms: it would take my being presented to myself in intuition and experience as a persisting object. But persisting objects can be presented only in space and time: as objects not just of inner, but also of outer sense. Does this mean, then, that as an object of inner *and outer* sense, I am a person? To answer this question, we need to look at the major premise more closely.

6.3 Consciousness of Identity and Personhood

What emerges from the preceding analysis is that it is an a priori property of my thoughts (because a necessary condition for my engaging in any activity of thinking at all) that I should be able to attribute them to myself, and that in attributing 'think' to 'I' I should think of myself as one and the same subject of my thoughts at different times. But this in no way guarantees that these thoughts that I am now ascribing to myself, have at different points in time indeed been thought by one and the same *entity* which I could justifiably claim to be identical to *me*, the current thinker of the proposition 'I think' or 'I think p.'

In all three of the paralogisms analyzed so far, in A Kant endorses the major premise as the statement of an a priori conceptual criterion for characterizing an object in a certain way: as a substance (the conceptual criterion: an entity is a substance if and only if it can be represented only as subject and cannot count as predicate of something else); as simple (the conceptual criterion: an entity is simple if and only if its action cannot be regarded as the concurrence of many acting things); and now as a person (the conceptual criterion: an entity is a person if and only if it is conscious of what is, in fact its own numerical identity at different times). About these conceptual criteria Kant agrees with the rationalist metaphysician. His complaint is that the rationalist metaphysician leaves unarticulated, and thus remains conveniently oblivious to, the kind of justification needed for asserting that *an existing object* does satisfy the conceptual criterion. In contrast, Kant makes explicit that the conceptual representation can in each case justifiably be asserted to be true of an existing object only if the object is presented in intuition. Now, because he is satisfied with a purely conceptual justification for the application of the concept to an existing object, the rationalist is prone to the illusion that the existing entity thought under the concept 'I' satisfies, as the existing entity it is, the criterion stated in the major premise. Kant agrees that 'I,' as used in 'I think,' refers to an existing entity. But that entity is *not* presented in intuition and thus does *not* present the characteristics that would justify applying to it the concept defined in the major premise. Once the requirement for such a justification is made explicit, then the inference takes on the explicitly paralogistic form:

MP_{id}^*: That which is represented to itself (conscious of itself), *in judgments justified by intuition and experience*, as numerically identical in different times, is a person.
mP_{id}^*: I, as thinking, am represented to myself (conscious of myself), in a judgment ('I think') *that is not justified by intuition and experience*, as numerically identical at different times.
C_{id}^*: So I, as thinking, am a person.

At the beginning of his comments on the paralogism of personality in A, Kant reminds us that the necessary condition for being conscious of the numerical identity through time of an object of outer sense, is being conscious of it as an object that persists while its states change:

If I want to cognize through experience the numerical identity of an external object, then I will attend to what is persisting in its appearance, to which, as subject, everything else relates as a determination, and I will notice the identity of the former in the time in which the latter changes. (A362)

This reminder is immediately followed by Kant's explanation of the very different nature of the consciousness of identity of oneself in 'I think,' analyzed in 6.2 of the present chapter. Having explained why the "identity of person is...unfailingly encountered in my own consciousness," Kant then explains why such a merely conceptual consciousness cannot count as a consciousness of the real identity of an entity.

But if I consider myself from the standpoint of another (as object of his outer intuition) only then [*allererst*] does this external observer consider me in time, for in apperception time is represented properly speaking only in me.[11] Thus from the I that accompanies, and indeed with complete identity, all representations at every time in **my** consciousness, although he takes it into account, he will not conclude to the objective permanence of my self. For since the time in which the observer posits me is not the time that is to be encountered in my own, but in his sensibility, the identity that is necessarily combined with my consciousness is not for that reason combined with his, that is to say with the external intuition of my subject. (A362-3)

Note that Kant is not just laying out the conditions under which *another* can regard me as persisting through time. Rather, his point is that I, myself, need to—mentally—occupy the standpoint of another on myself ("If I consider myself from the standpoint of another...") in order to confirm that what I take to be the representational states of one and the same entity, myself at different times, have indeed been states of one and the same entity, rather than states transferred from one entity to the next in a series of entities, collectively generating the representational unity expressed by the thought 'I think.' Indeed, only if the "standpoint of another" mentioned at the beginning of the quoted text is a standpoint *I* take on *myself* does it even make sense to say that "from the I that accompanies—with complete identity—all my representations," that "other" (in "the standpoint of another") will not infer the objective permanence of myself. Why would this inference even be in question for someone who is *really* another than myself? But of course, it is in question for me, the current thinker conscious of my own thoughts. *For me* it is *not* legitimate to infer the real identity of my (metaphysical) subject from the "complete identity" of the object I suppose to be the object of the concept 'I' to which I ascribe all my representations. In other words, neither the fact that all logically connected representations are necessarily, as such, attributed to one and the same "logical subject = I" in 'I think,' nor even the fact that for me, every temporal determination (whether the temporal determinations of my subjective states, or the objective temporal determinations of the outside world) is in the purview of one unity of apperception whose conceptual expression is the judgment 'I think'—neither of these facts guarantees that the concept 'I' refers to one and the same *real* subject of representations: a persisting, numerically identical entity. Such a guarantee can be obtained only from a third-person, objective standpoint, and this is a standpoint I do *not* have in referring to myself, the thinker of 'I think,' in using 'I' in 'I think.' This is why Kant concludes, immediately after the passage cited above:

> The identity of the consciousness of myself in different times is therefore only a formal condition of my thoughts and their connection, but it does not at all prove the numerical identity of my subject. (A363)

As we saw in Chapter 2, Evans took this passage to indicate that Kant's view was an ancestor of his own. According to Evans, consciousness of oneself as an embodied entity is a necessary condition for any use of 'I.' This is because, says Evans, a necessary condition for any use of 'I' is that I be able to pick out its referent as an individual entity distinct from other individual entities (one of the two aspects of the "generality constraint" applied to 'I').[12] And a necessary condition for the latter is that the referent of 'I' be identified as a physical object, distinct from other physical objects individuated by their positions in space and time. Evans warned, however, against the "verificationist" taint in Kant's version of this point, according to which I must be an object *of outer sense* in order for 'I' to have a referent. For Evans, the condition of spatiotemporal individuation is not only epistemic, but also semantic and therefore metaphysical. In order for 'I' to have a referential use, I must both *be* and *be conscious of myself as* a physical object among physical objects. Now for Kant, just as for Evans, it is true that I can identify and re-identify myself as an individual entity, one and the same at different times, only if I am conscious of myself as a spatiotemporal object. But this is not an a priori semantic condition on the referential use of 'I.' Rather, it is an epistemic condition on my being presented to myself as an object. What Evans did not notice is that Kant, in making the spatiotemporal condition on identification an epistemic rather than a semantic condition, leaves room for a referential use of 'I' in 'I think' that does *not* depend on this epistemic condition.[13]

Of course, Evans could justifiably reply that a referential use that does not include the possibility of an epistemic identification and re-identification through time of the entity being referred to is a very impoverished one. And this is certainly true of the use of 'I' in 'I think' as Kant understands it, in opposition to the rationalist metaphysician. Evans is partly correct in claiming that in that context, 'I' expresses only "a formal condition of my thoughts," the condition of formal unity of my thoughts and representations. Nevertheless, the fact that the use of 'I' in 'I think' should express that formal condition does not prevent 'I' from referring to an existing entity, myself as thinking. The difference between Kant's view and Evans's is that for Kant, for all we know on the basis of our mastering the use of the mere concept 'I' as used in 'I think,' that entity could be numerically different in each instance of the use of 'I.'

Indeed, immediately after the sentence cited above (A363), Kant remarks that even though necessarily, in thinking 'I think,' I think of myself as numerically identical throughout my thoughts, this does nothing to prove my real numerical identity through time. Let me now cite the passage in full.

The identity of the consciousness of myself in different times is therefore only a formal condition of my thoughts and their connection, but it does not at all prove the numerical identity of my subject, in which—*despite the logical identity of the I*—a change can go on that does not allow it to keep its identity; and this even though all the while the identical-sounding 'I' is assigned to it, which in every other state, even in the replacement of the subject, still keeps in view the thought of the previous subject, and thus could also pass it along to the following one.* (A363)

The asterisk sends us to the following footnote:

* An elastic ball that strikes another one in a straight line communicates to the latter its whole motion, hence its whole state (if one looks only at their positions in space). Now assuming substances, on the analogy with such bodies, in which representations, together with consciousness of them, flow from one to another, a whole series of these substances may be thought, of which the first would communicate its state, together with its consciousness, to the second, which would communicate its own state, together with that of the previous substance, to a third substance, and this in turn would share the states of all previous ones, together with their consciousness and its own. The last substance would thus be conscious of all the states of all the previously altered substances as its own states, because these states would have been carried over to it, together with the consciousness of them; *and in spite of this it would not have been the very same person in all these states.* (A363–4n)

Note that Kant's strategy in opposing the rationalist metaphysician's view is similar to his strategy in the second paralogism. In the paralogism of simplicity, Kant extended to thinking substances a point that the rationalist metaphysician accepted in the case of material substances but was unwilling to extend to the case of thinking substances. In his response to the rationalist fallacy, Kant maintained that just as one motion can be (as anyone, including the rationalist, would readily acknowledge) the concurrence (the composition of the motions) of several moving things, similarly one thought might well be the concurrence (the composition of the actions) of many thinking substances. The simplicity (indivisibility, non-compositionality) of the representation 'I' that reflects the unity of apperception does nothing to counter this fact. For the indivisibility of 'I,' as well as the indivisibility of the unity of apperception 'I' expresses, belongs to the first-person standpoint each thinker has on the contents of her own thoughts. It does not say anything one way or the other about the kind of entity that might be the bearer of that unitary, indivisible standpoint she has on the content of her thoughts.

Similarly, in the case of the paralogism of identity or personality, Kant extends to the case of apperception a point that the rationalist metaphysician, like anyone else, would have no difficulty accepting in the case of motion. Just as one motion can be transferred from one material substance (whether simple or composite) to the next in a series of material substances, so, says Kant, could the unity of apperception, the act of unifying a collective whole of representations, be transferred from one substance to the next in a series of substances. The last substance in the series could legitimately think of all the states thus transmitted, together with their unity, as its own states. "And yet it would not have been the same person in all these states."

In commenting (above, 6.2) on A362, in which Kant analyzes the consciousness of the identity of oneself at different times expressed by using 'I' in the proposition 'I think,' I noted that Kant moves seamlessly from using the mere reflective expression "of myself" or "of oneself" (as in: "consciousness of myself" *"Bewusstsein meiner selbst"*; or "intuition of myself," *"Anschauung meiner selbst"*) to using the concept "self" as if it were the concept of an entity, as in "the numerically identical self" (*"das numerisch identische Selbst"*) or "the unity of my self" (*"die Einheit meines Selbst"*).[14] This is because the step is short from the consciousness (conception) of the identity of oneself that is nothing over and above the consciousness of the unity of the contents of one's thoughts, to the supposition of a numerically identical object for the concept 'I.' That object (the object of a mere concept, the concept 'I') is then called a 'self.' That object itself has only as much (conceived) identity and unity at different times as there is *Zusammenhang*, collective unity, of the contents unified by the act of thinking. We can then understand why Kant maintains that the consciousness of (that is, the conceiving of) the unity and identity at different times of one's *self* does not warrant asserting the unity and identity at different times of oneself *as a person*. In the texts cited above, Kant illustrates his point by comparing the transmission of representations "together with the consciousness of them" from one substance to another, with the transmission of motion from one substance to another. One and the same unity of consciousness, with richer and richer content as each substance in the series contributes additional content, might be transferred from one substance to the next, and thus a concept of self conceived as one and the same throughout, albeit a self with richer and richer content, may emerge,. That consciousness of identity would be expressed by the thought 'I think.' But this would not mean that there is, from one state to the next, identity of *person*.

What, then, *is* the identity of person, for Kant? His discussion of the paralogism of personality is not meant to provide an answer to this question. Its point is primarily negative: the consciousness of identity carried by our use of the concept 'I' in 'I think' is *not* the consciousness of what is, in fact, a numerically identical person. But from Kant's argument for this negative point, we might gather the components of a positive view. In the empirical world—the world of spatiotemporal entities, accessible to us through our senses, identifiable and re-identifiable via the judging processes expounded in the Transcendental Analytic—the identity of persons depends on two factors, equally indispensable but which can conceivably come apart (in which case there just is no numerically identical person at different times): (1) the unity of apperception, namely, the unity of consciousness of the contents of mental states, which makes it possible to accompany them with the thought 'I think'; and (2) the numerical identity through time of a spatiotemporal entity, a living being endowed with mental states. Correspondingly, the *consciousness* of what is, in fact, a numerically identical person (which is, by the definition provided in the major premise of the third paralogism, the definition of 'personhood') rests on the two factors just listed. I could have *no* consciousness of my own numerical identity as an empirically determinate entity persisting through time unless I had the capacity to bind the contents of my own mental states in just the way that also makes it possible for me to accompany them with the thought 'I think.' Absent that capacity, I would not be a person "in the psychological sense."[15] But absent the actual numerical identity at different times of one and the same entity, conscious of what is, in fact, the numerical identity of herself as an entity persisting in space through time, the concept 'person' would remain an empty concept.

That the concept 'person,' if it is to apply to any entity at all, applies to an empirically determinate entity, seems to be confirmed by a text from the paralogism of simplicity. After criticizing Mendelssohn's purported proof of the immortality of the soul (from its simplicity), Kant continues: we do have knowledge of the persistence of the soul. But that is only insofar as we have knowledge of the persistence of the human being through the duration of her life. And this again is a standpoint we have on ourselves when we consider ourselves "from the outside," not a standpoint on ourselves we can have through mere inner sense.

> Thus the persistence of the soul, merely as an object of inner sense, remains unproved and even unprovable, although its persistence in life, where the thinking being (as a human being) is at the same time an object of outer sense, is clear of itself; but this is not at all sufficient for the rational psychologist, who undertakes to prove from mere concepts the absolute persistence of the soul even beyond life. (B415)

Admittedly, this text is not about the *personality* (consciousness of one's own identity through time) of the soul, but about its *persistence* (substantiality). The point Kant makes in this text is that there is no available criterion of the persistence of the soul independently of the persistence of the human being who has the soul (or, in Kant's terms, the self) as an object of inner sense, at least insofar as she has the unity of her own inner states as an object of inner sense. But it seems natural to say that, similarly, there is no available criterion of personhood (consciousness of the numerical identity through time of oneself as the thinking being one is) except as the consciousness of the numerical identity through time *of the human being* that thinks. This numerically identical entity is not a soul, the object of the concept 'I,' as an object of inner sense. It is an object of outer sense. Only our consciousness of that external object provides the warrant for asserting the continuing existence of a (relatively permanent) bearer for our mental states, the transient objects of inner sense. But as I said earlier (see 6.1.5), the concept of such a bearer *as an object of inner sense*, remains empty. The only corresponding object of intuition, persisting through time, is the living body we take to be our own insofar as it provides the empirical standpoint on the world from which we (as empirically determinate human beings) think and act.

And yet this is not Kant's conclusion. After completing his criticism of the fallacious inference he attributes to the rationalist metaphysician, Kant notes:

> Meanwhile, the concept of personhood [*Persönlichkeit*], just like the concepts of substance and of the simple, can remain, insofar as it is merely transcendental, i.e. a unity of the subject that is otherwise unknown to us, but in whose determinations there is a thoroughgoing connection of apperception, and to this extent this concept is also necessary and sufficient for practical use; but we can never boast of it as an extension of our self-knowledge through pure reason, which dazzles us with the uninterrupted continuous duration of the subject drawn from the mere concept of the identical self. (A365–6)

It is quite clear that the concept of "personhood" Kant says "can remain" is the rationalist concept derived from the mere concept 'I' in 'I think,' albeit deprived of any claim to yielding knowledge of any existing entity. It is a concept of personhood that lies beyond our access to empirically determinate persons. But why *should* it remain, if we do have that other, empirical concept available? Kant's expressed worry is that the more modest concept of person as an empirically accessible entity conscious of its own identity at different times is *not* "necessary and sufficient for practical use"—perhaps *neither* necessary *nor* sufficient. Now I will suggest that, here, Kant is in the grip of his own paralogism, a paralogism of pure practical reason. This is my next point.

6.4 Kant's Person, and the Moral Standpoint

Kant's justification for his claim that the rationalist notion of a person is "necessary and sufficient for practical use" is not given in the third paralogism, but in the solution to the third antinomy of pure reason, which is common to A and B.[16] The justification is roughly this. If our existence were only that of spatiotemporal entities belonging to the sensible world subject to universal causal laws, then there would be no room for metaphysical freedom (for being an uncaused cause, a cause that has the power to start a causal chain without being itself determined to do so), and thus no room for moral accountability. If everything we do were determined according to universal causal laws, we would deserve neither reward nor punishment. Only by supposing that we exist as pure intelligences belonging in an intelligible world can we at least think the possibility that we are free and morally accountable, and thus deserving of moral praise or blame. But thinking of ourselves in this way—as pure intelligences belonging in an intelligible world—just is thinking of ourselves as the kinds of entities that have immediate consciousness of their own numerical identity at different times: persons in the rationalist sense. This is presumably why Kant says, at the end of his criticism of the paralogism of personality, that the notion of person defended by the rationalist can nevertheless remain, as "necessary and sufficient for practical use." In the concluding remarks to the paralogisms of pure reason in B, Kant adds:

> Suppose there subsequently turned up—not in experience but in certain (not merely logical rules but) laws holding firm *a priori* and concerning our existence—the occasion for presupposing ourselves to be **legislative** fully a priori in regard to our own **existence**, and as self-

determining in this existence; then this would disclose a spontaneity through which our actuality is determinable without the need of conditions of empirical intuition; and here we would become aware that in the consciousness of our existence something is contained a priori that can serve to determine our existence, which is thoroughly determinable only sensibly, in regard to a certain inner faculty in relation to an intelligible world (obviously one only thought of). (B430-1)

This is of course a reference to the argument of *Groundwork of the Metaphysics of Morals*, published just one year before the second edition of the *Critique of Pure Reason*, in which Kant expounds the three formulations of the categorical imperative of morality as expressions of a law our rational will sets itself. The passage also foreshadows Kant's claim in the *Critique of Practical Reason*, published just one year *after* the second edition of the *Critique of Pure Reason*. Kant there claims that the moral law we find in ourselves is the *ratio cognoscendi* of freedom: our consciousness of the moral law we find in ourselves just is our consciousness of our own freedom.[17]

In *Groundwork*, Kant explains that having a will that is thus determined under the moral law is what makes us *persons* in the moral sense: individuals capable of self-determination and thus accountable for their actions. Strictly speaking, then, the notion of person that was defined in the major premise of the third Paralogism is *not* sufficient for practical use. That notion is a *necessary* but not a *sufficient* condition for the practical use of reason. The notion of person that is "necessary and sufficient" for practical use includes, on Kant's own account, not only the "psychological" notion (a person is an entity that is conscious of what is, in fact, her own identity at different times as the entity she is), but also the "moral" notion (a person is a conscious being that has a rational will, a faculty of desire determined under the moral law).

That the psychological notion of a person, defined by consciousness of one's own numerical identity at different times, and the moral notion, defined by moral accountability, are essentially related, was of course stressed by both Locke and Leibniz. After maintaining that the identity of person or self is "made by consciousness" rather than being in any way dependent on the identity of substances or even of human beings at different times, Locke notes that person is "a forensic notion" on which depends the distribution of blame and punishment, praise and reward. He then acknowledges that reducing the identity of person to the identity of consciousness would lead to insuperable paradoxes of accountability unless one could count on God's benevolence to ensure that on the day of Last Judgment, identity of consciousness will map identity of actual agency.[18] Correspondingly, one of the reasons Leibniz, in his response to Locke, does not accept dissociating identity of consciousness from identity of substance is precisely that God's benevolence could not have allowed that consciousness and actual agency be systematically dissociated.[19] In both cases, there is a strong connection between psychological personhood (consciousness of one's own numerical identity at different times), and moral personhood (accountability for one's actions).

In short, the connection between the two aspects (the psychological aspect and the moral aspect) of the notion of person is not proper to Kant. What is proper to Kant is the prima facie bizarre combination we find in his solution to the paralogism of personhood. On the one hand, Kant criticizes the rationalist illusion according to which one's consciousness (conception) of one's identity at different times, expressed in the concept 'I' in 'I think,' gives any access to one's actual identity at different times as a person. He seems thereby to open the way to another notion of person, in which only consciousness of one's numerical identity *as a spatiotemporal entity* can provide the justification for subsuming the referent of 'I' under the "psychological" concept of a person: an entity conscious of what is, in fact, her own numerical identity at different times. But on the other hand, Kant endorses, on behalf of the practical use of reason, the idea that I, as thinking, fall under the rationalist concept of a person. It is tempting to suspect him of a paralogistic inference similar to those he criticizes in the first three Paralogisms of Pure Reason. Is this plausible, and if so, what would the inference look like?

We might find guidance in Kant's lecture notes on metaphysics from the late 1770s, published in the Academy edition under the title *Metaphysik L₁*. There, Kant offers the lineaments of an a priori doctrine of the soul. Such a doctrine, he says, can be derived from the mere concept 'I' by applying to it the a priori transcendental concepts of substance, simplicity, identity, and spontaneity (absolute freedom). We thus obtain a rational psychology, distinct from the empirical psychology that studies the psychological states and capacities of the thinking being as an object of inner *and* outer sense: a living being that thinks.[20] In empirical psychology, the soul (the object of inner sense) is considered in its connection with the body (an object of outer sense). The soul and the body taken together constitute the human being, "the I *in sensu latiori*." In contrast, in rational psychology the soul is considered as pure intelligence, independent of the body. It is "the I *in sensu stricto*." The I *in sensu stricto*, the object of rational psychology, is known a priori by analysis of the pure concept 'I.'

> When we speak of the soul *a priori*, then we will talk of it only to the extent we can derive all from the concept of the I, and to the extent we can apply the transcendental concepts to this I.... We will thus cognize *a priori* nothing more of the soul than the I allows us to cognize. (AA28-1, 266)

We thus know a priori that the soul is substance:

> The I is *the universal subject* of all predicates, of all thinking, of all actions, of all possible judgments that we can pass of ourselves as a thinking being. I can only say: I am, I think, I act. Thus it is not at all feasible that the I would be a predicate of another being. (ibid.; Kant's emphasis)

We know in the same way that the soul is simple:

> If I say: I think, then I do not express representations which are divided among many beings. (ibid.)

We also know that it is numerically one:

> The soul is a *single soul* [*eine einzelne Seele*]..., i.e. *my consciousness is consciousness of a single substance*.... The I expresses unity [*Das Ich drückt Unität aus*]; I am conscious of One subject [*ich bin mir Eines Subjekts bewusst*]. (ibid., 267; Kant's emphasis)

These are precisely the derivations that Kant refutes in the first three paralogisms of pure reason, in the *Critique of Pure Reason*. The fourth paralogism, which concerns the relation between mind and body,[21] is also an inference that is endorsed in *Metaphysics L₁*. But it is presented in a different division than the first three I just listed: not in division 1, which is concerned with the soul considered on its own or "absolutely," but in division 2, concerned with the relation of the soul to other entities, whether those entities are "corporeal natures" or "thinking natures."[22] In division 1, the fourth title concerns the spontaneity of the soul, and it, too, is derived from a priori features of the concept 'I.'

> Now the question is: whether I can think of myself as soul? Whether I have transcendental spontaneity [*spontaneitatem transcendentalem*] or absolute freedom [*libertatem absolutam*]?
>
> Here the I must again help out.... The I proves that I myself act; *I* am a principle and not a thing that has a principle [*Ich bin ein Princip und kein Principiatum*].... When I say: I think, I act, etc., then either the word is brought about falsely [*das Wort Ich wird falsch angebracht*] or I am free. Were I not free, then I could not say: *I* do it; but rather I would have to say: I feel in me a desire to do, which someone has aroused in me. But when I say: I do it, that means spontaneity in the transcendental sense. (AA28–1, 268–9; Kant's emphasis on *I*)

So why is this fourth derivation of a property of the soul from the role of the concept 'I' not the object of a refutation in the *Critique of Pure Reason*? Why does it not become the fourth paralogism of pure reason?

Kant is justified in postponing the discussion of metaphysical freedom to his discussion of the antinomies of pure reason:[23] Freedom is spontaneous (uncaused) causality, and the question of the possibility of such an uncaused cause belongs in the discussion of the concept of a world as a complete series of causally connected entities and events, the topic of the antinomies of pure reason.[24] But transferring the issue of freedom to the discussion of the antinomies also conveniently excuses Kant from answering the embarrassing question: Why does the fourth property ascribed to the soul in *Metaphysik L₁* escape the critique to which the first three were subjected in the first three paralogisms?

A paralogism of spontaneity might look something like this:

> What is conscious of its own self-determination is to that extent absolutely free (an uncaused cause).
> I, as thinking (The soul), am (is) conscious of my (its) own self-determination.
> So I, as thinking, am absolutely free.

Just as in the other paralogisms, Kant could endorse both the major premise and the minor premise, while pointing out that after disambiguation of the middle term ("conscious of one's own self-determination"), the inference appears invalid. In the major premise, something "conscious of its own self-determination" means something that is conscious of being, in fact, the absolute beginning of a series of causes without itself being caused to act. In the minor premise, 'conscious of my own self-determination' means 'conscious, in thinking the moral "I ought to," of prescribing to myself the highest law of my actions.' This is a first-person standpoint on oneself that offers no insight into any kind of objective causal determination. The conclusion thus does not follow: I, as thinking (or more precisely, I, as willing), do not fall under the subject-concept of the major premise and thus do not fall under its predicate-concept, "absolutely (transcendentally) free." Just as from the mere use of 'I' in 'I think' no objective determination of myself as a thinking entity could be derived, so from the mere use of 'I' in 'I do' or even 'I (morally) ought to,' no objective determination of myself as a thinking (and willing) entity, let alone a claim to be an uncaused cause, can be derived.

Kant would of course reply with what he maintains in the *Critique of Pure Reason*: Absolute freedom is needed for any claim to moral accountability to gain any traction at all. This is precisely why, he would claim, the rationalist concept of a person could, indeed should, remain, as necessary and sufficient for practical use (at least if one adds to the psychological notion the moral notion of person). Now suppose we found a way to account for the notion of self-determination as it appears in the minor premise *without* appealing to Kant's notion of absolute spontaneity. Then Kant's reason to preserve the rationalist notion of a person as "necessary and sufficient for practical use" would disappear, and the obvious similarity of structure between the paralogism of spontaneity and the first three paralogisms of pure reason would give just as much ground to discount the former as it gives ground to discount the latter. What would remain is a notion of person, in the moral sense, as an entity belonging in the empirical world (a human being conscious of prescribing herself the law).

We can find such a notion of person, in the moral sense, in many texts posterior to the first edition of the *Critique of Pure Reason*. In *Groundwork of the Metaphysics of Morals*, Kant writes:

> The worth of any object *to be acquired* by our action is always conditional. Beings whose existence rests not on our will but on nature, still have, if they are non-rational beings, only a relative worth, as means, and are therefore called *things*, whereas rational beings are called *persons* because their nature already marks them out as ends in themselves, i.e. as something that may not be used merely as a means, and hence to that extent limits all choices (and is an object of respect). (*Groundwork*, AA4, 429)

It seems clear that *persons*, here, are empirically determinate entities, distinguished from those other kinds of empirical entities that are mere *things* by the fact that as rational beings they are ends in themselves, and objects of respect.

The notion of a person as an empirically given entity can also be found in the *Anthropology from a Pragmatic Standpoint*:

> The fact that the human being can have the 'I' in his representations, raises him infinitely above all other living beings on earth. Because of this, he is a *person*, and by virtue of the unity of consciousness through all alterations that may affect him, one and the same person, i.e. a being that is in rank and dignity entirely different from *things*, such as irrational animals, with which one can do as one likes. (AA7, 127; Kant's emphasis)

In the *Metaphysics of Morals*, Kant relates the anthropological notion of a person to the moral and juridical one: a person is a participant in a system of human legislation in which she has rights and obligations.

> A *person* is a subject whose actions can be *imputed* to him [*dessen Handlungen einer Zurechnung fähig sind*]. *Moral* personality is therefore nothing other than the freedom of a

rational being under moral laws (whereas psychological personality is merely the capacity to become conscious of one's identity in the different states of one's existence); from which it thus follows that a person is subordinated to no other laws than those he gives himself (either alone, or at least along with others. (AA6, 223)

It is with respect to persons so understood that the degree of praiseworthiness or blameworthiness of an action is evaluated, depending on the force of the drives that had to be overcome to engage in a morally required action, on the one hand, and the force of the rational demand potentially in conflict with those drives, on the other.[25] For such an evaluation to make sense, it has to be the case that the *person* whose action is thus being evaluated is a particular living being that has to bear up under the pressure of natural drives and keep in sight the demands of rational self-determination.

It thus remained open to Kant to say that being a person in the moral sense depends on two equally indispensable components that may or may not come apart (and if they do come apart, there just is no person in the moral sense): (1) being an empirically determined, persisting entity, conscious of its own numerical identity through time (person in the psychological sense); (2) having the capacity to prescribe the moral law to oneself, as the principle under which one's maxims are determined. Correspondingly, *consciousness* of being a person is inseparably consciousness of my own numerical identity as a persisting living, thinking, willing entity, and consciousness of the moral "oughts," that is to say, consciousness of the unconditional maxims, which I assign myself under the discriminating principle provided by the moral law.

I am not here taking a stand on the validity of Kant's moral law as a principle of morality. I am only suggesting a way in which it was open to Kant to derive a notion of person in the moral sense along lines parallel to those I suggested for his notion of person in the psychological sense. A natural objection is that such a notion of person would be radically inadequate to preserve the notion of freedom that, for Kant, is indispensable for moral accountability. But my point has been that in insisting on the indispensability to morality of that notion of freedom, Kant was prey to a paralogism of practical reason along just the same lines as the paralogism of pure theoretical reason of which he was accusing rationalist metaphysicians (including, as we just saw, himself in his pre-critical period). For he tries to subsume under a concept of self-determination understood in an objective, causal sense (in the major premise of what I have described as the paralogism of spontaneity) a concept of self-determination that is a necessary condition for understanding oneself as morally accountable for one's actions, but which belongs entirely, *not* to an objective standpoint on causal determination, but to the subjective, albeit universally (subjectively) valid standpoint that each agent has on her own action.

Defenders of Kant's view will no doubt reply that Kant is prey to no such paralogism. For nowhere does he claim objective validity, as a piece of theoretical cognition, for the concept of freedom as absolute spontaneity. In the remarks following his criticism of the paralogism of personality in A, Kant allows that the concept of personhood he has just criticized can remain as "necessary and sufficient for practical use," but only with the restriction: "insofar as it is only transcendental, that is to say a unity of the subject that is unknown to us" (A365–6). In the concluding remarks of the paralogisms in B, the rational concepts of substantiality, simplicity, and personality of the soul are granted validity, but only as concepts that are "merely thought about [*bloß gedachte*]." In *Groundwork*, thinking of ourselves as free is a "standpoint" we take on ourselves, a standpoint that is distinct from the theoretical standpoint according to which our actions are empirically determined according to universal causal laws. And, finally, in the *Critique of Practical Reason*, transcendental freedom is an object of rational *belief*, not a concept whose objective validity is asserted from the standpoint of theoretical cognition.

All of this is true. I acknowledge that it makes the paralogism I reconstructed above distinctly Kantian, not classically rationalist. Nevertheless, the inference does involve—albeit admittedly from a practical standpoint that makes no claim to objective validity from the standpoint of theoretical reason—an equivocation on the middle term, "self-determining," which, if I am right in the analyses I offered above, Kant had the resources to avoid.

6.5 Kant and Strawson on Persons

In insisting that Kant had the resources for defending a concept of person, both psychological and moral, that remained within the confines of an empirically determined, spatiotemporal, embodied entity, I find myself in some proximity to Peter Strawson's assessment of Kant's argument in the third Paralogism of Pure Reason. And yet the concept of person I have in mind is different from Strawson's. It is thus worth trying to sort out the similarities and differences between Strawson's assessment of Kant's view and mine.

According to Strawson, Kant had the groundbreaking insight that the self-ascription of currently experienced or directly remembered states of consciousness rests on no criteria of identity through time of the referent of 'I.' Kant saw that this makes the self-ascription of mental states different from the attribution of states or properties to objects of experience.

> There is nothing that one can...encounter or recall in the field of inner experience such that there can be any question of one's applying criteria of subject-identity to determine whether the encountered or recalled experience belongs to oneself—or someone else. (I think it could be said, without serious exaggeration, that it is because Kant recognized this truth that his treatment of the subject is so greatly superior to Hume's).[26]

Kant, says Strawson, also saw that this criterionless self-ascription of conscious states is not the only way we ascribe states to ourselves. When we take an objective standpoint on ourselves we are, for ourselves, human beings having a mind and body, empirical objects whose persistence through time can be known only by applying empirical criteria of identification and re-identification. Kant mentions this point only fleetingly, however. And what he does not emphasize clearly enough, according to Strawson, is the crucial point that even in criterionless self-ascription of conscious states, "the link to criteria is not in practice severed."

'I' can be used without criteria of subject-identity and yet refer to a subject. It can do so because—perhaps—it issues publicly from the mouth of a man who is recognizable and identifiable as the person he is by the application of empirical criteria of personal identity; or, even if used in soliloquy, is used by a person who would acknowledge the applicability of those criteria in settling questions as to whether he, the very man who now ascribes to himself this experience, was or was not the person who, say, performed such and such an action in the past. 'I' can be used without criteria of subject-identity and yet refer to a subject because even in such a use the links with those criteria are not in practice severed.[27]

That the links are not "in practice" severed presumably means that in ordinary self-ascription of conscious states, criteria of identification are always *available* even if not currently *used*. They are available to the interlocutor to whom the sentence 'I feel pain' is directed (to the question from a third party: 'Who feels pain?' the interlocutor will thus be in a position to reply: 'The guy just there in the corner'), and they are available to the speaker or thinker when the phrase transitions from statements about the present to statements about the past. But because they are not currently in use, it is all too easy to suppose that immediate self-ascription is *not* ascription to a subject so identified. This is an error to which philosophical reflection, cut off from the actual practice of human beings, is especially prone:

The links between criterionless self-ascription and empirical criteria of subject-identity are not *in practice* severed. But in philosophical reflection they may be. It is easy to become intensely aware of the immediate character, of the purely inner basis, of such self-ascription while both retaining the sense of ascription to a subject and forgetting that immediate reports of experience have this character of ascriptions to a subject only because of the links I have mentioned with ordinary criteria of personal identity. (Strawson 1966, 166)

Kant, says Strawson, had the "unparalleled" insight that the criterionless self-ascription of mental states, when severed from its link to empirical criteria of identification of the subject of the ascription, is the source of the rationalist illusion that the subject to which those states are ascribed is a special kind of subject: not the empirical, spatiotemporal, embodied subject, whose identification does rest on criteria of identification, but rather "an absolutely simple, identical, immaterial individual" (ibid.). But this insight is obscured by a "shortcut" Kant wrongly takes. Instead of developing his "unparalleled" insight and making clear that the rationalist illusion stems from abstracting the use of 'I' in self-ascription of thoughts and experiences from its ordinary setting, its connection to the identification of empirically determined subjects, Kant relates that use to a concept he had developed in the context of the transcendental deduction of the categories: the transcendental unity of apperception. The use of 'I' on which the rationalist illusion is based is a use "expressing" the transcendental unity of apperception that, according to Kant's transcendental deduction of the categories, makes experience possible.

Now this aspect of Kant's view, says Strawson, is not completely without merit. On Strawson's own reading of the transcendental deduction, the thought 'I think,' or more generally the self-ascription of representations and experiences, depends on a connectedness of experiences that makes possible the distinction between experiences, as subjective states, and what those experiences are *of* (a world of independently existing objects). That connectedness of experiences, he says, is not a *sufficient* condition for the thought 'I think.' But it is a *necessary* condition, for it is a necessary condition both for acquiring empirical concepts of independently existing objects and for acquiring the empirical concept of a subject of experience. Now if one abstracts from this empirical concept of a subject of experience (a person), what remains is the connectedness of experiences, and the possibility emerges, as Kant says, to confuse "the unity of experience with an experience of unity,"[28] the mere connectedness of one's mental states with the experience of a unitary subject. According to Strawson, the truth is that the experience of a unitary subject so characterized is abstracted out of the *full* experience of a subject, which is that of an empirical subject identified according to empirical criteria.

The "shortcut" Strawson charges Kant with is that of having *directly* derived the concept 'I' in 'I think' from the "unity and connectedness" of experiences, without considering that that unity and connectedness must first make possible the distinction between experience and what experience is *of*, a distinction which itself depends on the representation of the location in space and time of an empirical subject traveling through the world. *Only* by abstraction from *that* empirical subject can the concept of a subject ascribing thoughts and experiences to herself, without criteria of subject identity, emerge. According to Strawson, because Kant ignored this long route of derivation and instead took a shortcut through the idea that 'I' in 'I think' "expresses" the unity of apperception, he is led to say that the concept 'I' is "empty of content." Because of this, instead of characterizing the rationalist illusion as stemming from the illusory severance of the use of 'I' in 'I think' from its link to empirical criteria and thus to the empirical human being, Kant characterizes the rationalist illusion as being one in which an object is supposed where there is, in fact, none at all—just the "expression" of the unity of apperception, or unity of consciousness.

Now given the analysis I have offered so far, it should come as no surprise that I would disagree with Strawson's assessment of Kant's argument against the rational psychologist. Strawson thinks that Kant takes an ill-advised "shortcut" to the unity of consciousness instead of taking the proper way, that is to say, the long road through empirical consciousness of oneself as a person, to explain the possibility of self-ascription. In contrast, I think that Kant's view that 'I' in 'I think' expresses the unity of consciousness (the "transcendental unity of apperception") that is the condition for *any* representation of an object, including the representation of *oneself as a person* (an empirical entity endowed with consciousness and unity of consciousness, traveling through the world),[29] is both correct and a discovery we have yet to fully absorb—Strawson's criticism being a case in point. As I argued in Chapter 2, the unity of consciousness is the condition not only for the use of 'I' in 'I think' but also for *any* use of 'I,' including uses that are based on consciousness of oneself as an empirical, embodied entity.

If I am correct, then the ill-advised shortcut is Strawson's, not Kant's. The shortcut Strawson sees in Kant's reasoning consists in Kant's relating the use of 'I' in 'I think' to the connectedness of our representations and thereby ignoring the fact that there is no *direct* route from that connectedness to a referential use of 'I.' Instead, says Strawson, any referential use of 'I' starts with the self-awareness of an empirically determined, numerically identical person. The person's awareness of the connectedness of her representations depends, in turn, on her awareness of her biographical path through a world of physical objects. The "pure" use of 'I,' says Strawson, is just abstracted out of that empirical self-consciousness. In contrast, I think Strawson is taking a shortcut by ignoring the fact that the very awareness of oneself as an empirical entity traveling through the world, insofar as it allows a self-referential use of 'I,' is premised on the unity of consciousness which, when conceptually expressed, is expressed by the proposition 'I think' and its cognates ('I believe,' 'it seems to me,' and so on). The mistaken shortcut, for Strawson, consists in grounding the use of 'I' in 'I think' directly on the unity of consciousness. The mistaken shortcut, according to the view I endorse and take to be in agreement with Kant's, consists in grounding all uses of 'I' directly on the consciousness of oneself as an embodied entity. My claim is that there is, in fact, a use of 'I' that is *not* abstracted from the empirical representation of oneself, but rather *just* reflects the consciousness of the unity of one's representations and thoughts. My claim is moreover that the consciousness of the unity of one's representations and thoughts is a necessary condition for the consciousness of oneself as an empirical entity traveling through the world: one cannot obtain the latter without making use of the former.

As I have insisted throughout, I do not mean that having the thought 'I think' is a necessary condition for any other use of 'I.' Nor do I mean that any thought must be prefaced by 'I think.' What I mean is that *the unity of consciousness* that eventually comes to be expressed in the proposition 'I think' is a necessary condition for any use of 'I.' In the terms discussed in Chapter 2, that unity of consciousness (but not the proposition 'I think') is a necessary condition for all uses of 'I,' whether "as a subject" or "as an object."

Strawson misunderstands Kant when he maintains that, for Kant, the use of 'I' that "expresses" the unity of consciousness is non-referential. Kant consistently insists that 'I' as used in 'I think' "represents" (in post-Fregean terms, refers to) "a thing that thinks" or "the I or he or it (the thing) that thinks." When Kant says that 'I' in 'I think' is "the emptiest concept," he just means that 'I' has the peculiarity of expressing, for the thinker herself whom 'think' is asserted of, the fact that the predicate 'think' is true of her, without any of the usual marks of a concept being contained in 'I' and without any manifold of intuition being thought under it. This is not far from our understanding of 'I' as an indexical defined by FRR: 'I' refers, in any instance of its use, to the individual currently thinking the thought or expressing the proposition in which 'I' is used. What is peculiar to the use of 'I' in 'I think' is that no further information about the nature of the referent is carried by the predicate attributed to 'I.' This is of course different from the cases in which the predicates attributed to 'I' are concepts of physical properties. Even in these cases, however, FRR holds: 'I' refers, in each instance of its use, to the individual thinking or saying 'I am F.' But if the predicate F is a concept of physical properties, the proposition 'I am F' indicates that the consciousness we have of the referent of 'I' includes consciousness of physical properties—properties of what Kant called, in *Metaphysik L₁*, the I *in sensu latiori*, and what he calls, in the *Critique of Pure Reason*, a human being (*Mensch*) considered both as an appearance belonging to the sensible world (and as such, having outer [physical] and inner [mental] states), and as the supersensible ground of that appearance, whatever the ontological nature of that supersensible ground may be.[30]

Now admittedly, in some respects the distance between my view and Strawson's may seem quite small, since Strawson grants that there is a use of 'I' in which we *may* abstract from the empirical person; and conversely, the conclusion of my discussion of the third paralogism is that Kant had the resources for restricting the concept of a person in the psychological sense to that of an empirical entity, a living being endowed with psychological states and unity of consciousness. Such a concept, I claimed, when complemented with the moral concept according to which a person, in the moral sense, is an individual capable of giving herself the law (the moral law), gave Kant what he needed to account for the normative demands, on human beings, of both knowledge and morality. Still, the difference between Strawson's view and mine lies in the credit we respectively give to the role Kant assigns to the unity of mental activity in his account of our use of the concept and word 'I.' According to Strawson, Kant's story of mental activity belongs to the "imaginary topic of transcendental psychology." According to my interpretation and defense of Kant's arguments, Kant's transcendental account of the structure of our mental capacities and activities is indispensable to his account of the possibility of knowledge and of morality. It is also the essential component in Kant's concept of a person: a person is a living being *endowed with unity of apperception and with a capacity to take a second order stance on the rules of her actions, subjecting them to the discriminating principle of the moral law*. The unity of apperception is a necessary condition for the consciousness of one's numerical identity at different times as an entity (and thus for instantiating the psychological concept of a person). The unity of apperception plus the second order stance on the hierarchy of one's rules for action is a necessary condition for being morally accountable for one's actions (and thus for instantiating the moral concept of a person). The concept of person I am offering agrees with Strawson's in that, according to this concept, the *referent* of 'I' turns out to be the person in the empirical sense. But the *consciousness* on which the use of 'I' is based can be either the consciousness of the empirically determinate person (use of 'I' *in sensu latiori*) or the consciousness of the unity of mental activity that generates objective knowledge and the hierarchy of one's rules for action (use of 'I' *in sensu stricto*). Most often, it is both. The consciousness of the unity of mental activity is not abstracted out of the consciousness of the human being. It is a consciousness in its own right, which is the condition for any use of 'I,' including the use of 'I' that depends on the full-fledged consciousness of the individual biography of the empirical human being. The rational psychologist's mistake, according to Kant, is to confuse the self-consciousness that is based on the consciousness of one's mental activity, for the consciousness of a special, ethereal, disembodied entity. In fact, it is the consciousness of being engaged in and committed to the unity and rational connectedness of a mental activity one takes oneself to be accountable for. That consciousness is a necessary condition for any use of 'I.'

Now of course, Kant goes further than this. He thinks that from a practical standpoint there is reason to believe that the consciousness of one's rationally structured mental activity, whether theoretical or practical, is a consciousness of a purely intelligible entity whose existence grounds that of the empirical human being.

He also claims that believing we are such a pure intelligence is subjectively justified by our consciousness of the moral law as a law we give to ourselves. Restricting, as I have proposed to do, the concept of a person both in the psychological and in the moral sense, to that of the empirical human being *endowed with unity of consciousness and with the capacity to subordinate the rules of her actions to the categorical imperative of morality*, is rejecting the concept of person that Kant wanted to salvage from his own criticism of the rationalist argument for the objective validity of that concept. How much remains of Kant's conception of morality once one has rejected that concept in favor of a strictly empirical concept of person? I will offer some tentative answers to this question in Chapter 8.

6.6 Concluding Remarks

Kant's criticism of the paralogism of personality does not only yield a negative result, namely, the refutation of what Kant takes to be the rationalist's purported proof that, as entities capable of thinking 'I think,' we are persons. It also yields a positive account of our use of 'I' in 'I think,' complementing the accounts offered in the first two paralogisms of pure reason. I have suggested, moreover, that *pace* Kant's ultimate endorsement of the rationalist concept of a person as "necessary and sufficient for practical use," Kant's criticism of the paralogism of personhood opens the way to substituting for the rationalist concept a rich and complex concept of a person as a spatiotemporal, living entity endowed with unity of apperception and with the capacity for autonomous self-determination. Before closing this chapter, let me take stock of what we've learned so far about both points: the use of 'I' in 'I think' and Kant's concept of a person.

In Chapter 2, I argued that Kant was correct in claiming that the unity of apperception that finds expression in the proposition 'I think' is a necessary condition for any conceptual representation and any judgment. I argued that the unity of apperception is therefore a necessary condition for any use of 'I,' whether "as subject" or "as object."[31] I maintained, *pace* Evans, that the use of 'I' in the proposition 'I think' does *not* depend on consciousness of oneself as an embodied entity but only on understanding the reference rule: 'I' refers to the current thinker or speaker of the proposition/sentence 'I think.' Kant's statement that 'I' expresses "only a formal condition of my thoughts and their holding together [*Zusammenhang*]" does *not* entail, I maintained, that for Kant there is no referential use of 'I' absent the consciousness of oneself as an embodied entity.

I now submit that all these points are confirmed by Kant's arguments in the Paralogisms of Pure Reason. Kant's endorsement of Descartes's *cogito* argument confirms that for Kant, just as for Descartes, consciousness of thinking is a sufficient condition for consciousness of one's own existence.[32] It is nevertheless true, of course, that in most cases 'I' is used in propositions predicating of oneself states or properties of a physical thing. These are uses of 'I' based on the consciousness of what Kant called, in *Metaphysics L₁*, the I *in sensu latiori*. We might call the corresponding uses of 'I' uses of 'I' *in sensu latiori*, that is to say, uses of 'I' in which the concept we have of ourselves is based not only on the consciousness we have of ourselves as the individual currently thinking, but also on the consciousness of ourselves as an embodied entity. Correspondingly, we might call the use of 'I' based on consciousness of oneself as thinking the use of 'I' *in sensu stricto*. The *referent* of 'I' is one and the same in both uses. But in its use *in sensu stricto*, no further information is needed to ground the use of 'I' than the fact that I (the referent of 'I') think. In its use *in sensu latiori*, the judgments in which we ascribe physical predicates to 'I' rest on information concerning the properties I (the referent of 'I') have as an embodied entity—a living, sensing being.

Now according to Kant, the self-consciousness that grounds the use of 'I' in 'I think' has features of its own. These features are not features objectively verifiable or falsifiable as features of the existing entity I am, insofar as I think. But they are, according to Kant, ways I am inevitably disposed to represent myself, in thinking. In referring to myself by 'I' (in 'I think'), I *cannot but* represent myself (think of myself) as subject, the author of my thoughts. In referring to myself by 'I' (in 'I think'), I *cannot but* represent myself (think of myself) as a singular, indivisible entity. In referring to myself by 'I' (in 'I think'), I *cannot but* represent myself (think of myself) as an entity that remains numerically identical through all its thoughts. In all these features, one could characterize the object of the concept 'I' as the *intellectual appearance* of the thinker *to herself*. But this appearance is a mere "object in thought" (A400). So the paradox of 'I' is this: 'I,' as used in 'I think,' refers to an existing thing, known by the I-user (the thinker) to exist, in virtue of the fact that the I-user, in each instance of thinking knows herself to exist. 'I,' as used in 'I think,' is even the only purely intellectual concept that does give access to an existing thing. But if, from the way we think of ourselves in using 'I' in 'I think,' we infer there is an object that we take to be, as a thinking thing, a substance, simple, and numerically identical through time, then we make a mistake: that object is a fiction. The error of the rationalist metaphysician (the error of Kant himself in his pre-critical incarnation) is to insist that on the basis of the thought 'I think' we have sufficient ground to assert that the fictitious object of that representation is transcendentally real: real in itself. The mere thought 'I think' in fact provides no such ground.

Now as we saw, even in his critical period and precisely after his criticism of the paralogisms of rational psychology, Kant ultimately endorses the rationalist notion of a soul as substance, simple substance, and the locus of personhood. He cautiously admits at least the possibility that what appears to us as divisible in space might be grounded in the existence of "a subject which is not composite, but is simple, and thinks" (A360). But he rejects as a category mistake the idea that this subject should be thought to be a mental entity distinct from the body. Rather, insofar as we can think it at all, we must consider it as the common ground of what, in the phenomenal world, appears on the one hand as an object of outer sense (body), and on the other as an object of inner sense (the empirically determinate sequence of our mental states, for which we suppose an underlying object as the bearer of those states—the soul).[33]

Kant's cautious endorsement of the rationalist notion, whose proof of objective validity he has taken such pains to criticize, is most clearly stated in the final paragraphs of the paralogism of personality: the notion of a person, as the rationalist understands it, "can remain (insofar as it is merely transcendental, i.e. a unity of the subject that is otherwise unknown to us)" and as such it is "necessary and sufficient for practical use" (A366). I have suggested that strictly speaking, on Kant's own account that concept is in fact *not* sufficient for practical use: for practical use we need to add, to the "psychological," the "moral" concept of a person.[34] But I have also suggested that from Kant's criticism of the third paralogism, we could derive a more modest notion of a person, in both the psychological and the moral sense: a living being endowed with unity of apperception and a capacity for autonomous determination of the rules of her actions. Accepting such a notion of person, in the psychological and the moral sense, would be consistent with the groundbreaking analysis Kant has offered of the illusions necessarily brought about by our use of 'I.' But it would certainly be incompatible with Kant's claim that transcendental freedom is an indispensable condition for the very possibility of morality.

In the opening paragraph of his "Freedom of the Will and the Concept of a Person," Harry Frankfurt complains that Strawson's concept of a person does not capture our ordinary use of the concept. As we saw above, in *Individuals*, Strawson defines the concept of 'person' as that of "a type of entity such that *both* predicates ascribing states of consciousness *and* predicates ascribing corporeal characteristics... are equally applicable to a single individual of that single type."[35] But our ordinary concept of 'person,' says Frankfurt, is richer than Strawson's. It includes, as an essential characteristic, the capacity to form "second-order desires" or "desires of the second order."[36]

What I have been suggesting is that Kant's concept of a person, both in the psychological sense (an entity capable of consciousness of her own identity at different times) and in the moral sense (an entity capable of moral accountability) is along Frankfurtian rather than Strawsonian lines. But it is richer than Frankfurt's notion, both because it connects, better than any of its predecessors, and, I would suggest, better than any of its successors, the cognitive and the conative, the psychological and the moral notion of person; and because it offers richer hypotheses as to the structure of the mental life that makes us persons.[37]

* * *

In the next two chapters I propose to explore a particular developmental account of the structure of mental life at work in our cognitive and conative activities—in what Kant calls the theoretical and the practical uses of reason. To do this, I will follow a lead I offered at the end of Chapter 2. Following Oliver Sacks's description of "the disembodied lady,"[38] I suggested that Freud's account of the structure of our mental life offered a good model for the two fundamental types of information that I suggested any use of 'I' is based on: the consciousness of one's own body (including, in some cases, a consciousness grounding judgments that are immune to error through misidentification relative to the first-person pronoun) and, conditioning *any* use of 'I,' the consciousness of being engaged in generating the rational unity of the contents of one's mental states. I now would like to pursue this suggestion further. In the next two chapters, I will argue that Freud's psychoanalytic account of the fundamental structure of our mental life offers resources for exactly the kind of naturalization of the notion of person I have just suggested could be derived from Kant's criticism of the rationalist paralogism of personhood. By "naturalization," I mean an understanding of the notion of person that does not draw on a supposed unknown and unknowable noumenal realm, but remains within the confines of the empirical domain of spatiotemporal entities. What remains of Kant's view of morality in light of Freud's account? Surprisingly more than one might think. Or so I will argue.

Notes

1. See Leibniz 1981 [1765], bk. 2, chap. 27, §9; Wolff 1972 [1740], §741; and Baumgarten 1913 [1747], §641. For other possible sources of Kant's discussion of the third paralogism, see Guyer and Wood's indications in Kant (A/B), 738n27.
2. "Paralogism der Personalität," A361. Kant also calls the third paralogism "Paralogism der Persönlichkeit," 'paralogism of personhood.' To our contemporary ears this is less misleading. For the paralogism is not about 'personality' in the sense of 'character,' but about the necessary and sufficient condition for counting as a person. At A365–6, Kant repeatedly uses the term *Persönlichkeit*. However, *Personalität*, used in the title of the paralogism, and often in the text, is the more direct German counterpart of Baumgarten's Latin term *Personalitas*. In an effort to do justice to the shift in terminology, I translate *Persönlichkeit* by the admittedly less common term 'personhood' (the property of being, or counting as, a person). I keep 'personality' whenever the German says *Personalität*. But both terms clearly have the same meaning in Kant's discussion.
3. Guyer and Wood give, for the subject-concept in the major premise: "What is conscious of the numerical identity of its Self at different times." The German text in the academy edition says: "Was sich der numerischen Identität seiner selbst in verschiedenen Zeiten bewusst ist." "Seiner selbst" is equivalent to the reflexive "of itself" in English. It does not seem to warrant the substantive form in the translation "of its self," much less the upper case S on "Self." Guyer and Wood indicate in a note to their translation that "seiner selbst," without upper case on "selbst," appears in the fourth edition (see A/B, 422n). In correspondence, Paul Guyer indicated to me that the first edition of the *Critique* capitalized "Selbst" in "seiner Selbst," and that the fourth edition, in which "selbst" is no longer capitalized, was the 1794 edition, which most probably appeared without Kant's supervision, since Kant was then busy trying to complete his system. Guyer notes: "What the original upper-case 'S' meant remains a matter of interpretation." I agree. For my part, I tend to think that even with the upper case on "selbst," "seiner selbst" should be read as a simple reflexive. When Kant means to say "of my self," he uses the expression "meines Selbst" (see, for instance, A362). Since the rationalist move from the consciousness one has of oneself (*seiner selbst*) in thinking, to a consciousness *of a self supposed to be an object*, a soul, is central to Kant's argument in the paralogisms, my own view is that it is best to stick to "of itself" when Kant says "seiner selbst"—despite the admittedly puzzling presence of the upper case on *Selbst* in the first three editions. In any event, even "consciousness of the numerical identity of itself" is ambiguous between: consciousness of the numerical identity of something called a self, and consciousness of one's own numerical identity at different times, where what that amounts to remains to be clarified, as Kant tries to do in his discussion of the paralogism. Many thanks to Paul Guyer and Allen Wood for their helpful correspondence on this point.
4. Cf. the text from the introduction to the Paralogisms of Pure Reason cited in 5.1.5: "I, as thinking, am an object of inner sense, and am called 'soul'" (A342/B400).

5. This interpretation is confirmed by the more compressed formulation of the second edition: "[By identity of person would be understood] the consciousness of the identity of one's own substance as a thinking being in all changes of states" (B408). On this point, I agree with Karl Ameriks: see Ameriks 2000, 130–1. See also Rosefeldt 2000, 96.
6. 'I,' for Kant, is a concept. He calls the content of a concept sometimes its *marks* (the concepts 'contained in' the relevant concept, e.g., 'rational, animal' are the marks of 'human'), sometimes the objects falling under the concept (e.g., human beings all belong in the content of the concept 'human,' or in contemporary terms, each particular human being is an instantiation of the concept 'human being,' or belongs in the extension of the concept). Now, the concept 'I' has no marks, it is an "empty concept." But it is characterized by its role in the propositions in which it appears, and, for the problem at issue in the paralogisms, by its role in the proposition 'I think.' 'I' is the "absolute subject" of the proposition 'I think' (see 4.3, n. 32; 5.1.3; 5.1.4; and 5.2.2.3, n. 44). As the subject-concept of the purely intellectual proposition 'I think,' 'I' is only a logical subject or a "subject in thought," and it has only a logical object (an "object in thought"), not a real object given in sensibility. Nevertheless, since 'I think,' in any instance of its being thought, entails 'I exist,' 'I' refers to an existing entity, the transcendental subject of thought = X. For these notions, see 5.1.3 and 5.1.4.
7. Note that what is translated as 'mind' here is the German *Gemüt*, not *Seele*. The *Gemüt* is just the system of representational capacities and states, whose intentional objects are objects of the outside world (objects of outer sense) and its own states and activities (objects of inner sense)—and thereby also a supposed object of inner sense, the soul (*Seele*). Cf. 5.1.5.
8. See n. 7 in this chapter.
9. This is, I submit, the response to the looming question of identity I mentioned in 2.3. As formulated in the main text above in this chapter, however, the response does not exactly answer the question at issue in the third paralogism. The question at issue in the paralogism is that of the identity of the *entity* that thinks. It is not the system of representational capacities (*das Gemüt*), that represents its own identity. Rather, we ourselves, insofar as we represent ourselves (our own mental states) in time (and so, as appearances in inner sense), represent our own identity insofar as we represent the unity of the contents of our mental states. Kant's point, in his criticism of the third paralogism, is that the numerical identity we thus represent is numerical identity only "in thought," the numerical identity of the supposed (but not intuited) unitary object of inner sense (the object of the concept 'I, as thinking,' thought to be an object of inner sense), whose states are supposed to be our inner (mental) states. More on this in the following.
10. The Guyer–Wood translation does not always respect that distinction. Of course, an additional difficulty is created by Kant's erratic use of capital letters.
11. The German says: "Wenn ich mich aber aus dem Gesichtspunkt eines anderen (als Gegenstand seiner äußeren Anschauung) betrachte, so erwägt dieser äußere Beobachter mich allererst **in der Zeit**, denn in der Apperzeption ist die Zeit eigentlich nur **in mir** vorgestellt." What Kant means is: it is only from a third-person standpoint that I am *in time*. As long as I consider myself from the first-person standpoint of apperception, time is *in me*, that is to say, within the purview of the unity of apperception expressed in the thought 'I think.'
12. See Evans 1982, 75, 209–10, 226, 228; cf. 2.1.4 in this volume.
13. Admittedly, saying that for Kant, spatiotemporal conditions on the identification and re-identification of objects are merely epistemic conditions is not, strictly speaking, accurate, given Kant's claim that "the conditions of possibility of experience are also conditions of possibility of the *object* of experience." Space and time are not just epistemic conditions on

our forming objective knowledge of objects, but also conditions on the very possibility of those objects, as appearances. So in describing space and time as a priori forms of our (sensible) intuition, Kant also makes space and time the basis for a *metaphysics*, an a priori knowledge of the fundamental features of the world, as a world of appearances. My point here is that this leaves open, for Kant, the possibility of a semantic analysis of the word 'I' that is not restricted to those conditions.

14. See A362, cited in 6.2. See also my comments, ibid. and n. 10.
15. On the expression: person, "in the psychological sense," see *Met. Mor.*, AA6, 223. The complete concept of a person includes "person, in the psychological sense," characterized by consciousness of one's own numerical identity at different times; and "person, in the moral sense," characterized by accountability for one's actions (ibid.; cf. Locke 1975 [1689], bk. 2, chap. 27, §26: "The name *person* is a Forensick Term appropriating Actions and their Merit"). I say more below about these two senses of the concept 'person' and their relation: see 6.4.
16. Cf. A533–4/B561–2; A549–58/B577–86.
17. On the categorical imperative as the principle of a will that is "universally legislating through all its maxims," see AA4, 432; on "the autonomy of the will as the supreme principle of morality," see AA4, 440. On the moral law as the *ratio cognoscendi* of freedom, and freedom as the *ratio essendi* of the moral law, see AA5, 4. This reciprocal characterization of freedom and the moral law—the latter is the ground of cognition of the former, the former is the ground of being of the latter—is Kant's solution to the "circle" he acknowledged might be seen as an objection to his deduction of the possibility of a categorical imperative in section 3 of *Groundwork* (see AA4, 450). Discussing the problem of the "circle" and the solution offered in the *Critique of Practical Reason* is beyond the purview of this book. Sufficient for my purpose is the explanation of *why* Kant claims, in the concluding remarks of the paralogism of personality, that the rationalist concept of a person is "necessary and sufficient for practical use," and *why* he adds, in the concluding remark to the paralogisms in B, the reference to "laws holding firm *a priori* and concerning our existence," the awareness of which might be the awareness of our relation to an intelligible world.
18. Locke 1975 [1689], bk. 2, chap. 27, §23.
19. Leibniz 1981 [1765], bk. 2, chap. 27, §23.
20. See AA20-1, 224.
21. A366–80/B409; on the differences between A and B concerning the fourth paralogism of pure reason, see 4.3.1 and n. 28; 5.2.2.3.
22. See AA28-1, 271. The fact that in his pre-critical lectures on rational psychology Kant considered the relation of mind and body *not* in the first, but in the second section of his lectures, thus not in the fundamental doctrine of the soul but in the doctrine of the relation of the soul to other entities, might find an echo in his hesitations about the very content of the fourth paralogism and the proper place of the refutation of Cartesian skepticism in the *Critique of Pure Reason*.
23. See above, first sentence under 6.4 and n.16.
24. A407–8/B434–5.
25. Kant writes: "*Subjectively*, the degree to which an action *can be imputed* (*imputabilitas*) has to be assessed by the magnitude of the obstacles that had to be overcome. The greater the natural obstacles (of sensibility) and the less the moral obstacle (of duty), so much the more merit is credited to the *good deed*; for example, if at considerable self-sacrifice I rescue a complete stranger from great distress.

    In contrast: the less the natural obstacle and the greater the obstacle from grounds of duty, so much the more is the transgression imputed (as culpable)" (*Met. Mor.*, AA6, 228).

Note that for Kant, moral demand is always a demand in a situation of internal conflict (natural drives versus rationally determined will).
26. Strawson 1966, 165.
27. Ibid. What Strawson means by 'subject' is of course the empirically identifiable and re-identifiable entity, the person as an embodied entity endowed with subjective states. Strawson has no room for the variety of uses of the term 'subject' in Kant's reasoning.
28. Strawson 1966, 162.
29. Cf. Strawson's definition of 'person' in *Individuals*: "What I mean by the concept of a person is the concept of a type of entity such that *both* predicates ascribing states of consciousness *and* predicates ascribing corporeal characteristics, a physical situation &c. are equally applicable to a single individual of that single type" (1959, 102). This is the concept of person we also found in Evans: see 3.3, n. 30. It is close to the concept of person I suggest Kant had the resources to revert to after his criticism of the rationalist illusion according to which one could derive from the concept 'I' a concept of person as a soul, distinct from the body. Strawson's concept is less rich than the concept of person (even only in the psychological sense) that I suggest Kant had the resources to revert to, since for Kant the concept of person as an empirical entity includes not just bodily and psychological states, but also unity of apperception. And, of course, the full concept of person, for Kant, includes the concept of person in the moral sense. See 6.4. I say more about Kant's psychological and moral concept of a person in the concluding remarks of this chapter, and in Chapter 8.
30. On the I *in sensu latiori*, see *Metaphysik L1*, AA28, 265. On Kant's remark that it might be more appropriate to say "human beings think" rather than "souls think," because one and the same supersensible ground might be common to both physical and mental properties (of empirical human beings), see A360. On the thinking being as a human being, in the empirical sense, see B415.
31. "As subject" and "as object" are taken here in Wittgenstein's sense amended by Shoemaker: see 2.1.2. For the discussion of Kant's 'I think' in that same chapter, see 2.2.
32. See Descartes 1984 [1641], 17; Kant A405, B418–19, B422n; and 4.1 and 4.3 in this volume.
33. See A359–60; and 5.1.5 in this volume.
34. See 6.4.
35. Strawson 1959, 101–2, cited in Frankfurt 1988, 11.
36. Frankfurt 1988, 12.
37. Admittedly, Frankfurt would not endorse the Kantian version of the empirical notion of person, with its emphasis on the moral law as the law of a free will. But he might be friendly to the naturalization of Kant's notion of a person along the Freudian line I offer in the final two chapters of this book. I at least take the latter to be friendly to Frankfurt's view. See Chapters 7 and 8.
38. Sacks 1998 [1985], 52: "She had lost, with her sense of proprioception, the fundamental organic mooring of identity—at least of that corporeal identity, or 'body-ego' which Freud sees as the basis of self. 'The ego is first and foremost a body ego.'" Cf. 2.3 in this volume.

PART III
...And Back Again

7

Kant's 'I' in 'I Think' and Freud's "Ego"

7.1 Preliminary Remarks

In the final section of Chapter 2, I suggested that Freud's structural view of the mind, expounded in *The Ego and the Id*, offered a psychological model for the two kinds of self-consciousness that are fundamental to any use of 'I' as subject, and thus to any use of 'I': consciousness of one's own body and consciousness of being engaged in bringing rational unity into the contents of one's mental states and activity. Moreover, Freud's model, I suggested, offered support for the view that I had been arguing we inherit from Kant, according to which consciousness of being engaged in the rational of the contents of one's mental activity is a necessary condition for any use of 'I.'[1]

In the present chapter, I will offer a more detailed defense of those claims. I will argue that Freud's concept '*Ich*' (translated by James Strachey as 'ego') bears a striking similarity to Kant's concept of the transcendental unity of apperception, and thus to Kant's analysis of the role of 'I' in 'I think.'[2] In the next chapter (Chapter 8) I will defend a parallel claim concerning the relation between Kant's analysis of the role of 'I' in the moral 'I ought to' and Freud's concept of super-ego. Because Freud's account of ego and super-ego displays structural similarities to Kant's account of the structures of mental life grounding the use of 'I' in 'I think' and 'I ought to,' I will suggest that Freud's model of the mind might be an additional resource for naturalizing Kant's notion of a person along the lines I suggested at the end of Chapter 6. How deep a revision of Kant's view of morality this may involve will be discussed in Chapter 8 and in the conclusion of this book.

In neither of these two chapters am I taking a stand on the scientific credentials of Freudian psychoanalysis. Nor am I taking a stand on the clinical virtues of psychoanalytic therapy. Of course, I would not attempt the comparison I am offering if I found no value in Freud's approach to the mind, and more specifically in the structural view of the mind Freud offers on the basis of his clinical experience. But a thorough evaluation of Freud's claims is beyond the purview of the present book.[3]

Nevertheless, I should acknowledge from the outset some of the glaring differences between Kant's and Freud's respective projects. Here I will list three that may seem especially damning to the comparison I am proposing.

First, concerning the *concepts* under investigation. Kant's 'I' is the concept 'I' that occupies the place of logical subject in the proposition 'I think.'[4] In contrast, as we will see, Freud's concept 'ego' ('*Ich*') refers to a specific kind of organization of mental processes whose contents obey elementary logical rules.

Second, concerning the *context* of investigation. In Kant, that context is the Transcendental Deduction of the Categories, an investigation of the conditions of possibility of synthetic a priori cognition.[5] In contrast, the context in which Freud coins his concept '*das Ich*' is that of an empirical/clinical investigation into the propensity of human beings to specific kinds of mental dysfunction.

Third, the *method* of investigation. Kant's method is that of an a priori investigation into the necessary conditions of synthetic a priori cognition.[6] In contrast, Freud's method is empirical. The relevance of his concept '*Ich*' is supposed to be supported by empirical evidence gathered primarily—albeit not exclusively—in the context of psychoanalytical therapy.

There are thus radical differences between Kant and Freud concerning *what* is under investigation, concerning the *context* of investigation, and concerning the *method* of investigation. This being so, what can we possibly learn from a comparison or confrontation between them? A preliminary answer is that, although it is important to keep in mind the contrasts I just outlined, on each of those three points the opposition between Kant and Freud appears, on closer scrutiny, to be less drastic than I just suggested.

Take Kant again. Although 'I' is the *concept* 'I' as it occurs in the proposition 'I think,' that proposition itself is the conceptual expression of the unity of apperception that is a "formal condition of thoughts and their connectedness" (see, e.g., A363). Now my claim will be that Kant's concept of 'unity of apperception' is the ancestor of Freud's concept of 'ego' ('*Ich*') as an organization of mental processes governed by logical rules. Of course, unlike Freud's ego, the "formal condition" Kant is talking about is not the object of an empirical investigation into the mental lives of human beings, but rather the object of an a priori, transcendental investigation into the conditions of justification of synthetic a priori judgments. Nevertheless, it seems fair to say that the link between the "formal condition of thought" and the mental lives of empirical persons is in practice not severed.

I am borrowing this last formulation from Peter Strawson.[7] The expression "in practice not severed" occurs in the course of Strawson's analysis of Kant's argument in the Paralogisms of Pure Reason. Kant, says Strawson, had the unparalleled insight that 'I' in 'I think' is used in such a way that there is no need for the I-user to appeal to empirical criteria of identification to determine which entity is thinking when she thinks 'I think.' This is because 'I think' expresses a "formal unity of consciousness" without any need for the thinker to have in mind the particular empirical person 'I' refers to. Unfortunately, says Strawson, Kant failed to see that the link with the empirical criteria for such reference is "in practice not severed." In other words, 'I' in 'I think' refers to *the very same entity* which, in other contexts, we would need to identify by appealing to empirical criteria of identification and re-identification to ascertain whether a proposition of the form 'I am F' is true, that is to say, more precisely, whether I, an empirically determinate person, am the entity of which F is true. Thus, Kant did not see that even in 'I think,' 'I' refers to a person, an empirically given entity, identifiable and re-identifiable in space and time.

Strawson's point was semantic and epistemological; in the present context mine is psychological. I borrow Strawson's expression (the link to empirical persons is "in practice not severed") to make a different use of it than Strawson does. My claim is that the link between Kant's unity of apperception and the actual functioning of empirical human minds is "in practice not severed." For the formal condition, that is, the transcendental unity of apperception, is realized in the mental activities of empirically determinate, particular persons.

In fact, the link between transcendental and empirical investigation is readily apparent in Kant's works, in both directions: from transcendental to empirical and from empirical to transcendental. For instance, Kant's transcendental investigation in the *Critique of Pure Reason* appeals to elements of empirical psychology that Kant borrowed from his predecessors and contemporaries—Locke, Hume, Baumgarten, and Tetens, to name only a few. This is especially apparent in Kant's exposition of the "threefold synthesis" in the first edition of the Transcendental Deduction, where apprehension, reproduction, and recognition are described as empirically observable operations of the mind that occur in time.[8] Conversely, Kant's *Anthropology from a Pragmatic Point of View*, a treatise in empirical psychology and anthropology, is informed by Kant's transcendental philosophy, for instance, when Kant explains the distinction between productive and reproductive imagination,[9] or when he describes the emergence of the capacity to say and think 'I,' which he takes to be a landmark in the psychological development of the child and an indicator of the rational capacity that distinguishes human beings from non-human animals.[10]

These are only a few examples of the ways in which the contrast between Kant's a priori, formal investigation and Freud's empirical investigation becomes less drastic once one considers the mutual reinforcement of transcendental and empirical investigation in Kant's own version of psychology. It remains of course true that the context of Kant's analysis of 'I' in 'I think' is that of a transcendental, not an empirical, investigation. But the transcendental investigation is not unrelated to more empirical forays into the workings of the mind. The a priori investigation into conditions of justification is not unrelated to an empirical investigation of what is, in fact, going on in the mental life and mental development of human beings.

The contrast between transcendental and empirical investigation can also be mitigated on Freud's side. *Das Ich und das Es* belongs to what Freud called his "metapsychology," whose goal was to "clarify and carry deeper the theoretical assumptions on which one might ground a psychoanalytic system."[11] This characterization of the goals of metapsychology brings Freud's investigation of 'ego' in the vicinity of Kant's investigation of the conditions of possibility of specific cognitive achievements. Indeed, my claim in this chapter will be that Freud's concept '*Ich*' (translated into Latinate English as 'ego') is meant to give an account of what makes it possible for us to develop the capacity to think in the first person, and thus to relate our thoughts to 'I' in 'I think.'

Kant is famous for assigning this capacity to an unknown and unknowable transcendental subject.[12] In contrast, I shall maintain that Freud offers a compelling account of the complex ways in which empirically given, causally determined persons develop precisely those capacities Kant thought could be accounted for only by appealing to the absolute spontaneity of an unknown and unknowable transcendental subject. A parallel story can be told about Freud's developmental explanation of our capacity for moral motivation and justification, and thus of our use of 'I' in the moral 'I ought to.' This part of the story will be handled in the next chapter. In the current chapter, I am concerned with Kant's 'I think' in relation to our knowledge of a world of objective facts, and with Freud's 'ego' as an organization of mental processes geared toward knowledge of objective facts.

One final disclaimer: what I am offering is an investigation of conceptual similarities and differences, not an account of historical influence. Such an account would have to consider the history of philosophy of mind and psychology from Kant to Freud. Important figures along the way would include, at a minimum, Schopenhauer, Nietzsche, Brentano, Herbart, Helmholtz, as well as other lesser-known figures in the history of philosophy and psychology. My goal in this chapter is not to offer such a history. It is only to substantiate my claim that Kant's notion of a person can be naturalized and that Freud offers, for a contemporary reader, important resources for such a naturalization of Kant's transcendental philosophy.[13]

I will proceed as follows.

In 7.2, I will consider four features of Kant's account of 'I' and the transcendental unity of apperception that are, I believe, especially relevant to Freud's own concept 'Ich' (Strachey's 'ego').

In 7.3, I will expound in its own terms Freud's account of 'Ich' in *Das Ich und das Es*.

In 7.4, I will examine the extent to which the four points I highlighted in Kant's view have parallels in Freud's view. I will argue that the comparison supports my suggestion that there are striking parallels between Kant's concept of 'transcendental unity of apperception' grounding our use of 'I' in 'I think,' and Freud's concept of 'ego' ('Ich').

7.2 Kant on 'I' in 'I Think'

I will consider four points: (1) Kant's view of the relations among unity of apperception (and thus 'I'), discursive (conceptual) thinking, and consciousness of one's representations; (2) Kant's view of the relation between discursive thinking and imagination; (3) The activity of imagination as an activity of which we are "mostly not conscious"; (4) Kant's view of the relation between unity of apperception and consciousness of one's own body.

On all four points I will later argue (in 7.4) that we find striking parallels in Freud's views of the structure of our mental life.

7.2.1 *'I,' Discursive Thinking, and Being Conscious of One's Representations*

Let me start again with the well-known sentence from §16 of the B Transcendental Deduction:

The *I think* must *be able* to accompany all my representations; for otherwise something would be represented in me that could not be thought at all, which is as much as to say that the representation would either be impossible or else at least, would be nothing to me. (B131–2)

In previous chapters I have offered extensive comments on this sentence, as part of my investigation of Kant's analysis of 'I' in 'I think.'[14] I now want to focus on the question: What kinds of representations is Kant talking about, and what does he mean by saying that unless the *I think* were able to accompany them, they would be "nothing to me"?

The statement, on the face of it, is surprising. Kant's concept of 'representation' refers to any mental state, whether or not it has representational content (or what we would call 'intentional' content: something the representation is *about* or directed at), and whether or not the subject of representation is conscious of having the representation.[15] Now isn't it the case that some representations, in this broad sense, are something to me (I am aware of them, I am aware of being in those states) even though the thought 'I think' does not and never will, indeed cannot, accompany them (for instance, an acute pain, fleeting feelings, or even fleeting images)? Don't we have reason moreover to suppose that non-human animals have representations (mental states) that are something to them (something that they feel, and to which they respond with specific kinds of behavior) even though we have no reason to believe they form concepts of them, much less reason to believe that the thought 'I think' can accompany them? Isn't this a point Kant himself explicitly acknowledges?[16]

To clarify Kant's meaning, it will help once again to take a close look at the cited sentence. The sentence is a compressed statement of two conditioning relations, laid out in the form of three counterfactual propositions. I will make the conditioning relations explicit by appropriately dividing the quoted sentence:

[Thesis] The **I think** must be able to accompany all my representations.
[1_c] [first counterfactual proposition]: For otherwise [namely, *if* the **I think** were *not* able to accompany all my representations],
[2_c] [second counterfactual proposition, for which [1_c] counts as a sufficient condition]: [*then*] Something would be represented in me that could not be thought at all.
[3_c] [third, disjunctive counterfactual proposition, for which [2_c] counts as a sufficient condition]: Which is as much as to say that [= *then*] the representation would either [$3_c a$] be impossible or at least [$3_c b$] be nothing to me.

Reformulating the counterfactuals as a sequence of conditionals, we get:

[Premise 1] For any of my representations, that representation is possible at all, or at least, is something to me *only if* what is represented in me can be thought (contraposition of the relation of sufficient condition between [2_c] and the disjunctive proposition [3_c]).
[Premise 2] For any of my representations, what is represented in me can be thought *only if* the 'I think' is able to accompany the relevant representation (contraposition of the relation of sufficient condition between [1c] and [2_c]).
[Conclusion] So, for any of my representations, that representation is possible at all or at least, is something to me *only if* the 'I think' is able to accompany it (from [1] and [2]. This is the thesis asserted at the beginning of B131-2 cited above.)[17]

Let me now offer comments on the premises and conclusion.

Premise 1. I propose to consider three questions. First, what are the "representations" Kant is talking about in this passage? Second, why the disjunctive proposition, which sounds like a partial disclaimer: "The representation is possible, *or at least* is something to me"? Third, is there a difference between "something is represented in me" and "the representation is something to me"? In other words, can something be "represented in me" without the representation being "something to me"? Clearly Kant means to argue that a necessary condition for the latter (a representation's being "something to me") is that the 'I think' be able to accompany it: this is the purported conclusion of the argument reconstructed above. Does Kant mean also to say that "something is represented in me" only if the 'I think' is able to accompany it? A related question is: What exactly is meant by "me" and "*my* representation"?

Answering question (1): What kinds of representations are we talking about? According to the *Stufenleiter*,[18] the genus 'representation' is first divided into the two species: representation "with consciousness," and representation "without consciousness."[19] Under representation "with consciousness" the division is: representation that is only "related to the subject, as a modification of its state" (mere sensation, *Empfindung*) or representation that is related to an object (cognition). Under "cognition" the division is between "intuition" and "concept."[20] I submit that the representations Kant is talking about in B131-2 (cited at the beginning of this section) could be any of the representations included under "representation with consciousness," and so either mere sensation (representation "related to the subject as a modification of its state," a representation by which a subject is aware of her own state), or cognition: intuition or concept. Correspondingly, the "something" that is "represented in me" could be, in the case of sensation, my own state; in the case of intuition, the "something represented in me" could be the intentional correlate of the intuition—the appearance as an "undetermined object of intuition" (A20/B34); in the case of the concept, the "something represented in me" could be the appearance *reflected under a concept*: the phenomenon.[21] These different ways "something is represented in me" point us to an answer to question (2).

Answering question (2): Why the disjunction "a representation is possible, or at least is something to me"? I submit that the first disjunct ("a representation *is possible* only if what is represented in me *can be thought*") concerns those representations that are, in the classification of the *Stufenleiter*, cognitions, namely, concepts or intuitions. The point is obvious in the case of concepts: a concept is possible only if its object can be thought. That is just what a concept is: it is a product of the activity of thinking. So a concept is possible, as a representation, only if what is "represented in me" not only *can* be thought but indeed is thought. Now what about intuitions? According to the argument of the Transcendental Deduction recounted in Chapter 4, an intuition is possible only if it belongs in the formal intuitions of space and of time, and the formal intuitions of space and of time (space and time as that in which not only a manifold, but also the unity of a manifold, is given) are possible only if they stand under the unity of apperception, and so under what makes thought in general possible.[22] This takes care of the first disjunct: a representation (an intuition or a concept) is possible only if what is represented in me (in virtue of my having that representation) *can be* thought.

What about sensation, the first kind of "representation with consciousness" according to the *Stufenleiter*? This is where the second disjunct ("*or at least* is something to me") gets its pull. A sensation, unlike a concept or an intuition, is possible even if it is not intentionally related to an object (even if it is not part of an objective perception, a cognition). Then it does not relate to other sensations as the "matter" of an intuition in the unity of space and time. Nor does it, therefore, stand under the unity of apperception that would make it thinkable. Even though it is "with consciousness," the sensation is then "nothing to me." Not because it is not felt, or because there is no "what it feels like" character to it, but because it appears and disappears without being acknowledged as such, and remains thus "less than a dream" (A112). So unless what is represented in me via sensation "can be thought" (stands under the unity of apperception), the sensation, although possible, is "nothing to me": less than a dream.

We now have the explanation for the full conditional in premise one: "A representation is possible, or at least is something to me, only if something is represented in me that can be thought." And we can address the third question: Is there a difference between the fact that "something is represented in me" and the fact that the relevant representation is "something to me"?

Answering question (3): As we just saw, sensation is certainly "something represented in me": according to the *Stufenleiter*, it is the representation of a modification of my state that is accompanied with consciousness. And yet it is "nothing to me" unless either it is, itself, intuited (and thus related in time to other sensations, as an object of inner sense); or it becomes the "matter" of an empirical intuition directed at an object of outer sense.[23] There is thus a difference between a representation's "being in me" (as a modification of my state, and even a modification of my state *accompanied with consciousness*, in the minimal sense of the first division of the *Stufenleiter*) and a representation's being "something to me" (insofar as its intentional content is intuited and eventually reflected under a concept, either as the object of an outer or an inner intuition).

The interpretation I have offered of Kant's statements at B131–2 is confirmed if we consider Kant's explanation of "being conscious of a representation."[24] In the *Jäsche Logic*, Kant calls "clear" a representation "of which I am conscious" and "obscure" (*dunkel*) a representation "of which I am not conscious" (AA9, 34), or more precisely "of which I am not immediately conscious, but can become mediately conscious, by inference" (*Met. Mongrovius*, AA29, 879). Kant's classic example is that I am not immediately conscious of the stars that compose the Milky Way, although I can mediately infer that their light affects my eyes and thus my sensibility. Now Kant also defines a "clear" representation as a representation "that I can distinguish from other representations." So, being conscious of a representation is being in a position to distinguish it from other representations. Sensations are conscious or "with consciousness" in just that way: they have a quality such that they can be immediately (non-inferentially) distinguished from other sensations. Non-human animals are capable of such discrimination. But they are not capable of consciousness of the identities and differences themselves, as such, of the representations they have discriminated.[25] Such consciousness is possible only through judging, which means ordering the sensations into intuitions and bringing those intuitions under concepts, by acts of judging. Only rational beings, of which human beings constitute a species, are capable of this higher degree of consciousness.[26]

I would thus suggest that, even though he does not make the distinction explicit in just the terms I am about to offer, Kant actually uses the term "consciousness," when applying the term to representations, in at least two different senses. In the first sense, consciousness, the property of a representational state (as in the expression: a representation is "with consciousness" or "without consciousness") is the subjective *quality* of that state in virtue of which the subject differentiates that state from other states. In terms familiar to contemporary philosophers of mind, a representational state is "with consciousness" when there is "something it is like for the subject" to be in that state, and that "something it is like" differs from other types of "something it is like." Consciousness in this first sense is a property of representational states encountered in non-human (non-rational) animals as well as in human beings. It is in accordance with this sense of 'consciousness' that, in the *Stufenleiter*, sensations belong under the genus "representation with consciousness."

In the second sense, a representation is "with consciousness" if we do not just discriminate things in virtue of the way they affect us, but we represent their identities and differences *as such*: as identities and differences in positions in space and time (in the case of intuitions and their objects); and as identities and differences of marks (in the case of concepts, and objects falling under those concepts: phenomena). Moreover, in this second sense the representation (the representational state) may itself be something of which we are conscious. In short: in the second sense of "representation with consciousness" it is the case both that representations are that by which we represent the identities and differences of objects, and that the representational states in virtue of which we are conscious of these identities and differences may themselves be *objects of* representation, insofar as we are conscious *of* having them.[27] Both of these aspects of the second sense of consciousness are what Kant has in mind, I submit, when in the *Logic* he defines consciousness as the "representation that another representation is in me" ([*Logic*], AA9, 33). This higher-order consciousness *depends* on the merely qualitative consciousness (the first sense identified above), the "what it's like for the subject of the representation" character of sensations. But it is not identical to it. I will suggest later that we find a similar duality of concepts of consciousness in Freud.

We can now make clearer what is meant by "*my* representation." In a minimal sense, a representation is "my" representation just insofar as it is "in me" as a modification of my state (sensation). But in a fuller sense, a representation is "my" representation only insofar as it is "something to me" (intuition, concept, and all forms of discursive thinking: judgment, inference, systematic unity of different cognitions). This is the sense of "my representation" that is at work in the Transcendental Deduction of the Categories. As for the entity (referred to by 'I') to whom 'my' representations belong, it is the thinker of 'I think,' considered as such: the "I, or he, or it (the thing) that thinks" (A346/B404).

We can now move to premise two, which is straightforward.

Premise 2: "For any of my representations, what is represented in me can be thought *only if* the 'I think' is able to accompany [the relevant representation]."[28] The argument for this premise has been examined at length in Chapter 4: there is no thought, no conceptualization, without the ongoing act that binds the contents of representations together and makes possible the acquisition of concepts. That act is conceptually expressed in the proposition 'I think.'

Conclusion: "so, for any of my representations, that representation is possible at all (intuition or concept), *or at least* it is something to me (sensation), only if the 'I think' is able to accompany it."²⁹ It is precisely in this disjunctive conditioning relation that any use of 'I' in thought and language originates: the *possibility* of thinking 'I think' is a necessary condition for any (conscious) representation (intuition or concept) to be possible, *or at least* it is a necessary condition for a (conscious) representation (sensation) to be something to me.

7.2.2 Discursive Thinking and Synthesis of Imagination

As we saw in Chapters 2 and 4, discursive thinking presupposes a pre-discursive, pre-conceptual process of synthesizing representations that Kant calls "transcendental synthesis of imagination." So, for instance, I see a bunch of flowers in bloom, and the next day I see a bunch of flowers, on what appears to be the same table, in what appears to be the same vase, but those flowers are faded; and I say: 'The flowers that were so beautiful yesterday have now died.' Such a statement, and the thought it expresses, depends on having kept in mind the image of the blooming flowers, and compared it with the sorry bunch I now have in front of me. This is how I come to perceive the present flowers as being one and the same bunch as the one I saw the day before. And if asked why I take it to be the same bunch, I can give my reasons. For instance, one might ask me: 'How do you know these are the same flowers? Didn't your little brother just pull a prank on you?' Or: 'Why do you say the flowers are faded? They seem fine to me!' And so on. I can reply by offering reasons readily available to me when I am thus pressed for them, because they rest on an ongoing activity of binding and comparing present and past perceptions. The activity itself need not be an activity I am immediately conscious of. It is manifest in its result: I do acknowledge the presence of one and the same bunch of flowers in different shapes, I do see these shapes as indicating the bunch has wilted, and, if pressed, I can give my reasons. This leads us to the third point.

7.2.3 We are "Seldom Even Conscious" of the Synthesis of Imagination

The binding or synthesizing activity is, in Kant's words, "the work of imagination, a blind though indispensable function of the soul, without which we would have no cognition at all, *but of which we are seldom even conscious [der wir uns aber selten nur einmal bewusst sind]*" (A78/B103; italics mine).

In 7.2.1 we encountered *representations* "with consciousness" and "without consciousness." Now we are told that a *function of the soul* is something "of which we are seldom even conscious." Does "consciousness" here have the same duality of meanings it had in the case of representations?

I suggest that it does. There is no "what it's like" character of our activity of binding representations, thus no phenomenal consciousness of that activity.³⁰ There is no intentional consciousness of that activity either: no higher order mental state *of* which this activity is the intentional object and that would differentiate that activity from other activities of the mind. We are conscious of the binding activity mostly through its results—for instance, our consciousness of the flowers *as the same flowers*

I saw yesterday, now faded, our consciousness *of the object as am seeing, as a tree*,[31] and so on. These results are not necessarily judgments. They may just be perceptions in the stricter sense of the term: empirical intuitions whose manifold is bound by the imagination according to some rule;[32] or they may be concepts under which we explicitly recognize those intuitions (I see the tree *as* a tree, I see the flower *as* faded, and so on); or they may be representations of the temporal order of the objects intuited and conceptualized (I see that the flowers have changed *from* being in bloom *to* being faded). Those results would not be available to us unless we were in a position to compare the current perception (faded flowers) with the previous one (flowers in bloom), or to take into account the surrounding conditions for our interpreting our perceptions as perceptions of a tree, and so on. The activity does not have to be, itself, present to us either phenomenally (qualitatively) or intentionally (as the object of a higher order attitude). But we do implicitly assume that we have engaged in such an activity whenever we confidently interpret our perception and perceive an object *as* falling under a concept or combination of concepts ('the flowers have faded').

Note that Kant does not say, in the text cited above, that we are *never* conscious of the activity of the imagination. He only says we are "seldom even conscious" of it. And in fact, in §25 of the B Deduction, he seems to offer an example in which we *are* conscious of our own synthesizing activity:

We also always perceive this in ourselves. We cannot think a line without *drawing* it in thought, we cannot think a circle without *describing* it, we cannot represent the three dimensions of space at all without *placing* three lines perpendicular to each other from the same point, and we cannot even represent time without, in *drawing* a straight line (which is to be the external figurative representation of time) attending merely to the action of the synthesis of the manifold through which we successively determine the inner sense, and thereby attending to the succession of this determination in inner sense. Motion, as action of the subject (not as determination of an object) consequently the synthesis of the manifold in space, if we abstract from this manifold in space and attend solely to the action in accordance with which we determine the form of *inner sense*, first produces the concept of succession at all. (B154–5)

In the cases described here, Kant maintains that our attention is consciously directed at the acts of synthesis that condition the possibility of both intuitions and concepts. Nevertheless, even in these cases, where Kant does point to what seems to be a direct consciousness of the *act* of synthesizing, what we are in fact directly conscious of, according to his own description of the cases, is the successive generation *of an image*. Only thereby are we conscious of our action of generating the image, and of the action as our own. Moreover, even under this guise (being conscious of a mental action as our own in virtue of being conscious of the intuited image generated by that action), we were told in the text cited at the beginning of this section that we are only "seldom conscious" of the function of the imagination. In most cases, we do not catch ourselves in the act, as it were, while performing it. The action remains something of which we are not conscious.[33]

In the text cited at the beginning of this section (A78/B103), Kant also described imagination as a "blind" function of the mind. One might think that this is the very same point: the imagination is a "blind" function of the mind insofar as we are "seldom even conscious" of it.

But in fact, the two points are distinct. After all, of intuitions, too, Kant says that, without concepts, they are "blind" (A51/B75). And yet, in his general classification of representations, he characterizes intuitions as representations "with consciousness" (A320/B376). So we can assume that Kant means two different things when he says of imagination that it is "blind" and when he says that we are "seldom even conscious" of its acts of synthesis. Presumably, the imagination is "blind" in the same sense in which intuitions are: imagination is blind when its syntheses are not explicitly subsumed under concepts.[34] This is not what makes it the case that we are "seldom even conscious" of its activity. For again, even though intuitions are "blind" insofar as they are not conceptualized, they are nevertheless representations "with consciousness." As I suggested above, in the case of intuitions this means two things. First, we are phenomenally (qualitatively) aware of the sensory quality of our intuitions. Second, we are able to represent to ourselves those intuitions as distinct intuitions by locating their objects at different points in one space and one time. A related aspect of the second sense of "with consciousness" is that by turning our attention to them we can be intentionally conscious of the intuitions themselves, as representational states.

Similarly, we might imagine combinations of representations in imagination that are blind (even though they may occur according to concepts, those concepts are not currently represented as such), but nevertheless those acts of combination may be something we are conscious of in one or several of the senses just outlined: (1) There is "something it is like for us" to engage in them—indeed the activity of the mind engaging in them may be *felt* and may be a source of pleasure or displeasure;[35] (2) we are conscious of their result, for instance, drawing lines for the sake of their pleasing patterns, combining richly varied colors, or in Kant's own example,[36] improvising harmonies on the keyboard; (3) in considering the results we can also turn our attention back to the activity of imagination that is or has been engaged in producing these results. All three of these kinds of consciousness of the activity of imagination are compatible with that activity's being "blind."

In short, the imagination's being a "blind" function of the soul and the imagination's being "something of which we are seldom even conscious" are two different features of imagination in its activity of synthesis. Nevertheless, there is a connection between the blindness of imagination and the fact that we are "seldom even conscious" of it. For when it is *not* blind, the fact that we reflect under concepts the rules according to which it is performed may help us in turning our attention back to those rules themselves, and in becoming aware of them, in the second sense stated above in the case of representations, being able to represent their difference from other rules.[37]

7.2.4 'I' and Consciousness of One's Own Body

In today's semantic parlance, the word and concept 'I' are defined by FRR: 'I' is a word or concept that refers, in any instance of its use, to the author of the thought or the speaker of the sentence in which 'I' is being used.[38] In Kant's parlance and in the context of his transcendental investigation, the central question is: What kind of *representation* do I have of myself when using 'I,' on what kind of *consciousness* does using the concept 'I' depend? As I showed in Chapter 2, for Kant, any use of 'I' depends on the capacity to think 'I think.' This being so, if our semantic parlance were available to him, Kant would agree that any use of 'I' obeys the fundamental reference rule: in any instance of its use, 'I' refers to whoever is thinking the token proposition 'I am F.'[39] But what we are *conscious of* in using 'I' is a different matter. In thinking 'I think,' I am conscious of myself *as a thinker* and need not be conscious of myself in any other capacity. On the other hand, in thinking 'I am standing in front of the arch at Washington Square,' I am conscious of myself as an embodied entity located in space and time.[40]

Kant is quite explicit about the fact that our representation of objects in the physical world depends not only on unifying representations under the unity of apperception (expressed in the thought 'I think'), but also on our consciousness of our own position, as a physical thing, among other physical things. So, for instance, in the Third Analogy of Experience, Kant claims that our experience of the spatial position of material things in space and our experience of our own spatial position with respect to them are mutually conditioning. He writes:

From our experience it is easy to notice that only continuous influence in all places in space can lead our sense from one object to another, that the light that plays between our eyes and the heavenly bodies effects a mediate community between us and the latter and thereby proves the simultaneity of the latter; and that we cannot empirically alter our place (perceive this alteration) without matter everywhere making the perception of our position possible. (A213/B260)

This 'we' is 'I' in the plural: a first-person plural, or a plurality of persons each of whom is in a position to refer to herself via the first-person pronoun 'I.' In this context, Kant means to indicate that we are conscious of ourselves not just as thinkers, characterized by no further predicate than that of (currently) thinking (even though we are, among other things, conscious of being engaged in thinking), but also as empirical entities: living, sensing, thinking entities located in space and time. In this context, even if it is used in the proposition 'I think' (e.g., 'I think this star I see up there is Venus'), 'I' is indexed, as it were, to a particular living, sensing, experiencing person, an embodied entity, from whose standpoint knowledge of the relevant objective statement is acquired ('this is Venus'), even while she makes a claim to the universal validity (the truth) of that statement.

* * *

Let me take stock. Kant's 'I' in 'I think' has the following four important features.

(1) A representation is "something to me," it is conscious in the strong sense, only if it is bound with other representations in such a way that it can be thought, which means also that the thought 'I think' can accompany it. But the scope of Kant's notion of consciousness extends beyond that of representations that are "something to me." Sensations, we saw, are among the representations that are "with consciousness" and yet they are "nothing to me" as long as they are not taken up in the unifying activity that makes them the matter of intuitions and thus makes it the case that "the I think" *can* accompany them.

(2) Conceptual representation, or what Kant calls "discursive thinking," presupposes a pre-discursive binding activity, the activity of imagination under the unity of apperception, or "transcendental imagination."
(3) We are "seldom even conscious" of the pre-discursive activity that grounds the discursive (conceptually organized) activity of the mind and the representation 'I.'
(4) In many cases of uses of 'I' in 'I think,' the 'I'-user need not be conscious of herself in any other capacity than that of being an agent of thinking or a "transcendental subject of thoughts = X which is cognized only through the thoughts that are its predicates" (A346/B404). But in other uses, the 'I'-user is conscious of herself as a determinate entity: a person—a living, sensing, thinking entity, a human being. Indeed in many cases, 'I think' (as in: 'I think this is a tree') is indexed to the standpoint of such an entity, even while making a claim to the objective validity of the statement that entity makes (in the example just cited, the statement: 'this is a tree'), that is, the validity of the statement not just from her standpoint, but as an objective statement, which anyone can accept to be true.

* * *

I will now offer a quick overview of Freud's concept 'ego' in *The Ego and the Id*, as a preliminary to a systematic comparison of Freud's concept 'ego' (*Ich*), on the one hand, to Kant's transcendental unity of apperception and its expression in the proposition 'I think,' on the other.

7.3 Freud on "das Ich" ("the Ego")

I will first briefly recount Freud's notion of '*Ich*' as expounded in the first two sections of his 1923 essay, *The Ego and the Id*. This will be mainly expository. I will then compare Freud's and Kant's '*Ich*,' following the guiding thread of the four core theses I have identified in Kant's view.

7.3.1 Consciousness and What is Unconscious

In section 1 of *The Ego and the Id*,[41] Freud starts by recalling "the fundamental premiss" of psychoanalysis: being conscious is not the fundamental characteristic of the mental, but only a transitory quality of mental states (*Ego and Id, SE*, 19:13–14; *GW*, 13:240).[42] In earlier phases of his work, he says, he had progressed from a merely "descriptive" contrast between conscious and unconscious representations to a "dynamic" contrast: the representations that are properly speaking *unconscious* are those that are repressed, prevented from access to consciousness by an active force that resists this access. Mental representations that are merely descriptively unconscious, namely, those that are temporarily unavailable to consciousness without being pushed out of consciousness by the force of repression, must be characterized as "preconscious" rather than, properly speaking, unconscious.

But, says Freud, the dynamic notion in turn has now proved to be incomplete. Clinical experience calls for yet a new approach to the mind, where dynamic concepts—repression, the unconscious as the domain of repressed mental activity and its contents—are complemented by structural concepts. The distinction between ego and id belongs to this new, structural approach, and takes precedence over the old division between conscious and unconscious mental states and events. Indeed, although the id (*das Es*) is unconscious, the ego (*das Ich*) is part conscious and part unconscious, for reasons I will now explain.

7.3.2 "Ego" and "Id"

In Freud's view, the ego (*das Ich*) is the result of an internal differentiation within a more primitive system of representations, the id (*das Es*). Freud writes:

> We shall now look upon an individual as a psychical id, unknown and unconscious, upon whose surface rests the ego, developed from its nucleus, the *Pcpt* system.[43] ... The ego is not sharply separated from the id, its lower portion merges into it.
>
> But the repressed merges into the id as well, and is merely a part of it. (*Ego and Id*, SE, 19:24; GW, 13:251)

Is the individual the id? One might think so, since Freud writes, at the beginning of the text just cited: "We shall now look upon an individual as a psychical id." This does not mean, however, that all there is to an individual is her psyche, much less her psyche in the inchoate state that is "the id." What is true is that in the context of the psychoanalytic therapy, what the analyst deals with is the unruly mass of emotions that is the core of the person's psyche. But of course, in a more usual sense, an individual, for Freud, is the whole person.

As a biological entity, a person has drives (*Triebe*). Drives are physiological forces, characterizing any living being. In human beings, as in other animals endowed with a central nervous system, physiological drives have representatives, as it were, in psychical life, in the form of emotions. The id, which is the core of any individual's psyche, is the set of mental representatives of drives. It also includes feelings of pleasure or displeasure: pleasure at having a drive satisfied (e.g., pleasure at having successfully avoided the object of fear, pleasure at obtaining the object of lust, pleasure at relieving one's hunger, and so on), displeasure at having the drive.[44]

The life of the mind as an id is subject to what Freud calls the pleasure principle: obtain pleasure and avoid unpleasure.[45] The principle leads the individual's mental processes to select hallucinatory representations over veridical ones if the former are pleasurable and the latter unpleasurable. But this is a threat to the drive for self-preservation. This drive for self-preservation is what determines the differentiation within the id of a part that continues to obey the pleasure principle and it alone (this is the id properly speaking), and a part that learns to seek information from external reality and life-preserving responses to reality. This is how, as indicated in the text cited above, the ego emerges from the id as the organization of mental processes whose role it is to guide the individual in navigating its own life-preserving activities in relation to the external world.

Freud writes:

> We have formed the idea that in each individual there is a coherent organization of mental processes; and we call this his ego. (*Ego and Id*, SE, 19:17; GW, 13:243)

And again:

> The ego is that part of the id [*des Es*] which has been modified by the direct influence of the external world through the medium of the *Pcpt.-Cs*.... Moreover, the ego seeks to bring the influence of the external world to bear upon the id and its intentions [*Absichten*] and endeavors to substitute the reality principle for the pleasure principle that reigns unrestrictedly in the id. For the ego, perception plays the part which in [the?] id falls to the drive. (*Ego and Id*, SE, 19:25; GW, 13:252–3)[46]

The ego is thus an organization of mental processes unified by the specific function it is called upon to perform: it is that part of the id that heeds the instructions of the external world; that is to say, it is that part of the psyche in which mental processes are organized in such a way that *what the world is like* finds representation in the mind. In contrast to the id, which functions according to the pleasure principle, the ego thus functions according to what Freud calls the "reality principle."[47]

Now the information from the world comes via the body. The body is itself part of the world. So the organization of mental processes that constitutes the ego includes processes that represent states and changes of states of the body. Here's what Freud writes:

> A person's own body [*der eigene Körper*], and above all, its surface, is a place from which both external and internal perceptions may spring. It is *seen* like any other object, but to the *touch* it yields two kinds of sensations, one of which may be equivalent to an internal perception. Psycho-physiology has fully discussed the manner in which a person's own body attains its special position among other objects in the world of perception.[48] Pain, too, seems to play a part in the process, and the way in which we gain new knowledge of our organs during painful illnesses is perhaps a model of the way by which in general we arrive at the idea of our body.
>
> The ego is first and foremost a bodily ego; it is not merely a surface entity, but it is itself the projection of a surface. (*SE*, 19:25–6; *GW*, 13:253)

Freud has said earlier[49] that the ego belongs to the "surface" of the psyche, the *Pcs.Cs* system by which the psyche communicates with the external world. But the ego is also the projection of a surface. That is to say, the representational contents of the perception/consciousness system are the projection of a "surface," the projection of the limit between the body and the world, literally its skin and eyes and ears. Because of this, "the ego is a bodily ego," its perceptual contents are one and all representations of some point of contact between the body and the world around it.[50]

Freud assigns two complementary roles, one negative and the other positive, to the selective organization of mental events he calls the ego (*das Ich*). The two roles are connected to one another. The negative role is to hem in the individual's striving for immediate satisfaction via hallucinatory representation or immediate discharge of action. The positive role is to promote an ordering of perceptions yielding objective representation and delayed action when necessary for life preservation. In both roles, the ego develops out of the perception-consciousness system, the system of representations whose role is specifically to allow the individual to successfully navigate her environment.

Freud adds, however, that in addition to the conscious component of the ego that develops out of the perception-consciousness system, there is also an unconscious component. This is the "ego ideal" or "super-ego" expounded in the third part of *The Ego and the Id*. This unconscious aspect of the ego is the source of much of our social adaptation and therefore the source of moral imperatives. As such, it is also a major source of neurotic behavior. Insofar as Freud's 'super-ego' bears an interesting relation to Kant's 'I,' it is to Kant's *moral* 'I,' the 'I' of 'I (morally) ought to.' In the present chapter, I consider only the relation between Freud's *Ich* (ego) and Kant's '*Ich*' in '*Ich denke*,' 'I' in 'I think,' which Kant takes to be the expression of the unity of consciousness necessary for any objective representation. My claim is that Freud's and Kant's respective views of cognition, of its dependence on a specific kind of ordering of mental contents, and of the relation between that ordering and the concept 'I,' turn out to be strikingly similar.

To show this, I will now scan Freud's conception of ego (*Ich*) through the lens of the four features of Kant's 'I' ('*Ich*') that I identified in 7.1.

7.4 Kant's '*Ich*' in '*Ich denke*' and Freud's '*Ich*'

First, once again a caveat concerning the *differences* between what Kant and Freud respectively mean by '*Ich*.' As we just saw, Freud's concept 'ego' ('*Ich*') refers to an organization of mental processes about which Freud makes statements in the third person. In contrast, Kant's 'I' (also '*Ich*') is the first-person pronoun, as used in the proposition 'I think.' That pronoun does not refer to an organization of mental processes, but rather to the "transcendental subject = X," of which, according to Kant, nothing more can be said than that it is "the thing that thinks" (A346/B404), whatever that thing may be. Still, what makes it possible for us to use 'I' in this way, according to Kant, is that we are engaged in the activity of ordering our representations under the unity of apperception, a logically structured unity of representational contents geared toward objective cognition. My claim is that what Freud calls '*Ich*' bears striking similarities to that unity of representational contents. Indeed, I submit that Freud's developmental account of the organization of mental processes he calls '*Ich*' gives us an interesting path into what a naturalized account of Kant's transcendental unity of apperception might look like.

Kant characterizes the latter as a "formal condition" (A363) of objective representations. He explains that the role of the concept 'I' in its position as the logical subject in the thought 'I think' is both to express and to promote the unity of the activity of thinking that sets its own norms directed at generating objective representation.[51] Now contrary to Kant, Freud does not have much to say (to my knowledge, he has nothing at all to say) about the role of the concept and word 'I' in ordering our thoughts. But if Kant is right in the role he assigns to our capacity to ascribe representations to ourselves in acquiring objective representations and in conducting any kind of reason-giving process of thought, then Freud's concept 'ego' ('*Ich*') designates, within our mental life, that organization of mental processes that accounts for the use of 'I' in Kant's proposition 'I think.' Indeed, this might explain why Freud gave the name '*Ich*' to that organization. He gives an account in the third person, and a causal account, of a chain of events, physiological and mental/psychological, that result in our acquiring the capacity to think in the first person, which according to Kant is the very capacity to provide, or at least seek, reasons for one's thoughts and actions.[52]

I will now attempt to support this suggestion by reviewing the four points I highlighted in Kant's view of 'I' and comparing them to Freud's view of 'ego.'

7.4.1 'I,' Discursive Thinking, and Consciousness of One's Representations

Kant's "transcendental unity of apperception," the unifying activity of thinking directed at objective representation and eventually expressed in Kant's 'I think,' has its counterpart in the organization of mental processes Freud calls 'ego,' governed by the reality principle. What Freud calls the 'reality principle' is a mode of ordering the contents of mental processes. In his 1911 essay, "Formulations on the Two Principles of Mental Functioning," Freud traces back to the reality principle our capacity to form judgments. After sketching out the process by which the reality principle gradually takes precedence over the pleasure principle in ordering the contents of our representations, Freud continues:

Instead of repression, which excluded from investment [*Besetzung*][53] some of the emerging representations as productive of unpleasure, there came forth an *impartial passing of judgment*, which had to decide whether a given representation was true or false,—that is, whether it was in agreement with reality or not—the decision being determined by making a comparison with the memory-traces of reality. (*Formulations*, SE, 12:221; GW, 8:233)

In *The Ego and the Id*, Freud contrasts the ordering of representations in the ego according to elementary logical rules, that is to say, the laws of secondary processes, with the laws of primary processes, in which mutually inconsistent representations may coexist, events have no temporal order, and images prevail over words and concepts. In contrast to the laws of primary processes, the functioning of the ego according to the reality principle is close to what Kant calls the "logical use of the understanding," in which intuitions are brought under concepts and then combined in judgments and inferences according to logical rules—the laws of identity, of non-contradiction, and excluded middle.

For Freud, a representation is conscious, or I am conscious of it, just in case it is taken up in the functioning of the ego, which makes it possible to "pass impartial judgment" on its truth or falsity (agreement or not with reality) by comparing it with memory traces of other representations. This notion of consciousness is similar to the second notion of 'consciousness' we considered in Kant, according to which I am conscious of a representation if it is taken up in the unity of consciousness that makes objective representation and thinking possible.[54] This notion of consciousness coexists, for Freud, just as for Kant, with a purely qualitative notion, which was at work in the first classification of representations cited in 7.3.1.[55] There the distinction between conscious and unconscious representations was a distinction between representations having a "most immediate and certain character" and those lacking it. Only if one recognizes that Freud appeals to both notions of consciousness—consciousness as an immediate quality of mental states, on the one hand, and consciousness as the property of mental states whose content obeys the rules of the ego, on the other—can one make sense, I suggest, of some otherwise puzzling statements on Freud's part.

Freud says, for instance, that feelings are never unconscious. This seems strange, since feelings, if they threaten the "impartial passing of judgment" proper to the ego, are par excellence what is apt to elicit the resistance of the ego and to be pushed back into an aspect of our mental life that is neither qualitatively present (so not conscious in the first, immediate sense) nor discursively accessible (so not conscious in the second sense). However, if we keep in mind the difference between the two notions of consciousness I have identified both in Kant and in Freud, then we see that Freud might mean that feelings, in their qualitative aspect, *are never unconscious in the qualitative sense*. As a quality of affect governing our life, for a feeling to exist just is for it to be felt. But what is pushed back and made inaccessible to consciousness is the capacity to recognize feelings for what they are in their intentional content. They thus fail to be integrated into the life of the ego, that organization of mental contents in which they can be acknowledged, named, and dealt with.[56] They live their life in the id, that domain of mental life governed by the pleasure/un-pleasure principle that is unconscious in the sense of failing to be discursively accessed or assessed.

7.4.2 *Kant's Synthesis of Imagination and Freud's Perceptual Images Organized According to the Rules of the Ego*

We saw that, for Kant, the unity of consciousness that finds its discursive expression in concepts and judgments presupposes a pre-discursive activity of combination or synthesis, performed by the imagination. The pre-discursive combinations of representations depend on the very same acts of the mind that eventually lead to the reflection of representations under concepts, according to forms of judgments and inferences.[57] Similarly, for Freud, the ego, governed by the reality principle, includes not only discursive representations—judgments according to logical rules, and thus presumably also concepts and inferences—but also perceptual images and representations of imagination which, unlike the representations belonging to the id, are subject to rules of consistency and "impartial passing of judgment" according to the reality principle (*Ego and Id*, *SE*, 19:21; GW,13:248, and see in this chapter, 7.4.1). These images are thus either pre-conscious (latent images that are associated with word traces but not explicitly recognized in words) or conscious. They become conscious, or images we are conscious of, in the second sense of consciousness outlined above,[58] only if they are associated with words. Only then are they *also* qualitatively present, namely, conscious in the first sense (they have an "immediate and certain character"). When they are not associated with words, but remain accessible to such associations when needed, they belong in the pre-conscious. Both pre-conscious and conscious representations belong in the ego, in that aspect of our mental life governed by the reality principle. The pre-conscious is essentially made up of memory images, ready to be reflected, whenever needed, in combinations of concepts (associated with words) in judgments, namely, in the proper functioning of the ego.

Certainly Freud offers nothing like Kant's sophisticated transcendental analysis of the role of imagination in the generation of knowledge, with its three aspects: representing the unity of space and time as a condition for locating any individual object in space and in time, generating figures in space, and recollecting images for associations to be appropriated in judgment. Nevertheless, Freud does contrast a use of images *for judgment*, and a use of images captured by the pleasure/unpleasure principle, according to the laws of primary process proper to the id. One might say that whereas Kant has the richer view of the role of imagination in the mental activities by which an objective view of the world is acquired (ordinary perceptual judgments and their relation to scientific knowledge), Freud has an incomparably richer view of the structural features of the play of imagination when it is *not* governed by the reality principle, but rather by the conflicting pleasure/unpleasure principle, characteristic of the id and the super-ego.[59] For present purposes (the consideration of Freud's ego and its relation to Kant's transcendental unity of apperception), what I want to draw attention to is the fact that, for Freud, in one of its aspects—the aspect whose functional role is to contribute to objective cognition—the activity of imagination itself is governed by the reality principle and belongs in the structural context of the ego. This is comparable, mutatis mutandis, to that aspect of imagination that for Kant is under the unity of apperception.

7.4.3 Mental Activities of Which We are "Seldom Even Conscious"

We saw that the pre-discursive binding or synthesizing activity that goes on in the mind is, according to Kant, the work of imagination, that "blind though indispensable faculty of the soul" of which "we are seldom even conscious." I noted that one should distinguish Kant's statement that we are "seldom even conscious" of the workings of the imagination, from his statement that imagination is "blind." I suggested that with the first statement, Kant means that, in most cases, we have *neither* qualitative *nor* intentional consciousness of the workings of our imagination, whereas with the second statement, he means that imagination may work without the explicit guidance of concepts and be, in this sense, "blind," just as intuitions, according to Kant, even though they are representations "with consciousness," are "blind" if they are not subsumed under concepts.[60] I also noted that there is nevertheless a connection between the "blind" character of imagination, or of intuitions, on the one hand, and the lack of (or "seldom") consciousness *of* them, on the other. Synthesizing according to a concept (as when we draw a line or a circle) may be one way we are both phenomenally (qualitatively) and intentionally conscious of the activity of synthesizing. And in general, it is true for Kant that we become conscious of the mental activities that have gone into our cognitive achievements *by being conscious of their results*, by being conscious of those achievements themselves—drawing a line, knowing that this object is a tree, knowing that the proof is valid, and so on.

Now Freud states repeatedly, not only in *The Ego and the Id* but throughout his writings, and already in *The Interpretation of Dreams*, that the complex operations that go on in our minds are mostly unconscious. And here he clearly means that they do not have the *quality* of consciousness.

> Some of the activities whose successful performance in dreams excited astonishment are now no longer to be attributed to dreams but to unconscious thinking, which is active during the day no less than at night.... The intellectual achievement is due to the same mental forces

which produce every similar result during the daytime. We are probably inclined greatly to over-estimate the conscious character of intellectual and artistic production as well. (*Interpretation*, SE, 5:613; GW, 2–3:618)

Thought processes are in themselves without quality, except for the pleasurable and unpleasurable excitations which accompany them, and which, in view of their possible disturbing effects upon thinking, must be kept within bounds. In order that thought processes may acquire quality, they are associated in human beings with verbal memories, whose residues of quality are sufficient to draw the attention of consciousness to them and to endow the process of thinking with a new mobile investment from consciousness. (*Interpretation*, SE, 5:617; GW, 2–3:622)

Similarly, in *The Ego and the Id*:

All perceptions which are received from without (sense-perceptions) and from within—what we call sensations and feelings—are Cs. from the start. But what about those internal processes which we may—roughly and inexactly—sum up under the name of thought-processes? They represent displacements of mental energy which are effected somewhere in the interior of the apparatus as this energy proceeds on its way towards action. (SE, 19:19; GW, 13: 246–7).

It is important to note that the unconscious character of mental activities concerns not only the activities belonging in the id, but *all* mental processes, including those at work in the highest productions of the ego. The latter become conscious only when their contents are not only associated with word-traces (as they are in the preconscious), but also explicitly formulated in words (in conscious judgments). To say that they become conscious means three things: they acquire qualitative presence (via the visual and auditory qualitative presence of the words or symbols in which they are explicitly formulated), their intentional content becomes an object of consciousness or is "invested" (*besetzt*) by consciousness; and they, themselves, may become objects of a second-order consciousness. What distinguishes the mental processes that belong in the specifically Freudian, dynamic unconscious (the domain of repressed representations), is that they *first* need to reach the level of the preconscious, by leaving the realm of primary processes and entering that of secondary processes. Then only can they reach the level of conscious thought:

The question: 'how does a thing become conscious?' would...be more advantageously stated: 'how does a thing become preconscious?' And the answer would be: 'Through becoming connected with the word-presentations corresponding to it.' (*Ego and Id*, SE, 19:20; GW, 13:247)[61]

It is worth noting again that the term "conscious" has the same ambiguity in Freud as it has in Kant, and the ambiguous meaning is applied not only to representations (the case we considered in 7.4.1), but to the thought processes themselves (the processes through which the representational contents of our mental states come to be combined and connected in judgments). On the one hand, thought processes are unconscious in that they have no immediate qualitative character. On the other hand, they come to have quality insofar as they are associated with verbal memories, which do have qualities (sensory qualities: sounds, or visual shapes); they can then also become *objects* of consciousness. In the course of the cited passage from *The Ego and the Id,* Freud cites his earlier paper, "The Unconscious," in which he discussed the accessibility of unconscious thought processes to consciousness. There Freud said that once it has entered the pre-conscious, a thought process can eventually "become the object of consciousness."[62]

Admittedly, there is a difference between Freud's and Kant's characterization of the access to consciousness. Freud talks about language and words, Kant talks about thought and concepts. According to Freud, representations and thought processes become accessible to consciousness when they are associated with words and thus integrated into the ego. According to Kant, intuitions and the synthesizing activities of imagination make the transition from being "obscure" and "blind" to being "clear" when they are subsumed under concepts and thus brought to the unity of apperception.[63] But access to words is precisely, for Freud, the way a representation enters the realm of "reason and level-headedness" (*SE*, 19:25), "*Vernunft und Besonnenheit*" (*GW*, 13:253): reflective thinking, which appeals to concepts. And for Kant, there is no thought without language.[64] Words are the means to fix concepts and their use.

7.4.4 'I' and the Body

As we saw, Kant indexes the transcendental unity of apperception to one's own body represented as an object like any other in the world, albeit an object with respect to which or in connection with which alone the location in space and time of all other objects can be represented. For information about that location is provided via the sensory information carried by a state of our body. This role of sensory information concerning the state of our body in providing information about the world finds its psychological counterpart in the privileged role Freud assigns to the representation of one's own body in the organization of mental processes that constitutes the ego. Recall his formulation: "the ego is first and foremost a bodily ego."[65] So, here again, there is a direct parallel between Kant's view and Freud's.

But in virtue of what has been said about the id, *das Es*, another aspect of the role of the body plays an important role in Freud's view of mental representations. As an entity capable of representations, the individual is endowed not only with the organization of mental processes and representations Freud calls ego, but more primitively and fundamentally, she is endowed with an id. Now insofar as the system of our representations is id (*Es*) rather than ego (*Ich*), we are, says Freud—following a formulation of the German psychiatrist Groddeck—"lived by unknown, uncontrollable forces" (*SE*, 19:23; *GW*, 13:251). These forces, as belonging to the id, are the representational counterparts of physiological forces characteristic of the body. This is not a body we take to be our own in virtue of the "projection of [its] surface," which plays a prominent role in the system of representations called the ego, *das Ich*. Rather, it is a body that owns us, as it were: a body that, insofar as its representative in our mental life is the id rather than the ego, keeps the fragile surface of our mental life, the ego, under the spell of the id's conflicting demands. Is there a counterpart, in Kant, for this overbearing presence of the body?

There is, as we can see if we turn from the *Critique of Pure Reason* to the *Anthropology from a Pragmatic Standpoint.*[66] In section 5, "On the representations which we have, without being conscious of them," Kant notes that we may fail to be conscious of some of our representations not only because they are too weak to appear illuminated on the "large map of our mind" (AA6, 135), but also because we "have an interest in keeping in the shadow, in front of imagination, objects that are liked or disliked." Then Kant goes on:

> However, more often we ourselves are a play of obscure representations, and our understanding is unable to save itself from the absurdities into which they have placed it, even though it recognizes them as illusions. Such is the case with sexual love, in so far as its actual aim is not benevolence but rather enjoyment of its object. How much wit has been wasted in throwing a delicate veil over that which, while indeed liked, nevertheless still shows such a close relationship with the common species of animals that it calls for modesty?... Here imagination may prefer to walk in the dark, and it takes uncommon skill when, in order to avoid cynicism, one does not want to run the risk of falling into ridiculous purism.
>
> On the other hand we are often enough the play of obscure representations that are reluctant to vanish even when understanding illuminates them. To arrange for a grave in his garden or under a shady tree, in the field or in dry ground, is often an important matter for a dying man; although in the first case he has no reason to hope for a beautiful view; and in the other no reason to fear catching a cold from the dampness. (*Anthropology*, AA7, 137)

In these passages, Kant singles out sexual desire and fear/denial of death as sources of representations of imagination with respect to which we are passive, and over which the efforts of our understanding have limited control. There is thus an aspect of our mental life in which one might say that even for Kant, our bodies own us rather than the other way around: our nature as causally determined, natural beings limits the power of our theoretical understanding and practical reason to impose its rules on our representations. Does this mean that Kant actually went, on his own resources, in the direction of the kind of naturalized account of the life of our minds, including in their theoretical and moral-practical capacities, I am claiming we can get from Freud? I will say more about this point in Chapter 8.

7.5 Concluding Remarks

I submit, then, that Freud's '*Ich*,' 'ego,' offers resources for interpreting Kant's '*Ich*' ('I' in 'I think') in terms of what McDowell has called a "naturalism of second nature."[67] Kant claimed that 'I' in the proposition 'I think' is used to express, endorse, and commit oneself to the rational unity of the contents of an activity of thinking one takes to be one's own, geared toward objective representation. Freud's explanatory account of the emergence of the particular organization of mental events he calls '*Ich*,' governed by the reality principle, offers a causal-developmental account of the capacity to think in the first person, and of the odds against which it is constantly regained—or not. Freud's account can be read as a model for a naturalization of Kant's transcendental unity of consciousness because Freud's concept '*Ich*' refers to an "organization of mental processes"[68] occurring in an empirically determinate person. There is no need to suppose an unknown and unknowable transcendental subject to account for that organization. But Freud's account is a naturalization where "nature" includes "second nature" because the person's ego is the result of a developmental process that occurs in a social context, and in the course of which each person acquires her unique capacity for cognition and action: a normative capacity that includes the capacity to acknowledge error and failure, to take responsibility for them and eventually to correct them.

A full account of this developmental process, especially in its social aspect, calls for more than what I have talked about here. It calls for an account of that structure of mental life Freud calls sometimes "super-ego," sometimes "ego ideal." If we follow Freud's developmental story, just as our use of the concept 'I' in 'I think' depends on the mental structure Freud calls "*Ich*," so our use of the concept 'I' in 'I ought to' depends on the mental structure Freud calls "ego-ideal" and "super-ego." Here Freud's developmental account puts him in a more polemical relation to Kant's moral 'I ought to' than he is to Kant's 'I think.' The ego of morality, for Freud, namely, the super-ego and ego ideal, is identification driven, emotion driven, and in large part illusion driven. As such, it is prone to neurosis: the irrational repetition of early scenarios of love and loss and the retreat from reality. The remedy to the threat of neurosis is analytical therapy, whose success depends on progress in self-knowledge, including knowledge of oneself in the determination of one's goals driven by the reality principle—and thus the development of the ego at work in cognition, the operations of which I have tried to sketch out in this chapter. In other words, in matters of morality Freud's ambition is to substitute for Kant's mix of Enlightenment ideals and pietism the empathetic and objective attitude of the clinical psychologist and biological scientist.

To what extent does the comparison I have proposed between Kant and Freud still hold in light of that other aspect of the use of 'I'? This is what we will examine in the next chapter.

Notes

1. See 2.3.
2. The *locus classicus* for Freud's concept "*Ich*" is his *Ego and Id*, SE, 19:1–66.
3. For important contributions to such a discussion, see Grünbaum 1984; Neu 1991b; D. Sacks 1991; Brook 1992, 1995; and Lear 2015. For a comparison between Freud's and Kant's views of the mind along lines sometimes similar to, and sometimes different from, the lines offered here, see Brook 2003. For a discussion of the fate of Freudian psychoanalysis in light of cognitive psychology and neuroscience, see Widlöcher 1996; Ansermet and Magistretti 2004; Naccache 2006; Kandel 2006; Alberini, Ansermet, and Magistretti 2013. For a discussion of Freud in the context of nineteenth- and twentieth-century biology and psychology, see Sulloway 1979; and Arminjon 2010.
4. On Kant's characterizing 'I' in 'I think' as a concept, albeit a "wholly empty representation" (A346/B404), see 4.3.1, n. 32.
5. See 2.2 and 4.2.
6. See again 4.2.
7. See Strawson 1966, 165. On the differences between Strawson's interpretation of this point and mine, see 6.5.
8. Cf. 4.2.
9. *Anthropology*, AA7, 167.
10. Ibid., AA7, 127.

11. See Freud, *Metapsych. Suppl., SE*, 14:222n; *GW*, 1:412n.
12. See B158n; and A346/B404.
13. I say more about what I mean by 'naturalization' in the final section of this chapter. See 7.5. In case the reader wonders whether Freud had even read Kant, the answer is that he definitely had. Brook (2003) notes that Kant is the philosopher Freud refers to most frequently. Here's Brook's comparative count: "Plato (17), Aristotle (19), Schopenhauer (25), Lipps (26), Nietzsche (17), Kant (28+, 16 by name plus at least a dozen more to his doctrines)." Brook notes, in addition, that the books Freud took with him to London included a copy of Kant's *Kritik der reinen Vernunft* (that copy, exhibited at the Freud museum in London, is annotated by Freud) and a collection of Kant's writings on the philosophy of nature. See Brook 2003, 36nn1–2. Freud studied philosophy in Vienna under Brentano at a time when the influence of Kant's critical philosophy was prevalent in all German-speaking universities (a situation Brentano bemoaned). In a March 15, 1875, letter to his friend Eduard Silberstein, Freud recounts a visit to his teacher in which Brentano made recommendations concerning philosophical authors he should read: "Two figures from the skeptical period, *Hume* and *Kant*, were indispensable, *Hume* being the most precise thinker and most perfect writer of all philosophers. Kant, for his part, did not deserve the great reputation he enjoys, he was full of sophisms and was an intolerable pedant, childishly delighted whenever he could divide anything into three or four parts, which explains the inventions and fictions of his schemata; what people praise in him Brentano was ready to credit to *Hume*, what is entirely Kant's own he rejected as harmful and untrue" ([*Letters*], 104). In a letter from April 11, 1875, Freud dismisses Kant's refutation of the proofs of the existence of God on the ground that the refutation "rests on the assumption of synthetic a priori judgments and stands or falls with them" ([*Letters*], 110). Freud sides with "the empiricist school" in rejecting the possibility of such judgments. Undoubtedly under the influence of Brentano, he thinks that an empiricist and scientific philosophy leads to a proof of the existence of God. But he also expresses discomfort at the incompatibility of Brentano's theist view with his own materialist convictions. He hopes one day to come up with a refutation of theism. These are youthful letters, and should not be taken to reflect Freud's mature views or even his mature attitude toward philosophy. But they do show that philosophy loomed large in his early education and preoccupations.
14. See 2.2 and 4.2.
15. See the *Stufenleiter*, the scale of representations at A320/B376–377. Under the generic concept 'representation,' Kant first introduces the division between representation "with consciousness" and (implicitly) representation "without consciousness." He calls the former "perception (*perceptio*)" and divides it in turn into "sensation (*sensatio*)," namely, "a perception (*perceptio*) that refers to the subject as a modification of its state," and "cognition (*cognitio*)," namely, an "objective perception." "Objective perception," or cognition, in turn, is divided into intuition or concept. Clearly, in this text, "perception" (*Wahrnehmung*, for which Kant also gives the Latin *perceptio*) is not the concept of perception as empirical intuition Kant defines, for instance, in the Anticipations of Perception, in the Transcendental Analytic (A165/B207). It is a broader concept, since it includes in its extension 'sensation,' which does not relate to an object, as well as 'intuition' and 'concept,' which do. 'Perception' ('*perceptio*') here refers to any conscious representation. What Kant means by "conscious" will be analyzed below in the main text.
16. In *Anthropology*, AA9, 136, Kant says that "the field of representations of which we are not conscious ... that is, *obscure* representations in the human being (and thus also in animals) is immense." This passage seems to indicate that, conversely, representations of which the subject of representation is conscious belong not only to human beings but also to

non-human animals. This point is confirmed by Kant's description of "degrees of cognition" in *Logic*, AA9, 64–5: "The *first* degree of cognition is: to *represent* something; the *second*: to represent something with consciousness, or to *perceive* (*percipere*); the *third*: *to be acquainted* with something (*noscere*), or to represent something in comparison with other things, both as to sameness and as to *difference*; the *fourth*: to be acquainted with something *with consciousness*, i.e. to *cognize* it (*cognoscere*). Animals are *acquainted* with objects too, but they do not *cognize* them" (Kant's emphasis). Kant goes on to list three more "degrees of cognition," which are: to understand, to have insight through reason, and to comprehend. These final degrees are not relevant to my discussion. My goal here is to draw attention to the fact that for Kant, non-human animals not only have "representations with consciousness," they also represent something (with consciousness) *in comparison with other things*, that is to say, they discriminate things that affect them as to the identities and differences among those things. But they are not conscious of those identities and differences as such; more on this below. Note also that in this list of "degrees of cognition" Kant uses the term "cognition" (*Erkenntnis*) in an even broader sense than the one I will discuss in n. 20 in this chapter, since even representations *without consciousness* count as a "degree of cognition." This is unfortunate for our effort to get clear about the relevant distinctions. The reason for the broadened use of the word here is probably that all these degrees of "cognition" jointly contribute to the final outcome, which is cognition properly speaking: intuitions recognized (*erkannt*) under concepts, judgments as contents of acts of judging.

17. In Longuenesse 2013, I offered a more compressed reconstruction of the conditioning relations at B131–2. Because it was too compressed it gave a somewhat confusing account of the conditioning relations. This is the needed reformulation.
18. A320/B376–7. Cf. n. 15 in this chapter.
19. The disjunct: representation "without consciousness" is only implicit. Representations "without consciousness" are also what Kant calls "obscure" (*dunkle*) representations. See n. 16 in this chapter, and later in the main text.
20. In classifying 'intuition' and 'concept' as two species of the genus 'cognition' (*Erkenntnis*), that is to say, two species of conscious representation directed at an object, Kant gives the term 'cognition' a broader sense than the sense he gives to it at the beginning of the Transcendental Analytic, where he says that "Intuition and concepts...constitute the elements of all our cognition, so that neither concepts without intuition corresponding to them in some way nor intuition without concepts can yield a cognition" (A50/B75). In the broad sense presented in the *Stufenleiter*, intuitions and concepts are two types of cognition, namely two types of conscious representation with intentional content (directedness at an object). In the narrower sense, only the application of a concept to an intuition, or the recognition of (the object of) an intuition under a concept, is a cognition. In the narrow sense, cognition thus has the form of a judgment, in which a combination of concepts is justified by the relation of those concepts to the intuitions (pure or empirical—in fact, strictly speaking only empirical intuitions can yield cognitions in the proper sense: cf. B147) falling under them. For an excellent discussion of the two senses of 'cognition' for Kant, see Grüne 2009, 27–30. Note again that in [*Logic*] cited in n. 16 in this chapter, Kant made an even broader use of the term 'cognition.'
21. On this distinctions, see A248–9. For comments, see Longuenesse 1998, 25, 71, and 109–10.
22. What I am claiming here does not entail that the content of intuitions is conceptual. An intuition, or its intentional content, does not need to be thought, i.e., conceptualized, in order to be the intuition it is. Nevertheless, an intuition is given, as an intuition, only if it belongs in one space and one time with other intuitions. But the unity of space and time stands under the unity of apperception that makes thought *possible*. See 4.2.

23. Moreover, having a determinate intuition of objects of outer sense is a condition for having a determinate intuition of one's inner states. Cf. 4.3.
24. Here my explanation owes a great deal to Grüne 2009. See esp. 36–42, 71–102.
25. See the text from *Logic*, AA9, 64–5 cited in n. 16 in this chapter. Cf. already in *False Subtlety*, AA2, 59–60: "It is quite another thing to *differentiate* things from one another and to *cognize* (*erkennen*) the difference of things. The latter is possible only through judging and cannot happen on the part of any irrational beast... The dog differentiates the roast from the bread because it is affected by the roast differently than from the bread (because different things cause different sensations) and the impression from one is the cause of a different desire from the impressions of the other, according to the natural connection of his drives with his representations." See also *Logic Blomberg*, AA24-1, 236, §201: "We cannot have insight into [universal characters of things] merely through the senses, but actually merely through judgment. Non-rational animals have no experience, then, but instead only sensations."
26. See also B414n. Kant talks of "degrees of consciousness" for what really seem to be, on his own account, different types of consciousness or discriminating capacity: one that is based on the mere quality of the sensation; the other that is based on a higher order act that calls on the unity of apperception. The second, however, depends on the first, indeed on the degree of the first, since a sufficient degree of the sensation, namely, its qualitative vivacity, is necessary for consciousness of the difference, as such, to arise. But the mere qualitative vivacity does not suffice for consciousness of the differences as such (such as location of intuited objects in one space, or generation of concepts).
27. One might ask how the two aspects I have distinguished in Kant's concept of consciousness relate to Sartre's "non-thetic" and "thetic" consciousness, discussed in Chapter 3. The comparison is not straightforward. For Sartre, non-thetic (self-)consciousness and thetic consciousness of object are two sides of one coin: consciousness as intentionality. I suspect he would maintain that there is no (conscious) sensation without intentionality, and so no non-thetic (self-)consciousness without thetic consciousness of object, just as there is no thetic consciousness of object without non-thetic (self-)consciousness. For Kant, in contrast, sensation, as a conscious representation, or what he calls representation "with consciousness," may well be a mere "modification of my state" (A320/B376), a mere qualitative feel, without any directedness at an object. Such directedness is obtained only when the sensation is taken up in an intuition, as the "matter" of the intuition. This being so, Sartre's non-thetic and thetic consciousness seem to find a home at the level of what Kant calls intuition and thinking, namely, cognition, not at the more elementary level of what Kant calls mere sensation.
28. Recall that this is the second of the conditioning relations laid out in my reconstruction of B131–2, at the beginning of the present section.
29. This is the conclusion as laid out in the reconstruction of B131–2, offered at the beginning of the present section.
30. For consciousness as the "what it's like" character of mental states, see Nagel 1979b. For describing this aspect of consciousness as "phenomenal" consciousness, see Block 2002 and 2007.
31. This is an example I used in Chapter 2. See 2.2.
32. See B162.
33. In a similar vein, Kant says that "The schematism of our understanding with regard to appearances and their mere form is a hidden art in the depth of the human soul, whose true operations we can divine from nature and lay unveiled before our eyes only with difficulty" (A141–2/B180–1).

34. I specify "*not explicitly*" subsumed because syntheses of imaginations can occur according to concepts or be guided by concepts without the concepts being explicitly thought *as* concepts, i.e., *as* universal and reflected representations. On this point, see Longuenesse 1998, 196–7.
35. See *Judgment* AA5, 217–18.
36. B415n.
37. In the preceding I find myself in agreement with Claudio La Rocca's "Unbewußtes und Bewusstsein by Kant" (see La Rocca 2008), on the following points: distinguishing different senses in which representations are "with consciousness" or "without consciousness" for Kant; distinguishing consciousness from self-consciousness (sensations are "with consciousness" but may be "nothing to me"—they are not, unless they are taken up in intuition and thought under concepts, accompanied with *self*-consciousness); and in relating Kant's concept 'I' to a unifying activity of which we are mostly not conscious (the activity of transcendental imagination). La Rocca notes moreover that even while opening the way to Freud's notion of the unconscious, Kant remains far from Freud's concept of the unconscious insofar as the latter refers to representations and mental activities that are not only below the level of consciousness, but are repressed and as such, have their proper organization (primary process, pleasure/unpleasure principle). As we shall see in what follows (see 7.4.4), in fact Kant does consider the case of representations that are pushed back from consciousness by the force of repression. But the notion of repression is of course not developed in the systematic way it is developed in the Freudian view of mental life. And Kant does not elaborate on a specific organization of mental contents according to the pleasure/unpleasure principle, which according to Freud is proper to the id. I would add that the unconscious representations and mental activities we have been examining so far in Kant would be closer to the contemporary notion of a cognitive unconscious than to the Freudian dynamic unconscious. But as I will argue later in this chapter, there is also room in Freud's view of the mind for such a cognitive unconscious, distinct from the domain of unconscious representations that result from repression.
38. Cf. 2.1.4.
39. But note that FRR is not a rule in any of the senses Kant gives to the term: it is not a procedure followed in synthesizing intuitions, and it is not a universal proposition under which particular instances might fall. A reference rule just characterizes what makes it the case that an entity counts, in fact, as the referent of a concept or a word, in this case the concept and word 'I.' But strikingly, this makes FRR especially relevant to the way Kant thinks we use 'I,' or to the role of 'I' in all propositions in which, necessarily, 'I' is (in Kant's predicative logic) in the subject-place. For according to Kant, 'I' is the only concept that we apply to an existing entity *without* needing any rule in his usual sense of 'rule': either for synthesizing intuitions, or for recognizing an object as falling under a concept. Understanding the word 'I' just is knowing that 'I' refers, in any instance in which I use it, to myself as the thinker of the token proposition in which 'I' appears; as well as to any other 'I-user,' in any instance of their use of 'I.' FRR is not a rule for *application*. It is a rule of reference. And this is precisely what makes it appropriate (anachronism notwithstanding) for characterizing the way Kant thinks we use 'I.'
40. For an explanation of these two kinds of self-consciousness and the uses of 'I' they ground, see Chapter 2.
41. *Ego and Id*, SE, 19:13–18; GW, 13:239–45.
42. It is actually quite strange that Freud should present this as a groundbreaking discovery of psychoanalysis. As we saw in 7.2, the idea that the greatest part of our mental representations and our mental activities remain representations and activities "of which we are not

conscious" played a central role in Kant's view of the mind. The same is true of Schopenhauer and Herbart, to cite only two of the authors whom Freud had undoubtedly read (see the correspondence with Silberstein cited in n. 13 in this chapter). Brook (2003) suggests that in repeatedly chastising philosophers' resistance to the very idea of unconscious mental representations, Freud probably had in mind his teacher Brentano, even though he mentions him on only one occasion in his published writings (see Brook 2003, 35). In his student years, Freud had been an admirer of Brentano and had despaired of his own ability to refute Brentano's theism (see again n. 13 in this chapter). Brentano notoriously took the idea of unconscious mental representations to be an absurdity.

43. Freud uses the abbreviation "*W*" for "Wahrnehmung," translated by Strachey as "*Pcpt*" for "perception" in the expression: "perception system" ("*W* System" or "System *W*" in Freud's German text). He sometimes also uses "*W-Bw*" (translated "*Pcpt-Cs*") for "perception-consciousness" system. The "perception system" is the system of mental representations derived from sensory information.

44. On Freud's notion of drive, and the relation between the somatic drives and their psychic "representatives," see Laplanche and Pontalis 1973, 214–17, 364–5.

45. *Ego and Id*, *SE*, 19:25; *GW*, 13:252. Cf. the 1911 essay: "Formulations on the Two Principles of Mental Functioning," *Formulations*, *SE*, 12:219; *GW*, 8:231–2.

46. For the abbreviation *Pcpt.-Cs*, see n. 43 in this chapter. I differ from Strachey in translating "Absicht" as "intention" (Strachey says: "tendency," perhaps because he is skeptical about attributing "intentions" to the id). I also differ from Strachey in translating "Trieb" as "drive" rather than Strachey's "instinct."

47. See again *Ego and Id*, *SE*, 19:25; *GW*, 13:252. And *Formulations*, *SE*, 12:219; *GW*, 8:232.

48. A central reference for Freud here is certainly Theodor Meynert, who introduced the idea, supported by empirical research in neuroanatomy, that a representation of the body is projected in the brain. See Arminjon 2010, esp. pt. 1, chap. 2, on the influence of Meynert on Freud. Freud studied neuroanatomy under Meynert, who was director of the psychiatry clinic at the University of Vienna. Freud eventually distanced himself from Meynert's views on the articulation of psychological and neural phenomena. See Arminjon 2010, 72–3.

49. Cf. 7.3.2, citation from *Ego and Id*, *SE*, 19:24, *GW*, 13:51.

50. Of course, it is not the case that all the representations governed by the laws of secondary processes are perceptual representations. But perceptual representations are an important, perhaps the most important component, in that system of representations, on which all other representations depend, especially word-representations (*Wortvorstellungen*). More on this in the following.

51. Admittedly, I am reformulating Kant's view in my own terms here. In saying that the concept 'I' both expresses and promotes the unity of apperception, I mean that we have to be already engaged in unifying representations under the unity of apperception in order to be able to attach to those representations the thought 'I think'; but conversely, attaching to them the thought 'I think' is endorsing and further promoting the unity under which these representations already stand. One might object that in fact, 'I' in 'I think' often expresses not so much a *unity* of the process as a *taking responsibility* for the process. For when pressed, we may recognize that we in fact lost track of time, we lost count, we let go of the proof. So to the question: 'Are you sure?' we might respond: 'Well, perhaps I'm not so sure after all.' We still use 'I' to say: 'I'm not so sure... I lost track.' 'I' in this case does not seem to express unity, but rather just the fact of taking responsibility. But I submit that taking responsibility and attempting to keep track (= *promoting* unity) are one and the same. It is on *our doing* that the keeping track depends, and if we do lose track, we take responsibility for having lost track so and make it our commitment to get back on track. This is why

I propose that for Kant, 'I' in 'I think' serves both to *express* and to *promote* (to commit oneself to) the unity of a process on which justification depends. I am grateful to Ned Block for pressing me on this point.

52. One might object that Freud's use of the term '*Ich*' to designate a particular mental structure was not original to him. His own teacher in neuroanatomy at the University of Vienna, Theodor Meynert, designated as "primäres Ich," "primary ego," the "central representation of the body, the kernel of individuality." By this he meant the representation of the body in the brain. Starting from that core "ego" (*Ich*) and under the influence of the external world through the perceptual system, each living individual develops, according to Meynert, a system of memorized images and associated emotions that "form solid combinations, the kernel of a secondary individuality whose reproduction and psychomotor influence is surprisingly easy, in contrast to all the passing impressions and less intense sensations" (Meynert 1888, 183, quoted in Arminjon 2010, 71; cf. Meynert 1884, 162. English translation mine). I have suggested earlier in this chapter (see n. 48) that Freud is inspired by Meynert when he refers to the "homunculus," the image of the body in the brain, and says that "The ego is first and foremost a bodily ego." My claim, however, is that Freud's using '*Ich*' to designate the part of our mental life whose content is governed by the reality principle and logical rules, makes his concept of 'ego' quite different from Meynert's, both because it is mental not neural (even though Freud never loses sight of its neural basis), and because the emphasis is now on its structure as a system of mental representations and mental functioning, not on its physiological basis. The connection of 'ego' with discursivity and the laws of "secondary processes" is the justification I offer for relating Freud's ego to its Kantian ancestor, the transcendental unity of apperception expressed in 'I think.' This concept of 'ego' finds its fully developed exposition only with *The Ego and the Id*, even though we find the term 'ego' (*Ich*) much earlier in Freud's writings. Freud uses the term as early as the 1893 *Studies on Hysteria*, where it refers to that function of the psyche whose role is to defend the psyche against painful memories by pushing them below the level of consciousness: see, for instance, *Hysteria*, SE, 2:290-1; GW, 1:294-5. The term "ego" ("*Ich*") appears prominently again in the 1895 *Project for a Scientific Psychology*, where it refers to the organization of neurons whose function is to inhibit hallucinatory representations and facilitate the indicators of reality provided by the perceptual system (here the influence of Meynert is evident). Freud also introduces, in the *Project*, the distinction between primary and secondary processes, where the latter are proper to the 'ego' (see *Project*, SE, 1:327; *Entwurf*, 406-11). The contrast between primary and secondary processes appears again in chapter 7 of *The Interpretation of Dreams* (see *Interpretation*, SE, 5:601-2; GW, 2-3:607-8), where it is now developed as a mental, not a neural structure, and without reference to a concept of ego. For an analysis of the development and transformations of Freud's concept 'ego' from the early writings to 1923 (*The Ego and the Id*), see Laplanche and Pontalis 1973, 130-43.

53. Strachey translates *Besetzung* by *cathexis*. *Besetzung* is a common German term, which *cathexis* is not in English. I am translating *Besetzung* by 'investment,' taking the term in its quasi-military sense: psychic energy 'invests' some representations, takes possession of them or settles in them, and rejects others as unsuitable (unpleasurable) places to settle in or to invest. Throughout this passage I have significantly altered Strachey's translation.

54. See 7.2.1.

55. Cf. *Ego and Id*, SE, 19:13; GW, 13:240: "'Being conscious' is in the first place a purely descriptive term, resting on perception of the most immediate and certain character. Experience goes on to show that a psychical element (for instance, an idea) is not as a rule conscious for a protracted length of time. On the contrary, a state of consciousness is characteristically very transitory; an idea that is conscious now is no longer so a moment

later. Although it can become so again under certain conditions that are easily thought about."
56. See *Unconscious*, SE, 14:178; GW, 10:276-7. But see also *Ego and Id*, SE, 19:22-3; GW, 13:250, where Freud does talk about unconscious feelings, but distinguishes them from unconscious representations (or ideas) by claiming that they do not transition through the pre-conscious to become conscious: they do not need the support of word-traces to become conscious. I suggest, however, that this can be reconciled with the statements of *Unconscious* if one considers that in the latter, Freud considers three possible fates for repressed feelings: either they disappear altogether; or they find their way to abreaction; or they continue to live in the unconscious, but the representations to which they were attached are displaced by others according to the pleasure/unpleasure principle and the laws of secondary process. When Freud talks, in *Ego and Id*, of feelings *becoming* conscious directly, without transitioning through the pre-conscious, he may mean that they erupt, as feelings, to consciousness, after having *disappeared* from consciousness altogether—which would mean, after not even existing as feelings. On the other hand, in the other fate considered by Freud, in which they continue to live their life, but in the unconscious, what does need to transition through the pre-conscious to become conscious is the representations that elicited them in the first place. But they themselves, as feelings, are just as phenomenally present as they were before repression.
57. Cf. A79/B104-5: "The same function that gives unity to the different representations *in a judgment* also gives unity to the mere synthesis of different representations *in an intuition*.... The same understanding, therefore, and indeed by means of the very same actions through which it brings the logical forms of a judgment into concepts by means of the analytical unity, also brings a transcendental content into its representations by means of the synthetic unity of the manifold in intuition in general."
58. Cf. n. 55 in the present chapter.
59. See Freud, *Interpretation*, chap. 6: "The Dream Work," SE, 4-5:277-509; GW, 2-3:283-513. Freud's view of dreams or the various ways in which thought processes similar to those at work in dreams may also be at work in parapraxes, slips of the tongue or neurotic symptoms, is beyond the purview of the present chapter. In Freud's relation to Kant, what is most relevant to this chapter is the other aspect of imagination: its role in producing and binding images in what Freud calls the "pre-conscious" and thus the *ego*, when images and their associations are associated with words and thus available for judgment. I should add, however, that another point on which the comparison of Freud with Kant would be worth pursuing is the role of imagination in aesthetic production and appreciation. See Kant *Judgment*, AA5, 314-17; and Freud *Formulations*, SE, 12:224; GW, 8:236-7.
60. The distinction between a representation's being conscious by virtue of being qualitatively or phenomenally present—there is something it is like to have it—and its being conscious by virtue of being conceptualized is comparable to Ned Block's distinction between phenomenal and access consciousness: see Block 1995 and 2002.
61. Freud makes an exception for feelings (*Gefühle*): see n. 56 in this chapter.
62. See *Unconscious*, SE, 14:190-5; GW, 10:288-94.
63. On the relation between the "blind" character of imagination (and intuitions) and the fact that imagination is a function of the mind "of which we are seldom even conscious," see 7.2.3.
64. Cf. *Logic*, AA9, 109, §30.
65. *Ego and Id*, SE, 19:25; GW, 13:253. See 7.3.2 and 2.3.
66. I am grateful to an anonymous reader for urging me to acknowledge this point.

67. McDowell (1996), 85–6, 94–5. In a footnote to part IV-2 of (1996), McDowell makes reference to Freud. It is interesting to compare that brief reference to my own account of the resources we can find in Freud for a naturalization of Kant's transcendental philosophy. McDowell's goal, in the text to which the footnote is appended, is to clarify what he meant when he "refused to credit non-human animals with orientations toward the world." He did not mean, he says, to demean animal mentality, nor did he deny that animals "can be, in their way, clever, resourceful, inquisitive, friendly, and so forth" (ibid., 182). What he denies non-human animals is spontaneity in the Kantian sense, "the freedom that consists in potentially reflective responsiveness to putative norms of reason." Of course, he goes on, it is also true that in some respects "The lives of mature human beings simply match the lives of mere animals; it would be absurd to suppose that *Bildung* effects a transfiguration, so to speak, of everything that happens in a human life" (ibid., 183). And now comes the footnote: "Even those aspects of mature human life that are shaped by *Bildung* show unassimilated residues from their evolution out of mere nature (first nature). That is a way of putting a central thought of Freud." My own point about Freud is twofold. First, Freud does not *just* acknowledge the presence of "first nature" even at the core of "second nature," or *Bildung*. He also offers a fully naturalized account of *the mental structure that governs first-person thought*, the highest achievement of *Bildung* according to Kant, whereas Kant ultimately had to ground the latter—and the very possibility of *Bildung*—in a noumenal realm. Second, even where Freud's account reveals within *Bildung* "unassimilated residues" from first nature, those residues, as they appear in our mental life, are themselves fully acculturated, in the form of the laws of primary processes characterizing the id. In other words, even though Freud, strikingly, attributes an id as well as an ego to non-human animals (*SE* 19:37; *GW* 13:265–6), what differentiates the ego and id of humans, according to him, is that the latter is no less than the former a product of culture, or of what McDowell calls "second nature." Both are products of "second nature" in their structure (the laws of secondary processes in the ego and of primary processes in the id) as well as in their content (the emotions, images, and words bound by those laws).
68. Cf. *Ego and Id*, *SE*, 19:17; *GW*, 13:243; and see 7.3.2 in the present chapter.

8

Kant's 'I' in the Moral 'I Ought To' and Freud's "Super-Ego"

8.1 Preliminary Remarks

As we saw in Chapter 7, there are striking parallels between Kant's characterization of what he calls the "unity of apperception," expressed by the thought 'I think,' and Freud's characterization of what he calls "Ich" (translated in English as "ego"), an organization of mental processes governed by the reality principle. I have emphasized four main points of similarity. First, both Kant's "unity of apperception" and Freud's "ego" refer to organizations of mental processes that find expression in conceptualizing and judging: in what Kant calls "discursive thinking" and Freud calls "secondary process," which are governed by logical rules. Second, in both Kant's "unity of apperception" and Freud's "ego," discursive thinking presupposes a pre-discursive activity whose structure makes possible the emergence of discursive thinking: the transcendental synthesis of imagination for Kant, the ordering of images in pre-conscious mental life for Freud. Third, in both Kant's "unity of apperception" and Freud's "ego," the pre-discursive activity is below the threshold of consciousness. It becomes conscious when representations are brought under concepts (Kant) and when images are connected with words (Freud). Fourth and finally, representations of one's own body play a prominent role in the representational content of both Kant's "transcendental unity of apperception" and Freud's "ego." I have argued that those parallels give support to the claim I have been defending: we find in Freud's concept of "ego" resources for naturalizing Kant's "transcendental unity of apperception." For with that concept, Freud provides a model for explaining our psychological development as living beings belonging to a natural and social world. He provides a model for explaining how we acquire a capacity to make both ourselves and other human beings accountable for the justification of our beliefs and actions.

Now an essential part of this story remains to be told. For Kant's 'I' is not only 'I' in 'I think,' but also 'I' in 'I ought to,' and, more specifically, the moral 'I ought to.' Its counterpart in Freud is not only the ego that is related to the external world and is governed by the reality principle, but also that component of the ego which Freud calls the "super-ego," "*Über-Ich.*" The thesis I will defend in the present chapter is that just as we found in Freud's account of the "ego" a causal-developmental account of Kant's "transcendental unity of apperception," and thus of the role of the concept and word 'I' in 'I think,' similarly we can find in Freud's concept of "super-ego" a causal-developmental account of the structure of mental life that, according to Kant, finds expression in the concept and word 'I' in the moral 'I ought to.'

I have to grant, however, that in relating Kant's view of morality to Freud's concept of the super-ego I am opening the door to even more challenging objections than those I faced in relating Kant's concept of the unity of apperception to Freud's concept of the ego. I addressed some of the objections concerning the latter at the beginning of Chapter 7. In defense of the comparison I was offering, I noted that even though Freud's "ego" and Kant's "unity of apperception" belong to different types of investigation, psychological concepts are not foreign to Kant's transcendental account of cognition, and conversely, Kant's investigation into the a priori conditions of the possibility of experience is not foreign to Freud's metapsychological investigation of the structures of mental life that, he claims, provide the background for both healthy and neurotic mental functioning.[1]

But the central objection against relating Kant's view of morality and Freud's concept of super-ego is of a more radical nature than the objections considered earlier against relating Kant's "unity of apperception" and Freud's "ego." Now the objection is not just that Kant's and Freud's investigations have different contexts, method, and goals. Rather, the objection is that Freud's theory of the super-ego undermines the central tenet of Kant's moral philosophy.

Kant's view of morality starts from the idea that moral imperatives are categorical. As such they differ from prudential and instrumental imperatives. The latter have in common that they take as their basis our interests and desires, and formulate what we ought to do in order to best serve those interests and desires. In short, prudential and instrumental imperatives are *hypothetical* imperatives: *if* I want to satisfy desire X, *then* I ought to Y. *If* I want to obtain object Z, *then* I ought to W. Kant claims that moral commands are irreducible to those kinds of imperatives. They bind us *unconditionally*; they are *categorical* imperatives. But what is their basis, if they are not premised on our interests and desires? Kant's response: their basis is reason itself, making itself, or rather making its own claim to normative universality, the discriminating principle for determining the rules according to which we ought to act. The normative universality proper to the moral principles is expressed in the system of formulations of the categorical imperative that Kant offers in section 2 of *Groundwork*, and already in the first formulation of the categorical imperative in section 1: "I ought never to proceed except in such a way *that I could also will that my maxim should become a universal law*" (*Groundwork*, AA4, 402; Kant's emphasis).

Now Freud agrees with Kant that what distinguishes moral imperatives is their categorical nature. But he thinks that the idea that we are bound by *categorical* imperatives, imperatives that bind us unconditionally, is the result of the internalization, at a very early stage in the development of the small child, of the stern parental command to give up the libidinal and aggressive drives directed at both parents. "The domination of the super-ego over the ego," Freud writes, "manifests itself in the form of a categorical imperative" (*Ego and Id*, SE 19:35; GW 13:263). If Freud is right, Kant's claim concerning the authority of morality, namely, the normative grip on us of principles that are irreducible to rules governed by self-interest, seems to be significantly deflated. Morality, far from having its origin in the very nature of reason in its purest exercise, has its origin in the most archaic of our emotional responses: love, aggression, and fear, experienced by the child in the most helpless phase of its life. Categorical rules are just a fact of our life, not the highest achievement of our rational capacity. This being so, how can the mental structure that yields the use of 'I' in Kant's moral 'I ought to' have anything at all in common with Freud's "super-ego"? The latter seems, rather, to belong in the lineage of Nietzsche's radically skeptical genealogy of morality, summarized by Nietzsche in the damning statement: "The categorical imperative smells of cruelty" (1998 [1887], 41). According to Nietzsche, the genealogy of morality is a history of cruelty directed at the vital force in human beings that Nietzsche calls the will to power. To a reader of Nietzschean persuasion, Freud's statement that "the domination of the super-ego... manifests itself in the form of a categorical imperative" might well be just another way of saying that behind Kant's lofty notion of pure practical reason looms a history of domination and subjugation.

Such a reading of Freud's view would not necessarily be incompatible with the claim I want to defend, the claim that one finds in Freud a naturalized version of the structure of mental life that yields the moral 'I ought to' as Kant understands it. For it could be, after all, that that mental structure is actually obtained by the kind of violent training described by Nietzsche. But such a reading would certainly amount to a deflation of the Kantian claim to the autonomy of pure practical reason, and thus a radical challenge to the value of the moral attitude. Nietzsche, for one, explicitly intended his genealogy of morality to have such a result.

I hope to show, however, that reading Freud's view of morality along the Nietzschean lines just sketched out, is a mistake. I should add that my primary object here is not to discuss Kant's moral philosophy, nor is it to discuss Freud's views about morality. My primary object is, as it has been throughout this book, to discuss fundamental mental structures governing our use of 'I.' Nevertheless, to forestall the objections outlined above, it will help to lay out from the beginning a few of the reasons why I think it is a mistake to take Freud's view to be radically skeptical or deflationary with respect to the normative hold on us of specifically moral norms.

Freud thinks that the recognition of categorical norms is an indispensable stage in the development of the child. Unlike Kant, however, he thinks that the categorical nature of moral commands is grounded in the deepest, most archaic, and universal structure of the intersubjective relations a human infant encounters when it comes into the world: the emotional relation of the infant to the adult figures it depends on for its very life and well-being. The internalization[2] of that structure of intersubjective relations gives rise to the mental structure Freud calls the super-ego. As we shall see, the super-ego thus has its root in what Freud calls "the id" (*das Es*): the system of mental functioning generated by the non-rational, emotional attachments and dependencies of the infant and small child. And nevertheless the super-ego belongs in the ego, in the reasoning part or aspect of the developing human being's mental life. In the best developmental outcome we can hope for, the commands of the super-ego gradually become open to rational evaluation and endorsement—or, for that matter, dismissal. Their being thus open to rational assessment belongs in the kind of developmental account Freud has in view, I will suggest below, when he writes, "*Wo es war, da soll ich werden*" ("where it was, there I must come to be"), which we may perhaps reformulate in terms of the contrast between the two fundamental types of mental structure: "where the id was, there the ego must come to be" (*New Intr.*, SE, 22:79; *GW*, 15:86).

This being said, Freud takes no stance on what the correct formulation of moral principles might be, or what kind of assessment or justificatory system the ego ought to build for them. This is not within the purview of his investigation, indeed it would be quite contrary to his role as a clinical psychologist. As a clinical psychologist, he is led to uncover some of the effects that the pressures of the categorical commands of morality may exert on the human psyche, as well as their role in the etiology of various types of neurotic behavior. But he also describes morality as pertaining to "the higher side of man," to the side that is apt to promote human beings' intellectual and emotional development.[3]

In suggesting a parallel between Kant's and Freud's respective views of the structure of mental life that yields the categorical imperative, or imperatives, of morality, I find myself in broad agreement with Samuel Scheffler's argument in chapter 5 of his 1992 book, *Human Morality*. In this book, Scheffler argues for an account of the "content, scope, authority, and deliberative role"[4] of morality, an account that would do justice to our common moral intuition according to which moral motivation is different in kind from motivation based on our desires and interests. Against neo-Humean and consequentialist views, Scheffler argues that Kant's view of morality has the merit of doing justice to the irreducibility of moral motivation to ordinary belief–desire motivational sequences. But against Kant, Scheffler argues that we can find in ordinary human psychology sufficient resources to explain how our capacity for moral motivation was developed. And he suggests that Freud's account of mental development might offer a general outline for such an explanation. Unlike the Kantian account, the Freudian account is naturalistic because it holds that "our motivations for behaving morally all depend on . . . our possession of certain kinds of psychological features" (Scheffler 1992, 92). But it is a "fine-grained" naturalistic account because it has richer resources than those of ordinary belief–desire psychology to explain the moral motivation as a distinct type of motivation.

Whatever its own merits may be, the psychoanalytic account of moral motivation suggests a way in which it may be possible to reconcile a sophisticated naturalistic account of some kind with at least one important element of our traditional understanding of morality. More specifically, the psychoanalytic account reveals that a sophisticated form of naturalism may be capable of denying that the only way in which a consideration can motivate someone to act is conditionally on the presence of a suitable desire. Freud's remarks about the categorical imperative are of interest in this connection because, when taken in the context of his theory as a whole, they suggest that there may be room within a naturalistic account for a distinction between such *desire-based* motivation and motivation that works in another way. The other way in which a consideration could motivate, according to this distinction, would be if the architecture of one's personality included an authoritative structure or set of standards, by virtue of which one regarded the consideration as providing one with a reason to act. Let us call this sort of motivation *authoritative* motivation. (Scheffler 1992, 86)

One might object that given the role of love, aggression, and fear in the generation of the super-ego, Scheffler's so-called "authoritative motivation" is just a more complex form of motivation by desire. Scheffler anticipates this objection. He replies that, according to the view of morality inspired by the Freudian account, a specific *structure* of personality functions as that in virtue of which a consideration directly and categorically counts as a motive to act or refrain from acting in a certain way. This is a very different kind of motivation from ordinary motivation by particular desires or interests. He adds, moreover, that the Freudian account allows a distinction between what Scheffler calls "genuinely authoritative" motivation, on the one hand, and motivation by fear of the authoritative self (or desire for its approval), on the other. The latter keeps traces of its origin in the helpless status of the infant and the original circumstances (unfulfilled longing, aggression, fear of loss, fear of punishment) in which it appeared and developed. Only the former bears the mark of an integration of the super-ego within the ego, the rational functioning of our mental life. Scheffler's distinction here is in agreement with the interpretation I suggested earlier for Freud's formulation: "*Wo es war, da soll ich werden.*"[5]

Scheffler's discussion of Freud is only one element in the complex web of arguments that support his view of morality, which he calls "human morality." My own goal is not to argue for a particular view of the content, scope, or authority of morality. In line with the general argument of this book, my primary purpose is to elucidate fundamental aspects of the use and meaning of 'I.' My central claim in this chapter, as in the previous one, is that Freud's metapsychology offers resources for a naturalistic account of the structure of mental life that supports the use of 'I' in just those aspects Kant thinks are least amenable to an account in terms of our belonging to a natural world governed by causal laws. The previous chapter was concerned with the resources Freud offered for a naturalistic account of Kant's 'I' in 'I think.' This chapter will be concerned with the resources Freud offers for a naturalistic account of Kant's 'I' in the moral 'I ought to.' Let me now return to this main line of my argument.

I will proceed as I did in Chapter 7. I will first lay out the role of 'I' in Kant's moral 'I ought to' (8.2). To do this, I will focus on four features that are prima facie similar to the four features I identified for 'I' in 'I think.' The first is the relation of 'I' to discursive thinking. The second is the dependence of discursive thinking on a pre-discursive mental activity. The third is the fact that the pre-discursive mental activity is mostly below the level of consciousness. And finally, the fourth is the relation of 'I' to bodily consciousness. However, it will be quickly apparent that these four features have more complex ramifications in the case of Kant's analysis of 'I' in 'I ought to' than in the case of Kant's analysis of 'I' in 'I think.' It will turn out that this greater complexity of Kant's 'I' in the moral 'I ought to' once again finds corresponding complexity in Freud's account of what he calls the "super-ego."

In 8.3 I will introduce the comparison between Kant's and Freud's views by first outlining the terms Freud uses in *The Ego and the Id* (8.3). In 8.4 I will compare Freud's view of what he calls the "super-ego" to the four features of our mental life grounding Kant's 'I' in 'I ought to,' outlined in 8.2. My working hypothesis is that this will help complete the naturalized account of Kant's 'I' that I have claimed we could derive from Freud's account of the "ego."

8.2 Kant's 'I' in 'I Ought To'

8.2.1 The Moral 'I Ought To' and Mental Conflict

I said above that according to Kant's argument in the *Critique of Pure Reason*, ascribing one's thoughts to oneself, the referent of 'I' in 'I think,' expresses the consciousness of being engaged in generating the unity of a rule governed synthesis of one's representations, for which one takes oneself, explicitly or implicitly, to be accountable. The same, I suggest, can be said of ascribing 'ought' to oneself, the referent of 'I' in 'I ought to': it expresses the consciousness of being engaged in formulating and assessing rules for one's own actions, for which one takes oneself to be accountable. This is clearly true when 'I ought to' is the conclusion of a piece of hypothetical reasoning of the form 'If I want Y, then I ought to X; I want Y, so I ought to X,' the form of reasoning on which the prudential and instrumental self-prescribed rules that Kant calls "hypothetical imperatives"[6] depend. But it is also true, a fortiori, of those self-prescribed rules whose permissibility is assessed under the standard of the moral, categorical imperative: "I ought never to proceed except in such a way *that I could also will that my maxim should become a universal law*" (*Groundwork*; AA4, 402; Kant's emphasis). Both the formulation of the categorical imperative and the assessment of one's maxims under the standard of that imperative depend on keeping in view the unity of the propositional and inferential contents of one's thoughts. Whatever kind of entity the subject that attributes 'ought' to 'I' might be, its capacity to enter into the kind of assessment stated above depends on its taking itself to be accountable for the whole sequence of reasoning culminating in the moral 'I ought to X.'

But there is in this case—'I ought to'—another connotation of the use of 'I,' one that is absent from the use of 'I' in 'I think.' The mental action involved in formulating an 'ought,' whether hypothetical (instrumental or prudential) or categorical (moral), is not only *thinking* (generating concepts, acts of judging, and inferential sequences), but it is also *willing*. The faculty involved is not just the faculty of cognition (generating intuitions and conceptual representations of objects), it is also the faculty of desire, which Kant defines as "a being's *faculty to be by means of its representations the cause of the reality [Wirklichkeit] of the objects of these representations*" (*Pract. Reason*, AA5, 9n; Kant's emphasis). The faculty of desire is an essential characteristic of all living beings. Indeed, it is, for Kant, definitional of life: life just is "the faculty of a being [*das Vermögen eines Wesens*] to act in accordance with laws of the faculty of desire" (AA5, 9n). The faculty of desire is thus common to all animals, human and non-human (non-rational). In non-human animals, the representations involved in "causing the reality of the object" may be sensations (say, the sensation of hunger) accompanied by a feeling of displeasure (at the unfulfilled biological need) or of pleasure (when the hungry beast is satiated). Or the representations may be intuitions, perhaps even intuitions in mere imagination, of the object that might satisfy the need (say, the rabbit to be chased). Of course, the animal will not literally *cause the reality* of the rabbit. But at least the animal (say, the fox) will cause (if successful) the presence of the rabbit in the needed proximity (by chasing it) so that it can make it a dead rabbit, and devour it.

In human animals, the representations involved in "causing the reality of the object" include not only sensations, associated feelings of pleasure or displeasure, and intuitions of the object, but they also include concepts, judgments, and inferences. Human beings are thus not only capable of bringing about the proximity of the object, but they are also capable of literally causing the reality of the object by producing it in accordance with the concept they have formed of it and in virtue of the inferential patterns that allow representing relations of means to ends. Thus, only human beings have a faculty of desire in which the representations of objects to be obtained or avoided are discursively ordered: ordered in judgments and inferences. In other words, only human beings have a will, defined by Kant as a faculty of desire in which representations of objects to be obtained or produced involves the exercise of reason: "A will is a kind of causality of living beings insofar as they are rational" (*Groundwork*, AA4, 446). But this determination by reason can occur in two ways. In the first way, the rational capacity only serves to determine the best systematic correlation of means to ends in order to obtain the objects of sensible inclinations. So employed, the rational capacity generates a system of hypothetical imperatives—if I want X, I ought to Y—adjudicating priorities among maxims according to the respective strength of the relevant inclinations. In the second way, the rational capacity is, by itself, motivating for the faculty of desire. So employed, it orders all particular, hypothetical maxims of action under the one governing principle: "I ought never to proceed except in such a way that I could also will that my maxim should become a universal law" (*Groundwork*, AA4, 402).

Like the hypothetical 'I ought to,' the categorical, moral 'I ought to' is the expression of a thinking and desiring being that sets itself the rules for its actions and in doing so, is engaged in systematically ordered sequences of practical reasoning. Whether as the consequent in a hypothetical imperative, or as categorically asserted in a categorical imperative, the expression 'I ought to' is the expression of a will that is divided against itself. In hypothetical imperatives, various incentives and inclinations may be mutually incompatible. The will, as the faculty of desire of a rational being, is engaged in promoting the inclinations or interests that are stronger or perhaps more consistent with long-term goals. This self-imposition or self-discipline is expressed by the normative 'ought.' But the moral 'I ought to' expresses a self-imposed rule in a more radical sense. Here, the command is to give precedence, over *all* inclinations, to the categorical prescription to ascribe to myself *only* those maxims that I *could also will* to be a universal law.

So in all cases, what is proper to the thinker of 'I ought to X' is that she takes herself not only to be accountable for a sequence of *reasoning*, but also to be both the *author* and the *addressee* of the 'ought.' This is true in the case of the hypothetical imperatives resulting from the practical reasoning in the generic form just laid out. But it is also true, in a more radical sense, in the case of the *categorical* imperative, the unconditional self-prescription of the moral law that determines the assessments of permissibility or impermissibility of a maxim under the standard of that law. In Kant's own terms, in thinking the moral 'I ought to' I take myself to be both the *author* of the law and *subject* to the law.

> According to this principle [*the idea of the will of every rational being as a universally legislating will*], all maxims are rejected that are not consistent with the will's own universal legislation. Thus the will is not just subject to the law, but subject in such a way that it must also be viewed

as *self-legislating*, and just on account of this as subject to the law (of which it can consider itself the author) in the first place. (*Groundwork*, AA4, 431; Kant's emphasis. The emphasized clause in brackets belongs in the previous sentence in the text.)

Note that we find here a new sense of 'subject': 'subject' in this passage does not connote the metaphysical subject. 'Subject to the law' is taken in the moral-political sense, where it means 'subordinated to the law' or 'accountable for observance of the law.' But the will, as "subject to the law" in this new sense, is also the author of the law. The will (faculty of desire determined by reason) is the property of an entity that is both *prescribing* the law and *receiving* the law. In receiving the law, that entity is *limited* by the law with respect to the choices it can take to be permissible.

This dual status of the will that prescribes to itself the moral 'ought' is made especially salient by the contrast between the expressions of the imperative in section 1 and in section 2 of *Groundwork*. In section 1, the categorical imperative is formulated in the first person, indicating that the current thinker of the imperative is also taking responsibility for prescribing it to herself: "I ought never to proceed except in such a way that *I could also will that my maxim should become a universal law*" (*Groundwork*, AA4, 402; Kant's emphasis). In section 2, the categorical imperative is reformulated in the second-person imperative: "*Act only according to that maxim through which you can at the same time will that it become a universal law*" (AA4, 421; Kant's emphasis). The second-person formulation now makes more salient the fact that the individual referring to herself by using 'I' in 'I ought to,' in the formulation of the imperative offered in section 1 of *Groundwork*, is conscious of herself not only as the agent of the prescription but also as its patient as it were: the individual receiving the law as a command. That one and the same individual can be conscious of herself both as the author and the recipient of the law expressed as an imperative is explained in section 3 of *Groundwork*. In prescribing the categorical imperative to ourselves, we have to think of ourselves as belonging to a world of pure intelligences that are not causally determined according to empirical causal laws. As recipients of the categorical imperative, we know ourselves to belong to a causally determined world of spatiotemporal, material entities—living beings (AA4, 451–3).

This second characterization of the use of 'I' in the moral 'I ought to,' where the thinker of the current thought 'I ought to X' thinks of herself as both the author and the recipient of the categorical imperative, by no means makes irrelevant or redundant the first, where the thinker is conscious of being engaged in the sequence of practical reasoning yielding the thought 'I ought to X.' In the practical, just as in the theoretical use of reason, and in the moral-practical, just as in the technical-practical (prudential and instrumental) use, using the word and thinking the concept 'I' expresses the capacity to keep in view the unity of a mental process of connecting premises and conclusions for which one is in a position to give justification if called upon to do so. The aspect of the use of 'I' proper to the practical use of reason is itself dependent on the rational capacity to keep in view a discursive process of setting up norms for one's thoughts and actions. In that sense, the use of 'I' in the practical 'I ought to,' just as in the strictly theoretical 'I think,' is premised on the general capacity for discursive thinking.

However, just as the theoretical 'I think' was premised on a pre-discursive activity of imagination, so the discursive activity of practical reasoning is premised on a pre-discursive knowledge of one's duty that involves both imagination and feeling.

8.2.2 'I Ought To' and Pre-Discursive Determination of the Will

Kant devotes section 2 of *Groundwork* to laying out the different formulations of the categorical imperative and explaining how one would determine the maxims of one's actions under the standard set by one or the other of those formulations (AA4, 406–45). This does not mean, however, that knowing in each case what is morally permissible or impermissible depends on computing one's duty under the universal standard set by the categorical imperative. On the contrary, Kant insists that common moral wisdom just knows, without any reasoning, what ought to be done. True moral wisdom consists in character and action rather than in discursively expressed knowledge (*Groundwork*, AA4, 405). Kant goes as far as to ask whether it would not be better to just leave common wisdom to its insights rather than confusing it with the unnecessarily complex arguments of philosophers (AA4, 404). He answers in the negative: even though common moral understanding does not need sophisticated reasoning to know what is morally permissible or impermissible, it does need reasoning to reinforce itself against the sophistries of false prophets and moral skeptics:

Innocence is a glorious thing, but then again it is very sad that it is so hard to preserve and so easily seduced. Because of this, even wisdom—which otherwise surely consists more in conduct than in knowledge—still needs science as well, not in order to learn from it, but to obtain access and durability for its prescriptions. (AA4, 404–5)

The immediate insight into what one ought to do is experienced as a feeling of a unique kind: respect for the moral law. Respect is both *caused* by the moral law and *directed at* the moral law. As caused by the moral law, it is the effect of pure practical reason, whose form is the moral law, on our faculty of feeling pleasure and pain. The feeling thus elicited is both pain (humiliation at the realization that one is radically inadequate to the sublime command of the law) and pleasure (satisfaction at feeling the sublimity of practical reason in oneself).[7] Kant insists that the feeling of respect does not motivate us to act in accordance with the law, but, on the contrary, the fact that the law affects our faculty of desire is the cause of the feeling of respect for the law.[8]

But how can a rational faculty cause a feeling, and moreover through a mere form: the form of the law? Kant, I suggest, means something like the following. The effect of the faculty of pure practical reason on our faculty of desire just consists in the hierarchy established among our maxims, the dismissal of some as impermissible and the endorsement of others as permissible. This effect is experienced by the agent as a feeling of respect *for her duty*, as an incentive to do, in any given instance, just what she ought to do, and to do so only *because* this is what she ought to do. In other words, for common moral understanding, respect for the law is not respect for the law in its universal formulation (one or the other of the formulations of the categorical imperative as stated in section 2 of *Groundwork*), but respect *for duty*, that is, in any given instance, the subjective acknowledgment (by feeling not reasoning) of *the normative necessity of doing this particular action and no other.* Moreover, Kant moves seamlessly from respect *for duty* to respect for *persons*: for individuals whom we take to exemplify a motivation that gets its structure solely from the form of the law.[9]

And yet, whether an agent has in any given instance actually acted from a motive of duty remains radically unknowable, both by others and by the agent herself. This is the third feature of Kant's view that I now want to consider.

8.2.3 Motivated Blindness to the Grounds of One's Actions

There are two importantly different senses in which, for Kant, we are blind to the nature of our motivation. First, common moral understanding may have a correct representation of what duty commands without having a clear representation of the universal moral principle under which this command is justified. This is just the general situation explained in the previous section, in which imagination and feeling give us access to the commands of pure practical reason without a clear conceptual representation of those commands. Nevertheless, that conceptual representation can be made clear. Indeed, as we just saw, Kant takes it to be an important role of philosophical investigation to make it clear and thus better fixed in the moral agent's mind. Then its relation of congruence or conflict with instrumental or prudential motivations may come to light: the latter, too, may be "obscure," and then become clear when they are conceptually represented.[10]

But there is another, more radical blindness, which is what I call in the title of this section "motivated blindness to the grounds of one's actions." Even though the formal structure of motivation under the moral law is present as a capacity in each human being and negatively attested at least by the sense of our own imperfection when we obviously act *against* what morality would require, it is impossible positively to know whether an action has ever been accomplished *from* duty rather than merely in external conformity with the commands of duty. Indeed, we have, according to Kant, a natural propensity to deceive ourselves and to conveniently present to ourselves as an action done *from* duty what is really only an action *in conformity* with duty. Self-deception is the most common of moral failures.

[There is] a certain *perfidy* on the part of the human heart (*dolus malus*) in deceiving itself as regards its own good or evil disposition and, provided that its actions do not result in evil (which they could well do because of their maxims), in not troubling itself on account of its disposition but rather, considering itself justified in front of the law.... This dishonesty, by which we throw dust in our own eyes and which hinders the establishment in us of a genuine moral disposition, then extends itself also externally, to falsity or deception of others. (*Religion*, AA6, 38)

Already in section 2 of *Groundwork*, Kant wrote:

In fact, it is absolutely impossible by means of experience to make out with complete certainty a single case in which the maxim of an action otherwise in conformity with duty rested simply on moral grounds and on the representation of one's duty. It is indeed sometimes the case that with the keenest self-examination we find nothing besides the moral ground of duty that could have been powerful enough to move us to this or that good action and to so great a sacrifice;

but from this it cannot be inferred with certainty that no covert impulse of self-love, under the mere pretense of that idea, was not actually the real determining cause of the will; for we like to flatter ourselves by falsely attributing to ourselves a nobler motive, whereas in fact we can never, even by the most strenuous self-examination, get entirely behind our covert incentives, since, when moral worth is at issue, what counts is not actions, which one sees, but those inner principles of action, that one does not see. (*Groundwork*, AA4, 407)

The situation described here is not just that, because our motivation to act is present in us in the "blind" form of feeling and desire, we are not fully conscious of its true nature. Nor is it merely that even the most strenuous reflection will not allow us completely to elucidate it. Rather, the situation described is that, just as we have sensible motives to act against the moral law, we also have sensible motives (motives of self-love, escalating into self-conceit) to deceive ourselves about the motivation of our actions. Thus, the very effort at self-reflection and conceptually clear elucidation of one's motivation all too naturally turns into a mere tool for moral pretense, where discursive formulation of one's purported motivation by one or the other formulations of the moral imperative is just a complacent mask for another kind of motivation whose explicit conceptual formulation is conveniently blocked. The procedure is made all the more effective by the fact that one and the same mental activity, that of reason in its practical use (its use in determining maxims for actions), and one and the same faculty of desire or will, the faculty of desire affected by reason, are at work in, on the one hand, endeavoring to enforce the structural priority of the moral imperative, and, on the other, implementing the counterinfluence of hypothetical imperatives of self-love. In other words, the battle rages within one and the same mind, in which one or the other overall structure of motivation may win the day, depending on whether the force of sensible motives or the force of the motive of duty has the final say.

It remains that, even in the situation of motivated blindness just described, the conflict within the will remains within the purview of reason. The conflict is between types of motivations that *can* be discursively formulated (motivation under hypothetical imperatives of prudence or skill versus motivation under the categorical imperative of morality). So it is worth asking: Is there room in Kant for another type of unconscious motivation, where the system of unconscious desires is radically a-rational?

As we saw in the previous chapter (7.4.4), in his 1798 *Anthropology from a Pragmatic Point of View*, Kant notes that representations of sexuality and death are actively removed from our clear consciousness and live on in the shadows of our mind, where they generate uncontrolled fantasies and irrational conduct. In a similar vein, in his 1786 *Conjectural Beginning of Human History*, Kant offers "conjectures" ("*Muthmaßungen*": see *Conjectural Beginning*, AA8, 109) concerning the earliest steps in the development of reason in human beings. The second step is the one that interests me most, but let me first quickly summarize all four.[11]

In the first step, the first "stirrings of reason" result in the multiplication of the ways to satisfy needs. With those first stirrings, the capacity to represent the relations of means to ends is developed and, with it, possible choices are multiplied indefinitely.[12] In the second step, human beings learn that sexual restraint prolongs and increases sexual desire, helps the development of imagination, and prevents "the boredom that comes with the satisfaction of merely animal desires." In the third step, the capacity to anticipate the future is accompanied with fear of death, alleviated only by the creation of families and the representation of the continuation and improvement of life in one's posterity. In the fourth step, human beings are in a position to consider themselves "although only darkly" as the "true end of nature," insofar as they are able to use the rest of nature, including other animals, as means to their own preservation and to the improvement of their condition. In doing so, every human being becomes able to think of herself as equal to any other human being, and to think of all other human beings as equal to herself: they are, one and all, to be treated as ultimate ends of nature. These four steps, says Kant, are the stages by which humankind steps out of the "guardianship of nature to the state of freedom" (*Conjectural Beginning*, AA8, 115).

The second of the steps just listed is the most important for the question I was asking earlier: Is there room, in Kant's view of human motivations, for radically a-rational motivation, just as there was room (as we saw in Chapter 7) for representations obeying the laws of fantasy rather than those of reason? Here's what Kant writes about the second step.

The human being soon found that the stimulus to sex, which, with animals, rests merely on a transient, for the most part periodic impulse, was capable for him of being prolonged and even increased through the power of the imagination, whose concern, to be sure, is more with moderation, yet at the same time works more enduringly and uniformly the more its object is *withdrawn from the senses*, and he found that it prevents the boredom that comes along with the satisfaction of a merely animal desire. The figleaf (*Genesis* 3:7) *was thus the product of a far greater expression of reason than that which it had demonstrated in the first stage of its development* [my emphasis; recall that the first stage is the multiplication of choices of means for the satisfaction of one's ends: an instrumental use of reason]. For to make an inclination more inward and enduring by withdrawing its object from the senses, shows already the consciousness of some dominion of reason over impulse and not merely, as in the first step, a faculty for doing service to it within a lesser or greater extension. *Refusal* was the first artifice for leading the merely sensed stimulus over to the ideal one, from merely animal desire gradually over to love, and with this from the feeling of the merely agreeable over to the taste for beauty, in the beginning only in human beings but then, however, also in nature. Moreover, *propriety*, an inclination by good conduct to inspire in others respect for us (through the concealment of that which could incite low esteem), as the genuine foundation of all true sociability, gave the first hint toward the formation of the human being as a moral creature.—A small beginning, which, however, is epoch-making, in that it gives an entirely new direction to the mode of thought—and is more important than the entire immeasurable series of extensions of culture that followed upon it. (*Conjectural Beginning*, AA8, 112–13)

The restraint imposed on the satisfaction of the sexual instinct and the withdrawal of sexual organs from sensory perception are not a means to satisfy a particular end. They are an entirely new way of structuring one's representations and desires. It is, says Kant, "the product of a far greater expression of reason" than that which occurred in the first step, where the "expression of reason" was strictly instrumental, consisting in finding a greater and greater variety of means to a greater and greater variety of possible ends. The second step, in contrast, consists in the imagination's being given free range to fantasize about sexuality. This free range given to imagination is to the greater benefit of reason in opening the space for reason's own higher end, treating human beings as the ultimate end of nature, indeed as ends in themselves, not merely means for other people's ends.

I propose, then, that there is room in Kant's view of the human mind, considered not only in its cognitive capacities but also in its faculty of desire, for determinations that radically escape the domain of clear (conceptual) representations and instead belong in what Kant calls, in the *Critique of Pure Reason*, the "blind, but indispensable function of the soul" (A78/B103), imagination, an imagination that here, unlike its role in cognition, is not ruled by concepts but by desire and fantasy. Note, however, that in Kant's presentation, reason remains the underlying *cause* of the substitution of the fantasies of imagination for the immediate satisfaction of animal sexual instinct: the development of fantasy over immediate sensory representation is the "product of the [by far greatest] expression of reason." There is thus an underlying teleology of reason determining even the most a-rational functions of the soul. This will be important for our comparison of Kant with Freud.

Let me now take stock of this section. I have tried to elucidate the ways in which, according to Kant, we are *not* conscious of our motives in thinking 'I ought to X.' But it should not be forgotten that in most cases of *hypothetical* practical reasoning, we are clearly aware of our motives. I know what I ought to do and why I ought to do it when I set myself a goal and come up with a clear representation of the means necessary to reach that goal. The absence of awareness appears at the two extremes of the spectrum of our motivational patterns. First, at the rational end of the spectrum of motivations, even though every human being has it in herself to *feel* respect (there is thus a "what it's like" character, a phenomenal character, to our consciousness of the moral law), human beings cannot claim to have a clear consciousness of the nature of their motivation, much less to *know* without a doubt that they are acting from a motive of duty. On the contrary, human beings are motivated to *keep out of clear representation* the true nature of their motivation. Second, at the opposite end of the spectrum of motivations (in the sense that the motivations here are non-rational or a-rational), we are motivated to remove from clear (conceptual) consciousness the sexual fantasies spun by our imagination and motivating some of our behaviors.

We will find similar complexities in the types of *self*-consciousness entering into the thought "I ought to."

8.2.4 'I' in 'I Ought To' and Consciousness of One's Body

We saw that the unity of apperception expressed in the thought 'I think' is, as a matter of empirical fact, indexed to a particular body.[13] This indexing extends to self-consciousness in instrumental and prudential reasoning. The latter involves consciousness of one's own body on two counts. First, our *desires* and relevantly related maxims are determined by incentives[14] that consist in the pleasure one expects or the displeasure one seeks to avoid. Second, the *cognitions* on which the hypothetical imperatives rest depend on the body as well, insofar as these cognitions are empirical.

In contrast, the use of 'I' in the moral command depends on the consciousness of oneself as the subject of an activity of reasoning that determines the maxims of one's actions under the unconditional command of the categorical imperative. Considered under this aspect, the subject referred to by 'I' is conscious of herself (thinks of herself) as the subject (in the metaphysical sense) of a will determined by reason alone. Of course, the *content* of the obligations determined under the categorical imperative is nevertheless derived from the empirical nature of the agent. But the motivation expressed by the categorical imperative is a motivation by reason alone.

There is thus, according to Kant, a contrast between the consciousness of oneself as a sensibly determined agent grounding the use of 'I' in prudential and technical reasoning, and the consciousness of oneself as a purely rational agent grounding the use of 'I' in the formulation of the categorical imperative. We find an echo of this contrast in the three kinds of "original predisposition to the good in human nature" that Kant expounds in part 1 of *Religion*.[15] There is a good proper to *animality*, and a corresponding predisposition to that good in any human being considered merely as a living being. There is a good proper to *humanity*, and a corresponding predisposition to that good in any human being considered as a living *and rational* being. And finally, there is a good proper to *personhood*, and a corresponding predisposition to that good in any human being, considered as a rational being. To each of these predispositions corresponds a notion of self.[16] First, the embodied self, present in our disposition to animality, characterized by self-love under three guises: self-preservation, sexual drive, and the disposition to community with other human beings. Second, the embodied *and* rational self of instrumental and prudential reasoning, which is the self of humanity, characterized as both sensible and intellectual. And finally, the moral self, radically independent of any corporeal impulse, indeed actively opposing any determination of the will by mere sensible impulse. Only insofar as they are ordered under the human being's predisposition to personhood can the other two predispositions escape the propensity to evil they otherwise contain.

Nevertheless, precisely because of its role in ordering the technical and prudential maxims under the unconditional command of the moral law, there is a sense in which even the moral self is indexed to an animal and human self, and thus to a living, sensing, thinking body. This is apparent in Kant's discussions of duties in *Groundwork of the Metaphysics of Morals* as well as in the *Metaphysics of Morals*. Although duties are determined under the moral law and thus under the command of our pure rational nature, their content is clearly provided by our sensible nature: for instance, the duty to keep one's promise and pay back a loan, the duty not to take one's own life, the duty to develop one's talents, the duty to extend help to one's fellow human beings, and so on.

* * *

Let me now take stock of the four points examined in 8.2. I have argued that we can identify four features of the kind of self-consciousness that grounds, according to Kant, the use of 'I' in the moral 'I ought to,' parallel to the four features I identified in Chapter 7 for the use of 'I' in 'I think.' Nevertheless, the specifications of those four features are quite different in the case of 'I' in 'I ought to' from what they were in the case of 'I think.' Let me briefly recount the main contrasts. (1) The use of 'I' in the moral 'I ought to' expresses the consciousness of the conflicted nature of the moral agent, both prescriber and receiver of the moral imperative. (2) The discursive activity expressed in the moral 'I ought to' depends on a pre-discursive consciousness that is a *feeling* (the feeling of respect for the moral law) rather than the consciousness of an activity of imagination, as it was in the case of 'I think.' Nevertheless, it can be the latter as well (for instance, imagining a character that exemplifies respect for the moral law and is thus, itself, an object of respect). (3) Whether moral motivation (determination of the will under the moral law) is at all in play in the determination of action is more radically inaccessible to consciousness than was, in the case of 'I think,' the synthesis of imagination under the unity of apperception. This is because we are actively invested in remaining blind to the motivations of our own actions. (4) The self-consciousness expressed by 'I' in the moral 'I ought to' is, just like the self-consciousness expressed by 'I' in 'I think,' indexed to a body. At the same time, in both cases using 'I' expresses the consciousness of myself as a pure intelligence, a thinking being. Still, only of our consciousness of the moral law does Kant say that it is *ratio cognoscendi* of freedom, i.e. that it is the way we come to be aware of ourselves as exercising a type of causality distinct from the causal determinism of the natural world.

In Chapter 6, I argued that we could find in Kant's solution to the third Paralogism of Pure Reason resources for a concept of person as an empirical being belonging in a natural world, and endowed with unity of apperception and the capacity to determine her actions under the discriminating principle of the moral law. I also suggested that we could find in Freud's account of the structures of mental life, resources for a causal-developmental, naturalistic explanation for just those capacities that Kant thought could be accounted for only by appealing to an unknown and unknowable transcendental subject, belonging in a noumenal world grounding the phenomenal world and thus our existence as empirical beings. In Chapter 7, I supported my point by arguing that Kant's concept of 'unity of apperception' finds its counterpart in Freud's concept of 'ego.' In the present chapter, I now propose to show that, similarly, Kant's conception of the structure of mental life that enters into the self-ascription of the categorical imperative of morality finds its counterpart in Freud's concept of 'super-ego.'

I now turn to Freud's concept of 'super-ego.' I will proceed as I did in the previous chapter. I will first expound Freud's explanation of the structure of mental life that he calls 'super-ego' (*Über-Ich*). I will then scan it through the lens of the four features I identified as central to Kant's view of the structure of mental activity expressed in the moral 'I ought to.'

8.3 Freud's Super-Ego

In the first two sections of *The Ego and the Id*, Freud explains how he moved from a descriptive, to a dynamic, and finally to a structural distinction between conscious and unconscious mental representations. According to the structural distinction, unconscious processes are those whose sequences are determined according to the pleasure principle and whose contents are connected according to the laws of what Freud calls "primary processes." In contrast, sequences of conscious/pre-conscious mental processes are determined according to the reality principle and their contents are structured according to the laws of secondary processes, elementary logical rules connecting the contents of mental states.[17]

Freud defines as "ego" the organization of mental processes according to the laws of secondary processes. The ego, he claims, emerges from the id (the system of mental processes governed by the pleasure principle and laws of primary process), as a response to the individual's need for structuring the contents of her representations in such a way that they will serve life-preserving action rather than immediate gratification. Given this characterization of "ego" and "id," it seems that the ego just is the system of conscious representations, and the id, the system of unconscious representations. And yet, Freud goes on:

> If the ego were merely the part of the id modified by the influence of the perceptual system, the representative in the mind of the external world, we should have a simple state of things to deal with. But there is a further complication.
>
> [We have been led to assume] the existence of a stage [einer Stufe] in the ego, a differentiation within the ego, which may be called the "ego ideal" or "super-ego." The fact that this part of the ego is less firmly connected with consciousness is the novelty which calls for explanation. (Ego and Id, SE, 19:28; GW, 13:266)

The ego, then, is not just a system of conscious representations. There is a stage or aspect of the ego that is not necessarily conscious: the super-ego. The explanation Freud goes on to offer is roughly the following.[18] One grounding feature of the child's early development is the necessity of finding resolution to the so-called "Oedipus complex." The "Oedipus complex" is a structure of emotional attachments in which the child finds his original love object in the parent of the opposite sex and experiences the parent of the same sex as a threatening rival toward whom the child experiences aggressive impulses.[19] In the effort to give up the impossible love object and curb his aggressive impulses, the child turns those emotions toward himself. In so doing, he revives older, archaic identifications with his parents, dating from the time when he experienced himself as one with the loving, nurturing parent. The child thus forms the representation within his mental life of an "ego ideal" ("Ich Ideal"), which he strives to emulate, but to which he also experiences himself as radically inadequate. This sense of inadequacy is brought about by another identification: the identification with the stern figure of the competing parent that forbids the satisfaction of the loving attachment.[20]

When introducing the concept of the super-ego in section 3 of *The Ego and the Id*, Freud relates it to the categorical imperative:

> The super-ego retains the character of the father, while the more powerful the Oedipus complex was and the more rapidly it succumbed to repression (under the influence of authority, religious teaching, schooling and reading), the stricter will be the domination of the super-ego over the ego later on—in the form of conscience or perhaps of an unconscious sense of guilt. I shall presently bring forward a suggestion about the source of its power to dominate in this way—the source, that is, of its compulsive character, which manifests itself in the form of a categorical imperative. (Ego and Id, SE, 19:34–5; GW, 13:263)

Freud's "suggestion about the sources of the [super-ego's] power to dominate" is further explained at the beginning of section 5, entitled "the ego's relations of dependence." Here, Freud writes:

[The super-ego] is a memorial of the former weakness and dependence of the ego, and the mature ego remains subject to its domination. As the child was once under a compulsion to obey its parents, so the ego submits to the categorical imperative of its super-ego. (*Ego and Id, SE*, 19:48–9; *GW*, 23:277–8)

In *The Economic Problem of Masochism*, which dates from the same period, Freud is even more explicit: "Kant's categorical imperative," he writes, "is the direct heir of the Oedipus complex" (*Masochism, SE*, 19:167; *GW*, 13:380).

Now one may wonder in what tone of voice Freud makes this remark. Is this an ironical statement, meaning to indicate that, Kant's grandiose statements about morality as autonomy notwithstanding, obeying the categorical imperative is being subject to irrational compulsion? The answer, I submit, is no. Rather, as I suggested in the introductory remarks to this chapter, Freud means exactly what he says: the categorical imperative is the *heir* of the Oedipus complex. The sense of unconditional normative constraint appears as early as the Oedipus complex.

What about the *content* of Kant's categorical imperative? Is there any plausibility at all in supposing that such a purely rational content is "the direct heir" of the story of drives and their frustrations that is, according to Freud, the core of the Oedipus complex and its resolution? We will be in a better position to answer this question after comparing Freud's explanation of the super-ego to the four theses I laid out concerning Kant's explanation of the structure of mental activity that finds expression in the moral 'I ought to.'

8.4 Kant's 'I' in 'I Ought To' and Freud's Super-Ego

8.4.1 Mental Conflict

We saw in 8.2.1 that the use of 'I' in Kant's moral 'I ought to' expresses the consciousness of being both the author and the recipient of the categorical imperative. This twofold aspect of the consciousness of oneself in the moral 'I ought to' has its counterpart, in Freud, in the twofold aspect of the super-ego we just analyzed. On the one hand the super-ego is a component within the ego. It contributes to shaping the character of the individual and her capacity to act according to norms experienced as her own. And yet the super-ego is also experienced as a force external to the ego and sternly imposing on it a standard of conduct that the individual experiences herself as hopelessly inadequate to satisfy.

Just as the command of the categorical imperative is, for Kant, an *unconditional* command, independent of any particular end *to be achieved*, but rather grounded in an *existing end*, humanity as an end in itself, similarly the commands of the super-ego, which Freud describes as "categorical imperatives," are commands experienced as overriding any particular ends and determining the shape one can give to all aspects of one's life, including the particular life-preserving ends whose representation is generated by the ego. Of course, according to Kant, what makes morality unconditionally binding is its foundation in pure practical reason and thus in our freedom as rational beings (recall Kant's formulation in the *Critique of Practical Reason*: freedom is the *ratio essendi* of the moral law, the moral law is the *ratio cognoscendi* of freedom).[21] In contrast, according to Freud, what gives the commands of the super-ego their unconditional character is, originally at least, our being bound by what we experience as the standards set by the idealized figure of the lost parent or any other original nurturing authority figure. So, whereas the unconditional character of morality is, for Kant, originally grounded in pure reason affecting the faculty of desire, it is, for Freud, originally grounded in the raw emotion that binds us to the figure from which we have learned the rules of our socialization.

Nevertheless, might it not be that the development of rational capacities, characteristic of the ego, results in a change in the nature of the moral command, from compulsive to rationally assessed and endorsed? Recall the distinction that Scheffler suggested can be derived from Freud's analysis, between "genuinely authoritative" motivation on the one hand, and motivation by fear of the internalized figure of the super-ego and longing for its approval, on the other.[22] Only the former bears the marks of the integration of the super-ego into the ego, a development that depends both on favorable emotional circumstances and on the development of rational capacities enabling the individual to assess the justification of moral commands: "*Wo es war, da soll ich werden*"—"where it was, there must I come to be."[23] As I interpret it, Freud's developmental account of the super-ego and its evolving integration into the ego supports Scheffler's distinction. Further support for this view is offered by Freud's account of the relation between discursive and pre-discursive or non-discursive mental activity in shaping the content and authority of the moral 'I ought to.'

8.4.2 Discursive, Pre-Discursive, Non-Discursive Mental Activity

For Freud, the internalization of the parental figure in the form of an ego ideal is accompanied by the recognition of the inadequacy of the individual ego to that ideal. The stronger the early attachments, the more powerful the figure of the ego ideal and super-ego, and the more crushing the experiential manifestation of the sense of inadequacy.[24] What makes the feeling a moral feeling is its role in curbing libido and aggression, and in developing what Freud calls the "supra-personal side of human nature."[25] Similarly, for Kant, as we saw, the moral attitude has its primary manifestation in the feeling of respect, which is elicited in children by presenting to them characters exemplifying the idea of a will determined by the moral law.[26]

Still, the capacity to spell out universal principles of morality is indispensable, for Kant, for protecting common moral understanding from the sophistries of false prophets. Now again, we find something similar in Freud. The super-ego becomes part of the ego. As such, the rules of the super-ego can come to be expressed in words and enter into conscious reflective thinking.[27] This means that the standards set by the ideal and the harsh judgments passed by the super-ego eventually come to be formulated in explicit principles and moral judgments according to those principles. This is where Freud's remark, "The categorical imperative is the direct heir of the Oedipus complex," finds its full meaning. I suggest what Freud means is that Kant's categorical imperative is a late formulation, influenced by the eighteenth-century ideals of rationality, of a more primitive moral attitude that has historically taken many other forms. Supposing Freud was right: What would that make of Kant's claim to have derived his formulations of the categorical imperative, determining the standard by which all our particular maxims are to be assessed, from an a priori argument constructed from the very notion of a categorical imperative?[28]

A plausible answer would be to say that the practice of reason giving and justification, which is characteristic of a developed ego, is unsurprisingly also in play when it comes to finding a formulation for the categorical character of the moral imperative. If Kant is correct in thinking that the formulation that does justice to the categorical character of the moral imperative is the set of formulas he proposes in section 2 of *Groundwork*, then that formulation is indeed just the most adequate formulation for a mind set on finding justification for the universal authority, the normative hold on us, of moral imperatives. Explaining the causal history of the very idea of a categorical imperative is not incompatible with providing an argument to the effect that a rational formulation, one that does justice to its content *qua* imperative commanding categorically, has to be something like the one Kant proposes. Once we have reached the point at which we are capable of justifying moral imperatives on purely rational grounds, does the question of what brought us to that point really matter, at least from the standpoint of moral philosophy?[29] Can't we just accept to throw away the ladder?

Well, maybe the causal history is not just a ladder. Maybe the relation between emotion and reason stays with us no matter what stage of ontogenetic or phylogenetic development we find ourselves at, because the grounding role of emotion is not a mere chronological fact but also an ontological order of precedence that stays with us. For Kant, the moral feeling of respect is the experiential manifestation of our metaphysically grounding rational nature imposing its standard on our sensible nature.[30] For Freud, the moral feelings of inadequacy and guilt are the experiential manifestation of our renunciation of exclusive emotional attachments, a renunciation that is a groundbreaking event in the developmental history of each individual human being. For Kant, morality is the manifestation of the highest in us: our rational self. For Freud, morality is the manifestation of the highest in us: our "social sense" and our capacity to live by norms we endorse. But it is also the "direct heir" of the most helpless in us: the system of emotional dependences that shape us. As such, it is also a primary source of the neuroses generated by unresolved conflicts. In other words, if it is true that Kant's categorical imperative is the direct heir to the Oedipus complex, then, according to Freud, the awe it inspires should be inseparable from a vigilant suspicion directed at the harshness of its demands.[31]

8.4.3 Motivated Blindness

Freud describes the super-ego as an *unconscious* component of the ego even though it is not repressed but rather repressing.[32] This peculiarity of the super-ego is in fact one major reason, according to Freud, for preferring the structural to the dynamic characterization of the unconscious. It is still true that repressed processes are unconscious, but it is not the case that all unconscious processes are repressed. Rather, what is common to all unconscious processes is that they occur according to the pleasure principle rather than the reality principle, and that their representational contents obey the rules of primary processes rather than those of secondary processes. The super-ego, insofar as it is unconscious, is unconscious in just this sense: its contents are opaque to the subject of mental representations because they do not obey conceptual/logical rules of combination. For instance, an overbearing super-ego may be manifest in a feeling of guilt whose origin is not accessible to consciousness but which finds expression in the (qualitatively) conscious phenomena of neurotic symptoms and dreams. The structure of the latter is not that of logically ordered secondary processes but that of primary processes: condensation, displacement, overdetermination, symbolization.[33]

But the feeling of guilt may also find access to conscious representation via its connection to pre-conscious word representations, and thus eventually it may find access to conscious propositional representations, where it comes to be expressed as categorical moral imperatives. Freud writes:

> One may ... venture the hypothesis that a great part of the sense of guilt must normally remain unconscious, because the origin of conscience is intimately connected to the Oedipus complex, which belongs to the unconscious. (*SE*, 19:52; *GW*, 13:281)

However,

> The super-ego is part of the ego and remains accessible to consciousness by way of ... word-presentations (concepts, abstractions). But the *invested energy*[34] does not reach these contents of the super-ego from auditory perception (instruction or reading) but from sources in the id. (*Ego and Id*, *SE*, 19:52–3; *GW*, 13:282)

In other words, even though moral commands come to be discursively formulated in terms that are comprehensible to the subject, their motivating power remains premised on their origin in the resolution of the Oedipus complex. The latter remains unconscious, both in the dynamic sense (it is repressed) and in the structural sense (the representational contents it generates are bound together according to rules of primary processes).

This is clearly not the same as what I called, in 8.2.3, the "motivated blindness" to the nature of our motivation as understood by Kant. According to Kant, we have a natural propensity to present to ourselves as moral motivation what is really a motivation according to rules of instrumental or prudential reasoning. So although we do know (by virtue of the immediate access we have to the moral law in us) that we have a disposition to determine our action from a motive of duty, we never know whether we have actually so determined our action. This kind of blindness to one's own motivation is different from Freud's notion of the unconscious. The conflict between motivations and the propensity to self-deception, as articulated by Kant, remains within the purview of reason. The issue in Kant's characterization of self-deception is: Do I deceive myself when I claim to be performing or to have performed an action from a motive of duty? Isn't it really performed according to hypothetical imperatives of prudential or instrumental reason? Both kinds of motivations are open to discursive formulation.[35] Freud's unconscious motivational pattern, in contrast, is unconscious precisely in the sense that it is inaccessible to discursive formulation. The discursive formulation of moral commands is an alteration of the originally unconscious motivation and thus makes it part of the life of the ego. This is a positive development, which opens our moral attitude to discursive thinking and to rational assessment. It remains, nevertheless, that whereas the ultimate self-deception is, for Kant, presenting to oneself as motivated by duty an action that is actually performed from a motive of self-love, for Freud, the more radical self-deception is to believe that reason is by itself motivating and that the moral attitude has its origin in a "pure" reason that is the source, in virtue of its influence on the faculty of desire, of the unconditional character of moral imperatives.

From the preceding we can discern the shape of the difference between Kant and Freud concerning the relation of the 'I' of the moral 'I ought to' to consciousness of one's own body.

8.4.4 *'I' in 'I Ought To,' Freud's "Super-Ego," and Embodiment*

In the previous chapter, I argued that there are two different ways in which, for Freud, the ego is a bodily ego. First, the body image is at the core of the system of mental representations constituting the ego. Second, the body is the locus of the drives represented as emotions in the id. Under the first aspect, Freud's view of the relation between ego and body is comparable to Kant's view of what I have called the indexing of the transcendental unity of apperception to a particular body. Under the second aspect, Kant's view offers only tentative ancestors of the relation between ego and the body that, I suggested in Chapter 7, owns us rather than our owning it.[36] Under both aspects, I argued that Freud's developmental account of ego offers a model for a naturalization of Kant's transcendental unity of apperception and its expression in 'I think.'

The same is true, I now argue, of Freud's super-ego in relation to Kant's account of the structure of mental life generating the moral 'I ought to.' We saw earlier in this chapter that the consciousness of oneself grounding the use of 'I' in the moral 'I ought to' has to be indexed to an animal and human self from which it receives the contents of its maxims (see 8.2.4). It remains, however, that for Kant, what defines the thought 'I ought to' as an expression of moral obligation is the purity of its motivation. The consciousness of oneself that grounds the use of 'I' in the moral 'I ought to' is thus at least in part the consciousness of oneself as a pure intelligence belonging to a purely intelligible world. In contrast, for Freud, the sense of unconditional moral command is rooted in the effort to overcome the loss of the beloved figure of authority and curb the feeling of aggression that is in part a reaction to that loss. The *content* of moral obligations is eventually discursively expressed, and this may open the way to assessing what the proper structure of moral justification might be. Such an assessment depends on the exercise of our rational capacity. Nevertheless, for Freud, what makes it the case that morality has a hold on us is the process by which the id morphs into the super-ego and the ego ideal, and by which both the super-ego and the ego ideal are integrated into the ego. The moral self, then—the concept we have of ourselves in ascribing the moral 'ought' to ourselves—is not only, as it is for Kant, *indexed to* a body in virtue of the fact that the maxims among which we exercise our discriminating capacity receive their content from our empirical existence as embodied entities. The moral self also has its *ontological ground* in our body as the locus of drives that find their representatives in the emotions shaping the id and the super-ego.

So Freud's story concerning the origin of morality, unlike Kant's, locates its roots in our living, sensing, emotion-driven bodies. What does that tell us, indeed does it tell us anything at all, about Freud's view of moral justification? Does Freud claim to offer any response at all to the question: Are Kant's formulations of the categorical imperative of morality worthy candidates for the proper criterion of moral permissibility or impermissibility? Is this even a proper question for him to ask, or for us to ask his view to offer a response to?

It's actually not *just* nor even *first* the Kantian version of the categorical imperative of morality that Freud sees as originating in the internalization by the child of the lost parental figure. It is also the whole set of religious and social norms. All of them have, for the individual, the character of being *categorical*, namely, *not* determined by the particular goals of particular individuals, but binding, period. They have the form of categorical judgments: not the hypothetical form '*If* I want X, *then* I ought to Y,' but 'I ought to Y,' period. Indeed, historically and in countless cases until the present day, moral norms, however categorically expressed and experienced, were not easy to distinguish from social and religious norms. According to Freud, "Religion, morality, and a social sense—the chief elements in the higher side of man—were originally one and the same thing" (*Ego and Id, SE,*19:37; *GW,* 13:265).

Now Kant's ambition was to give a formula for morality that would be independent of any particular religious or social belief or command. This is why he gave it the absolutely universal forms we find in *Groundwork*. He wanted a formula for what is *categorical* about morality that would not ground morality in a particular religion or in a particular social order, but would present it as binding for mankind as such.

One might object to Kant and his followers that the very idea of a universal foundation for morality is itself relative to a particular society and to a particular stage in the history of humankind. The idea of universal law, equally binding for all human beings, is an idea that is born from the eighteenth-century Enlightenment. Kant's model for morality is inspired by Jean-Jacques Rousseau's political model of the Social Contract, based on giving up individual will in exchange for participating in the constitution of a universal will. So one might say that in his formula for the categorical imperative, Kant just internalizes to the moral command the idea of universality that originates in the political ideal of the social contract: take to be permissible only those rules of action you could accept that everybody else takes, to be permissible for themselves as well.

Kant would reply that the very possibility of formulating such a political model as Rousseau's conception of the Social Contract depends on the capacity of human beings to take themselves and others to be bound by the same universal laws. Political and juridical laws bind externally (by way of state institutions and the use of punishment to enforce the law), whereas the moral law binds internally (by respect and rational endorsement). The existence of the former helps inculcate human beings with the latter. But the capacity to be bound by the latter is a condition for the emergence of the former, and in fact the ground of its justification.

Nothing in what Freud says about the categorical nature of morality is incompatible with this kind of response. Transforming the emotional ground of our categorical normative attitudes into the discursive formulation of categorical principles we can share, indeed we ought to share, is the proper work of the ego. That this process should be historically dependent on the actual development of social and political models of human interactions is no surprise. Still, Freud's genealogy of morality is a sobering warning. On the one hand, the lasting merit of Kantian morality is to seek moral principles that do not depend on particular religious beliefs or on the cultural norms of particular societies. It is to make the criterion for the moral permissibility of an action the answer to the question: could you accept that all human beings give themselves the very same rule according to which you are currently determining yourself to act? On the other hand, according to Freud, the danger inherent in the Kantian account of the moral attitude is the illusion that the authority of morality comes from reason alone. By 'authority' I mean both the motivating *force* and the discursive *justification* of the moral command as a categorical 'ought.' According to Freud, as far as its motivating force is concerned, the moral attitude is rooted in emotion, in the attachment of the young child to the parental figure whose exclusive love she or he has to give up. Because of this, the moral attitude, with its typical features as Kant understood them—categorical command, conflict with inclinations, potential for self-deception, and lack of clarity about one's own motives—is, for Freud, to be handled with care. Rational justification is an ideal to strive for even while recognizing that it derives its very energy and the richness of its resources from what is radically irrational in us: the inexhaustible surge of our emotional life, both dangerous and creative.

8.5 Concluding Remarks

In the previous chapter, I related Kant's 'I' in 'I think' to Freud's concept of ego. In this chapter, I have related Kant's 'I' in 'I ought to' to Freud's concept of super-ego. I have argued that, just as Freud's account of the structure of mental life he calls 'ego' can be seen as providing a developmental story for just the unity of apperception that grounds the use of 'I' in 'I think,' so Freud's account of the structure of mental life he calls 'super-ego' can be seen as providing a developmental story for the conflicted structure of mental life that grounds, according to Kant, the use of 'I' in the moral 'I ought to.' However, the relation of Freud's 'super-ego' to Kant's moral 'I ought to' is more complex than the relation of Freud's 'ego' to Kant's 'I think.' Freud turns around the fundamental ground of the moral 'I ought to' as Kant understood it by arguing that the origin of the very categorical nature of morality lies not in reason but in emotion, indeed in the most archaic roots of our emotional life. I have argued that this story of origin does not entail an indictment of the Kantian account of moral justification. After all, in internalizing the norms of rationality she receives from the parental figure, the developing infant internalizes a capacity not only for the rational evaluation of existing norms, but also for the promotion and invention of heretofore unformulated moral norms. The latter capacity is in turn shaped by the opportunities offered by the historical development of human societies. In that context, it might well turn out that the Kantian account of moral justification is among the highest that the ego—the reasoning part of our mental life—can aspire to. Freud takes no position on this point; this is not the kind of question he sets himself the task of answering. Whatever the answer one might give to that question, it remains that when all is said and done, the key to a healthy ego, for Freud, is the ordering of mental states and their contents according to the reality principle, over against the fantasies and hallucinatory satisfactions of the id.

I submit, then, that we do find in Freud a general outline for a naturalization of Kant's critical account of 'I': *naturalization* because there is no need to suppose an unknown and unknowable transcendental subject to account for the possibility either of our using 'I' in 'I think,' or of our using 'I' in the moral 'I ought to.' *Naturalization* also because our capacity for setting norms of cognition and our capacity for setting norms of practical agency both have a developmental history. *Naturalization of second nature* because the content of the norms is brought about not only by our relation to nature and our existence as biological entities, but also by the internalization of the parental figures and the learning of language, and thereby the internalization of the social and symbolic tools that are necessary not only for learning existing norms, but also for acquiring and creating new ones. Nature does not do any work in our individual development that is not already informed by the world of social norms into which we are born and educated. It is that world that makes possible the development, in the kinds of living beings we are, of a capacity to set and assess norms of truth in cognition and norms of justification in action for which we take ourselves and all other human beings to be equally accountable. In Freud's terms: "*Wo es war, da soll ich werden.*" Where it was, there must I come to be. Where the id was, there must the ego come to be.

Notes

1. See 7.1.
2. What I mean here by "internalization" is the fact that the child's emotional attachment to, and dependence on, the parental figure or figures, result in her adopting as her own the categorical norms she experiences as imposed by the parent. More will be said about this process in 8.3 and 8.4.
3. *Ego and Id*, SE, 19:37; GW, 13:265. The full sentence reads: "Religion, morality, and a social sense—the chief elements in the higher side of man*—were originally one and the same thing." The asterisk sends the reader to the following remark in a footnote: "I am at the moment putting science and art on the side." Should we suppose that Freud uses the expression "the higher side of man" with some degree of irony? I don't see any reason to suppose he does. He certainly takes "a social sense" to be an achievement that is indispensable to the phylogenetic and ontogenetic development of human beings. Religion and morality are part of that development, even if the particular forms taken by either may be damaging to the flourishing of human beings. The fact that Freud puts "science and art" among the elements that also belong to the "higher side" confirms that he does not take the latter expression ironically. The fact that he is "at the moment putting them aside" is due to the fact that they call for explanations that are not directly connected to the concept of the super-ego that he is developing in part 3 of *Ego and Id*.
4. Scheffler 1992, 5.
5. *New Intr.*, SE, 22:79; GW, 15:86. See 8.1 in the present chapter.
6. *Groundwork*, AA4, 414–15.
7. *Groundwork*, AA4, 80–1.
8. Cf. *Pract. Reason*, AA5, 76: "And so respect for the law is not the incentive to morality [*Sittlichkeit*], but it is morality itself, considered subjectively, insofar as practical reason, in striking down the pretentions of self-love in its opposition to morality, insures consideration for the law, which now alone has influence." Surprisingly enough, a few pages later Kant seems to offer a conflicting view: "Respect for the moral law is therefore the sole and

also undoubted moral incentive" (AA5, 58). The apparent inconsistency in formulation is unfortunate. But the context makes Kant's meaning fairly clear. Kant has just contrasted respect with other feelings, such as love (AA5, 76) or admiration (AA5, 76–7), neither of which, he maintained, can count as moral feelings or moral incentives. Only respect is a properly moral feeling, and thus only it is a moral incentive. But this is because respect is "effected only by reason [*lediglich durch die Vernunft bewirkt*]" (*Pract. Reason*, AA5, 76; cf. *Groundwork*, AA4, 31n). And a few pages later: "Therefore respect for the moral law must be regarded as also a positive though indirect *effect of the moral law on feeling* insofar as the law weakens the hindering influences of the inclinations by humiliating self-conceit, and must therefore be regarded as a subjective ground of activity" (*Pract. Reason*, AA5, 79; my emphasis). Thus, if respect is an incentive, it is one only insofar as it is, itself, the effect rather than the cause of the moral law's influence on us. I say more about the nature of that influence below in the main text. Thanks to Allen Wood for pressing me on this point.
9. Cf. *Groundwork*, AA4, 401n. *Pract. Reason*, AA5, 78–9.
10. On obscure and clear representations, and the relation of clear representations to conceptualization, see 7.2.1 and 7.2.3.
11. I am grateful to Allen Wood for bringing this text to my attention. It is important to keep in mind that it presents only a set of "conjectures" in response to Johann Gottfried Herder's 1784 *Ideas for a Philosophy of the History of Humanity*. Those conjectures, says Kant, are a product of "the power of imagination, indulged in for the recreation and health of the mind, but not for a serious business." Kant presents them in the form of a commentary, somewhat tongue in cheek, on the biblical text of Genesis 3 to 6, sometimes inspired almost word for word by Rousseau's 1754 *Discourse on the Origins and Foundations of Inequality among Men*. Still, Kant's comments are quite telling of the way he thinks of the historical development of reason in its relation to imagination and to repressed sexual instinct. On the circumstances of the publication of this text, see Allen Wood's preface to *Conjectural Beginning*, 160–2. See also Wood 2008, 230–4.
12. *Conjectural Beginning*, AA8, 111.
13. See 6.3. Cf. also Kant's reasoning in the Third Analogy of Experience (B260): light playing between our eyes and celestial objects is the empirical condition for our perceiving the simultaneous existence of those objects. "Our eyes" means, for each of us: the eyes belonging to me, who can think 'the moon exists simultaneously with the earth' and can reinforce the statement by also thinking 'I think the moon exists simultaneously with the earth.' 'I' refers to the entity thinking 'I think the moon exists simultaneously with the earth,' conscious of her own thinking, and also conscious that she is entitled to think that thought in virtue of being conscious of her own position with respect to the moon and the earth, namely in virtue of her being conscious of her own body.
14. *Triebfeder*: cf. *Pract. Reason*, AA5, 71.
15. See *Religion*, AA6, 26–7.
16. I speak here of "notion of self" rather than "notion (or concept) of 'I'" because Kant himself talks, in the case of the first two predispositions to the good, of "self-love" (*Selbst-Liebe*). See also *Groundwork*, where he talks of "the dear self" (*das liebe Selbst*) as what might be the actual end of the action, lurking behind the purported moral motivation of that action (see *Groundwork*, AA4, 407). I suggest this "dear self" is the concept of oneself under which one represents oneself (where "oneself" means whoever is currently thinking 'I think' or 'I ought to') and in accordance with which one privileges technical or prudential maxims of action over maxims determined under the moral law. In contrast, the moral self is the concept of oneself under which one represents oneself when one gives due precedence to the categorical imperative in selecting the maxim of one's actions.
17. Cf. 7.3.1 and 7.3.2.

18. Freud introduced and developed this explanation in earlier works, among which are *On Narcissism: An Introduction* (1914), *Mourning and Melancholy* (1917), and *Group Psychology and the Analysis of the Ego* (1922).
19. The situation is actually more complex than that: the infant has attachments to both parents and thus also experiences each of them as a competitor for the affection of the other. This is related, says Freud, to the "constitutional bisexuality of each individual" (*Ego and Id*, *SE*, 19:31; *GW*, 13:260).
20. I have recounted Freud's narrative in the masculine gender, since Freud tells the story mostly as applied to the little boy, although he makes clear that there is a corresponding story for the little girl: see *Ego and Id*, *SE*, 19:31-2; *GW*, 13:260-1. As Freud himself reminds us (*SE*, 19:28; *GW*, 23:266), the notion of ego ideal was introduced for the first time in *Narcissism* (see *SE*, 14:94; *GW*, 10:161-2) and further developed in *Group Psychology* (1921). In *Narcissism*, Freud distinguishes the ego ideal from the "special psychical agency...which...constantly watches the actual ego and measures it by that ideal" (*Narcissism*, *SE*, 14:95; *GW*, 10:162). As we can see from the citation above, in *Ego and Id* Freud takes the internalized ideal and the critical agency to belong to one and the same mental configuration, which he calls indifferently "ego ideal" and "super-ego." Considering in this way the super-ego (judgmental agency) and the ego ideal (the ideal standard against which the super-ego judges the ego, that is to say, the individual judges herself) is especially interesting if one compares, as I propose to do, Freud's structure of super-ego to the structure of mental life which is, according to Kant, characteristic of morality.
21. See *Pract. Reason*, AA5, 4. Cf. 6.4, n. 19.
22. Cf., 8.1. On "internalization," see n. 2.
23. Cf. 8.1. *New Intr.*, *SE*, 22:79; *GW*, 15:86.
24. *Ego and Id*, *SE*, 19:37, 53; *GW*, 13:265, 282-3.
25. Ibid., *SE*, 19:35; *GW*, 13:264.
26. In personal correspondence, Allen Wood has objected that, for Kant, the feeling of respect is a feeling of our own freedom. It thus has a positive connotation quite different from Freud's analysis of the feeling of guilt. I agree. But the feeling of respect, according to Kant, *also* has a connotation of self-accusation and guilt. "So little is respect a feeling of pleasure that we give way to it only reluctantly with regard to a human being. We try to discover something that could lighten the burden of it for us, some fault in him to compensate us for the humiliation that comes upon us through such an example" (*Pract. Reason*, AA5, 77). And earlier (AA5, 74): "What in our own judgment infringes upon our self-conceit humiliates. Hence the moral law unavoidably humiliates every human being when he compares it with the sensible propensity of his nature." It is true that in both cases, Kant immediately goes on to say that insofar as we recognize the moral law in ourselves, then we are elevated in our own eyes: "The soul believes itself elevated in proportion as it sees the holy elevated above itself and its frail nature" (AA5, 77). But we find the same duality in Freud as we find in Kant: while being crushed by the sense of our own inadequacy under the severe judgment of the super-ego, our narcissism is nevertheless satisfied by our identification with the ego ideal, generating a sense of empowerment and enthusiasm. The fact that Freud takes the elevated image of oneself to be largely illusory is reminiscent of Kant's suspicion of our tendency to self-deception about our own motivations. For what remains of the fundamental difference between the two, see 8.4.3.
27. *Ego and Id*, *SE*, 19:52; *GW*, 13:282.
28. Cf. *Groundwork*, AA4, 420.
29. Thanks to Allen Wood for pressing me on this point.
30. Therefore the feeling of freedom as well as inadequacy. See n. 26.

31. In personal correspondence, Allen Wood offers the following cautionary comment. "You are clearly right about what Freud intends. But in anything good, is there not always the danger that it will be misused or perverted? And things can always be misused or perverted in more than one way. To every virtue there corresponds a vice of excess and a vice of deficiency. The demands made by morality can be perverted either by being made harsh and cruel, or by being made too lenient and self-indulgent. Kant seems more worried about the latter, Freud more worried about the former. Kant probably saw complacent laxity and selfishness among the nobility and bourgeoisie who frequented his dinner table. Freud treated patients who were victims of cruel parents and overbearing religious traditions. Why can't we just acknowledge that both worries are justified? Does one of them have to be right, and the other wrong? Where is there even an issue here?" I agree that Freud and Kant may both be right in the evils they denounce. Neither claim is thereby undermined, *at least up to a point*. Kant's claim as to the rational principle of morality and his denunciation of moral laxity may be correct even if Freud's story of origins and his worry about neuroses generated by harsh moralism are correct, and vice versa. Nevertheless, if one accepts Kant's formulations of the categorical imperative and at the same time accepts a story of origin along lines broadly similar to the one Freud is offering, then this story has consequences for the way we understand Kant's formulations of the categorical imperative, and therefore the way to apply them. For instance, what does "humanity" mean in the "principle of humanity" (second formulation of the categorical imperative: see *Groundwork*, AA4, 429)? As I said at the beginning of this chapter, my goal here is not to offer a discussion of Kant's moral philosophy. But I do think the position we take on the question, "What is a human being?" has consequences for the way we evaluate Kant's formulations of the categorical imperative and their application. For more on this point, see Longuenesse 2005, chap. 9: "Moral Judgment as a Judgment of Reason."
32. Cf. *SE*, 19:28; *GW*, 13:256.
33. On primary vs. secondary processes, cf. *Interpretation*, *SE*, 5:588–609; *GW*, 13:593–614. *Formulations*, *SE*, 12:213–26; *GW*, 8:229–39. *Ego and the Id*, *SE*, 19:21–5; *GW*, 13:235–89.
34. About my translating "*besetzte*" by "invested" rather than "cathectic," see Chapter 7, n. 53.
35. On the difference between self-deception, which remains within the purview of propositional psychology, and Freud's notion of the unconscious, which does not, see Gardner 1993, chap. 1. As described by Kant, both kinds of motivation—motivation from motives of self-love according to hypothetical imperatives, motivation from the motive of duty according to the categorical imperative—are amenable to propositional formulation, even if that formulation is not clearly represented in the agent's mental functioning.
36. Cf. 7.4.4.

9
Epilogue

Before closing, let me first briefly recap the main steps taken in this book. I will then consider some of the questions that might be raised concerning the path thus taken.

In the first part of the book, I considered a few influential recent analyses of our uses of the first-person pronoun 'I,' in relation to Kant's analysis of self-consciousness on the one hand (Chapter 2), and in relation to Sartre's phenomenological description of different types of consciousness and self consciousness on the other hand (Chapter 3). Kant's groundbreaking legacy, I argued, is to have identified a type of self-consciousness that is distinct from bodily self-consciousness although intimately connected with it. That type of self-consciousness is the consciousness of being engaged in bringing rational unity into the contents of one's mental states.

In the second part, I submitted to close scrutiny Kant's view of self-consciousness, focusing on the two chapters of the *Critique of Pure Reason* in which that view is developed most extensively: the Transcendental Deduction of the Categories on the one hand, and the Paralogisms of Pure Reason on the other. In the Transcendental Deduction, Kant develops his analysis of the type of self-consciousness grounding the proposition 'I think' and the role of 'I' in that proposition. In the Paralogisms, he criticizes what he takes to be the implicit inferences grounding rationalist metaphysical conceptions of the soul as a thinking substance distinct from the body. I argued that the lessons to be derived from Kant's criticism were not only negative. Rather, they have a twofold positive outcome. The first positive outcome is the contrast Kant draws between the conception of ourselves we inevitably develop insofar as we are engaged in thinking and willing, on the one hand; and the conception of ourselves that can be justified objectively, from what we would call a third-person standpoint, that of science or that of metaphysics. The error of rationalist metaphysicians, Kant maintains, is to have formed the illusory belief that one could derive a priori metaphysical views from the first-person standpoint one has on oneself in thinking.

The second positive outcome is one Kant himself does not endorse, at least not in the context of his criticism of the paralogism of personhood. It is nevertheless an outcome I have claimed we can derive from Kant's criticism of the rationalist view. Kant criticizes the rationalist inference from features of 'I' in 'I think' to the thesis that we are persons in the psychological sense—entities conscious of their own numerical identity at different times—and in the moral sense—entities capable of moral accountability—to the extent that we are thinking beings, distinct from bodies. I have maintained that from Kant's criticism one could derive a positive notion of a person not just as a thinking being, but as an embodied entity, endowed with unity of apperception and with the capacity to bring rational hierarchy into the maxims of its actions.

In the third part of the book, I have argued that Kant's view of the structure of our mental life, grounding the use of 'I' in 'I think' and in the moral 'I ought to,' found a descendant in Freud's notions of ego and super-ego, respectively. I have argued that one thus found in Freud's metapsychological analysis of mind the outline of a naturalization of Kant's analysis of 'I' in its theoretical and practical uses—in 'I think' and 'I (morally) ought to.'

Let me now consider some of the questions that might be pressed, and that in any event are worth taking some time to address. The first (9.1) concerns the scope of Part III: why stop with Freud, and in fact, why bother with Freud at all? In what ways does the consideration of Freud's view of the mind constitute a way "back" from Kant "to" present times?

The second question (9.2) concerns the relation between Part I and Part III. Does the analysis of the role of 'I' in language and mind have any connection at all with the metapsychological considerations inspired from Freud, offered in Part III? Do they really belong in one and the same book?

A third question (9.3) concerns the reasons for focusing on the two kinds of self-consciousness privileged in all three parts of the book—consciousness of one's own body, consciousness of being engaged in bringing rational unity into the contents of one's mental states and attitudes—rather than on what might perhaps be equally important types of self-consciousness, for instance the awareness one has of one's emotions, sensations, and feelings?

A fourth question (9.4) is even more radical: is it possible at all to consider self-consciousness, let alone uses of 'I,' without taking into consideration the relation of individual (self-)consciousness to consciousness of other (self-)conscious beings?

And finally, a fifth question (9.5): supposing (in response to 9.3) one has established that indeed the two kinds of self-consciousness explored in this book are fundamental, why is this point important? What does it help us understand? Why is it of any consequence at all that there should be those two fundamental types of self-consciousness?

9.1 The Temporal Scope of Part III

One might think that the subtitle of the book, "Back to Kant, and Back Again," constitutes false advertising. The reader is led to expect that Part III will take her "back" from Kant "to" contemporary philosophy, just as Part I led "from" contemporary philosophy "back to" Kant. Instead, Part III takes us at best halfway. Stopping with Freud, we are left hanging in the early twentieth century, and, moreover, in the company of a controversial figure in early twentieth-century approaches to the mind.

There are really two questions in one here: (1) Why does Part III stop with Freud? (2) Why does it consider Freud at all? My response to the first question is that in fact, the discussion offered in Part III does not stop altogether with Freud. In considering Freud's model of the mind, I have offered comparisons with developments in contemporary philosophy of mind and moral psychology, for instance concerning conscious and unconscious representations, the structure of the will, and the authority of morality. My intention in appealing to Freud has not been to make his account of the structure of mental life an end point. Rather, my intention has been to argue that by paying due attention to Freud's structural view of the mind, we stand to gain insights into possible ways in which Kant's view of the normative capacities we exercise in cognition and action, which Kant thought we could account for only by taking ourselves to belong in a purely intelligible world grounding the world of appearances, might turn out to be compatible with an account of our existence as living beings belonging to the natural world.

My response to the second question (why consider Freud at all?) is that it would be a mistake to underestimate Freud's place in the history of psychology and philosophy of mind. Freud—whose training was, for the first two years of his university education, in philosophy; and for the rest of his education and for his professional training, in biology and neurology—is part of the groundbreaking nineteenth- and early twentieth-century movement in psychology pressing the biological and neurological nature of the mental. In this respect, he is the heir of Hermann von Helmholtz and Theodor Meynert.[1] But he is also a pioneering figure in the investigation of the complex relations between emotions and rationality, and of the role of language in the expression of the former and the development of the latter. Nevertheless, undoubtedly, more needs to be said than I have in this book about the independent plausibility of Freud's account of the mind, and about the degree to which Freud's view remains relevant in light of contemporary cognitive psychology and neuroscience. I made reference in Chapters 7 and 8 to some of the research available on those issues. Discussing that research is beyond the ambition of the present book. I hope to pursue such discussion in future work.

Relating Kant's transcendental philosophy, via Freud, to contemporary moral psychology, is a program that differs from the program of exploring the relations between Kant's transcendental philosophy, Freud's metapsychology, and contemporary cognitive psychology and neuroscience. The latter program calls for exploring the subpersonal mechanisms that undergird the mental activities Kant and Freud explore at the personal, folk-psychological level. The former program remains within the framework of the ordinary folk-psychological concepts of belief, desire, and related normative attitudes while urging the necessity to break free of the limitations of those concepts. The two programs can be mutually illuminating and are worth pursuing jointly.

9.2 "Back to..." and "...Back Again"

A second question might concern not just Part III of the book, but the relation between Part I and Part III. As discussed in Part I, several contemporary analytic philosophers of mind and language not only are willing to grant the connections between current analyses of the uses of 'I' in language and thought on the one hand, and Kant's investigation of 'I,' self-consciousness, and the self on the other; they also have themselves made strong claims to such a connection. Similarly, as discussed in Part III, several contemporary philosophers, psychologists, and psychoanalysts have recognized the connections between Freud's view of the mind and Kant's. But the views discussed in Part I and Part III belong to quite different types of investigation, the first mostly in analytic philosophy of language and mind, the second mostly in psychoanalytic theory, moral psychology, and moral philosophy. What makes it appropriate to include them in one and the same book?

My answer is that the connection is precisely where it should be, namely, through Kant, whose view is extensively discussed in Part II. In Part I, I argued against the view that 'I' is a non-referential expression (see the discussion of Wittgenstein and Anscombe in Chapter 3), but also argued against the view that it is a necessary condition on the very possibility of a referential role for 'I,' that its referent be an embodied, spatiotemporal entity, and that the I-user be aware of herself as such an entity (see the discussion of Evans's view in Chapter 2 and of Cassam's view in the Preface). I have nevertheless acknowledged that consciousness of oneself as thinking is, as a matter of empirical fact rather than as a matter of a priori argument, intimately connected to awareness of one's own body.

Now, both aspects of the view I defend—the distinction *and* connection between consciousness of oneself in thinking, and consciousness of one's embodied existence—are prominent in Kant's view of self-consciousness. In Part II of the book, I examined at length Kant's argument against the rationalist metaphysicians' characterization of the thinking being as a soul, distinct from the body. The negative result is that even though, in thinking, we develop an implicit or explicit conception of ourselves as the agent of our thoughts, indivisibly present in all instances of our thinking, numerically identical in different times and distinct from our bodies, that conception has neither a priori metaphysical support, nor empirical support. But that negative result, I have argued, is intertwined with a positive thesis, inherited from the Transcendental Analytic and recurrent in the course of Kant's arguments in all four Paralogisms of Pure Reason: the only way we are objectively justified in believing ourselves to be entities that persist through time, and the only way we are able to track our own existence through time, is by adopting a third-person standpoint on our own existence as the existence of an embodied entity. We cannot derive any objectively justified belief in our persisting existence from the mere consciousness of ourselves in thinking.

In other words, Kant's argument, as I understand it, is a strong defense of the distinction, but also the intimate connection, between consciousness of oneself in thinking and consciousness of oneself as an embodied entity. An added complexity of Kant's view is of course that, for him, our existence in space and time, and so, our existence as embodied entities, is only the appearance of our existence as purely intelligible entities or things as they are in themselves. My argument has been, however, that Kant's explanation of the way we conceive of ourselves in thinking, and conceive of the structure of mental life that grounds our uses of 'I' both in the theoretical and in the practical use of reason, can be preserved without stepping out of our existence as empirically knowable, spatiotemporal entities. There is no need to think of ourselves as the appearances of a purely intelligible entity, no need to appeal to the notion of purely intelligible entities at all.

This is where the connection lies between Part I and Part III of the book. Freudian metapsychology, I claim, offers at the very least a blueprint, obviously to be amended, completed, and refined, for a developmental account of the two aspects of self-consciousness extensively analyzed by Kant from the standpoint of his transcendental philosophy: consciousness of oneself in thinking and consciousness of one's own embodied existence. By drawing on Freud's insights, we keep in view those two fundamental aspects of self-consciousness without appealing to a noumenal realm to account for consciousness of one's rational capacities in thinking or in determining one's actions. This, then, is the connection between Parts I and III of the book, via Part II: Part I discusses recent and contemporary answers to questions concerning the use of 'I' in language and thought; Part II gives Kant's original answers to those questions and provide tools to evaluate contemporary philosophers' claims to build on Kant's insights; Part III offers a developmental account of Kant's insights into the structures of mental life accounting for our uses of 'I.' That account, I claim, preserves the power of Kant's insights without paying the price of Kant's partial return to the metaphysics his critical analysis disavowed.

As I said in Chapter 1, it remains that each of the three divisions of the book, as well as each of its main chapters individually, offer self-standing textual interpretations and systematic arguments that readers, depending on their particular interests, may opt to study and discuss separately. I see nothing wrong with that way of approaching the book. My hope is, nevertheless, that many readers will develop an interest in following the complete arc of the argument—from philosophy of language and mind, back to Kant, and back again to twentieth-century developments in Freudian metapsychology—with a view to further investigation of its relation to contemporary cognitive and moral psychology.

9.3 Why Not Consider Other Kinds of Self-Awareness?

A third question might concern the privilege given, in grounding any use of 'I,' to the unity of consciousness (as exemplified by Kant's "transcendental unity of apperception" and Freud's "ego"), on the one hand; and to consciousness of one's own body, on the other. Weren't other sources of self-awareness worthy of consideration as well? What about sensations, emotions, feelings? I offered answers to this question in Chapter 2; it may help to briefly recall those answers.[2]

Many mental states are such that being aware of them just is being aware of being, oneself, in those states (e.g., normal cases of feeling pain). However, such awareness would not suffice to ground a use of 'I' in language or in thought. The availability of the concept 'I,' as the concept referring, in any instance of its use, to the entity of which the predicate in the proposition currently thought, 'I am F,' is true—the availability of that concept presupposes the capacity to think at all. Thinking is unifying and articulating the contents of mental states into concepts, propositions, and inferential patterns. Sensations, feelings, and emotions become propositionally self-ascribed, using the concept and word 'I' ('I have tooth-ache,' 'I am angry,' 'I see red,' and so on) only when the content of the relevant state is conceptually articulated into propositions, and the thinker of the propositions thereby thinks of herself, the thinker and speaker, as the entity of which the relevant predicate (e.g., '—have tooth-ache,'—am momentarily going to be hit by that snowball') is true. This means that any use of the concept 'I' presupposes the exercise of the capacity for unifying and conceptualizing mental contents that Kant calls "transcendental unity of apperception." The exercise of that capacity is itself conceptually expressed in the proposition 'I think.'

The question I have been trying to address has been: Does the self-consciousness expressed in 'I think' depend on the consciousness of one's own body? My answer, which I have argued is in tune with Kant's own, has been twofold. On the one hand, satisfying the reference rule for 'I' calls for nothing more than being, in any instance of the use of 'I,' the thinker of the thought and speaker of the sentence in which 'I' is used; correspondingly, having available the fact that one is, oneself, in any given instance of one's use of 'I,' the entity satisfying its reference rule, calls for nothing more than the awareness of one's being engaged in thinking. On the other hand, however, in many uses of 'I' the predicate that is self-ascribed is a predicate referring to some bodily property; correspondingly, asserting that predicate to be true of oneself is expressing one's consciousness of a property of the body one takes to be one's own. In such cases, of course, consciousness of one's own body is involved in the use of 'I' in the particular proposition under consideration. But this consciousness is not a necessary condition on the use of 'I.' Rather, it is what is expressed in the content of the predicate of the proposition in which 'I' is in the argument-place.

Nevertheless, another aspect of bodily consciousness is more directly relevant to the use of the concept and word 'I' itself, whatever is predicated of it. Lacking an integrated consciousness of one's own body is deeply unsettling for the standpoint from which the unity of mental contents can be achieved. It is thus deeply unsettling both for the acquisition of a consistent view of the world (including a consistent view of one's own place and agency in the world), and for the sense of self that supports the use of 'I'—as was evident in the example of Sacks's "disembodied lady" and in the related examples of deafferented patients discussed in Chapter 2. So, here, it does appear that there is a connection between the consciousness of one's own body and the consciousness of oneself as a self, namely, as an entity that counts as the referent of 'I' whenever 'I' is used by that entity. But even this fact does not make consciousness of one's own body a necessary condition for using, or being capable of using, 'I,' and thus counting, for oneself and for others, as a self. Consciousness of a well-integrated body one takes to be one's own is only an empirical condition, given the kinds of entities we are, for the use of 'I.'

9.4 Self-Consciousness and Intersubjectivity

As should be obvious, this book makes no claim to offer an exhaustive approach to the nature of self-consciousness. Nor does it make any claim to offer an exhaustive account of the relation between Kant's conception of self-consciousness and later developments in the history of philosophy up to our own time. Even so, one might regret that no consideration should be given to the connection between, and mutual conditioning of, self-consciousness and intersubjective consciousness. This might seem to be one aspect of self-consciousness that it is mandatory to discuss in any treatment of the topic, no matter how non-exhaustive it claims to be.

Here, I would first note that particular aspects of the relation between self-consciousness and intersubjectivity are in fact discussed at various points in the book, for instance, in the discussion of Sartre's view of the body as "for itself," "for another," and "for another for itself" in Chapter 3; in the discussion of Kant on first-person and third-person standpoints on oneself in Chapter 6; or in the discussion of Freud on the internalization of parental norms in Chapter 8. It remains that those discussions do not amount to a systematic investigation of the role of intersubjectivity in the acquisition of the word and the concept 'I.' A common trait of the approaches I have been discussing in all three parts of the book is that they give precedence to the mental capacities and the structure of mental activity constitutive of self-consciousness understood as the capacity of any individual thinker to implicate herself, the thinker, in the content of her thought. Without doubt, both the development and the actual use of those capacities depend on the intersubjective learning of the uses of 'I' and 'you,' on the capacity to recognize other entities as minded entities, and on the capacity to recognize others as I-users who, in all instances of their using 'I,' use it according to the same reference-rule according to which I, myself, use 'I,' thereby locating themselves in the content of their own thought. But no amount of exposition to the uses of 'you' and 'I' in language, and no amount of intersubjective recognition of others as thinkers like me, would yield an understanding of the complex rules of reference for 'I' and 'you' if the language user did not have the capacity to judge and to think of herself, in each instance of judging, as the author of the judgment, referred to by 'I.' This capacity is what has been at the forefront of the discussions offered in this book. A systematic discussion of the relation between self-consciousness and intersubjectivity, whether in Kant or in any aspect of his philosophical posterity, was not part of the project. This is in no way a judgment on the importance of the topic from a systematic standpoint, nor does it indicate its lack of importance in Kant's own work. What the choice of topic of the present book does indicate is that in agreement with Kant, I take the capacities at work in generating the kind of self-consciousness that grounds any use of 'I,' to be fundamental conditions for the intersubjective learning of 'I' to be available at all.

9.5 Overall Import of the Investigation

Finally, one might ask what all the fuss is about: Why does it seem so important to have identified a type of self-consciousness that, while being intimately connected to consciousness of one's own body, is nevertheless distinct from it and is, moreover, the condition for any use of 'I'? A first reply is that the duality in the types of self-consciousness, and the grounding role, for any use of 'I,' of the consciousness of being engaged in rationally unifying the contents of one's mental states, are a matter of intrinsic interest, intriguing facts about the make-up of our minds. Any philosopher or psychologist should be interested in sorting out what makes such duality and grounding role possible, and what their function is.[3] A second reply is that, as Kant has argued, and as Wittgenstein, Shoemaker, Peacocke, and others have argued again on different grounds, elucidating the nature of those two types of self-consciousness and their respective grounding role may help resolve, or as the case may be, dissolve, a good deal of ordinary as well as philosophical problems about the relation between mind and body.

A third reply, perhaps the most important, concerns specifically the role of consciousness of being engaged in rationally ordering the contents of one's mental states. Insofar as my use of 'I' is based on this type of self-consciousness, in using

'I,' I express my consciousness of myself, not only as an *individual* (the author of the current thought 'I think' or 'I [morally] ought to'), but also as an individual thinking "with a universal voice."[4] To repeat an example I used in Chapter 2: In thinking and asserting the proposition 'I think the proof is valid,' I assert the predicate '—think the proof is valid' to be true of me, the current thinker of the proposition 'I think the proposition is valid,' on the basis of my consciousness of having, myself, just checked the steps and endorsed the proof. But the implicit thought, when I say 'I think the proof is valid,' is that anyone endowed, like me, with a capacity rationally to connect her thoughts, ought to endorse the proof. *I* think, but I think *for all* and *with all* rational beings. Similarly for the moral 'I ought to': I think 'I ought to p' on the basis of consciously acknowledging, for myself, a moral obligation. But the idea behind the moral 'I ought to' is that any individual capable of rationally evaluating the motivations for her actions would have to come up, in similar circumstances, with a similar assessment of her duty. This is quite different from the use of 'I' in which I assert of myself, the thinker of the thought 'I am F,' a predicate I know to hold of me as the particular, embodied entity I am. There I speak and think *for myself alone* and about myself as the particular individual I am, even though the capacity to think I am exercising in forming any judgment at all, including a judgment about myself as the particular entity I am, depends on the very same rational capacities that allow me also to elevate myself to thinking *for all* and *with all* rational beings. This is the kind of contrast Kant had in mind when, in the moral context, he distinguished 'the dear self,' giving priority to its particular inclinations as a living, thinking being, and 'the proper self' (*das eigentliche Selbst*) (*Groundwork*, AA4, 407, 457). The "dear self" is the referent of 'I,' an entity presented to itself insofar as it is conscious of its individual sensations, feelings, and desires, and is motivated to act accordingly. The "proper self" is the same entity insofar as it is consciously ordering its thoughts and actions according to norms of rationality that ought to hold for all rational beings. If Kant and Freud are right, the latter capacity is what makes human beings referents for 'I,' namely selves, entities capable of using the first person at all. But sane reflection and awareness of our own limitations tell us that even while exercising, to the best of our ability, our "universal voice," we remain anchored in our individual body—our biological, socially shaped, historically determined, and symbol-laden body.

Notes

1. See Arminjon 2010, chaps. 1 and 2.
2. See 2.2; and n. 30 in Chapter 2.
3. I have discussed these questions in Longuenesse 2012a. See also Longuenesse and Rösler 2008.
4. I borrow the expression "universal voice" from Kant, who uses it to describe the kind of claim we make when passing an aesthetic judgment of reflection. See *Judgment*, AA5, 216. I am using it here to describe, instead of the claim we make in aesthetic judgment (where, says Kant, one "believes oneself to have a universal voice"), the claim we make when reinforcing a statement 'p,' for which we take ourselves to have provided valid justification, by saying 'I think that p.'

Bibliography

Works by Kant

All citations of Kant's works use the pagination of the standard Akademie edition (Akademie Ausgabe), cited by volume and page. Individual works are identified by the abbreviations listed below in brackets. The only exception is the *Critique of Pure Reason*, for which citations use the standard A/B format to refer to pages in the first (A) and the second (B) editions. For that work, in addition to the Akademie Ausgabe I have on one occasion used the Meiner edition, indicated by A/B 1971 (see full reference below). Kant's Lectures on Metaphysics are identified by *Met.*, followed by the particular identification of the lectures cited. I have made use of the translations and editions listed below, but have occasionally corrected them. I mention the corrections only when they are especially relevant to the interpretation of Kant's argument

[AA] *Kants Gesammelte Schriften*. Ausgabe der Königlich-Preußischen Akademie der Wissenschaften, später Deutschen Akademie der Wissenschaften Berlin, später Akademie der Wissenschaften der DDR, jetzt Berlin-Brandenburg Akademie der Wissenschaften. 29 vols. Berlin, 1900–.

[A/B] *Critique of Pure Reason*. Translated and edited by Paul Guyer and Allen W. Wood. Cambridge: Cambridge University Press, 1998.

[A/B 1971] *Kritik der reinen Vernunft*. Hamburg: Felix Meiner, 1971.

[*Anthropology*] *Anthropology from a Pragmatic Point of View*. Translated and edited by Robert B. Louden. Cambridge Texts in the History of Philosophy. Cambridge: Cambridge University Press, 2006.

[*Conjectural Beginning*] *Conjectural Beginning of Human History*. Translated by Allen Wood. In *Anthropology, History and Education*, edited by Robert B. Louden and Günter Zöller, 160–75. The Cambridge Edition of the Works of Immanuel Kant. Cambridge: Cambridge University Press, 2008.

[*False Subtlety*] *The False Subtlety of the Four Syllogistic Figures*. In *Theoretical Philosophy, 1755–1770*, translated and edited by David Waldorf and Ralf Meerbote, 85–105. The Cambridge Edition of the Works of Immanuel Kant. Cambridge: Cambridge University Press, 1992.

["First Introduction"] "First Introduction to the *Critique of the Power of Judgment*." In *Critique of the Power of Judgment*, edited by Paul Guyer, translated by Paul Guyer and Eric Matthews, 3–50. Cambridge Texts in the History of Philosophy. Cambridge: Cambridge University Press, 2008.

[*Groundwork*] *Groundwork of the Metaphysics of Morals*. A German–English edition. German text from the second original edition (1786). English translation by Mary Gregor, revised by Jens Timmermann. Cambridge: Cambridge University Press, 2011.

[*Judgment*] *Critique of the Power of Judgment*. Edited by Paul Guyer. Translated by Paul Guyer and Eric Matthews. Cambridge: Cambridge University Press, 2000.

[*Logic*] *The Jäsche Logic*. In *Lectures on Logic*, translated and edited by J. Michael Young, 521–640. The Cambridge Edition of the Works of Immanuel Kant. Cambridge: Cambridge University Press, 1992.

[*Logic Blomberg*] *The Blomberg Logic*. In *Lectures on Logic*, translated and edited by J. Michael Young, 1–246. The Cambridge Edition of the Works of Immanuel Kant. Cambridge: Cambridge University Press, 1992.

[Metaphysics] *Lectures on Metaphysics*. Translated and edited by Karl Ameriks and Steve Naragon. The Cambridge Edition of the Works of Immanuel Kant. Cambridge: Cambridge University Press, 1997.
[Met. L$_1$] *Metaphysik L$_1$*. In *Metaphysics*, 19–106.
[Met. Mongrovius] *Metaphysik Mongrovius*. In *Metaphysics*, 109–286.
[Met. Mor.] *The Metaphysics of Morals*. Translated by Mary Gregor. Cambridge: Cambridge University Press, 1991.
[Pract. Reason] *Critique of Practical Reason*. Translated and edited by Mary Gregor. Revised by Andrews Reath. Cambridge: Cambridge University Press, 2015.
[Prol.] *Prolegomena to Any Future Metaphysics That Will Be Able to Come Forward as Science*. Translated and edited by Gary Hatfield. Cambridge: Cambridge University Press, 2004.
[Religion] *Religion within the Boundaries of Mere Reason*. Translated by Allen Wood and George Di Giovanni. With an introduction by Robert Merrihew Adams. Cambridge: Cambridge University Press, 1998.

Other Works

Alberini, Cristina M., François Ansermet, and Pierre Magistretti. 2013. "Memory Reconsolidation, Trace Reassociation, and the Freudian Unconscious." In *Memory Reconsolidation*, edited by Cristina M. Alberini, 293–310. London: Elsevier.
Allison, Henry E. 2000. "Where Have All the Categories Gone? Reflections on Longuenesse's Reading of Kant's Transcendental Deduction." *Inquiry* 43(1): 67–80.
Ameriks, Karl. 2000. *Kant's Theory of Mind: An Analysis of the Paralogisms of Pure Reason*. New ed. Oxford: Oxford University Press.
Anderson, R. Lanier. 2015. *The Poverty of Conceptual Truth: Kant's Analytic/Synthetic Distinction and the Limits of Metaphysics*. Oxford: Oxford University Press.
Anscombe, G. E. M. 1994. "The First Person." In *Self-Knowledge*, edited by Quassim Cassam, 140–59. Oxford: Oxford University Press. Originally published in *Mind and Language: Wolfson College Lectures, 1974*, edited by Samuel Guttenplan, 140–59. Oxford: Oxford University Press, 1975.
Ansermet, François, and Pierre Magistretti. 2004. *Biology of Freedom: Neural Plasticity, Experience, and the Unconscious*. Translated by Susan Fairfield. New York: Other Press.
Aristotle. 1973. *The Categories*. Translated by Harold P. Cooke. Loeb Classical Library, 9–109. First printed in 1938.
Arminjon, Mathieu. 2010. *Les Intentions du corps: Psychanalyse, biologie et sciences de l'esprit*. Paris: Liber.
Baumgarten, Alexander Gottlieb. 1913 [1747]. *Erläuterungen zur Psychologia empirica*. In *A. G. Baumgartens Metaphysica*. In Kant, AA15, 7–54.
Bayne, Tim. 2010. *The Unity of Consciousness*. Oxford: Oxford University Press.
Bayne, Tim, and David Chalmers. 2003. "What Is the Unity of Consciousness?" In *The Unity of Consciousness: Binding, Integration and Dissociation*, edited by A. Cleeremans, 23–58. Oxford: Oxford University Press.
Bermúdez, José Luis, Anthony J. Marcel, and Naomi M. Eilan, eds. 1995. *The Body and the Self*. Cambridge, MA: MIT Press.
Block, Ned. 1995. "On a Confusion about a Function of Consciousness." *Behavioral and Brain Sciences* 18(2): 227–87.
Block, Ned. 2002. "Concepts of Consciousness." In *Philosophy of Mind: Classical and Contemporary Readings*, edited by David Chalmers, 206–19. Oxford: Oxford University Press.
Block, Ned. 2007. "Consciousness, Accessibility, and the Mesh between Psychology and Neuroscience." *Behavioral and Brain Sciences* 30: 481–548.

Brakel, Linda A. W. 2013. *The Ontology of Psychology: Questioning Foundations in the Philosophy of Mind.* New York: Routledge.

Brook, Andrew. 1992. "Psychoanalysis and Commonsense Psychology." *Annual of Psychoanalysis* 20: 273–305.

Brook, Andrew. 1995. "Explanation and the Hermeneutic Sciences." *International Journal of Psychoanalysis* 76: 519–33.

Brook, Andrew. 2003. "Kant and Freud." In *Psychoanalytic Knowledge*, edited by Man Cheung Chung and Colin Feltham, 20–39. Basingstoke: Palgrave Macmillan.

Burge, Tyler. 2000. "Reason and the First Person." In *Knowing Our Own Minds*, edited by Crispin Wright, Barry Smith, and Charles Macdonald, 243–70. Oxford: Oxford University Press.

Cassam, Quassim, ed. 1994. *Self-Knowledge.* Oxford: Oxford University Press.

Cassam, Quassim. 1997. *Self and World.* Oxford: Oxford University Press.

Chalmers, David. 2002a. *The Conscious Mind: In Search of a Fundamental Theory.* New York: Oxford University Press.

Chalmers, David, ed. 2002b. *Philosophy of Mind: Classical and Contemporary Readings.* Oxford: Oxford University Press.

Chignell, Andrew. 2007. "Belief in Kant." *Philosophical Review* 116(3): 323–60.

Cole, Jonathan. 1995. *Pride and the Daily Marathon.* Cambridge, MA: MIT Press.

Cole, Jonathan, and Jacques Paillard. 1995. "Living Without Touch and Peripheral Information about Body Position and Movement: Studies with Deafferented Subjects." In *The Body and the Self*, edited by José Luis Bermúdez, Anthony J. Marcel, and Naomi M. Eilan, 245–66. Cambridge, MA: MIT Press.

Coliva, Annalisa, ed. 2012a. *The Self and Self-Knowledge.* Oxford: Oxford University Press.

Coliva, Annalisa. 2012b. "Which 'Key to All Mythologies' about the Self?: A Note on Where the Illusions of Transcendence Come From and How to Resist Them." In *Immunity to Error through Misidentification*, edited by Simon Prosser and François Recanati, 22–45. Cambridge: Cambridge University Press.

Coorebyter, Vincent de. 2000. *Sartre face à la phénoménologie: Autour de "L'Intentionnalité" et de "La Transcendance de l'ego."* Brussels: Ousia.

Damasio, Antonio R. 1994. *Descartes' Error: Emotion, Reason, and the Human Brain.* New York: G. B. Putnam.

Descartes, René. 1984–91. *The Philosophical Writings of Descartes.* Translated by John Cottingham, Robert Stoothoff, and Dugald Murdoch. 3 vols. Cambridge: Cambridge University Press.

Descartes, René. 1984 [1641]. *Meditations on First Philosophy.* Translated by John Cottingham. *Objections and Replies.* Translated by John Cottingham. In *The Philosophical Writings of Descartes*, 2:3–383. Cambridge: Cambridge University Press.

Descartes, René. 1985 [1637]. *Discourse on the Method.* Translated by Robert Stoothof. In *The Philosophical Writings of Descartes*, 1:111–51.

Descartes, René. 1985 [1644]. *Principles of Philosophy.* Translated by John Cottingham. In *The Philosophical Writings of Descartes*, 1:177–291. Cambridge: Cambridge University Press.

Emundts, Dina. 2006. "Die Paralogismen und die Widerlegung des Idealismus in Kants *Kritik der reinen Vernunft*." *Deutsche Zeitschrift für Philosophie* 54: 295–309.

Evans, Gareth. 1982. *The Varieties of Reference.* Oxford: Clarendon Press.

Evans, Gareth. 1985. *Collected Papers.* Oxford: Clarendon Press.

Frankfurt, Harry. 1988. "Freedom of the Will and the Concept of a Person." In *The Importance of What We Care About*, chap. 2, 11–25. Cambridge: Cambridge University Press.

Freud, Sigmund. [*GW*] *Gesammelte Werke, chronologisch geordnet.* Edited by Anna Freud, E. Bibring, V. Hoffer, E. Kris, and O. Isakowa, with the collaboration of Marie Bonaparte. 18 vols. London: Imago, 1952. Reprint, Frankfurt: S. Fischer Verlag, 1991.

Freud, Sigmund. [SE] *The Standard Edition of the Complete Psychological Works of Sigmund Freud*. Edited by J. Strachey, A. Freud, C. L. Rothgeb, and A. Richards. 24 vols. London: Hogarth, 1953–74.

Freud, Sigmund. [*Anfänge*] *Aus den Anfängen der Psychoanalyse: Briefe an Wilhelm Fliess, Abhandlungen und Notizen aus den Jahren 1887–1902*. London: Imago 1950.

Freud, Sigmund. [*Ego and Id*] *The Ego and the Id* [1923]. In *SE*, 19:1–66; *GW*, 14:237–89.

Freud, Sigmund. [*Entwurf*] *Entwurf einer Psychologie* [1895]. In *Aus den Anfängen der Psychoanalyse*, 379–466.

Freud, Sigmund. [*Formulations*]. *Formulations on the Two Principles of Mental Functioning* [1911]. In *SE*, 12:213–26; *GW*, 8:229–39.

Freud, Sigmund. [*Group Psychology*] *Group Psychology and the Analysis of the Ego* [1922]. In *SE*, 18:69–144.

Freud, Sigmund. [*Hysteria*] *Studies on Hysteria: Breuer and Freud* [1893]. In *SE*, 2:3–309; *GW*, 1:77–313.

Freud, Sigmund. [*Interpretation*] *The Interpretation of Dreams* [1900–1901]. In *SE*, 4–5; *GW*, 2–3.

Freud, Sigmund. [*Letters*] *The Letters of Sigmund Freud to Eduard Silberstein, 1871–1881*. Cambridge, MA: Harvard University Press, 1990.

Freud, Sigmund. [*Masochism*] *The Economic Problem of Masochism* [1924]. In *SE*, 19:159–72.

Freud, Sigmund. [*Metapsych. Suppl.*] "Metapsychological Supplement to the Theory of Dreams" [1915]. In *SE*, 14:222–35; *GW*, 10:412–26.

Freud, Sigmund. [*Mourning*] *Mourning and Melancholy* [1917]. In *SE*, 14:243–59.

Freud, Sigmund. [*Narcissism*] *On Narcissism: An Introduction* [1914]. In *SE*, 14:73–102.

Freud, Sigmund. [*New Intr.*] *New Introductory Lectures on Psychoanalysis* [1933]. In *SE*, 22:7–250.

Freud, Sigmund. [*Project*] "Project for a Scientific Psychology" [1895]. In *SE*, 1:295–397.

Freud, Sigmund. [*Remembering*] *Remembering, Repeating, and Working Through* [1914]. In *SE*, 12:145–56.

Freud, Sigmund. [*Unconscious*] "The Unconscious" [1915]. In *SE*, 14:166–235.

Garber, Daniel, and Béatrice Longuenesse, eds. 2008. *Kant and the Early Moderns*. Princeton, NJ: Princeton University Press.

Gardner, Sebastian. 1993. *Irrationality and the Philosophy of Psychoanalysis*. Cambridge: Cambridge University Press.

Garrett, Don. 2003. "Locke on Personal Identity, Consciousness and 'Fatal Errors.'" *Philosophical Topics* 31(1–2): 95–125.

Glock, H.-J., and P. M. S. Hacker. 1996. "Reference and the First Person Pronoun." *Language and Communication* 16: 95–105.

Grier, Michelle. 2001. *Kant's Doctrine of Transcendental Illusion*. Cambridge: Cambridge University Press.

Grünbaum, Adolf. 1984. *The Foundations of Psychoanalysis: A Philosophical Critique*. Berkeley: University of California Press.

Grüne, Stefanie. 2009. *Blinde Anschauung: Die Rolle von Begriffen in Kants Theorie sinnlicher Synthesis*. Frankfurt am Main: Vittorio Kostermann.

Guyer, Paul, ed. 2010. *The Cambridge Companion to the Critique of Pure Reason*. Cambridge: Cambridge University Press.

Horstmann, Rolf-Peter. 1993. "Kants Paralogismen." *Kant-Studien* 83: 408–25.

Howell, Robert. 1992. *Kant's Transcendental Deduction: An Analysis of Main Themes in Kant's Critical Philosophy*. Synthese Library, vol. 222. Dordrecht: Kluwer Academic Publishers.

Howell, Robert. 2001. "Kant, the 'I think,' and Self-Awareness." In *Kant's Legacy: Essays in Honor of Lewis White Beck*, edited by Predrag Cicovacki, 117–52. Rochester, NY: University of Rochester Press.

Husserl, Edmund. 2012 [1913]. *Ideas: General Introduction to Pure Phenomenology*. Translated by W. R. Boyce Gibson. With a new foreword by Dermot Moran. London: Routledge.

James, William. 1981 [1890]. *Principles of Psychology*. Cambridge, MA: Harvard University Press.

Kandel, Eric R. 2006. *In Search of Memory: The Emergence of a New Science of Mind*. New York: Norton.

Katz, Jerome. 1990. "Descartes' Cogito." In *Demonstratives*, edited by Palle Yourgrau, 154–81. Oxford: Oxford University Press.

Kitcher, Patricia. 2011. *Kant's Thinker*. Oxford: Oxford University Press.

Laplanche, Jean, and Jean-Bertrand Pontalis. 1973. *The Language of Psychoanalysis*. Translated by Donald Nicholson-Smith. New York: Norton.

La Rocca, Claudio. 2008. "Unbewußtes und Bewusstsein bei Kant." In *Kant-Lektionen: Zur Philosophie Kants und zu Aspekten ihrer Wirkungsgeschichte*, edited by Manfred Kugelstadt, 47–68. Würzburg: Königshausen und Neumann.

Lear, Jonathan. 2015. *Freud*. 2nd ed. Oxford: Routledge.

Leibniz, Gottfried Wilhelm. 1981 [1765]. *New Essays on Human Understanding*. Translated by Peter Remnant and Jonathan Bennett. Oxford: Clarendon Press.

Leibniz, Gottfried Wilhelm. 2014 [1714]. *Leibniz's Monadology: A New Translation and Guide*. Edited by Lloyd Strickland. Edinburgh: Edinburgh University Press.

Locke, John. 1975 [1689]. *An Essay Concerning Human Understanding*. Edited with an introduction by Peter H. Nidditch. Oxford: Clarendon Press.

Longuenesse, Béatrice. 1998. *Kant and the Capacity to Judge*. Princeton, NJ: Princeton University Press.

Longuenesse, Béatrice. 2005. *Kant on the Human Standpoint*. Cambridge: Cambridge University Press.

Longuenesse, Béatrice. 2006. "Self-Consciousness and Consciousness of One's Own Body: Variations on a Kantian Theme." *Philosophical Topics* 34: 283–309.

Longuenesse, Béatrice. 2007. "Kant on the Identity of Persons." *Proceedings of the Aristotelian Society* 107(pt. 2): 149–67.

Longuenesse, Béatrice. 2008. "Kant's 'I Think' versus Descartes' 'I Am a Thing That Thinks.'" In *Kant and the Early Moderns*, edited by Daniel Garber and Béatrice Longuenesse, 9–31. Princeton, NJ: Princeton University Press.

Longuenesse, Béatrice, ed. 2010a. *Le Moi, the Self, le soi*. Special issue of *Revue de Métaphysique et de Morale* 4.

Longuenesse, Béatrice. 2010b. "De Différentes manières de se rapporter à soi." *Le Moi, the Self, le soi*, special issue of *Revue de Métaphysique et de Morale*, edited by Béatrice Longuenesse, 4: 419–34.

Longuenesse, Béatrice. 2012a. "'I' and the Brain." *Psychological Research* 76: 220–8.

Longuenesse, Béatrice. 2012b. "Kant's 'I Ought To' and Freud's Superego." *Aristotelian Society Supplementary Volume* 86: 19–39.

Longuenesse, Béatrice. 2013. "Kant and Freud on 'I.'" In *Proceedings of the 11th Kant Congress*, 1:287–308. Berlin: Walter de Gruyter.

Longuenesse, Béatrice, and Frank Rösler. 2008. "Neurone vergeistigen: Geist und Gehirn im Gespräch." *Jahrbuch des Wissenschaftskollegs zu Berlin*, 241–58.

McDowell, John. 1996. *Mind and World*. With a new introduction by the author. Cambridge, MA: Harvard University Press.

Melnick, Arthur. 2009. *Kant's Theory of the Self*. Abingdon: Routledge.
Merleau-Ponty, Maurice. 1962. *Phenomenology of Perception*. Translated by Colin Smith. London: Routledge.
Meynert, Theodor. 1884. *Psychiatrie: Klinik der Erkränkungen des Vorderhirns begründet auf dessen Bau, Leistungen und Ernährung*. Vienna: Wilhelm Braumüller.
Meynert, Theodor. 1888. *Psychiâtrie: Clinique des maladies du cerveau antérieur basée sur sa nature, ses fonctions et sa nutrition*. Translated by Georges Couzot. Brussels: A. Manceaux.
Naccache, Lionel. 2006. *Le Nouvel inconscient: Freud, Christophe Colomb des neurosciences*. Paris: Odile Jacob.
Nagel, Thomas. 1979a. *Mortal Questions*. Cambridge: Cambridge University Press.
Nagel, Thomas. 1979b. "What Is It Like to Be a Bat?" In *Mortal Questions*, 165–81. Originally published in *Philosophical Review* 4 (1974): 435–50.
Neu, Jerome, ed. 1991a. *The Cambridge Companion to Freud*. Cambridge: Cambridge University Press.
Neu, Jerome. 1991b. Introduction to *The Cambridge Companion to Freud*, edited by Jerome Neu, 1–7. Cambridge: Cambridge University Press.
Nietzsche, Friedrich. 1998 [1887]. *On the Genealogy of Morals: A Polemic*. Translated by Maudemarie Clarke and Alan J. Swensen. Indianapolis, IN: Hackett.
Pariente, Jean-Claude. 1973. *Le Langage et l'individuel*. Paris: Armand Colin.
Pariente, Jean-Claude. 1988. "Problèmes logiques du Cogito." In *Le Discours et sa méthode*, edited by N. Grimaldi and J.-L. Marion, 229–69. Paris: Presses Universitaires de France.
Pariente, Jean-Claude. 2002a. *Le Langage à l'œuvre*. Paris: Presses Universitaires de France.
Pariente, Jean-Claude. 2002b. "La Première personne et sa fonction dans le Cogito." In *Le Langage à l'œuvre*, 89–113. Paris: Presses Universitaires de France.
Peacocke, Christopher. 1999. *Being Known*. Oxford: Oxford University Press.
Peacocke, Christopher. 2008. *Truly Understood*. Oxford: Oxford University Press.
Peacocke, Christopher. 2010. "Self-Consciousness." In Longuenesse, *Le Moi, the Self, le Soi*, 521–52.
Peacocke, Christopher. 2012a. "Subjects and Consciousness." In Coliva, *The Self and Self-Knowledge*, 74–101.
Peacocke, Christopher. 2012b. "Conscious Events and Self-Ascriptions: Comments on Heal and O'Brien." In Coliva, *The Self and Self-Knowledge*, 180–6.
Peacocke, Christopher. 2014a. *The Mirror of the World: Subjects, Consciousness, and Self-Consciousness*. Oxford: Oxford University Press.
Peacocke, Christopher. 2014b. "Paralogisms and First Person Illusions." In *The Mirror of the World: Subjects, Consciousness, and Self-Consciousness*, 154–87. Oxford: Oxford University Press.
Perry, John. 1993a. *The Problem of the Essential Indexical and Other Essays*. New York: Oxford University Press.
Perry, John. 1993b. "The Problem of the Essential Indexical." With a postscript by John Perry. In *The Problem of the Essential Indexical and Other Essays*, 33–52. Originally published in *Noûs* 13 (1979): 3–21.
Perry, John. 2002a. *Identity, Personal Identity, and the Self*. Indianapolis, IN: Hackett.
Perry, John. 2002b. "Self-Knowledge, Self-Notions, and the Self." In *Identity, Personal Identity, and the Self*, chap. 10, 189–213.
Proops, Ian. 2010. "Kant's First Paralogism." *Philosophical Review* 119(4): 449–95.
Prosser, Simon, and François Recanati, eds. 2012. *Immunity to Error through Misidentification*. Cambridge: Cambridge University Press.
Röder, Brigitte, Frank Rösler, and Charles Spence. 2004. "Early Vision Impairs Tactile Perception in the Blind." *Current Biology* 14: 121–4.

Rosefeldt, Tobias. 2000. *Das logische Ich: Kant über den Gehalt des Begriffes von sich selbst*. Berlin: Philo.
Sacks, David. 1991. "In Fairness to Freud: A Critical Note on *The Foundations of Psychoanalysis* by Adolf Grünbaum." In *The Cambridge Companion to Freud*, edited by Jerome Neu, 309–38. Cambridge: Cambridge University Press.
Sacks, Oliver. 1998. *The Man Who Mistook His Wife for a Hat, and Other Clinical Tales*. New York: Touchstone, Simon & Schuster. First published in 1985.
Sartre, Jean-Paul. 2003a. *Being and Nothingness*. Translated by Hazel Barnes. Introduction by Mary Warnock. With a new preface by Richard Eyre. London. First published, in French, in 1943.
Sartre, Jean-Paul. 2003b. "Conscience de soi et connaissance de soi." In *La Transcendance de l'ego et autres textes phénoménologiques*, edited by Vincent de Coorebyter, 135–65. Paris: Librairie Philosophique Vrin. First published in 1947.
Sartre, Jean-Paul. 2003c. "Une Idée fondamentale de la phénomenologie de Husserl: L'intentionnalité." In *La Transcendance de l'ego et autres textes phénoménologiques*, edited by Vincent de Coorebyter, 87–9. Paris: Librairie Philosophique Vrin. First published in 1939.
Sartre, Jean-Paul. 2003d. *La Transcendance de l'ego et autres textes phénoménologiques*. Critical edition by Vincent de Coorebyter. Paris: Librairie Philosophique Vrin. First published in 1937.
Sartre, Jean-Paul. 2004. *The Transcendence of the Ego*. Translated with an introduction by Sarah Richmond. London: Routledge. First published, in French, in 1937.
Scheffler, Samuel. 1992. *Human Morality*. Oxford: Oxford University Press.
Shoemaker, Sydney. 1996a. *The First Person Perspective and Other Essays*. Cambridge: Cambridge University Press.
Shoemaker, Sydney. 1996b. "Introspection and the Self." In *The First Person Perspective and Other Essays*, 3–24.
Shoemaker, Sydney. 2003a. *Identity, Cause and Mind*. Oxford: Clarendon Press.
Shoemaker, Sydney. 2003b. "Persons and Their Pasts." In *Identity, Cause and Mind*, 19–48. Oxford: Clarendon Press.
Shoemaker, Sydney. 2003c. "Self-Reference and Self-Awareness." In *Identity, Cause and Mind*, 6–19. Oxford: Clarendon Press.
Spinoza, Baruch. 1995. *The Letters*. Translated by Samuel Shirley. Introduction and notes by Steven Barbone, Lee Rice, and Jacob Adler. Indianapolis, IN: Hackett.
Strawson, Peter. 1959. *Individuals: An Essay in Descriptive Metaphysics*. London: Methuen.
Strawson, Peter. 1966. *The Bounds of Sense*. London: Methuen.
Sturma, Dieter. 1985. *Kant über Selbstbewusstsein: Zum Zusammenhang von Erkenntniskritik und Theorie des Selbstbewusstseins*. Hildesheim: Georg Olms Verlag.
Sulloway, Frank J. 1979. *Freud: Biologist of the Mind*. New York: Basic Books.
Treisman, Anne, and Garry Gelade. 1980. "A Feature Integration Theory of Attention." *Cognitive Psychology* 12(1): 97–136.
Widlöcher, Daniel. 1996. *Les Nouvelles cartes de la psychanalyse*. Paris: Editions Odile Jacob.
Wittgenstein, Ludwig. 1958a. *The Blue and Brown Books*. Oxford: Blackwell.
Wittgenstein, Ludwig. 1958b. *Philosophical Investigations*. Translated by G. E. M. Anscombe. Oxford: Blackwell.
Wittgenstein, Ludwig. 1993. "Notes for Lectures on Private Experience and Sense Data." In *Wittgenstein: Philosophical Occasions*, edited by J. C. Klagge and A. Nordmann, 200–88. Indianapolis: Hackett.
Wolff, Christian. 1968 [1738]. *Psychologia empirica*. Critical edition by Jean Ecole. Hildesheim: Georg Olms Buchhandlung. First published 1732. Olms 1968 is based on the second edition (1738) of the original text.

Wolff, Christian. 1972 [1740]. *Psychologia rationalis*. Critical edition by Jean Ecole. Hildesheim: Georg Olms Verlag. First published in 1734. Olms 1972 is based on the second edition (1740) of the original text.

Wolff, Christian. 1983 [1751]. *Vernünftige Gedanken von Gott, der Welt und der Seele des Menschen, auch allen Dingen überhaupt*. Critical edition by Charles A. Corr. Hildesheim: Georg Olms Verlag. First published in 1720. Olms 1983 is based on the 11th edition (1751) of the original text.

Wood, Allen. 2008. *Kantian Ethics*. Cambridge: Cambridge University Press.

Wright, Crispin, Barry Smith, and Charles Macdonald, eds. 2000. *Knowing Our Own Minds*. Oxford: Oxford University Press.

Wuerth, Julian. 2010. "The Paralogisms of Pure Reason." In Guyer, *The Cambridge Companion to the Critique of Pure Reason*, 210–44.

Wuerth, Julian. 2014. *Kant on Mind, Action, and Ethics*. Oxford: Oxford University Press.

Yourgrau, Palle, ed. 1990. *Demonstratives*. Oxford: Oxford University Press.

General Index

Note: Footnotes in page entries are indicated by 'n'

action awareness 86, 101n59, 134n16
animality, good proper to 217
antinomies of pure reason 155
    second 135n25, 139n52
    third 152, 155
apperception, transcendental unity of xii, 2, 3, 7, 10, 31, 69n40, 78, 79, 103–4, 149, 150, 159, 162, 165, 169n29, 178, 179, 191, 193, 198n26, 205, 218, 224, 231, 235
    condition for any objective representation 79, 90
    formal condition of thought 133n14, 174, 175
    and 'I think' 11, 12, 13, 35, 36, 42n32, 80, 96n14, 97nn19, 22, 24, 104, 105, 106, 107, 108, 133, 142, 160, 163, 173, 176, 184, 185, 189, 197n22, 200n51, 201n52, 204, 216, 226, 236–7
    and logical functions of judgment 80, 96n19
    as "mere feeling" 88, 90
    pure vs. empirical apperception 104
        see also 'I think'; self-consciousness
autonomy 43n38, 51, 163, 165, 168n17, 206, 220
awareness of oneself
    and consciousness xi, 34, 46, 61, 86, 101n59, 134n16, 153
    as embodied entity xii, xiii, 19, 20, 26, 34, 37, 40n26, 44, 45, 51, 52, 68n21, 134n14, 148, 160, 161, 163, 164, 184, 234
    as located in space 20, 27
    as numerically identical xii, 10, 83, 98nn27, 32, 105, 112, 140, 141, 143, 144, 145, 147, 148, 149, 150, 151, 161, 164, 234
    as object xi, 46
    as thinking subject xi, xii, 89, 92, 145, 236
    as "what-it's-like-for-the-subject-of-thinking" 89
    see also action-awareness; consciousness; self-awareness; self-consciousness

binding 4, 14n5, 29, 31, 32, 41nn29, 30, 42n32, 81, 89, 96n11, 97nn19–21, 103, 144, 145, 151, 180, 181, 185, 191, 202n59, 205, 220, 221, 225
    see also synthesis
bodily ego (or body ego) 5, 14n6, 34, 35, 36, 169n38, 187, 193, 201n52, 224
    see also body; consciousness
body
    as being in the world (Sartre) 54, 55, 56
    body image 33, 37, 43n38, 224
    body for itself (Sartre) 44, 50, 55–6, 57, 58, 59, 64, 65, 69nn45, 49
    body for me/body for others (Sartre), comparison with Evans 53, 54, 57, 58, 64
    body and moral self (Freud) 217, 224
    body for others 53, 54, 57, 58, 64
    and 'I ought to' (Kant) 216–17
    as object of outer sense (Kant) 109–10, 111, 117, 151, 154, 164, 167n7
    three ontological dimensions of (Sartre) 54–8, 64, 68n33
    and unity of apperception (Kant) 12, 176, 193, 216, 224
    see also consciousness; embodied entity

categorical imperative 13, 14, 153, 163, 168n17, 205, 207, 209, 210, 211, 212, 214, 217, 225, 228n16, 230nn31, 35
categorical religious, social, moral norms, compared to universal categorical imperative
    for Kant 225
    compared to Freud 226
    and hypothetical imperative 205, 209, 210, 214, 216, 223, 230n35
    of Kant
        and Freud's super-ego 11, 205, 218, 219, 220, 221, 222
        a priori derivation of formulas of 222
    Nietzsche on 206
categories 116
    and logical functions of judgment 80, 96–7n19, 103, 106, 133n6, 137–8n44
    transcendental vs. empirical use of 116–17
cathexis (investment) 201n53, 230n34
cogito xiv
    Descartes's *cogito* argument xv, 6, 48, 50, 73–7, 82–6, 93, 94, 95nn1–2, 7, 95–6n8, 96n9, 99n50, 100n52, 102, 163
    existence in 'I think, I exist' is not the category of existence, for Kant 89, 90
    Kant's response to Descartes's *cogito* argument 73–7, 82–94, 96n9, 100n52, 103, 163
    Anderson on Longueness on 93–4
    Sartre's pre-reflective 5, 6, 44, 48, 59, 66, 67n9, 12, 92, 97n22
    Wolff on the cogito argument 99nn39, 40
    see also 'I think'
cognition
    for Freud 191, 195
    for Kant 11, 25, 26, 29, 30, 37, 40n21, 78, 86, 87, 88, 91, 97n24, 100n48, 103, 106, 107, 111, 118, 128, 157, 158, 168n17, 174, 178, 179, 180, 181, 188, 196n15, 197nn16, 20, 198n27, 205, 209, 216, 227, 233
    of non-rational animals 198n25, 203n67
    see also representation

248 GENERAL INDEX

combination 14n5, 41n29, 85, 96n11, 97, 97n24, 103, 104, 105, 106, 108, 133n7, 183, 190, 197n20, 223
   and binding 14n5, 41n29, 96n11, 97
   see also synthesis
consciousness
   of activity of thinking 32, 81, 92, 108, 116, 131, 132, 142
   degrees of and types of, in Kant 197n20, 198n26
      compared with Sartre 198n27, 231
   empirical 29, 94, 107, 160
      vs. transcendental consciousness 107
   for Freud
      conscious and unconscious feelings 202n56
      and what is unconscious 185, 189–93
   of identity 10, 133n7, 140, 141
      and consciousness of unity 150
      in different times 142–6
      of the act of combination 133n7
      and personhood 146–52 *see also* identity of person
   and intentionality 6, 46, 54, 55, 66nn6–7
   Kant on being conscious of one's representations 176, 178
   of mental unity 2, 11, 12, 20, 35, 36, 37, 44, 45, 59, 64, 65, 66, 102, 103, 104, 131, 138n47, 150, 162, 165, 173, 232
   as mode of existence of the body, for Sartre 55
   multiple meanings of, for Sartre 68n34
   of my own thinking 7, 85–7, 91, 92, 94, 164
   non-thetic consciousness of one's own body xiv, 5, 44, 47, 50, 51, 54–9, 64, 65, 69nn45–9
   non-thetic (self-)consciousness and 'I' 44, 45, 46, 47, 48, 50, 51, 62, 66, 68n22
   of oneself, as embodied entity xii, xiii, 26, 27, 44, 45, 47, 50, 161, 164, 184, 185, 228n13, 232
   of oneself, expressed in 'I ought to,' for Kant 37, 155, 209, 216, 217, 218, 224, 228n16, 238
   of oneself, as object xi, xii, xiii, 1, 2, 5, 11, 19, 31, 32, 37, 44, 45, 46, 47, 50, 52, 53, 60, 62, 67n9, 69–70n49, 166n3
   of oneself, as physical entity xi, 45, 54
   of oneself, as subject xi, xii, xiii, 1, 2, 4, 14n2, 19, 20, 26, 28, 31, 32, 34, 36, 37, 44, 45, 50, 66, 67nn7, 12, 109, 124, 125, 142
   of oneself, as thinking xi, xiii, 1, 145, 164, 184, 185, 234 *see also* 'I think'
   of one's own body xi, xiv, 1, 2, 11, 32–5, 42n37, 42–3n38, 44, 132, 148, 183, 216, 228n13
   of one's own numerical identity at different times xii, 10, 83, 95, 98nn27, 32, 105, 112, 132, 140, 141, 142, 143, 144, 145, 146, 147, 148, 149, 150, 151, 152, 161, 164, 234
   see also person

   of one's mental/physical agency 6, 50, 94, 101n59
   phenomenal consciousness and access consciousness 202n60
   reflective consciousness 47, 48, 50, 57, 67n9, 145
      in Anscombe 61, 63, 64
      compared with Sartre 68nn45, 49
   that I am 86, 97n24
   thetic (positional) consciousness of object vs. non-thetic (non-positional) self-consciousness 45, 46–51, 55, 64
   of thinking 1, 7, 9, 87, 88, 92, 163
      as an indeterminate perception, or feeling 86, 88, 91, 94, 100n48, 101n60, 106, 121, 132n11
   three kinds of, of one's own thinking 86–92, 133n12, 134n16
   transcendental consciousness 29, 107
      vs. empirical consciousness 107
   transcendental unity of 67n9, 194
   two senses of
      for Freud 180, 189
      for Kant 180, 199n37
   unity of xiii, 2, 3, 12, 35, 37, 41n29, 43n39, 44, 123, 150, 151, 156, 160, 161, 162, 163, 174, 188, 189, 190, 194, 235
      and Freud's 'ego' 2, 67n9
   see also apperception; ego
   as "what it's like for the subject" (or phenomenal consciousness) 66–7n7, 180, 181, 198n30, 216
   see also self-consciousness

dream 179, 202n59
   see also imagination
drives 13, 157, 169n25, 186, 198n25, 200n44, 205, 220, 224

ego
   as bodily ego (or body ego)
      for Freud 5, 12, 14n6, 35, 36, 169n38, 187, 193, 201n52, 224
      for Sacks 5, 14n6, 34, 35, 169n38
      compared to Kant 224
   Freud's 'ego' xiii, xiv, 2, 3, 5, 11, 12, 13, 34, 35, 36, 37, 43n42, 67n9, 169n38, 173, 174, 175, 176, 185–8, 189, 190–5, 202n59, 203, 204–8, 218–27, 229n20, 232, 235
   development of Freud's notion of 201n52
   "Ich" and the brain 201n52
   Meynert on the "primary ego" and "secondary individuality" 201n52
   and Kant's transcendental unity of apperception 2, 11, 12, 13, 35, 36, 173, 174, 176, 185, 188, 189, 190, 191, 193, 194, 204, 205, 218, 235
   and Kant's 'I' in 'I think' 12, 174, 188–94, 226, 232
   and naturalism of second nature 194, 224
   of non-human animals 203n67

GENERAL INDEX   249

Sartre's 'ego' xiii, 50, 67n9, 67n10
  see also body; 'I'; id; 'I think'; reality principle; unity of apperception
ego ideal 188, 195, 219, 221, 224, 229nn20, 26
  see also super-ego
embodied xi, 27, 158, 159, 169n27, 217, 224, 231, 238
  consciousness of oneself as xii, xiii, 5, 10, 19, 20, 26, 34, 37, 39n13, 40n26, 44, 45, 51, 52, 68n21, 132, 134n14, 148, 160, 161, 162, 163, 164, 184, 234–5
  Sacks's "disembodied lady" 5, 33, 34, 37, 42n34, 165, 236
  see also consciousness
expression xii, 67n12, 96n14, 105, 137n40
  and conceptual representation 1, 67n12, 133nn9, 14
  'I' as expression of the unity of apperception (Strawson) 160

faculty of desire 153, 209, 212, 216
  determined by reason = will 209–11, 214, 221, 224
feeling
  distinct from sensation 100n48
  never unconscious for Freud 190, 202nn56, 61
first person xi, xvii, 15n11, 21, 22, 39n11, 41n28, 83, 137n44, 139n50, 142, 143, 184, 238
  pronoun 'I' xi, xii, 1, 4, 7, 35, 47, 61, 184, 188, 231
    and its role in *cogito* argument 70, 73, 76, 82
    statements in 49, 51, 52, 69n44
    standpoint on oneself in thinking, vs. third person standpoint on oneself 9, 10, 38n10, 95, 125, 128, 130, 131, 147, 148, 149, 155, 167n11, 231, 234
  thinking 12, 37, 53, 61, 69n44, 145, 175, 188, 194, 203, 211
  see also cogito; consciousness; of identity; 'I'; identity; 'I think'; immunity to error through misidentification relative to the first person pronoun; self-consciousness
freedom
  absolute 154, 155, 156, 157
  metaphysical, for Kant 152, 155
  moral law as *ratio cognoscendi* of freedom, freedom as *ratio essendi* of moral law 153, 168n17, 218, 220
  and non-thetic consciousness, for Sartre 59
  see also moral law
FRR (fundamental reference rule for 'I') see 'I'
function of judging 80n18

generality constraint 24, 52, 54, 68n24, 148
good proper to animality, humanity, and personhood 217

human beings 169n30, 175, 179, 180, 186, 196–7n16, 215, 216
"what is a human being?" and formula of humanity 230n31
humanity, good proper to 217
hypothetical imperative 205, 209, 210, 214, 216, 223, 230n35

'I' xii, xiii, 7, 37, 107–8
  as author and recipient of the law 211
  blindness to motivation 213–18
    relation to body 216–18
  different types of use of, as subject 32, 36, 44, 68–9n40, 173
  as empirical entity 160, 161, 162, 174
  four features of 'I' in 'I think,' according to Kant 184–5
  and Freud's super-ego xv, 3, 12, 173, 188, 195, 204, 206, 208, 220–6, 232
  Freud on two types of information that ground use of 36, 37, 38n10, 165, 173
  compared to Kant 173
  fundamental reference rule (FRR) for 23, 26, 30, 31, 42n32, 61, 63, 76, 161, 183, 184, 199n39, 237
  from grammatical features of, to rationalist illusions in the Paralogisms 98n32
  in 'I ought to' xv, 12, 13, 173, 175, 195, 204, 206, 208, 209–18, 220–1, 224–7, 228n16, 232, 238
  in 'I think' xii, xv, 1, 2, 4, 6, 7, 9, 10, 11, 12, 13, 19, 25, 26, 27, 28, 29, 30, 31, 32, 34, 35, 36, 41nn26, 28, 44, 50, 67n9, 73, 74, 76, 77, 81, 82, 83, 84, 89, 90, 95, 98nn27, 32, 99n39, 100nn45, 47, 102, 106, 107, 108, 109, 110, 111, 112, 115, 116, 118, 119, 120, 121, 122, 123, 124, 125, 128, 129, 131, 132, 132n3, 134n14, 135n30, 136–7n40, 137nn43, 44, 140, 141, 142, 143, 144, 146, 147, 148, 149, 150, 152, 156, 160, 161, 163, 164, 167n6, 173, 174, 175, 176, 180, 184, 185, 188, 194, 195, 195n4, 200–1n51, 204, 208, 209, 211, 217, 218, 226, 227, 228n13, 231, 232, 238
I-thoughts 49
  for Anscombe 63
  "Cartesianly preferred" vs. bodily 63–4, 66
  for Evans 23, 39n12
  Kant on syntactical and logical property of concept 'I' 119, 121, 128, 129, 137n44, 139n50
  Kant's analysis of xii, 2, 4, 7, 26, 41n28, 132n3, 135n30, 141, 173, 175, 176, 208, 232
  and moral conflict 218, 220, 226
  as pure intellectual concept 89
  referent of 'I,' an embodied, spatiotemporal entity 234

'I' (cont.)
  referent of 'I,' a pure intelligence, for Kant 154, 162, 218, 224
  referring or non-referring use of 21–2, 25, 26, 45, 49, 60, 67–8n21, 68–9n40, 69nn43–44, 96n8, 131, 161, 234
  refers to a thing that thinks xiv, 7, 9, 25, 27, 93, 108, 161, 180, 188
  refers to "transcendental subject of thought = X," 25, 108, 131–2, 167n6, 185, 188
  refers to unknown and unknowable entity 108, 137n43, 175, 227
  related to feeling 49, 90, 100n48, 218
  role of, in Descartes's *cogito* argument 6, 73, 76–7, 81, 82, 84, 96n8
  role of, in Kant's 'I think,' in Transcendental Deduction 4, 6, 73, 77, 81, 83, 107, 116, 131
    compared to its role in Descartes's cogito argument 6, 77, 81–2
  for Sartre, I, me, and ego (je, moi, ego) 67nn9–10
  in *sensu stricto* and *in sensu latiori* 154, 161–2, 163, 164, 169n30
  and soul 1, 15n11, 73, 83, 95, 97n27, 102, 107, 109–10, 111–13, 117, 126, 129, 132n3, 141, 154, 155, 166n4, 169n29
  as subject/absolute subject in all possible judgments 113–16, 137–8n40, 154
  and transcendental imagination 199n37
  and unity of apperception 11, 31, 36, 68–9n40, 69n43, 107, 108, 134, 142, 149, 159, 160, 163, 173, 174, 176, 200n51, 204, 226, 235
  and unity of consciousness xiii, 2, 35, 37, 44, 161, 188, 235
  and unity of apperception (Strawson) 160
  use of, and identity propositions 6, 22, 38n9, 51, 52, 53, 59, 61, 62, 65, 70n49
  use of, as subject/as object xiii, 1, 2, 4, 5, 11, 19, 20, 21, 22, 23, 28, 31, 32, 34, 35, 36, 37, 38nn7, 10, 39n13, 44, 45, 48, 49, 50, 51, 52, 62, 65, 68nn21–22, 69n40, 143, 169n31, 173
  see also cogito; consciousness; ego; 'I think'; soul; subject; synthesis
id 12, 13, 35, 186, 187, 190, 191, 192, 199n37, 200n46, 206, 207, 219, 223, 226, 227
  and the body 193, 224
  of non-human animals, according to Freud 203n67
  see also pleasure and unpleasure principle; primary process(es)
identification 21, 22, 148, 158, 159, 167n13, 174, 195, 219, 229n26
  two senses of 51–3
  see also identity; proposition grounding uses of 'I'
identity
  conceptual criterion of 146
  consciousness of *see* consciousness

  of consciousness of myself, a formal condition of my thought 148
  empirical criteria 158, 159, 160, 174
  "'I am E.A.' is not an identity proposition" 59, 61, 63, 65, 70n49
  numerical 9, 10, 28, 102, 140, 141, 142, 143, 144, 146, 147, 148, 149, 151, 152, 153, 154, 157, 162, 166n3, 167n9, 168n15, 231
    of myself xii, 10, 25, 141
  of oneself and unity of the contents of one's thoughts 143–4, 150, 160
  of persons 140, 142, 146, 150
    for Locke 141
  of person unfailingly to be encountered in my consciousness 145, 146, 147
  presumption of, at different times of the referent of 'I' in 'I think' 143
  proposition grounding uses of 'I' 6, 22, 38n9, 51, 52, 53, 59, 61, 62, 65, 70n49
  real 140, 146, 147, 148
  spatio-temporal criteria 10, 28, 147, 148, 149, 167
  see also person
IEM *see* immunity to error through misidentification
'I exist' contained in 'I think' 6, 7, 73, 74, 75, 76, 77, 81, 82, 84–6, 88, 89, 91–4, 95nn1–2, 98n27, 99nn39, 42, 102, 118, 133n10, 137n43, 167n6
  as an intelligence conscious of its activity of thinking 108
  see also cogito; consciousness; 'I think'; self-consciousness
illusion of reason 132n3
imagination 3, 12, 41n29, 79, 80, 86, 97n21, 103, 109, 132n5, 175, 176, 185, 199n37, 209, 212, 213, 215, 218
  and aesthetic production, in Freud and in Kant 202n59
  comparison of Kant and Freud 191, 204
  and practical reason 228n11
  relation to sexual love and fear of death, in Kant 194
  ruled not by concepts but by desire and fantasy 216
  synthesis of 199n34
    discursive thinking and 181
    Kant's 190–1, 193, 204
    we are "seldom even conscious" of 181–3, 202n63
  and understanding 202n57
  see also synthesis
immunity to error through misidentification relative to the first-person pronoun (IEM) xii, 4, 5, 7, 19, 21, 22, 23, 28, 30, 32, 34, 40n19, 49, 52, 64, 65, 165
  different types of 41n30
  and first person memory 38n11, 67–8n21
  of 'I' in 'I think' 131, 135n30
  "thin," of 'I think' 41n30

imputability of action 168n25
inner sense *see* sense
internalization 13, 205, 206, 221, 225, 227, 227n2, 237
investment/invest *see* cathexis
'I think' xiv, xv, 2, 7, 9–12, 29–32, 35, 40n22, 42n32, 48, 67n12, 75–95, 96n14, 99n41, 104–9, 111, 112, 116, 118–24, 129, 132, 133nn9–11, 134nn14, 18, 135n30, 137n43, 140–4, 146–51, 156, 160, 164, 169n31, 173–8, 180, 194, 195, 195n4, 200–1n51, 212, 215, 226, 228n16, 232, 238
  and action-awareness 86–7, 101n59
  act of spontaneity 80, 104
  as concept, and as proposition xii, 1, 4, 6, 9, 19, 26–8, 31, 32, 37, 41n30, 44, 45, 73–8, 80, 81, 83–92, 94, 95, 95nn1, 6, 98nn27, 32, 34, 36, 99n40, 100n48, 101n60, 102, 104–8, 110, 115–18, 121–3, 128, 131, 137nn40, 44, 140, 142–4, 146, 150, 161, 163, 167n6, 173, 174, 177, 181, 184, 185, 188, 231, 236
  and consciousness of oneself as remaining numerically identical at different times xii, 140, 141, 143, 144, 147
  as determination of my own existence 105
  as empirical proposition 84, 85, 88, 89, 99n40, 100n48
    for Leibniz and Wolff 99nn39, 40
  expresses act of determining my existence 86, 104, 105, 133n12
  expresses act of thinking 48, 67n12, 128, 137n40
  expresses consciousness of myself as subject, according to Kant 19, 20, 26, 28, 31, 32, 36, 45, 50, 67n12
  as formal proposition of apperception 25, 128
  'I am thinking' 6, 75, 76, 84, 92, 95nn1–2
  indeterminate empirical intuition that 84, 87, 88, 89, 91, 118
  inner perception that 87–91
  in Kant's Transcendental Deduction of the Categories 4, 6, 40n18, 73, 77–81, 102, 115, 134n18, 176–81, 231
  merely 'formal' according to Evans 4, 25
  merely problematic 98n36
    or assertoric 133n10
  perceiving that 6, 85–6, 92, 118, 133nn11–12
  and transcendental unity of apperception xii, 11, 12, 13, 78–81, 96n14, 97nn19, 22, 103–7, 133n14, 142, 160, 173, 174, 176, 181, 185, 189, 200n51, 201n52, 204, 224
  that 'I' must count as subject and not predicate of 'think' is an identical proposition 116, 122
  transition from, to 'I exist'

  in Descartes 75
  in Kant 84, 118, 133n10
  as type, vs. as occurrent thought 83, 122
  as vehicle of categories 106
  why attribute 'think' to 'I'? 77
  see also apperception; *cogito*; consciousness; 'I'
intuition 59, 75, 130n49, 151, 207
  for Kant 25, 29, 78–8, 84, 86–91, 96n18, 97nn19, 21, 24, 98n32, 104–6, 108, 110–12, 116–18, 120, 121, 123–5, 129, 130, 135n24, 136n33, 137–8n44, 139nn50, 51, 142–4, 146, 147, 150, 153, 161, 168n13, 178–84, 189, 191, 193, 196n15, 197nn16, 20, 22, 198nn23, 27, 199nn37, 39, 202nn57, 63, 209, 210
  see also cognition; representation

judgment 4, 5, 7, 11, 12, 21–6, 28, 29, 32, 36, 37, 38nn7, 10, 39n12, 39–40n13, 40nn14, 26, 41n29, 42n32, 44, 45, 47, 48, 50, 68n21, 77–9, 85, 96n11, 113–16, 118, 119, 121, 124, 125, 129, 132, 133nn9–11, 135n24, 137–8n44, 138n49, 142, 146, 147, 148, 154, 163–5, 174, 180, 182, 189–92, 196n13, 197nn16, 20, 198n25, 202nn57, 59, 210, 221, 225, 229nn20, 26, 237, 238, 238n4
  logical forms of, for Kant 3, 80–1, 83, 96n18, 96–7n19, 97n21, 98nn27, 36, 103, 105–8, 120, 122, 133n6, 135nn24, 31
  see also categories

metapsychology 3, 14, 35, 175, 208, 233–5
mind xii, xiii, 1, 2, 3, 7, 9, 12, 14, 25, 26, 30, 33, 35, 37, 42n32, 66n6, 67n7, 74, 75, 78, 79, 82, 85, 92, 97–8n27, 143, 144, 155, 158, 168n22, 173, 175, 176, 180–3, 185, 186, 187, 190, 191, 194, 195n3, 199n37, 200n42, 202n63, 213, 214, 228n11, 232, 233, 235, 237
  Gemüt 144, 167n7, 167n9
moral law 13, 153, 157, 162, 163, 169n37, 210, 212–14, 216–18, 221, 223, 225, 227–8n8, 228n16, 229n26
  ratio cognoscendi of freedom 153, 168n17, 218, 220
morality 206
  for Freud 12, 195, 206, 207, 208, 213, 222, 224–6, 227n3, 230n31, 232
    as higher side of man, for Freud 227n3
  for Kant 12, 153, 157, 162, 165, 166, 168n17, 173, 205, 207, 220–2, 224, 226, 227n8, 229n20, 230n31
    as categorical imperative 11, 13, 14, 163, 205, 207, 214, 218, 225, 226
  naturalistic account of 207
  respect for the law is morality itself, for Kant 227n8

morality (*cont.*)
  unconditional command
    for Kant 13, 217, 220
    and for Freud 221
  see also respect

naturalism of second nature 194–5, 218
naturalization
  of Kant's account of 'I' in its theoretical and practical uses 232–4
  of Kant's critical account of 'I' 227
  of Kant's view of the structure of human minds 14 *see also* person; Freud and naturalization of notion of; transcendental philosophy, Kant's; Freud and the naturalization of

object of consciousness xiii, 46, 58, 64, 65, 67n9, 192, 193
  see also consciousness; of oneself, as object;'I'; use of, as subject/as object
Oedipus complex 219, 223
  and categorical imperative 13, 14, 220, 221, 222

paralogisms of pure reason (Kant) xvii, xix, 6–9, 11, 14n8, 25, 40n18, 70, 73, 74, 77, 78, 82–4, 91, 94, 97–8n27, 98nn28, 31, 102–3, 107, 108, 111, 112–31, 132n3, 133n11, 134n18, 135nn19, 31, 136nn36, 39, 137–8n44, 138nn45–6, 140, 145, 146, 152, 154, 155, 163, 166nn3–4, 6, 174, 231, 234
  first and second 8, 9, 10, 82, 102–3, 105, 112–31, 142–4, 149, 154–6, 163
  third 9, 10, 15n11, 82, 103, 113, 123, 132, 140–5, 151–6, 158, 162, 165, 166nn1–2, 167n9, 218
  fourth 82–3, 97nn28, 31, 103, 123, 155, 168nn21–22
  comparison of A and B
    on first paralogism 122
    on second paralogism 129–30
    on all four paralogisms 123, 135n19, 136n39
  logical 8, 15n10, 113
  of personality 9, 82, 132, 140–2, 144, 147, 150, 152, 153–4, 157, 158, 163, 164, 166, 166n2, 168n17, 231
    comparison with simplicity 142–3, 150
  of pure practical reason 152, 154
  of rational psychology 113, 164
  of simplicity 8, 82, 125–31, 138n45, 142, 149, 151, 158
  of spontaneity 155, 156, 157
  of substantiality 8, 82, 112–25, 130, 138n45, 158
perception/consciousness system in Freud 187, 200nn43, 46

person
  anthropological, psychological, juridical, moral concept of 156–7
  consciousness of identity of *see* consciousness
  developmental account of, in Freud 218
  as empirical human being endowed with unity of consciousness 160, 162
  and capacity to prescribe oneself moral law 163, 165, 218
  as empirically determinate entity 11, 151, 152
  as ends in themselves 156, 216
  for Frankfurt, compared with Kant 165
  Freud and naturalization of notion of 166, 169n37
    compared with Frankfurt 169n37
  identity of xiv, 10, 28, 95, 140–1, 145, 146–54, 157, 159, 167n5
  in psychological and moral sense 153, 157, 165, 168n15, 231
  forensic notion for Locke 153, 168n15
  for Strawson 68n30, 140–1, 158–63, 169n29
  see also consciousness of identity; identity; self
personhood and personality 9, 112, 150–4, 156–8, 163, 164, 166, 168n17, 207, 208, 217, 231
  good proper to 217
  transcendental concept of personhood 152
  necessary and sufficient for practical use 152, 166n2
  see also person
pleasure and unpleasure principle 35, 186, 187, 189, 190, 191, 199n37, 202n56, 218, 219, 222
  see also id
pre-conscious *see* representations
primary process(es) 189, 191, 192, 199n37, 203n67, 218, 219, 222, 223, 230n33
  see also id; pleasure and unpleasure principle; unconscious
propositions, particular for Kant 135n24
psychology
  relation of Kant and Freud to contemporary moral psychology, cognitive psychology, and neuroscience 233
  transcendental 103, 162
    imaginary topic of, for Strawson 162

reality principle xiii, 3, 11, 12, 35, 187, 189, 190, 191, 194, 195, 201n52, 204, 218, 222, 226
  see also ego
Refutation of Idealism 83, 89, 91–2, 93, 94, 98n31, 133n8
representation(s)
  Freud's pre-conscious 12
  Kant's scale [*Stufenleiter*] of 178–80, 196n15, 197n20

GENERAL INDEX 253

obscure
  and clear 29, 30, 107, 179, 194, 196n16, 197n19, 228n10
  of which we are not conscious 196nn15–16, 19
  something is "represented in me" 77, 80, 176, 177
  vs. the representation is "something to me" 178–80
  unconscious representation 188, 189, 202n56, 219, 232
    comparison of Kant and Freud on 199n37
  Freud's error on philosophers' views of 199–200n42
repression 185, 189, 199n37, 202n56, 219
respect 156, 212, 213, 215, 216, 218, 221, 222, 225, 227–8n8, 229n26
  see also morality

schematism see synthesis
second nature 194, 203n67, 227
secondary process 189, 193, 200n50, 201, 202n56, 203n67, 204, 218, 219, 222, 223, 230n33
  see also ego; reality principle
self xiv, xvi, xvii, 5, 7, 29, 34, 35, 40n19, 46, 51, 55, 57–60, 63, 66nn4, 7, 87, 92, 103, 111–12, 120, 140, 144–7, 150–3, 169n38, 208, 222, 233, 236
  dear xviii
  and moral self 228n16
  and proper self xviii, 238
  identity of (or of oneself) 144, 145, 150, 152, 166n3
  vs. of person 150
  moral 217, 228n16
    comparison of Freud and Kant 224
  and predispositions to the good 217, 228n16
  proper xviii
  and soul 112, 113, 121
  and thinking subject xi, xii, 112
self-consciousness xi–xiv, 1–6, 23, 26, 29, 31, 32, 37, 40n14, 44–6, 50, 51, 58–64, 66nn4, 7, 67n9, 69n43, 70n49, 90–3, 104, 112, 161, 173, 199n40, 216–18, 231–7
  for Anscombe 60–1
    comparison with Sartre 69n43
  comparison of Kant and Sartre 92, 134n16
  consciousness of oneself as a thinking subject and as an embodied entity xi, 45, 50, 58–9, 64, 65, 231, 234, 235, 237, 238
  for Evans 5, 39nn12, 14, 45, 50
  and intersubjective consciousness 236
  Kant on, and use of 'I' xi, 1, 19, 45, 67n9, 68n22, 83, 87, 88, 90, 91, 92, 104, 112, 124, 125, 132, 144, 145, 162, 164, 199n37, 216, 217, 218, 231, 232, 233, 234, 236–7
  non-thetic (Sartre) xiii, xiv, 5, 6, 44, 45, 46, 50, 51, 58, 59, 62, 65, 66nn4, 7

  and Anscombe's "unmediated agent-or-patient conception of actions, happenings and states" 61–2
  reflective 45, 50, 70n49, 93
  and self-awareness 50
  thetic, or positional 45, 46, 47, 48, 50, 64, 65, 67n9, 70n49, 198n27
  thinking about oneself vs. knowing oneself (self-consciousness vs. self-knowledge) 125, 132
  in Transcendental Deduction and in the Paralogisms 145, 231
  transcendental unity of self-consciousness 67n9
  see also body; consciousness; consciousness of oneself; ego; first person
self-deception 113, 213, 223, 224, 226, 229n26, 230n35
self-location 23, 24, 30, 32, 34, 46, 39n11–12, 41n30, 134n14
self-love 13, 214, 217, 224, 227n8, 228n16, 230n35
sense, inner 32, 42n33, 86, 97n24, 109–12, 117, 118, 129, 143–5, 151, 154, 164, 166n4, 167nn7, 9, 179, 182
  vs. apperception 110
  vs. outer 109, 110, 111, 117, 146, 151, 154, 164, 167n7, 179
soul 11, 15n11, 43n44, 73, 83, 87, 95, 102, 103, 116, 120–2, 126, 130, 132n3, 135n25, 141, 154–5, 158, 168n22, 169n29, 181, 183, 191, 198n33, 216, 229n26, 231, 234
  object of inner sense 42n33, 109–12, 117, 118, 129, 144, 145, 151, 154, 164, 166nn3–4, 167nn7, 9, 179
  no persistence of, as object of inner sense/ persistence of human being as an object of outer sense 151
  Kant's pre-critical argument from 'I' to 154
  rationalist notion endorsed by Kant 164
subject xi, xii, xiii, 1, 2, 4, 5, 7–12, 14n2, 15n11, 19–23, 25–6, 28, 31, 32, 34–7, 38nn5, 7, 10, 39nn11–12, 39–40n13, 40nn14, 19, 41n30, 44–5, 48–52, 57, 58, 60–3, 65, 66, 66–7n7, 67n12, 68nn21–2, 69nn40, 49, 77, 81, 83, 87, 89, 96n10, 97n24, 98n27, 32, 34, 36, 100n48, 103, 104, 107–10, 112–16, 118–26, 128–32, 135nn23, 25, 136–7n40, 137n43, 137–8n44, 138n47, 139n50, 142–9, 152, 154, 155–65, 166n3, 167n6, 168n25, 169nn27, 31, 173, 175, 177, 178, 180, 182, 185, 186, 188, 190, 194, 196nn15–16, 199n39, 206, 209–12, 216–18, 220, 222, 223, 227, 227–8n8, 236
  absolute simplicity of the logical subject 'I' vs. real simplicity of the metaphysical subject 128

254 GENERAL INDEX

subject (*cont.*)
  according to Strawson 160, 169n27
  of consciousness xiii, 10, 124
  identity of logical subject 'I' vs. identity of real subject 148
  logical xii, 8, 96n10, 98n34, 108-9, 113, 122, 128, 130, 131, 137-8n44, 148, 167n6, 173, 188
    and subjective 'I' 130
  metaphysical 8, 96n10, 108, 110, 114, 115, 122, 128, 131, 145, 148, 211
  and substance 119-20, 122, 123, 135n25
  to the law 210, 211
  transcendental = X 12, 25, 108, 109, 131, 167n6, 175, 185, 188, 194, 218, 227
  see also consciousness; of oneself, as subject; 'I'; use of, as subject/as object; substance
  substance 6, 7, 8, 26, 33, 60, 83, 87, 88, 95, 98n27, 102, 105, 108, 113-24, 126, 127, 129, 130, 132n3, 135n23, 136nn33, 36, 137nn42-3, 137-8n44, 138n45, 139nn50-1, 140-2, 146, 149, 150, 152-4, 164, 167n5, 231
    in Aristotle 135n23
    and logical function of subject in categorical judgment 137-8n44
    and permanence 120, 121, 124, 136nn33, 36, 137n42, 137-8n44
    and subject 114, 115
    see also subject
super-ego xv, 11, 13, 205, 207, 218, 227n3, 229
  and categorical imperative 219-20
  and ego 3, 12, 13, 173, 204, 205, 206, 208, 219-24, 226, 232
  and ego ideal 188, 195, 219, 221, 224, 229n20,
  and Kant's moral 'I ought to' 13, 195, 204, 206, 218, 219, 220-6
  as part of the ego 221
synthesis 29, 41n29, 42n32, 46, 67n12, 78-80, 86, 92, 97n24, 105, 109, 115-17, 138nn44, 49, 144, 175, 182, 183, 202n57, 209, 218
  according to logical functions of judgment 80
  and concepts 199n34
  as condition for analysis 97n19
  discursive thinking presupposes a pre-discursive synthesis of imagination (for Kant) 12, 176, 181, 185, 190, 204
  as effect of imagination, "blind" function of mind 182, 183, 191
  and 'I,' for Kant 29, 31, 42n32, 107, 133n7
  Kant's, of imagination compared to pre-conscious images for Freud 12, 198, 204
  schematism, "hidden art in the depth of the human soul" 198n33
  for thinking 67n12
  and understanding 202n57
  unity of 80, 103, 106, 133n9, 143, 194
  of which we are "seldom even conscious" 181-2
  see also combination; imagination

thinking xii, 1, 6-12, 15n11, 21, 24-32, 34, 35, 37, 39n12, 39n13, 40nn14, 22, 41n30, 44, 48, 49, 52, 62, 63, 65, 67n12, 69n40, 70n49, 73, 75-7, 81, 82-95, 95nn1-2, 96n10, 97nn21, 24, 98n27, 36, 99n39, 100n48, 101n59, 102, 106-13, 115-29, 131-2, 132n3, 133nn11-12, 134n16, 137n40, 138nn44-7, 139n50, 140-7, 149-52, 154-8, 161, 163, 164, 166nn3-4, 167nn5, 9, 169n30, 174, 178, 184, 188, 191-4, 198n27, 209-11, 217, 218, 221-3, 228nn13, 16, 228n16, 231, 234-6, 238
  agent of xii, 185
  cannot be a composite of actions 126-7, 129
  discursive 12, 185, 204, 208, 211, 223
  and being conscious of one's representations 176-81
  and 'I' 189-90
  and synthesis of imagination 181
  "I, as thinking" 142-7
  'I think' = 'I exist thinking' 82-93
  mere consciousness of act of 86-7
  of oneself as numerically identical xii, 10, 83
  subject xi, xiii, 1, 2, 12n12, 89, 112
  three kinds of consciousness of my own thinking 86-92
transcendental investigation 3, 12, 37, 43n43, 174, 175, 183
  vs. empirical investigation 175
transcendental philosophy, Kant's 89
  Freud and the naturalization of 175, 176, 188, 194, 196n13, 203n67, 233, 234
transcendental subject (unknown and unknowable) 175, 185

unconscious in Kant and in Freud 185-7, 190-3, 199n37, 200n42, 202n56, 214, 219, 230n35, 232
  Freud's structural distinction between conscious and unconscious representations 185, 186, 189, 218
  inaccessible to discursive formulation 223
  motivated blindness to the grounds of one's actions, for Kant 213-16, 223
  structural vs. dynamic characterization of unconscious representations, in Freud 185, 218, 222, 223
  unconscious motivations 214, 223
  see also pleasure and unpleasure principle; primary process(es); representation(s)

Name Index

Note: Footnotes in page entries are indicated by 'n'

Adickes, Erich 136n32, 138n45
Alberini, Cristina M. 240
Allison, Henry 96n19, 240
Ameriks, Karl 120, 135n19, 136n37, 167n5, 240
Anderson, R. Lanier 93–5, 99n39, 100nn51, 53, 55, 101n60, 240
Andrade, Brooke xvii
Anscombe, G. E. M. 5–6, 45, 49, 50, 51, 59–64, 65–6, 67n20, 68n21, 69nn41–3, 45, 48–9, 70nn49–50, 96n8, 234, 240
Ansermet, François 195n3, 240
Aristotle 98n34, 108, 113, 135n23, 196n13, 240
Arminjon, Mathieu 195n3, 200n48, 201n52, 238n1, 240
Arnauld, Antoine 95n6

Barnes, Hazel 66n4
Baumgarten, Alexander Gottlieb 138n46, 140, 166nn1–2, 175, 240
Bayne, Tim 38n4, 41n29, 240
Beatles, the xvii–xviii
Benacerraf, Paul xvi
Bermúdez, José Luis 240
Beyssade, Jean-Marie xiv
Blattner, William xiv
Block, Ned xvi, 198n30, 200n51, 202n59, 240
Boghossian, Paul xvi
Boyle, Matthew xiv
Brakel, Linda A. W. 241
Bratman, Michael xv
Brentano, Franz 176, 196n13, 200n42
Brook, Andrew 195n3, 196n13, 200n42, 241
Burge, Tyler 41n28, 241
Burgess, John xv
Buss, Sarah xvi

Carroll, Karen xvii
Cassam, Quassim xi, xii, xiii, xvii, 15n9, 39n13, 40n22, 42n32, 101n59, 134n16, 234, 241
Chalmers, David 41n29, 240, 241
Chignell, Andrew 40n22, 241
Cole, Jonathan 5, 37, 42nn34, 38, 43n38, 241
Coliva, Annalisa 38n9, 41nn30, 32, 241
Conant, James xi
Cooper, John xvi
Coorebyter, Vincent de 66n6, 241
Cottingham, John 95n2

Damasio, Antonio R. 241
de Boer, Karin 136n36
De Pierris, Graciela xv

Descartes, René xv, xix, 6–7, 33, 42nn32, 37, 50, 73–7, 81, 82–6, 89, 92–4, 95n1–4, 95n6, 8, 96n9, 97n26, 98nn29–30, 99nn39, 42, 102, 114, 163, 169n32, 241
Descombes, Vincent xv
Dreyfus, Hubert xiv

Eilan, Naomi M. 240
Emundts, Dina xiv, 241
Evans, Gareth 4, 5, 6, 7, 14n4, 19, 20, 23–5, 26, 27, 31, 34, 37, 38nn1, 5, 39n12, 40nn14–17, 20, 25, 41n26, 44, 45, 49, 50, 51, 52–4, 56, 58, 63, 64, 65, 66, 66nn1–3, 67–8n21, 68nn24–5, 28, 30–2, 70n51, 132, 134n14, 148–9, 167n12, 169n29, 234, 241

Fichant, Michel xiv
Flanagan, Owen xvii
Foley, Richard xvi
Frankfurt, Harry xvi, 165, 169nn35–7, 241
Freud, Sigmund xiii, xv, xix, 2–3, 5, 11–14, 35–6, 37, 43nn41–3, 67n9, 165–6, 169n37, 169n38, 173–4, 175–6, 185–93, 194–5, 195nn2–3, 196nn11, 13, 42, 199n37, 200nn42–4, 200n48, 201n52, 202n56, 59, 61, 203n67, 204–8, 216, 218–21, 222–7, 227n3, 229nn18–20, 26, 230nn31, 35, 232–3, 234–5, 237, 238, 241–2

Gabbey, Allan 95n2
Garber, Daniel xiv, xv, xvi, 242
Gardner, Sebastian xv, 230n35, 242
Garrett, Don xvi, 242
Gelade, Garry 41n29, 245
Ginsborg, Hannah xiv
Glock, H.-J. 67nn17, 21, 242
Grice, Paul 41n26
Grier, Michelle 132n3, 242
Grimm, Dieter xvi
Groddeck, Georg 193
Grünbaum, Adolf 195n3, 242
Grüne, Stefanie xiv, 197n20, 198n24, 242
Guyer, Paul 136nn32–3, 136–7n40, 138n46, 139nn50–1, 166n1, 167n11, 242

Hacker, P. M. S. 67nn17, 21, 242
Harris, Sarah xvii
Harrison, George xvii
Heidegger, Martin 48
Helmholtz, Hermann von 176, 233
Herbart, Johann Friedrich 176, 200n42
Herder, Johann Gottfried 228n11

NAME INDEX

Hills, David xv
Hogan, Desmond xv
Horstmann, Rolf-Peter xiv, 134n15, 135n19, 137n43, 139n54, 242
Howell, Robert 242–3
Hume, David 158, 175, 196n13
Husserl, Edmund 45, 66nn4, 6, 243

James, William 69n46, 243
Jamieson, Dale xv, xvii
Johnston, Mark xv, xvi

Kandel, Eric R. 243
Kant, Immanuel xi–xv, xvii–xviii, xix, 1–3, 4, 6–14, 15n10, 19–20, 25–32, 34, 35, 36, 37, 38n1, 40nn18, 21–3, 41nn26, 28–30, 42nn32, 33, 43nn39, 43–4, 44, 45, 48, 50, 53, 67nn9, 12, 69n40, 73–4, 75, 77–95, 95n2, 96nn9–11, 18, 19, 97nn19, 21, 22, 27, 98nn27, 32, 36, 99n39, 100nn45, 47, 48, 52, 101nn59, 60, 102–32, 132nn3, 5, 133nn8–11, 13, 134nn14, 16, 18, 135nn19, 24–5, 30, 31, 136nn32–3, 136nn36, 39–40, 137n43, 137–8n44, 138n46–7, 139n50, 140–66, 166nn1–3, 167nn5–6, 9, 11, 167–8n13, 168nn17, 22, 168–9n25, 169nn27, 29–32, 37, 173–85, 188–95, 195nn3, 4, 196n13, 15, 16, 197n16, 19, 20, 198nn26–27, 33, 199nn37, 39, 200nn42, 51, 201nn51–2, 202n59, 203n67, 204–18, 220–2, 223–7, 228nn8, 11, 13, 16, 229nn20, 26, 230nn31, 35, 231–8, 238n4, 239–40
Katz, Jerome 95–6n8, 243
Kitcher, Patricia 38n1, 97–8n19, 243
Kukla, Rebecca xiv

Lachenmann, Helmut xvii
Laplanche, Jean 200n44, 201n52, 243
La Rocca, Claudio 199n37, 243
Lear, Jonathan 195n3, 243
Leibniz, Gottfried Wilhelm xix, 93, 99n40, 138n46, 140, 153, 166n1, 168n19, 243
Lipps, Theodor 196n13
Locke, John xix, 109, 140, 141, 153, 168n15, 18, 175, 243
Longino, Helen xv
Longuenesse, Béatrice xvi, xvii, 96nn12–13, 16, 18, 96–7n19, 97n20, 100nn52, 56, 133n6, 135n24, 197nn17, 21, 199n34, 230n31, 238n3, 242, 243–4

Macdonald, Charles 241, 246
Magistretti, Pierre 195n3, 240
Marcel, Anthony J. 240
Marion, Jean-Luc xiv
McDowell, John 38n1, 53, 194, 203n67, 244
Melnick, Arthur 133n7, 134n15, 137n43, 139n54, 244
Mendelssohn, Moses 73, 151
Menger, Pierre-Michel xiii, xvii
Merleau-Ponty, Maurice xiii, 244

Meynert, Theodor 43n42, 200n48, 201n52, 233, 244
Moran, Richard xiv, xvi
Moyar, Dean xvii

Naccache, Lionel 244
Nagel, Thomas 66–7n7, 198n30, 244
Narboux, Jean-Philippe xiv
Nehamas, Alexander xvi
Nelson, Michael xiv
Neu, Jerome 195n3, 244
Nietzsche, Friedrich 176, 196n13, 206, 244

Otto, Lynn xvii
Otto, Paul xvii

Paillard, Jacques 42n34, 42–3n38, 241
Pariente, Jean-Claude 69n40, 95nn6, 8, 244
Peacocke, Christopher xi, xv, 38n4, 41–2n30, 42nn31–2, 101n59, 237, 244
Perry, John 22, 38–9n10, 244
Pippin, Robert xiv
Plato 196n13
Pontalis, Jean-Bertrand 200n44, 201n52, 243
Prodoehl, Christopher xvii
Proops, Ian 137n44, 139n50, 244
Prosser, Simon xiii, 245

Recanati, François xiii, 245
Röder, Brigitte 245
Rosefeldt, Tobias xiv, xv, 115, 133n9, 135n27, 138nn46, 49, 139n50, 167n5, 245
Rosen, Gideon xv, xvi
Rösler, Frank xvi, 238n3, 244
Rousseau, Jean-Jacques 225, 228n11

Sacks, David 195n3, 245
Sacks, Oliver 5, 14n6, 19, 32–3, 34–5, 37, 42nn34–6, 43n39, 40, 44–5, 165, 169n38, 236, 245
Sartre, Jean-Paul 5, 6, 14n7, 44–8, 50–1, 53, 54–9, 62, 63–6, 66nn4, 6–12, 68nn33–5, 40, 69n43, 45, 47, 49, 70n49, 93, 97n22, 134n16, 198n27, 231, 236, 245
Schapiro, Tamar xv
Scheffler, Samuel xvi, 207–8, 221, 227n4, 245
Schmidt-Hempel, Paul xvii
Schopenhauer, Arthur 176, 196n13, 200n42
Schuth, Sam xvii
Schwarz, Bill xvii
Sebanz, Natalie xv
Shoemaker, Sydney xii, 4, 7, 14n3, 19, 20, 21, 31, 32, 38nn1, 2, 8, 9, 11, 39n11, 40n19, 41n30, 49, 67n15, 69n44, 169n31, 237, 245
Siewert, Charles xiv
Silberstein, Eduard 196n13, 200n42
Smit, Houston xiv
Smith, Barry 246
Smith, Michael xv
Spence, Charles 245

Spinoza, Baruch 245
Stout, Jeffrey xv
Stoofhof, Robert 95n2
Strachey, James 14n6, 35, 173, 200nn43, 46, 201n53
Strawson, Galen xi
Strawson, Peter 38n1, 41n26, 68n30, 140–1, 158–62, 165, 169nn26–9, 35, 174, 195n7, 245
Sturma, Dieter 245
Sulloway, Frank J. 195n3, 245

Taylor, Ken xv
Tetens, Johannes Nikolaus 175
Treisman, Anne 41n29, 245

Van Benthem, Johan xv, 43n44
Van Fraassen, Bas xvi
Velleman, David xvi

Warren, Daniel xiv
Waxman, Wayne xi
Widlöcher, Daniel 195n3, 245
Wilson, Margaret xvi
Wittgenstein, Ludwig 1–2, 4, 5, 14n1, 19, 20–2, 23, 28, 31, 38nn1, 3, 6, 7, 44, 45, 48–9, 50, 51, 58, 64, 67nn13, 14, 16–18, 68nn21, 40, 69n40, 169n31, 234, 237, 246
Wolff, Christian xix, 94, 99n39–40, 138n46, 140, 166n1, 246
Wong, Hong Yu xv, 42n34
Wood, Allen xv, 136n33, 136–77n40, 138n46, 139nn50–1, 166nn1–2, 167n11, 228nn8, 11, 229nn26, 29, 230n31, 246
Wright, Crispin 246
Wuerth, Julian 136n37, 246

Yourgrau, Palle 246

Printed and bound by CPI Group (UK) Ltd, Croydon, CR0 4YY